THE ROUGH GUIDE TO
SHANGHAI

**ROUGH
GUIDES**

This fourth edition updated by
Simon Lewis

Contents

Introduction to
Shanghai

In the Roaring Twenties, Shanghai was a place of opportunity, notorious for its cool style, risqué modernity and savvy business panache. Decades of war and neglect followed, until, in the 1990s, the city shook off its mothballs and set off on one of the fastest economic and urban expansions the world has ever seen. Today's Shanghai has certainly retaken its spot in the limelight – this dizzying metropolis has China's largest stock exchange, the world's longest metro network and over a thousand skyscrapers, more than any other Asian city. By 2020, it is expected to be the richest economic region in the world. While Shanghai may not brim with big-name tourist attractions, it is a fascinating, thrilling place to visit – fast, ever-changing and utterly unique.

Faced with all those ads, neon signs, showcase buildings and vast shopping plazas, it's hard to imagine that you are in a Communist country. Indeed, though dissent is quashed, outside the political arena anything goes, and frantic consumerism and the pursuit of novelty, gratification and wealth are the order of the day. Witness all the gleaming new restaurants and malls, the enthusiastic embrace of fashion and high culture, clubbing and fine cuisine.

Yet despite the rampant modernity, evidence of Shanghai's short and inglorious **history**, when it was carved up by foreign powers into autonomous concessions, is everywhere, and parts of the city appear distinctly European. Looking like a 1920s vision of the future, prewar Art Deco buildings dot the streets: once considered relics of foreign imperialism, these are now protected as city monuments and often sympathetically converted into fashionable shopping and dining venues; they stand in the shadows of brazen skyscrapers that, although built decades later, seem to share the same utopian aesthetic.

And Shanghai maintains its **international character**. The Shanghainese have always felt apart from the rest of the country and look abroad for inspiration as well as business; now, you'll find more English spoken here than in any other mainland city, see foreign mannerisms such as handshaking and air-kissing, and observe the obsession with

ABOVE CHINESE NEW YEAR LANTERNS

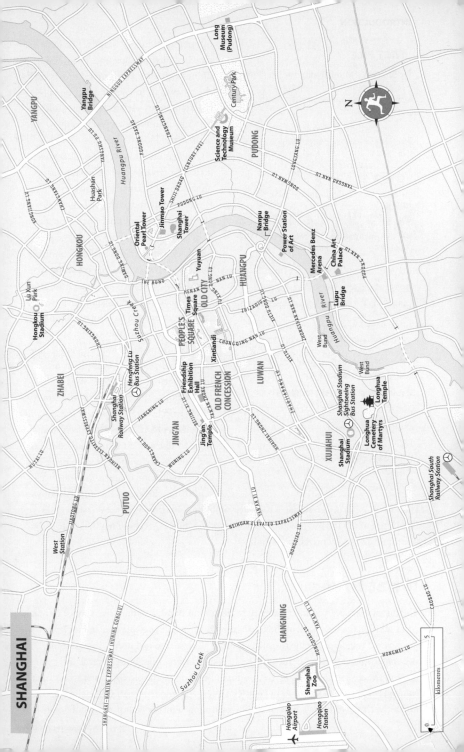

FACT FILE

- **Shanghai Municipality** encompasses 6300 square kilometres, which includes Shanghai city, eight surrounding districts and thirty islands.

- The city is **governed** by the Communist Party of China but enjoys a surprising degree of autonomy, to an extent which has begun to worry the central government in Beijing.

- The official **language** is Mandarin, but locals also speak a dialect called Shanghainese.

- The **population** of Greater Shanghai is 24 million, which includes five million migrant workers.

- Shanghai is the busiest **port** in the world, by cargo tonnage. The Shanghai region, including the adjoining provinces of Jiangsu and Zhejiang, accounts for almost a third of China's foreign **exports**, and a fifth of its **manufacturing output** is produced here. Each year, the city attracts a quarter of all China's foreign **investment**, more than any single developing country.

- The weight of its **skyscrapers** has caused Shanghai to sink 1.5m in twenty years, and the city continues sinking at the rate of 1.5cm a year.

- Shanghai's residents have the highest **life expectancy** of anywhere in China, at 82 years.

international luxury brands. But look closely and you'll also find a distinctly **Chinese identity** asserting itself, whether in the renewal of interest in traditional entertainments such as teahouses and acrobatics or in the revival of old architectural forms.

Unlike most Chinese cities, Shanghai is actually a rewarding place to **wander** aimlessly: it's fascinating to stroll the elegant Bund, explore the pockets of colonial architecture in the Old French Concession or get lost in the choked alleyways of the Old City, where traditional life continues much as it always has. The **art scene** is world-class, and you can visit a host of flashy galleries, from gleaming new structures designed to display billionaire collections to bohemian concerns housed in ramshackle old factories. But perhaps the city's greatest draw is its emphasis on indulgence – it's hard to resist its many temptations. There's a superb **restaurant** scene, with every Chinese and most world cuisines represented; whether you treat yourself to the latest outrageous concoction at a celebrity restaurant or slurp noodles in a neighbourhood canteen, you may well find that eating out is the highlight of your trip. There are many great places to go for **nightlife**, too, from dive bars to slick clubs featuring international DJs, and the **shopping** possibilities, at shiny malls, trendy boutiques and dusty markets, are endless.

What to see

The first stop on every visitor's itinerary is the famous **Bund**, an impressive strip of colonial edifices lining the west bank of the Huangpu River. As well as giving you an insight into the city's past, a wander along the riverside affords a glimpse into its future – the awesome, skyscraper-spiked skyline on the other side. Taking a river cruise from here will offer you a sense of the city's scale. Heading west from the Bund down the old consumer cornucopia of **Nanjing Dong Lu** will bring you to **People's Square**, the modern heart of the city. Here you'll find a cluster of world-class museums, all worth a few hours of your time, and the leafy and attractive Renmin Park. Not far away is the superb new Natural History Museum, set in an attractive sculpture park. Continuing west onto Nanjing Xi Lu brings you to the modern commercial district of **Jing'an**, where a couple of worthwhile temples and the shabby-chic Moganshan Arts District provide welcome respite from the relentless materialism.

Heading south from People's Square brings you to delightful **Xintiandi**, an upscale dining district housed in renovated traditional buildings, and a good introduction to the civilized pleasures of the **Old French Concession**, which stretches west. As well as the best (and most exclusive) shopping, hotels and dining, on these incongruously European-looking streets you'll find a host of former residences of Shanghai's original movers and shakers.

But Shanghai's history was not all about the foreigners, as you'll find if you explore the **Old City**, south of the Bund, where most of the Chinese lived during the Concession era. The old alleys are being torn down at speed, but you'll still find plenty of evidence of a distinctly Chinese way of life in the elegant old Yu Gardens, the bustling shopping bazaar that's grown up around them and a clutch of backstreet temples. By way of contrast, across the river in **Pudong** you'll see very little that's more than twenty years old; come here for the staggering views from the elegant Jinmao Tower or the colossal new Shanghai Tower.

A clutch of sights on the city's **outskirts** are also worthy of exploration, among them Duolun Culture Street in the far north, Century Park and the Long Museum in the east and Longhua Temple in the southwest. Not far from the last you'll find the West Bund, a riverside promenade that hosts some fantastic contemporary art venues. Meanwhile, Shanghai's extensive new metro network has bought some intriguing suburban sights within easy reach of the centre: foremost among them are the heritage town of **Qibao** and the lovely **Guyi Garden** in Nanxiang.

The city's hinterland, meanwhile, offers countryside, historic buildings and a chance to slow down. The cities of **Suzhou**, most famous for gardens and silk, and **Hangzhou**, with its gorgeous lake, are well worth an overnight stop, while for a day-trip you shouldn't miss the sleepy **water towns**, such as Zhouzhuang or Wuzhen.

ARCHITECTURAL WONDERS OF SHANGHAI

China Art Palace (2010) This extraordinary red, boxy crown was the grand Chinese showpiece of the 2010 Expo. It's now an art museum. See p.81.

Customs House (1927) Huge Doric columns accentuate this imposing Neoclassical building's height, and lead the eye towards the massive clocktower. See p.44.

Fairmont Peace Hotel (1926) Designed by Palmer & Turner as Sassoon House, this is the city's most glorious Art Deco masterpiece, with a magnificent interior. See p.42.

Jinmao Tower (1998) Beautiful tapering tower that uses the formal language of Chinese pagodas; the enormous barrel-vaulted atrium, lined with staircases arrayed in a spiral, is the city's most spectacular interior. See p.78.

Long Museum (West Bund) (2014) This new contemporary art museum, built around an old coal hopper, is a triumph of post-industrial chic. See p.88.

1933 Millfun (1933) An astonishing concrete slaughterhouse in Hongkou, reminiscent of an Escher drawing. See p.85.

Oriental Arts Centre (2004) French architect Paul Andreu designed this building to look like a butterfly orchid, with the petals being the exhibition halls. Lights on the roof change colour to match the cadences of the music played inside. See p.81.

Shanghai Tower (2015) At a whopping 632m, this is the world's second-tallest building; the observation deck is a must-see. See p.78.

Shanghai World Financial Centre (2007) This 492m-high edifice is a broad-shouldered wedge with very clean lines and a hole in the top – like God's own tent peg. See p.79.

Tomorrow Square (2002) One of the city's most distinctive landmarks, thanks to the pincers on the roof. See p.52.

When to go

The best times to visit Shanghai are in **spring** and early summer (late March till the end of May) and **autumn** (mid-September till the end of October). During these times, you can expect warm temperatures, blue skies and infrequent rain. **Summer** (June to mid-September) is very hot and humid – but bring an extra layer to combat the fierce air conditioning. During the "Plum Flower Rain" season from mid-June to early July you should expect frequent showers, and up till September a number of heavy storms – you'll need an umbrella. **Winters** are chilly and windy, though the temperature rarely drops below freezing and snow is uncommon. January and February are the coldest months.

Try to avoid visiting during the two "Golden Week" **holidays** – the first weeks of May and October – when pretty much the whole country is on holiday and tourist attractions are crowded. The city is lively during the run-up to **Chinese New Year** (between mid-Jan and mid-Feb) but travel during this time is tricky and expensive as most Chinese people head home for the holiday. New Year itself is best avoided as just about everyone stays at home with their family and most businesses are closed.

AVERAGE TEMPERATURES AND RAINFALL

	Jan	Feb	Mar	Apr	May	Jun	Jul	Aug	Sep	Oct	Nov	Dec
Max/min °C	8/1	8/1	13/4	19/10	25/15	28/19	32/23	32/23	28/19	23/14	17/7	12/2
Max/min °F	46/34	46/34	55/39	66/50	77/59	82/66	90/74	90/74	82/66	74/57	63/45	54/36
Rainfall (mm)	48	58	84	94	94	180	147	142	130	71	51	36

Author picks

Our author has been to all the trendy bars, backstreet eating holes and destination restaurants; and he's cycled the city's length and breadth via busy thoroughfares and narrow *longtangs*. Here is a list of his personal highlights.

Sip with the fast set Shanghai does after-dark glamour very well, and boasts some of the world's louchest cocktail bars. Head to a speakeasy such as *Senator* (p.145) and ask their expert mixologists to fix you up something to fit your mood.

Look up Shanghai is a treasure trove of fantastic Art Deco architecture, much of which, delightfully, has been spruced up after decades of neglect. Check out the *Fairmont Peace Hotel* – inside and out – to bask in this most refined design aesthetic (p.42).

Get lost Dense with incident and colour, central Shanghai's streets reward the urban flaneur – they're architecturally diverse, busy with stylish (or at least noteworthy) people and have plenty of shade thanks to all those plane trees. Start in the Old French Concession (pp.58–67) and see how far east you can get. Jump in a cab when you've had enough.

Hang out with the art crowd Don a black polo neck and statement glasses and see if you can schmooze your way into the smart art set – chat up the interns at the Moganshan galleries (p.73) and you might get yourself invited to some private views.

Dine in style Some of the world's greatest chefs work in Shanghai. Try to fit in at least one proper fine-dining experience: it'll be a lot cheaper than in the West and as good or better. We especially recommend *Table Number One* (p.132), *elEfante* (p.134) and *Mr and Mrs Bund* (p.130).

Get high At some point in your stay, try rising into the clouds. Pick a fine day or a dark evening, and head up a skyscraper to a viewing platform or pricey hotel bar. The absolute best views, for the moment, are from the Shanghai Tower observation deck (p.78).

Our author recommendations don't end here. We've flagged up our favourite places – a perfectly sited hotel, an atmospheric café, a special restaurant – throughout the guide, highlighted with the ★ symbol.

18

things not to miss

It's not possible to see everything that Shanghai has to offer on a short trip – and we don't suggest you try. What follows is a selective taste of the city's highlights: fascinating museums, spectacular buildings and a few ways just to indulge yourself. All highlights have a page reference to take you straight into the Guide, where you can find out more. Coloured numbers refer to chapters in The City section.

1 THE BUND
Page 39

This iconic riverside stretch of grand colonial mansions is the first stop on any itinerary.

2 YU GARDENS
Page 55

A classical garden of pavilions, ponds and rockeries – a calm oasis at the heart of an olde-worlde Chinatown-style shopping centre.

3 SHANGHAI MUSEUM
Page 49

Fabulous collection of paintings, jade, bronzes and other antiquties, housed in one of Shanghai's most stylish buildings.

4 XIAOLONGBAO
Page 128

These delicious dumplings are available from street vendors and fancy restaurants both.

5 TAILORING
Page 160

Clothes tailored to any design you can think of, for a tiny fraction of the price you'd pay at home – Shanghai's best bargain.

12

13

14

15

Itineraries

Shanghai has distinct districts, but the centre is pleasingly compact and easy to stroll around, if you don't mind crowds. Each of the following itineraries can be covered in a day, mostly by walking, with a few short hops by metro.

THE BUND TO RENMIN PARK

This is the classic Shanghai walk: heading from the Neoclassical elegance of the Bund, along brash shopping streets, to a park fringed with standout sights, it offers a sample of all the city's flavours.

❶ **Huangpu Park** This compact park alongside the Huangpu River is the perfect vantage point to take in Shanghai's two iconic skylines: the trim parade of the Bund's colonial edifices on this side and the dizzying modernity of Pudong's skyscrapers across the water. **See p.41**

❷ **Afternoon tea at the Peninsula hotel** A great way to sample the luxuries of an iconic hotel without breaking the bank. Take in the sumptuous, marble-columned lobby in the company of the local smart set, over tea, pastries and a glass of champagne. **See p.132**

❸ **Fairmont Peace Hotel** This historic hotel is once more the city's premier luxury destination. Don't miss the magnificent Art Deco lobby. **See p.42**

❹ **Nanjing Dong Lu** This vivid pedestrianized street is jammed with stores: even if you don't buy, it's great for people-watching – and at night it's a river of neon. **See p.46**

❺ **Renmin Park** A surprisingly quiet and civilized retreat bang in the middle of the city. Stop off for a coffee by the lotus pond at *Barbarossa* (see p.131) before checking out a show at the Museum of Contemporary Art (see p.000). **See p.000**

❻ **Park hotel** Ladislav Hudec's slim, tapering Art Deco masterpiece might have long since lost its

crown as highest building in the city, but it's still one of the most striking – and clearly an inspiration for modern structures such as the Jinmao Tower. **See p.51**

❼ **Shanghai Museum** Check out the Qing furniture and Tibetan masks at this stylish, modern museum. **See p.49**

❽ **Shanghai Urban Planning Exhibition Hall** Raise an eyebrow at the scale and scope of the plans for Shanghai's future, dramatically presented with models; you can't fault the ambition. **See p.51**

THE OLD FRENCH CONCESSION

These elegant streets and districts are great for strolling – you'll see why Shanghai got that "Paris of the East" moniker – and if you want to stop off for coffee or dinner, you'll be spoilt for choice.

❶ **Xintiandi** This complex of upmarket restaurants, in a complex of pastiche traditional architecture, is very attractive – and wildly popular. Splash out at *Ye Shanghai* (see p.137) or *Crystal Jade* (see p.133), and make sure to check out the Shikumen Museum. **See p.49**

❷ **Fuxing Park** One of the city's rare green spaces is a great place to unwind, and you'll probably see groups of elderly locals playing instruments or singing. **See p.63**

❸ **Tianzifang** The narrow *longtang* alleys here are a warren of cute shops and cafés. Browse in Harvest Studio (see p.161) for homeware and Nuomi (see p.159) for womenswear, then hit *The Bell Bar* (see p.144) for a drink. **See p.64**

❹ Maoming Nan Lu The Old French Concession is deservedly famous for its fashion stores; this street is dotted with proficient tailors who will knock up a *cheongsam* or a suit for a very reasonable price. **See p.65**

❺ Fuxing Xi Lu This charming street has a winning mix of bars, boutiques and villas, many in prewar buildings. Browse around Urban Tribe (see p.162) for ethnic knick-knacks, then dine at *Hot Pot King* (see p.134).

❻ Yongkang Lu A leafy residential strip that hosts some of the city's best expat bars and cafés, such as *Le Café des Stagiaires* (see p.137) and *Pain Chaud* (see p.138). It's appealingly boho and low key; in the evening everyone spills onto the street to mingle. **See p.143**

❼ Wukang Lu Join the smartest of the smart set for a cappuccino at *Farine* (see p.137) before exploring the Ferguson Lane boutiques and Former Residences nearby. **See p.67.**

PUDONG

It's hard to credit now, but forty years ago Pudong was mostly paddy fields. Today it's where the city is growing fastest, a forest of skyscrapers and new build.

❶ Jinmao Tower It might have been literally overshadowed by its newer, taller neighbours, but this stylish take on Art Deco is still the most glamorous skyscraper on the Lujiazui block. Lovely interior too; check out the observation deck and the *Grand Hyatt* lobby. **See p.78**

❷ Shanghai History Museum Down in the bowels of the Oriental Pearl Tower, this little museum does a great job of bringing to life the city's turbulent twentieth-century history. **See p.78**

❸ Shanghai Tower This giant new skyscraper is the tallest of a clutch of jaw-dropping Pudong edifices. The observation deck offers amazing views. **See p.78.**

❹ Science and Technology Museum A huge museum with an IMAX cinema and interactive and imaginative displays – the exhibit on China's space programme is fascinating. **See p.80**

❺ Fake market You'll find plenty of choice at this busy market specializing in fake designer-label clothes, shoes and watches. Bargain assertively but politely and you'll end up with some real steals. **See p.158**

❻ Century Park This well-maintained park is big enough to make for a proper escape from the teeming urban jungle. Rent a tandem and cycle sedately around the lake. **See p.80**

❼ Long Museum A long way out, but worth the trip: this museum displays the choicest items from a billionaire's collection, ranging from historical objets d'art to modern Chinese paintings. **See p.81**

MANSIONS AND VILLAS

Shanghai is blessed with some fantastic foreign-built mansions and villas from the Concession era. Many languished for decades and have only recently been renovated and repurposed, often as restaurants, bars and hotels.

❶ Mansion Hotel It might look the height of respectability now, but this genteel five-storey mansion, now a hotel, was once the home of Shanghai's most famous gangster, Du Yuesheng. There's a terrace bar, too. **See p.120**

❷ Arts and Crafts Museum This gracious white mansion, reminiscent of the White House, is one of Ladislav Hudec's masterpieces (see box, p.169). it's now a charming museum, exhibiting some great ivory carvings and snuff bottles. **See p.66**

❸ Normandie Apartments Built in 1926, this striking landmark apartment block is another Hudec classic; its unusual wedge shape resembles the prow of a ship. **See p.67**

❹ Song Qingling's Former Residence The private home of Song Qingling – a central figure in early twentieth-century Chinese politics – is now a museum of her life. After looking at the exhibits, check out the limos in the garage and the fine gardens. **See p.67**

❺ Former Residence of Sun Yatsen A museum of the great man, in a handsome old mansion; you can safely whizz over the displays, but take in the refined atmosphere of the house itself. **See p.63**

❻ Ruijin Guesthouse These urbane houses were built by a newspaper magnate; they then became a government guesthouse. Today the complex operates as a high-end hotel – the well-groomed grounds are perfect for a restful stroll. **See p.64**

❼ Fu 1039 Many of the smaller French Concession mansions have been converted into restaurants. This Shanghainese place, housed in a gracious villa, is one of the most successful. **See p.134**

STREET SCENE IN THE OLD CITY

Basics

Getting there

Shanghai has direct flights from many European capitals as well as a number of American and Australian cities. Fares vary with the season; prices are highest between Easter and October, around Christmas and New Year, and just before the Chinese New Year (which falls between mid-January and mid-February).

You can often cut costs by going through a **specialist flight agent** – either a consolidator, who buys up blocks of tickets from the airlines and sells them at a discount, or a **discount agent**, who may also offer special student and youth fares plus travel insurance, rail passes, car rentals, tours and the like. Prices quoted here assume midweek travel – flying at weekends tends to be slightly more expensive.

Flights from the UK and Ireland

Nonstop flights to Shanghai **from the UK** are offered by Virgin (🅦 virgin-atlantic.com), British Airways (🅦 ba.com), Air China (🅦 airchina.co.uk) and China Eastern (🅦 flychinaeastern.co.uk), leaving from London Heathrow (11hr). Direct Air China flights from Manchester are scheduled to start in 2017. Flying from other UK airports or **from the Republic of Ireland** you'll have to catch a connecting flight to London or your airline's hub city.

Return **fares** for direct flights from the UK start at around £450 in low season, rising to around £900 in high season. If you're flying from the Republic of Ireland, reckon on €1100 in low season, €1700 at peak times. Indirect flights can work out cheaper; Air China and Lufthansa (🅦 lufthansa.com), both of which stop in Frankfurt, are worth considering, as is Aeroflot (🅦 aeroflot .co.uk), which stops over in Moscow, Emirates (🅦 emirates.com), which stops over in Dubai, and China Southern (🅦 cs-air.com), which stops in Paris. Less-fancied airlines such as Qatar Airways (🅦 qatarairways.com) offer the most competitive fares, though you may have a lengthy stopover.

Flights from the US and Canada

From the US and Canada, Delta (🅦 delta.com), American Airlines (🅦 americanairlines.com), United Airlines (🅦 united.com), Air Canada (🅦 aircanada .com), Air China (🅦 airchina.com) and China Eastern (🅦 flychinaeastern.com) offer direct flights from San Francisco, Los Angeles, Chicago, Detroit, New York, Vancouver and Toronto. It takes around thirteen hours to reach Shanghai from the west coast; add seven hours or more to this if you start from the east coast. In low season, expect to pay around US$1000 from the west coast or US$1400 from the east, less for an indirect flight. In high season if you book your ticket early you probably won't need to pay more than US$300 above these low-season fares.

Flights from Australia, New Zealand and South Africa

From Australia, you can pick up direct flights to Shanghai from Sydney and Melbourne (about 11hr) with China Eastern (🅦 flychinaeastern.com), Emirates (🅦 emirates.com) and Qantas (🅦 qantas .com) – reckon on a starting price of Aus$1100. The cheapest flights (around Aus$900 in low season) are with carriers such as Malaysia Airlines (🅦 malaysia -airlines.com) and Royal Brunei (🅦 bruneiair.com), with a stopover in Hong Kong or Singapore. Flying from Perth to Shanghai with the major airlines can cost as little as Aus$900 in high season. **From New Zealand**, Air New Zealand (🅦 airnewzealand.com) flies direct from Auckland to Shanghai; flights cost around NZ$2200 in high season.

Flying **from South Africa** requires a change of planes. A flight from Johannesburg with a stopover in Hong Kong will cost around ZAR10,000 in high season.

AGENTS AND OPERATORS

China Highlights China ☎ +86 773 2831999, 🅦 chinahighlights .com. Three- to five-day tours of Shanghai and the surrounding area.

China Odyssey China ☎ +86 773 5854000, 🅦 chinaodysseytours .com. Short city and water town tours, plus longer trips taking in other destinations in China.

A BETTER KIND OF TRAVEL

At Rough Guides we are passionately committed to travel. We believe it helps us understand the world we live in and the people we share it with – and of course tourism is vital to many developing economies. But the scale of modern tourism has also damaged some places irreparably, and climate change is accelerated by most forms of transport, especially flying. All Rough Guides' flights are carbon-offset, and every year we donate money to a variety of environmental charities.

CTS Horizons UK ☎ 020 7868 5590, ⊛ ctshorizons.com. A range of tours including cheap off-season hotel and flight packages to Shanghai.
On the Go Tours UK ☎ 020 7371 1113, ⊛ onthegotours.com. Group and tailor-made tours that include Shanghai as part of a jaunt around China.
STA Travel UK ☎ 033 321 0099, US & Canada ☎ 1800 781 4040, Australia ☎ 134 782, New Zealand ☎ 0800 474 400, South Africa ☎ 0861 781 781; ⊛ statravel.com. Worldwide specialists in independent travel; also student IDs, travel insurance, car rental, rail passes and more. Good discounts for students and under-26s.
Trailfinders UK ☎ 020 7368 1200, Republic of Ireland ☎ 01 677 7888, Australia ☎ 1300 780 212; ⊛ trailfinders.com. One of the best-informed and most efficient agents for independent travellers.
Travel China Guide US & Canada ☎ 1800 892 6988, all other countries ☎ +800 6668 8666; ⊛ travelchinaguide.com. Chinese company with a wide range of three- and four-day group tours of Shanghai and around, and a useful app for train booking.

Arrival

Wherever you arrive, you're almost guaranteed a long journey into the centre. Fortunately, bus and metro connections are excellent, and there are plenty of taxis – though you should always catch a licensed cab from a rank.

By plane

Flying in from overseas, you'll touch down at glossy **Pudong International Airport** (PVG; ☎ 68341000, ⊛ shairport.com), 40km east of the city along the mouth of the Yangzi River. There are currently two terminals, with a third due to open in 2019. Banks and ATMs are on the upper floors. There are left-luggage offices in arrivals and departures (6am–11pm; ¥30 up to four hours, ¥45/day).

You'll be pestered in the arrivals hall by charlatan taxi drivers; ignore them and instead make for the official taxi rank, on your right as you go out, opposite exit 15. A taxi to Pudong or the Bund should cost around ¥180, to Nanjing Xi Lu around ¥150, and the ride will take around an hour, depending on traffic.

The most convenient public transport into town is the **airport bus**, which leaves from opposite the exit gates (every 15min 6am–7.30pm, reduced service 7.30–11pm; ¥20–30). The journey into town takes around ninety minutes. There are eight routes: bus #2 is generally the most useful as it goes to the Jing'an Temple metro station in the city centre. Bus #1 goes to Hongqiao Airport (see opposite); bus #3 to Xujiahui; bus #4 to Hongkou Stadium, in the north; bus #5 to Shanghai Railway Station; bus #6 to Zhongshan Park; and bus #7 to Shanghai South Railway Station. The only one that drops off in Pudong is bus #5 (at Dongfang Hospital).

You can also take the **metro** straight into town, although this isn't as convenient as it should be, as the trip takes ninety minutes (so isn't any faster than the bus) and you'll have to stop for up to twenty minutes at Guanglan Lu, where you have to change platforms, remaining on line #2.

The most exciting way to get into town is on the **Maglev** (see box opposite), though it's not

SHANGHAI TRANSPORT TERMINALS

AIRPORTS

Pudong Airport	浦东机场	pǔdōng jīchǎng
Hongqiao Airport	虹桥机场	hóngqiáo jīchǎng

TRAIN STATIONS

Hongqiao Station	上海虹桥火车站	shànghǎi hóngqiáo hǔochē zhàn
Shanghai Station	上海火车站	shànghǎi huǒchēzhàn
Shanghai South Station	上海火车南站	shànghǎi huǒchēnánzhàn

BUS STATIONS

Hengfeng Lu Bus Station	恒丰路汽车站	héngfēnglù qìchēzhàn
Pudong Bus Station	浦东汽车站	pǔdōng qìchēzhàn
Qiujiang Lu Bus Station	虬江路汽车站	qiújiānglù qìchēzhàn
Shanghai Long-Distance Bus Station	上海长途客运总站	shànghǎi chángtú kèyùn zǒngzhàn
Shanghai South Bus Station	上海南站	shànghǎi nánzhàn
Shanghai Stadium Sightseeing Bus Station	上海体育馆旅游集散中心	shànghǎi tǐyùguǎn lǚyóu jísàn zhōngxīn

THE MAGLEV

The **Maglev train** (daily 7am–9pm; every 20min), suspended above the track and propelled by magnetism, provides a glamorous way to get into town from Pudong airport. It whizzes from the international airport to Longyang Lu metro station, in eight minutes, accelerating to 300km/hr in the first four minutes, then immediately starting to decelerate. It is capable of an incredible 410km/hr, but to travel this fast you need to time your trip – trains go at full speed between 10.30am and 11.30am and 2.30pm and 3.30pm. It doesn't make much difference in journey time, of course.

Tickets cost ¥50 one way, or ¥40 if you show a plane ticket; a return is ¥90. Note that the Maglev terminal is three minutes' walk from the airport, and that Longyang Lu is still a long way from the centre of town.

recommended if you have heavy luggage, as there are escalators and corridors at the airport and at your arrival point at Longyang Lu metro station.

If you're heading straight out of the city, make for exit 18, opposite which **long-distance coaches** depart hourly for Suzhou, Hangzhou and other destinations (¥80–100).

Hongqiao Airport

Most **domestic flights** land at **Hongqiao Airport** (SHA; ☎ 62688899, ⓦ en.shairport.com/hongqiaoair), 20km from the Bund. It's on the metro, on lines #2 and #10. There are two terminals; most flights arrive at terminal 2, which is attached to Hongqiao train station. Luggage storage is available at arrivals and departures (7am–11pm; ¥30/hr, ¥45/day).

A taxi to Nanjing Xi Lu costs about ¥50 and takes around 45 minutes; to the Bund you'll pay about ¥60. At busy times, such as Friday nights, you can wait more than an hour for a cab at the rank – walk to departures and pick up a taxi that's just dropped someone off, or get on any bus for a couple of stops, disembark and hail one from there.

Buses leave from the parking lot: bus #1 goes to Pudong International Airport; the airport shuttle goes to Jing'an Temple metro station in the city centre; bus #925 goes to Renmin Square; and bus #941 goes to Shanghai train station. Journeys can take up to an hour depending on traffic.

Getting to the airports from town

Airport shuttle buses for **Pudong International Airport** leave from the terminal at 1600 Nanjing Xi Lu, opposite Jing'an metro station (daily 6am–7.30pm; every 30min; 45min; ¥20–22). It's faster, though, to take the metro to Longyang Lu on line #1 and then get the Maglev (see box, above). You could also take the metro the whole way (see p.22), or hop in a taxi (which will cost around ¥180). To get to **Hongqiao Airport**, take metro line #2 or catch a cab (¥60 or so from the centre; 45min).

Plane tickets

International and domestic **plane tickets** can be bought from any hotel or travel agent (where you will pay a small commission) or online at ⓦ elong .net, ⓦ travelchinaguide.com and ⓦ english.ctrip .com. You'll need to provide a phone number to confirm the booking.

By train

The main train station – **Shanghai Station** – is in the north of the city. It offers services to most cities in the country, a few high-speed trains to Nanjing and Xi'an, and services to Hong Kong. Its vast concrete forecourt is always a mass of encamped migrants, and it's not a particularly safe place to hang around at night. The best way to get out of the station area is by metro (lines #1, #3 and #4 run through it) or taxi (there's an official rank outside the station) – a cab into the city shouldn't cost more than ¥15–20.

If you've come on a slow train from Hangzhou, or many destinations in the south of China, you'll arrive at the impressive **Shanghai South Station**, which is on metro lines #1 and #3. And if you've come on the fast train from (for example) Beijing, Suzhou or Hangzhou, you'll arrive at the new **Hongqiao Station**, which is on metro lines #2 and #10.

You can **buy tickets** from the station itself, from a booking office or, for some destinations, online (see p.92). Most hotels will book tickets for you for a small fee.

By bus

Hardly any tourists arrive in Shanghai by bus. If you do you'll probably be dropped at either the **Shanghai South Bus Station** (which is underneath Shanghai South train station, on metro lines #1 and #3), or the **Shanghai Long-Distance Bus Station**, behind the main Shanghai train station north of

Suzhou Creek. Some buses arrive at **Hengfeng Lu Bus Station** – again, a short walk from the main train station. If you're unlucky, you might be dropped at **Pudong Bus Station** in the far east of the city ; a cab from here to town will cost ¥100 or so – it's cheaper to catch a cab to the nearest metro station, Chuansha Lu, a couple of kilometres southwest. A few services use the **Qiujiang Lu Bus Station**, next to the Baoshan Lu metro station. Sightseeing buses that serve the water towns use the **Shanghai Stadium Sightseeing Bus Station**; regular long-distance buses depart from the **Shanghai South Bus Station** (see p.97).

City transport

Shanghai's infrastructure is the best in mainland China. The metro system is the world's longest, and it's fast, extensive, air-conditioned and easy to navigate. Taxis are cheap and plentiful and drivers are honest, which means that it's easy to avoid the overcrowded bus system.

Cycling can be a good way to get around, though bear in mind that bikes are banned on most of the major roads in the daytime. **Walking** is more rewarding than in most Chinese cities – there are few of the tedious boulevards that tend to characterize Chinese city centres – but the sheer density of the crowds can be intimidating. Crossing the road is more stressful than it should be, as traffic is allowed to turn right even when the green man is flashing – you really have to stay on your toes. It's impossible to **rent a car** without a Chinese driving licence, and anyway you'd have to be nuts to voluntarily drive on these streets; you're much better off hiring a driver.

Tours of Shanghai can be a great way to see the sights, especially if you're short of time – a Huangpu **cruise** is one of the highlights of a visit and shouldn't be missed (see p.45). The train is the best way to get to most of the sights beyond the city, although for some you may have to take the bus (see p.97).

By metro

Shanghai's clean, modern **metro** operates from roughly 5.30am to around 11pm and includes both underground and light-rail lines. The system is easy to find your way around: station entrances are marked by a red "M" logo, all stations and trains are well signed in English and stops are announced in both English and Chinese when the train pulls in.

There are currently fourteen lines, with a couple more being built, although not all are particularly useful for visitors. **Line #1** runs north–south, with useful stations at the main railway station, People's Square, Changshu Lu (for the Old French Concession), Xujiahui and Shanghai Stadium. **Line #2** runs east–west with stations at Jing'an Temple, Henan Lu and, in Pudong, Lujiazui and the Science and Technology Museum. The lines intersect at the enormous People's Square station (take careful note of the wall maps here for which exit to use). Lines #4 to #7 are much less used by visitors, and mainly serve commuters. **Line #8** runs north–south, with handy stations at Hongkou Stadium, Qufu Lu and Laoximen (for the Old City). **Line #9** stops at tourist destinations in the far southern outskirts, such as Qibao and Sheshan, while **line #10** can get you to a clutch of tourist attractions in the centre – from Yuyuan it heads west to Xintiandi then on to the French Concession. **Line #11** is of limited interest, though it does end at the Disney resort. **Line #12** stops at Longhua and Shaanxi Nan Lu. **Line #13** is useful when it's going north–south – stops include the Natural History Museum, Xintiandi and the China Art Museum. You're not likely to use the other, suburban lines.

Note that there are a couple of line **intersections** that look like transit stations, as they share a name, but aren't. At these you have to leave the station, walk a short distance to another station and buy another ticket – unless you are using a stored-value card (see below), in which case you are still considered as being on the same journey. These "not quite" intersections are indicated on good metro maps by adjacent (rather than conjoined) circles. Ones you'll likely encounter are at the main train station (transferring between lines #3 and #4) and at Nanjing Xi Lu (transferring lines #2 and #12).

Tickets (¥3–10) can be bought from stations, either from touchscreen machines (there's an option for English) or from vendors who can also sell you a stored-value card for a refundable ¥20, which you can top up with as much as you like.

By bus

Shanghai has more than a thousand **bus** lines, all air-conditioned, and with services every few minutes, although they're often overcrowded, and you should be careful of pickpockets. Buses operate from 5am to 11pm, after which night buses take over. **Fares** are ¥2; you pay on board. There are on-board announcements in English, but be careful not to miss your stop as the next one will likely not be for another kilometre. Services with numbers in

USEFUL SHANGHAI BUS ROUTES

NORTH–SOUTH

#18 (trolleybus) From Lu Xun Park, across Suzhou Creek and along Xizang Lu.

#41 Passes Tianmu Xi Lu, in front of the Shanghai Railway Station, and goes down through the Old French Concession to Longhua Park.

#64 From Shanghai Railway Station, along Beijing Lu, then close to the Shiliupu wharf to the south of the Bund.

#65 From the top to the bottom of Zhongshan Dong Yi Lu (the Bund), terminating in the south at the Nanpu Bridge.

EAST–WEST

#3 From the Shanghai Museum across the Huangpu River to the Jinmao Tower.

#19 (trolleybus) From near Gongping Lu wharf in the east, passing near the *Astor House Hotel* and roughly following the course of Suzhou Creek to Yufo Temple.

#20 From Jiujiang Lu (just off the Bund) along Nanjing Xi Lu past Jing'an Temple, then on to Zhongshan Park metro station in the west of the city.

#42 From Guangxi Lu near People's Square then along Huaihai Lu in the Old French Concession.

#135 From Yangpu Bridge in the east of the city to the eastern end of Huaihai Lu, via the Bund.

#911 From the Yu Gardens to Huaihai Lu.

the 300s are night buses; those in the 400s cross the Huangpu. Most large fold-out city maps show bus routes, usually as a red or blue line with a dot indicating a stop. **Sightseeing buses** for tourist sights in the outskirts leave from the **Shanghai Stadium Sightseeing Bus Station.**

By taxi

Taxis are ubiquitous and very cheap – the rate is ¥2.4 per kilometre, a little more after 10pm, with a minimum charge of ¥14, or ¥18 at night. They can be hailed from the street, or booked in advance; the best **taxi company** is Dazhong (☎63183880), whose well-trained drivers wear uniforms and white gloves and drive newish Santanas (they also hire out cabbies at a day rate of around ¥600).

Locals these days often call **taxis** using a **smartphone app** (see box, p.37); these allow you to add a small tip if you want to get picked up more quickly, and are liked by cabbies. The upshot for low-tech roadside hailers – including most tourists – is that taxis are scarce at high-demand times, such as during downpours: those five empty cabs that just infuriatingly whooshed past your bedraggled, furiously waving form are all heading for an app booking.

When you do manage to hail a cab, bear in mind that drivers rarely speak English so you'll need your destination written down in Chinese characters. Otherwise, if you're heading anywhere near an intersection, just say the name of the two roads. The driver should flip the meter down as he accelerates away –

if he doesn't, say **dabiao** (dǎ biǎo). Having a map open on your lap deters unnecessary detours, but you shouldn't be paranoid as Shanghai cabbies are a decent bunch on the whole. If you get into a dispute with a driver, take his number, written on the sign on the dashboard – just the action of writing it down can produce a remarkable change of behaviour.

By bicycle

Cycling can be a great way to get around Shanghai, but you need to be wary – traffic is not disciplined and you'll no longer be one of a crowd of cyclists, as most locals seem to have abandoned bikes for scooters and cars. Pedestrians provide the biggest hazard, thanks to their tendency to step right out in front of you. Ringing your bell will elicit no response, so you need to yell – shouting in English gets a better response than trying to do it in Chinese (perhaps it sounds more alarming). Note that major thoroughfares are closed to cyclists between 7.30am and 5pm.

China Cycle Tours (☎1376 1115050, ⓦwww .chinacycletours.com), offers good **bike rental**, starting at ¥100 per day for a city bike (¥350 for a week); ¥150 for a mountain bike (¥500 for a week). They'll deliver to, and pick up from, your hotel, and rent you a helmet for ¥20 a day or ¥50 a week.

Otherwise some of the hostels **rent bikes**; the *Le Tour* youth hostel (see p.123) will rent to non-guests. Shanghai also has a citywide **bike-sharing** scheme, run by Forever Bikes (¥4/hr), though the bikes themselves are not great. To use it, head with passport ID to one of their booths – either at the Wukang Lu Tourist Information Centre, 393 Wukang Lu, near Hunan Lu in the Old French Concession (daily 9am–5pm) or, less centrally, at 1068 Zhaojia-bang Lu, outside Xujiahui station exit 14 (daily 9.30am–4.30pm). For a ¥200 deposit you'll receive a card that will unlock any of the orange clunkers at their bike stations, along with a map (in Chinese) that shows their locations – there are plenty in the centre.

A couple of companies run **cycling tours** of the city and out to the water towns (see below).

Tours

CITS, the government-run tourist office (see p.36), runs a wide range of tours and trips, as well as selling tickets for onward travel.

If you're short on time, the hop-on, hop-off double-decker bus sightseeing tours offered by **Big Bus** (W bigbustours.com) are a good option. The best route (¥350; ticket valid for 24 hours) trundles around the major sights, with 22 stops including the Shanghai Museum, Xintiandi, Jing'an Temple, the Cool Docks and Yu Gardens – a useful place to board is at the north side of People's Square, opposite Madame Tussauds (metro exit 7). A second (less interesting) route takes you around the less crucial sights of Pudong, and a third goes around the temples. Tickets can be bought through the website or at a hotel, and all include a free one-hour cruise down the Huangpu (see p.45) and entry to the Jinmao Tower observation deck.

Another company, Spring Tours, offers much cheaper bus tours (¥50 for a 48hr pass), but their departures are irregular and their service poor. The **Shanghai Stadium Sightseeing Bus Station**, close to the Caoxi Lu metro station on line #3, is the place to head for tours of the outlying areas, including the local water towns (see p.95).

Also good if you're short on time are the half-day and one-day **cycling tours** offered by China Cycle Tours (☎ 1376 1115050, W www.chinacycletours .com; from ¥400/person) which breeze around the major sights. For **overnight cycle tours** further afield, check out Bohdi Bikes (Building 15, 3F, 271 Qianyang Lu; ☎ 52669013, W www.bohdi.com.cn). Shanghai Insiders (172 Jinxian Lu; ☎ 1381 7616975, W shanghaiinsiders.com) offers intriguing tours in the sidecar of a vintage BMW **motorbike** (¥1500 for two hours).

Newman Tours (☎ 1381 7770229, W newmantours .com; around ¥200) leads guided English-language **walking tours** of the French Concession and the Bund, and an imaginative, if tenuous, evening Ghost Tour. Finally, for a **bespoke tour**, contact the reliable and helpful Timesavers (☎ 1592 1739908, W timesavers-sh.com) who can put together a personalized trip for you that might include after-hours access to tourist sites and talks from local experts.

The media

All media in China is censored. Journalists and bloggers who try to write about sensitive topics, and even the lawyers and NGOs who try to defend them, are often slung in jail, usually on a charge of "revealing state secrets". The Chinese state has put a mind-boggling amount of effort into fencing off the internet: more than two million people are employed in policing public opinion.

Newspapers and magazines

Xinhua is the Chinese news agency. You can read their reportage in the English-language **newspapers**, *China Daily* and *Shanghai Star*, available from most newsagents, including those on metro platforms. Both have a handy section listing mainstream cultural events.

Imported publications (sometimes censored) such as *Time*, *Newsweek* and Hong Kong's *South China Morning Post* can be bought at the bookshops of four- and five-star hotels and are sometimes available at the Foreign Language Bookstore (see p.163) – a particularly useful resource if you are moving to Shanghai or doing business here. A number of magazines aimed at expats are useful for listings (see p.36).

The internet

Tireless as ever in controlling what its citizens know, the government has built a sophisticated **firewall** – known as the "Golden Shield Project", but nicknamed the new Great Wall of China – that blocks access to undesirable websites. The way the firewall is administered shifts regularly according to the mood of the powers that be. In general, you can be pretty sure you **won't be able to access** stories deemed controversial from sites such as the BBC or CNN, or anything about Tibetan freedom or democracy. Neither can you get Facebook, YouTube, Twitter or anything Google, including Google Maps and Gmail. If you normally rely on a **Gmail** account, make sure you set up a temporary account before you go with a safe provider – Hotmail will do – and get your emails automatically forwarded to that.

Virtual private networks (VPNs)

The firewall isn't impenetrable, however; it's simply meant to make getting information deemed controversial enough of a hassle that most Chinese people won't bother. You can get around it simply by subscribing to a **Virtual Private Network**, or **VPN**, such as Astrill, ExpressVPN or Vypr, all of which cost a few pounds or dollars a month and offer a free limited-period trial – though you may need to pay a little more for "Stealth" mode to get the VPN to work properly. Technically, of course, this is illegal, but the government pays no attention to foreigners who do this – and just about every foreign business in China runs a VPN. For Chinese nationals, it's a different matter, and you will never find a public computer, such as one in an internet café, hotel or business centre, running a VPN.

Internet cafés and wi-fi

Shanghai has plenty of **internet cafés**, usually full of kids playing games. They're generally located in backstreets, not on the ground floor, and never signposted in English – look for the net character, **wǎng 网**. All are open 24 hours, and rates are cheap (around ¥3/hr), but they're heavily regulated – you'll need to show your **passport** before being allowed near a computer. There are a couple on Nanyang Lu, behind the Shanghai Centre, and another on Yunnan Nan Lu, just south of the intersection with Huaihai Zhong Lu.

Shanghai Library, 1555 Huaihai Zhong Lu (Ⓜ Hengshan Lu; daily 7am–2am) has a ground-floor room full of computers which cost ¥4 per hour to use; again, you'll have to show a passport. In addition, all large **hotels** have business centres where you can

get online, but this is expensive, especially in the classier places (around ¥30/hr). Better value are the **backpacker hostels** (see p.116), which all have a few grubby computers that are free for use by guests.

Just about every bar, café and restaurant has **free wi-fi**, as do shopping malls and hotel lobbies. While independent businesses will have a wi-fi password, in some chains – including *Starbucks*, *Costa* and *McDonald's* – you'll need a log-in code to access wi-fi. The code is sent to your mobile, so if you're not toting a mobile phone with a local number (see p.35) you'll have to get a member of staff to help you.

USEFUL WEBSITES

China Bloglist Ⓦ chinabloglist.org. Directory with links to more than five hundred blogs about China, most of whose writers have unique insights into the country, its people and culture.

China Business World Ⓦ cbw.com. Corporate directory site with a useful travel section, detailing tours and allowing you to book flights and hotels.

China Hush Ⓦ chinahush.com. Translations of what Chinese forums are saying about popular national press stories.

City Weekend Ⓦ cityweekend.com.cn/shanghai. Up-to-date listings and light-hearted, informative features aimed at expats.

Danwei Ⓦ danwei.org. English-language analysis of high-brow and "serious" goings-on in the Chinese media. Thorough and worthy, but a little humourless.

Expat Shanghai Ⓦ expatsh.com. Bags of useful info for the baffled big nose – how to register your pet, what's on TV and so on.

Middle Kingdom Life Ⓦ middlekingdomlife.com. Online manual for foreigners planning to live and work in China, providing a sane sketch of the personal and professional difficulties they're likely to face.

Shanghaiist Ⓦ shanghaiist.com. News and a forum, with lots of quirky local gossip; entertaining and informative.

Smartshanghai Ⓦ smartshanghai.com. The definitive nightlife site, with plenty of restaurant reviews, too; up to date, with events listings, bitchy user reviews, maps (a rare plus) and a personals section.

That's Shanghai Ⓦ thatsmags.com/shanghai. This extensive website is rather more useful than its sister print magazine, with a good "community" section, listings and features.

Time Out Ⓦ timeoutshanghai.com. Hip listings magazine for expats, well written and with in-depth restaurant and bar reviews.

Zhongwen.com Ⓦ zhongwen.com. A dictionary site useful for students of Chinese and anyone struggling to communicate.

Radio

On the **radio** you're likely to hear the latest ballads from the Hong Kong and Taiwan idol factories, or versions of Western pop songs sung in Chinese. The **BBC World Service** can be picked up at 12010, 15278, 17760 and 21660kHz. **Voice of America** can be tuned into on 5880, 6125, 9760, 15250, 15425, 17820 and 21840kHz. **China Drive** is a bilingual music station at 87.9FM – you'll probably hear it in a cab sometime.

Television

Chinese **TV** is heavy on domestic travel and wildlife programmes, along with elaborate song-and-dance extravaganzas. The most popular dramas are Korean; gung-ho Chinese war films, in which the Japanese are shown getting mightily beaten, at least have the advantage that you don't need to speak the language to understand what's going on. There are plenty of tacky dating shows, and pop idol-type shows are tremendously popular – though the latter are sometimes taken off the air by censors for vulgarity.

The only **English-language** programmes are news; CCTV9 is an English-language **news** channel, while local broadcaster SBN has a news update at 10pm daily. The CCTV5 sports channel often shows European football games. **Satellite TV** in English is available in the more expensive hotels, and most mid- and top-range hotels will have ESPN, BBC and CNN.

Festivals and public holidays

The rhythm of festivals and religious observances that used to mark the Chinese calendar was interrupted by the Cultural Revolution, and only now, more than forty years on, are old traditions beginning to re-emerge. The majority of festivals celebrate the turning of the seasons or propitious dates, such as the ninth day of the ninth lunar month, and are times for gift-giving, family reunions and feasting.

Traditional **festivals** follow dates in the Chinese lunar calendar, in which the month starts when the moon is a new crescent, and the middle of the month is marked by the full moon; by the Gregorian calendar, these festivals fall on a different date every year.

Generally **public holidays** have little effect on business, with only government departments and certain banks closing. Exceptions are New Year's Day, during the first three days of the Chinese New Year and National Day, when most businesses, shops and sights will be shut, though some restaurants stay open.

JANUARY & FEBRUARY

New Year's Day Jan 1.

Spring Festival Starts between late Jan and mid-Feb. Chinese New Year Celebrations extend over the first two weeks of the new lunar year (see box opposite).

MARCH & APRIL

Shanghai Literary Festival March; Ⓦ m-restaurantgroup.com/mbund/literary-festival.html. Held over three weekends in March at *M on the Bund* (see p.130), the city's literary festival has attracted some of the world's most fêted writers. A high point in the cultural calendar.

Guanyin's Birthday April 4, 2018; March 25, 2019; March 12, 2020. Guanyin, the goddess of mercy and probably China's most popular Buddhist deity, is celebrated on the nineteenth day of the second lunar month; festivities are held at the Yufo and Baiyunguan temples.

Qingming Festival April 4 & 5. "Tomb Sweeping Day" is the time to visit the graves of ancestors, leave offerings of food and burn ghost money – fake paper currency – in honour of the departed.

MAY

Labour Day May 1. A national holiday, during which all tourist sights are extremely busy.

Youth Day May 4. Commemorating the student demonstration in Tian'anmen Square in 1919, which gave rise to the nationalist, anti-imperialist May Fourth Movement.

JUNE

Children's Day June 1. Most school pupils are taken on excursions on this day, so if you're visiting a popular tourist sight, be prepared for mobs of kids in yellow caps.

Dragon Festival June 18, 2018; June 7, 2019; April 4, 2020. A one-day public holiday held on the fifth day of the fifth lunar month. Traditionally, a time to watch dragonboat racing.

Shanghai International Film Festival Mid-June; Ⓦ siff.com. This highly regarded movie festival brings a raft of interesting films to the city.

SEPTEMBER

Moon Festival Oct 4, 2017; Sept 24, 2018; Sept 13, 2019. Celebrated on the fifteenth day of the eighth lunar month, this national holiday is also known as the Mid-Autumn Festival. It's a time for family reunions, celebrated with fireworks and lanterns; in Shanghai there is an evening parade along Huaihai Lu. Moon cakes, containing a rich filling of sweet paste, are eaten.

Shanghai Biennale Sept–Nov 2018 & 2020; Ⓦ shanghaibiennale.org. An increasingly big deal on the international arts scene; the main venue is the Power Station of Art (see p.57).

OCTOBER

National Day Oct 1. Everyone has three days off to celebrate the founding of the People's Republic, and TV is packed with programmes celebrating the achievements of the Party. During the "golden week" expect massive crowds everywhere – it's not a convenient time to travel.

Double Ninth Festival Oct 28, 2017; Oct 17, 2018; Oct 7, 2019. Nine is a number associated with *yang*, or male energy, and on the ninth day of the ninth lunar month qualities such as assertiveness and

CHINESE NEW YEAR

The **Spring Festival**, which usually falls in late January or the first half of February, is marked by two weeks of festivities celebrating the beginning of a new year in the lunar calendar (and is thus also called **Chinese New Year**). In Chinese astrology, each year is associated with a particular animal from a cycle of twelve and the passing into a new astrological phase is a momentous occasion.

There's a tangible sense of excitement in the run-up to the festival, when Shanghai is at its most colourful, with shops and houses decorated with good-luck messages, stalls and shops selling paper money, drums and costumes, and skyscrapers festooned with neon. However, it's not a good time to **travel** – most of the population is heading to their home town, so don't even think about trying to get a plane or a train ticket during this period. For the days of the festival itself, Shanghai is eerily quiet and most businesses shut down.

The **first day** of the festival is marked by a family feast at which **jiaozi** (dumplings) are eaten, sometimes with coins hidden inside. To bring luck, people dress in red clothes (red being regarded as a lucky colour) – a particularly important custom if the animal of their birth year is coming round again – and each family tries to eat a whole fish, since the word for fish is a homonym for surplus. After eating everyone relaxes in front of the world's most watched entertainment TV show, the *New Year gala*. In the evening, firecrackers are let off to scare ghosts away – this is done again on the fifth day, to honour Cai Shen, god of wealth. (Another ghost-scaring tradition you'll notice during New Year is the pasting up of images of door gods at the threshold.)

The most public expression of the festivities – a must for visitors – is at the **Longhua Temple** (see p.89), held on the first few days of the festival. There are food and craft stalls and plenty of folk entertainments such as stilt walkers and jugglers. The highlight is on the evening of the first day, when the Longhua bell is struck.

New Year falls on February 16, 2018 (Year of the Dog); February 5, 2019 (Year of the Pig); January 25, 2020 (Year of the Rat); and February 12, 2021 (Year of the Ox).

strength are celebrated. It's believed to be a good time for the distillation (and consumption) of spirits.

NOVEMBER

Shanghai International Arts Fair Throughout Nov Ⓦ artsbird .com. This month-long fair sees a variety of cultural programming at the city's arts venues. At its best during the Shanghai Biennale (see p.26).

Sport and activities

Head to any public space in Shanghai in the morning and you'll see citizens going through all sorts of martial arts routines, playing ping pong and street badminton, and even ballroom dancing. Sadly though, facilities for organized sport are fairly limited.

Spectator sports

The Chinese say they're good at "small" ball games, such as squash, badminton and, of course, table tennis, at which they are world champions, but also admit there is room for improvement in the "big" ball games, such as **football**. That may be set to change though, as Premier Xi Jinping is a big footie fan, and – partly to curry favour with him – China's billionaires are throwing money into the Chinese Super League. In 2016, for instance, the Brazilian player "Hulk" signed for Shanghai SIPG, earning the world's third-highest football salary. SIPG play at the Shanghai Stadium in the south of the city (metro line #4). Their rivals are the more established Shanghai Shenhua, who play at Hongkou Stadium (see p.85) in the north (metro lines #3 and #8). It's worth catching a game, especially when the two Shanghai teams play each other, or bitter rivals Beijing Guo'an or Hangzhou's Greentown. You can see schedules at Ⓦ soccerway.com. Tickets, from ¥50, are available from the stadium ticket office or scalpers on the day, or in advance from Ⓦ mypiao.com. For more on Shanghai's football scene, check out English-language fanblog Ⓦ wildeastfootball.net.

Basketball has a massive following. You can see the Shanghai Sharks play at the Yuanshen Sports Centre, which is on metro line #6; the season runs from November to April. Tickets, from ¥80, are available on the night or in advance from Ⓦ mypiao.com.

Shanghai has an impressive **Formula One** track at Jiading, west of the city (**W** icsh.sh.cn). Races are held every September; tickets start at ¥50.

Activities

Most large hotels have **gyms**, with facilities at the *Westin* and *Pudong Shangri-La* being particularly impressive. Good private gyms with walk-in deals include Physical, 7F, Raffles City Mall, 268 Xizang Zhong Lu (**T**63403939) and Total Fitness, 5F, 819 Nanjing Xi Lu, near Taixing Lu (**T**62553535).

Yoga has taken off in a big way with the smart set. The most fashionable studio is Yplus (3F, 150 Hubin Lu, **T**63406161; 3F, 308 Anfu Lu, **T**64372121; **W** www.yplus.cn).

For swimming, try the **Olympic-size pool** in the International Gymnastic Centre at 777 Wuyi Lu (Mon–Fri 3.30–9.30pm, Sat & Sun 8.30am–9.30pm; **T**62289488) or the smaller Pudong Pool, 3669 Pudong Nan Lu (Mon–Fri 3.30–9pm, Sat & Sun 9am–9pm; **T**5889015856). One of the best of the luxury hotels for swimming is the *JW Marriott* (see p.117), which offers indoor and outdoor pools with views over People's Square. Entry is ¥150.

For fun, you can't beat the **Dino Beach water park** at 78 Xinzhen Lu, near Gudai Lu, Qibao town (mid-June to early Sept daily 9am–9pm; ¥200, ¥100 after 6pm; **T**64783333, **W**dinobeach.com.cn); with its slides, wave machines and 50m-long artificial beach. Rather incongruously, indie music gigs and raves are occasionally held here.

Golfers will find plenty of courses outside the city; the most prestigious is the Shanghai West Golf

---

MASSAGE AND SPAS

Shanghai has superb **massage and spa facilities**, with something for all budgets. The perfect places to go to unwind from the stresses of a noisy, overcrowded city – or even to cap a night out on the town – they're generally open from 10am till 10pm or later.

There will be a **foot masseur** in every neighbourhood – you can spot them by the poster showing big feet in the window. For around ¥25 you'll get your toes and legs bathed, then thoroughly rubbed and pummelled for around forty minutes.

The city also boasts a **massage neighbourhood**, Dagu Lu, in Jing'an off Maoming Bei Lu, where a whole strip of upscale massage venues offer every imaginable treatment. The branch of Dragonfly here is perennially popular.

At the upper end of the scale, there are some fantastic, lavish **spas**, with well-trained English-speaking staff. Look out for discounts and special offers in the expat magazines.

MASSAGE

Dragonfly 2F, 559 Nanchang Lu (**T** 54561318); 206 Xinle Lu (**T** 54039982); 458 Dagu Lu (**T** 62371193); 193 Jiaozhou Lu (**T** 52135778); **W** dragonfly.net.cn; daily 10am–midnight. This popular chain offers aromatherapy massage to relieve muscular aches and restore energy, as well as shiatsu and Chinese massages (all start at ¥188/hr). There's even a hangover relief massage (¥358 for 2hr).

Ganzhi Blindman Massage 1065 Beijing Xi Lu, near Jinagnin Lu (**T** 52287621); daily 10am–2pm. No-frills venue where the staff (all of whom are blind) know their stuff. Very good value at ¥78 for one hour.

Green Massage 58 Taicang Lu, near Jinan Lu (**T** 53860222, **W** greenmassage.com.cn); daily 10.30am–2am. Shiatsu and cupping among a wide range of inexpensive treatment massages, starting at around ¥188. Handily located just around the corner from Xintiandi.

Huimou Massage 1 Lane 117, Ruijin Er Lu (**T** 64664857); daily 11am–2am. Cheap and friendly – foot massage ¥60, body massage ¥80, aromatherapy massage ¥184 for an hour. They can also arrange house calls, for which the same rates apply plus the cost of return taxi fare.

Yiheyuan Massage 656 Jianguo Xi Lu (**T** 54651265); daily 10am–2am. Inexpensive foot, body, aromatherapy and traditional Chinese massages, from ¥60.

SPAS

Anantara Spa 3F, Puli hotel, 1 Changde Lu (**T** 32039999, **W** spa.anantara.com/shanghai); daily 10am–midnight. One of the best high-end spas, with a mix of Chinese and Thai techniques. A two-hour full body massage will cost ¥1500, a green tea wrap a little less.

Banyan Tree Spa 3F, Westin hotel, 88 Henan Zhong Lu (**T** 63351888, **W** banyantreespa.com); daily 10am–midnight. Thai-style oil massages, themed around the elements; prices start at ¥880.

ESPA 55F, Ritz-Carlton hotel, 8 Century Ave (**T** 20201888); daily 9.30am–10pm. This luxurious spa even has perfumed showers, and the relaxation rooms offer great views. English-speaking therapists specialize in treatments inspired by Chinese traditions, such as the Jade facial, which will set you back just over ¥1200.

Hilton Spa Hilton hotel, 250 Huashan Lu (**T** 62480000); daily 10am–10pm. Reasonably priced, no-nonsense and a bit more clinical than the other top-end places, this place is popular with men. Treatments include Chinese and Swedish massages and facials, from ¥880.

Club (☎0512 57203888, ⓦ shanghaiwest.com.cn). The more conveniently located Hongqiao Golf Club in the west of the city (☎64215522) has a driving range and is reasonably priced (¥480 for a round).

PUBLIC TOILETS		
toilet	厕所	cèsuǒ
man	男	nán
woman	女	nü

Culture and etiquette

Shanghai is cosmopolitan and sophisticated, and its inhabitants on the whole well-mannered. But because the streets are so crowded there is a widespread public brusqueness that can take some getting used to. Pushy vendors will shout at you, jump in front of you or even tug your arm, and it takes a while to train yourself to simply ignore them, as the locals do.

Businesspeople meeting for the first time exchange business cards, with the offered card held in two hands as a gesture of respect – you'll see polite shop assistants doing the same with your change.

If you **visit a Chinese house**, you'll be expected to give your hosts a small gift, though avoid giving anything too practical as it might be construed as charity.

There is a certain amount of **restaurant** etiquette (see p.126). Pricier restaurants will have a **no-smoking section**, but mid-range restaurants, cafés and bars often don't. **Public toilets** are sanitary on the whole, but if you blanch at going local, visit any decent hotel – there are always Western-style toilets in the lobby. You'll soon become familiar with the characters you need to know (see box, below).

Sex and gender

Women travellers in Shanghai usually find sexual harassment much less of a problem than in other Asian countries. Chinese men are, on the whole, deferential and respectful.

In terms of sexual mores, pretty much anything goes in Shanghai these days – the **LGBT scene**, for instance, is the best in the country (see p.147), though public displays of homosexual behaviour

Tipping is never expected, and though you might sometimes feel it's warranted, resist the temptation – you'll set a precedent.

will raise an eyebrow. **Prostitution**, though illegal, is widespread, with plenty of hairdressers and massage parlours operating as ill-disguised brothels. AIDS is common and the public remains largely ignorant of sexual health issues. Condoms are widely available.

Travel essentials

Children

Foreigners with kids can expect to receive lots of attention from curious locals – and the occasional admonition that the little one should be wrapped up more warmly. Local kids don't use **nappies**, just pants with a slit at the back, and when baby starts to go, mummy points him at the gutter. Nappies are available from modern supermarkets such as Parkson and City Shop (see p.147), though there are few public changing facilities. High-end hotels offer **baby-minding services** for around ¥200 an hour.

Sights that children would enjoy include the Shanghai Aquarium and Century Park in Pudong (see p.75), the zoo (see p.90), acrobat shows (see p.150), Disneyland (see p.94), Dino Beach (see p.28) and the Natural History and Science and Technology museums (see p.72 and p.80). If you're tired of worrying about your kids in the traffic, try taking them to pedestrianized Xintiandi (see p.59), Tianzifang (see p.64), South Bund (see p.87) or Moganshan Arts District (see p.73).

Costs

Though there's a minority in Shanghai who throw their money around – and plenty of places to spend it – it's quite possible to live cheaply, with most locals surviving on salaries of around ¥5000 a month.

Generally, your biggest expense will be accommodation. Food and transport, on the other hand, are cheap. The minimum **daily budget** you can comfortably maintain is around US$50/£38/¥330 a day, if you stay in a dormitory, get around by metro and eat in local restaurants. On a budget of US$85/£65/¥550 a day, you'll have a better time, staying in a room in a hostel or cheap business hotel, taking taxis and eating in decent restaurants. To stay in an upmarket hotel and eat in the trendiest places you'll need around US$250/£190/¥1700 a day.

Discounts on some admission prices are available to students in China on production of the red Chinese student identity card or ISIC card, and an international youth hostel card gets a small discount at hostels.

High-end restaurants and hotels add a ten or fifteen percent **service charge** (annoyingly though, it rarely goes to the staff), but **tips** are not expected.

Crime and personal safety

The main problem likely to affect tourists visiting Shanghai is **getting scammed** (see box, below). In terms of personal safety, Shanghai is safer than most Western cities, but you do need to take care as tourists are an obvious target for petty **theft**. Passports and money should be kept in a concealed money belt, and it's a good idea to hide away some cash, your insurance policy details and photocopies of your passport and visa. Be wary on buses, the favoured haunt of pickpockets.

Hotel rooms are on the whole secure, dormitories less so – in the latter case it's often fellow travellers who are the problem. Most hotels should have a safe, but it's not unusual for things to go missing from these.

On the street, flashy jewellery and watches will attract the wrong kind of attention, and try to be discreet when taking out your cash.

The police

The police, or **PSB** (Public Security Bureau) are recognizable by their dark blue uniforms and caps. You'll most likely have to seek them out for visa extensions (see p.31), to get a loss report or complain (uselessly) when you've been scammed

> ### EMERGENCY NUMBERS
> **Police ☎** 110
> **Fire ☎** 119
> **Ambulance ☎** 120
> Note that in an emergency you are generally better off **taking a taxi** (see p.23) to the nearest hospital than calling for an ambulance.

in a teahouse (see box, below). They are often extremely helpful, but can be officious. A convenient **police station** is at 499 Nanjing Xi Lu, beside the Chengdu Bei Lu overpass.

Electricity

The **electricity supply** runs on 220 volts, with the most common type of plug dual flat prong. Adaptors are widely available from neighbourhood hardware stores, or any of the tech malls (see below).

Entry requirements
Visa applications

To enter China, all foreign nationals require a **visa**. The Chinese embassy has outsourced its visa services to a Chinese visa service application centre (Ⓦ visaforchina.org), which will process your application much more quickly than the embassies used to, and accepts postal applications, but administration fees are substantial – as much as the cost of the visa itself. Offices are usually not far from the embassy or consulate and are open from Monday to Friday.

Single-entry tourist visas (L) must be used within three months of issue, and cost US$50–80 or the local equivalent. The standard L visa is valid for a month, but the authorities will sometimes grant a two- or three-month visa for the same price – though they might refuse at times of heavy

---

WARNING: SCAM ARTISTS

Getting scammed is the biggest threat to foreign visitors, and there are so many professional con artists targeting tourists that you can expect to be approached many times a day at places such as **Yuyuan Bazaar**, around **People's Square** and on **Nanjing Dong Lu**.

Commonly, a sweet-looking young couple, a pair of girls, or perhaps a kindly old man, will ask to practise their English with you, offer to show you round or just ask you to take a photo with their camera. After befriending you – which may take hours – they will suggest some refreshment, and lead you to a teahouse. Following a traditional-looking tea ceremony you will be presented with a bill for thousands of yuan, your new "friends" will disappear or pretend to be shocked, and some large gentlemen will appear. In another variation, you will be coaxed into buying a painting (really a print) for a ridiculous sum. Remember never to drink with a stranger if you haven't seen a price list.

tourist traffic. British travellers can get a two-year multiple -entry L tourist visa.

To apply for an L visa you have to submit an application form, either one or two passport-size photographs, your passport (which must be valid for at least another six months from your planned date of entry into China, and have at least one blank page for visas) and the fee. Offices also demand proof of entry and exit – such as a flight booking – and proof of accommodation bookings for the whole trip (though these can be cancelled later; bookings are straightforward on ⓦhostelbookers.com and can be cancelled for free). If you intend to stay with friends, you must provide photocopies of their passport information and visa page and a letter of invitation. You'll also be asked where you intend to visit; this is not binding, and is not checked – but it's safest not to put down sensitive areas such as Tibet or Xinjiang.

If you apply in person, processing should take between three and five working days. Postal applications are a little more expensive and take longer. You'll be asked your occupation – it's not wise to admit to being a journalist or writer as you may be forced to apply for the inconvenient **journalist visa (J)**, which restricts your movements. And at sensitive times, any media job can cause your application to be rejected. If you do make up a job, say that you are a freelancer – otherwise you might be asked to produce salary slips.

A **business visa (F)** is valid for six months and can be for either multiple or single entry; you'll need an official invitation from a government-recognized Chinese organization to apply. **Twelve-month work visas (Z)** again require an invitation, plus a health certificate from your doctor.

Students can get an **F visa** if they have an invitation or letter of acceptance from a college in Shanghai, though this is only valid for six months. If you're intending to study for longer, you need to fill out an additional form, available from Chinese embassies and online, and will need a health certificate; you'll be issued with an **X visa** which allows you to stay and study for up to a year.

If you are coming to Shanghai to live or work you'll need a **work visa** and a **residence permit** (see p.33).

Visa extensions

When you're in China, it's possible to get a **first extension** to a tourist visa, valid for a month; most Europeans pay ¥160 for this, and Americans nearly ¥1000. You need to start the application with at least seven days left on your original visa. To apply for an extension, go to the "Aliens Entry Exit Department" of

VISA-FREE TRANSIT

Currently, visitors from the US, Canada, UK and many European countries arriving on international flights can spend up to 72 hours in Shanghai in transit without a visa. To be eligible, you must have proof of onward travel to a third country (so you can't, for instance, be on a round trip from Hong Kong). You are also not allowed to leave the city's boundaries during your stay.

the PSB (Public Security Bureau) at 1500 Minsheng Lu, in Pudong, near Yinchun Lu (Mon–Fri 9–11.30am & 1.30–4.30pm). The visa office is on the third floor. You'll need a passport photo (a shop on the ground floor offers a photo service), proof of your address in Shanghai (take some pink hotel receipts), proof that you have plans to leave the country (ideally a plane ticket, if you have one) and an itinerary for what you plan to do for the rest of your stay (which can be ficti-tious, of course). You may also need to prove that you have health insurance and they may want to see train tickets, museum entrance tickets and such like to prove that you haven't been working illegally in Shanghai. The officious staff will keep your passport for at least a week – you can't change money, or even book into a new hotel, while they've got it. **Subsequent applications** for extensions will be refused unless you have a good reason to stay, such as illness or travel delays, but they'll reluctantly give you a couple of extra days if you have a flight out of the country booked.

Don't **overstay your visa** – the fine is ¥500 per day, and if you're caught at the airport with an out-of-date visa the subsequent hassle may mean you miss your flight.

Customs regulations

It's officially illegal to **import** printed or filmed matter critical of the country, but don't worry too much about this, as confiscation is rare in practice.

Meanwhile, **export restrictions** apply on any items over 100 years old that you might buy in China. As you'd be hard pressed to buy anything that old in Shanghai, you needn't be unduly concerned about the process – the "antiques" you commonly see for sale are all fakes (see p.158).

CHINESE EMBASSIES AND CONSULATES

Australia 15 Coronation Drive, Yarralumla, Canberra, ACT 2600 (ⓣ000612 6228 3999, ⓦau.china-embassy.org); consulates in Toorak, Surry Hills, Camperdown and East Perth.

Canada 515 St Patrick St, Ottawa, Ontario K1N 5 (☎ 613 7891911, Ⓦ ca.china-embassy.org); consulates in Calgary, Toronto and Vancouver.

New Zealand 2–6 Glenmore St, Wellington 6011 (☎ 064 21 528663, Ⓦ cnz.china-embassy.org); consulate in Auckland (☎ 09 525 1589).

Republic of Ireland 40 Ailesbury Rd, Dublin 4 (☎ 01 269 0032, Ⓦ www.ie.chineseembassy.org).

South Africa 972 Pretorius St, Arcadia, Pretoria 0007 (☎ 1243165000, Ⓦ chinese-embassy.org.za).

UK 31 Portland Place, London W1B 1QD (☎ 020 7631 1430, Ⓦ chinese-embassy.org.uk); consulates at Denison House, Denison Rd, Victoria Park, Manchester M14 5RX (☎ 0161 224 7480), 55 Corstorphine Rd, Edinburgh EH12 5QC (☎ 0131 3373220) and Belfast (Ⓦ belfast.china-consulate.org).

US 3505 International Place, Washington DC 20008 (☎ 202 495 2266, Ⓦ china-embassy.org); consulates in Chicago, Houston, Los Angeles, New York and San Francisco.

FOREIGN CONSULATES IN SHANGHAI

Australia 22F, 1168 Nanjing Xi Lu (☎ 22155200, Ⓦ shanghai .china.embassy.gov.au).

Canada 8F, ECO City Building, 1788 Nanjing Xi Lu (☎ 32792800).

New Zealand 2801-2802A and 2806B-2810, Corporate Ave 5, 150 Hubin Lu (☎ 54075858, Ⓦ nzembassy.com/china).

Republic of Ireland 700A Shanghai Centre, 1376 Nanjing Xi Lu (☎ 62798739, Ⓦ dfa.ie/irish-consulate/shanghai).

South Africa 222 Yanan Dong Lu (☎ 53594977).

United Kingdom 17F, The British Centre, Garden Square, Beijing Xi Lu (☎ 62797651, Ⓦ ukinchina.fco.gov.uk).

US 1469 Huaihai Zhong Lu (☎ 64336880, Ⓦ shanghai .usembassy-china.org.cn).

Health

The most common health hazard in Shanghai is the **cold and flu infections** that strike down a large proportion of the population in the winter months, but **diarrhoea** can also be a problem. It usually strikes in a mild form while your stomach gets used to unfamiliar food, but can also be a sudden onset accompanied by stomach cramps and vomiting, which indicates food poisoning. In both instances, get plenty of rest, drink lots of water and in serious cases replace lost salts with oral rehydration solution (ORS); this is especially important with young children. Take a few sachets with you, or make your own by adding half a teaspoon of salt and three of sugar to a litre of cool, previously boiled water. If you are struck with diarrhoea, avoid milk, greasy or spicy foods, coffee and most fruit, in favour of bland food such as rice, plain noodles and soup. If symptoms persist, or if you notice blood or mucus in your stools, consult a doctor.

To avoid stomach complaints, eat at places that look busy and clean and stick to fresh, thoroughly cooked food. Beware of food that has been precooked and kept warm for several hours. Sadly, you'd be advised to avoid all **street food** – it's often cooked with reclaimed gutter oil, which is just as disgusting as it sounds. Shellfish is a potential hepatitis A risk, and also best avoided. Fresh fruit you've peeled yourself is safe; other uncooked foods may have been washed in unclean water. Shanghai's **tap water** can be a little suspect – too many heavy metals – so try to avoid drinking it. Boiled or bottled water is widely available.

Finally, note that though Shanghai is a relatively permissive place, there is widespread ignorance of sexual health issues; always practise **safe sex**.

Hospitals, clinics and pharmacies

Medical facilities in Shanghai are pretty good: there are some high-standard international clinics, big hotels have a resident doctor, and for minor complaints, there are plenty of pharmacies that can suggest remedies. Most doctors will treat you with Western techniques first, but will also know a little Traditional Chinese Medicine (TCM).

Chinese **hospitals** sometimes charge high prices for simple drugs and procedures that aren't necessary – they'll put you on a drip just to administer antibiotics – so be wary of price gouging. In an **emergency** you're better off taking a cab than waiting for an ambulance – it's quicker and will work out much cheaper. The United Family Hospital (1139 Xianxia Lu; 24hr hotline ☎ 22163999, Ⓦ shanghai.ufh.com.cn) in Xujiahui, near Beixinjing metro station, is staffed entirely by English-speaking doctors trained in the West. They also have a clinic in Pudong at 525 Hongfeng Lu. Huashan Hospital (12 Wulumuqi Zhong Lu; ☎ 62489999, Ⓦ huashan .org.cn) has some English-speaking staff and a specialist foreigners' clinic on the eighth floor (daily 8am–10pm; ☎ 62483986); some English is also spoken at the Ruijin Hospital (197 Ruijin Er Lu; ☎ 64370045, Ⓦ www.rjh.com.cn). Expect to pay around ¥700 for a **consultation** at all of the above.

Expats with medical insurance use **private clinics** – reliable, English speaking, international standard and expensive. The largest is Parkway (24hr hotline ☎ 64455999, Ⓦ parkwayhealth.cn), with seven clinics. The most central are at 2F, Shanghai Centre, 1376 Nanjing Xi Lu (Mon–Fri 9am–7pm, Sat & Sun 9am–5pm) and 2258 Hongqiao Lu (Mon–Fri 9am–7pm, Sat & Sun 9am–5pm). A consultation will cost around ¥1000. Parkway manages one hospital, the East International Medical Centre (150 Jimo Lu, near Pudong Dadao; 24hr hotline ☎58799999, Ⓦseimc.com.cn), which accepts travellers with medical insurance.

Dental treatment will often not be covered on your travel insurance – but thankfully treatment is a little cheaper than in the West. Head to Parkway, or the United Family Hospital, where it's cheaper but you'll have more of a wait. For surprisingly affordable dental treatment from English-speaking staff, head to CAD (daily 9am–6pm; Block G, Zhonglian Villa, 1720 Huaihai Zhong Lu, near Wuxing Lu; ☎64377100) or KOWA, which has branches (both daily 8.30am–8.30pm; Ⓦen.kowa-dental.com) at 11F, HONI Plaza, 199 Chengdu Bei Lu, near Weihai Lu (☎80 09881120) and 3N1–3N5, Jinmao Tower, 88 Century Ave (☎51082222).

Pharmacies are marked by a green cross. Be wary of backstreet pharmacies as counterfeit drugs are common (check for spelling mistakes in the packaging or instructions). There is a 24-hour pharmacy at 201 Lianhua Lu, Changning (☎62941403), and another outside the Huashan Hospital (see above). Watson's (daily 9am–9pm) is a good pharmacy for over-the-counter medicines – there are large branches at 787 Huaihai Zhong Lu and 616 Nanjing Dong Lu, and in the basements of the Times Square Mall on Huaihai Lu, Raffles Mall on Fuzhou Lu and Westgate Mall on Nanjing Xi Lu.

Insurance

With medical cover expensive you'd be wise to have **travel insurance**. There's little opportunity for dangerous sports in Shanghai (though crossing the road might count) so a standard policy should be sufficient. Check if your policy includes dental treatment, as many don't.

Laundry

All hotels provide a **laundry service** for around ¥50–150. Hostels have self-service laundries. There are few public laundries, though a hotel concierge can usually point you towards a local entrepreneur who runs a service from home. Laundry Town (Ⓦlaundrytown.com) will pick up and deliver, and charges ¥25 a kilo.

Living and working in Shanghai

If you want to stay on in Shanghai, you'll need a **residence permit**, which your employer will help you sort out. You have to show your passport and **Z** (working) visa, health certificate, employment certificate, work permit and your employer's business licence at the main PSB (see p.30). The issued green card is then valid for a year.

Foreigners often live in housing targeted towards them. Rent in these suburban compounds is expensive, usually at least US$2000 a month, which gets you a tolerable imitation of a Western apartment. Living in ordinary neighbourhoods is cheaper: a central, furnished two-bedroom apartment costs around US$900 a month. The easiest way to find an apartment is through a real-estate agent, who will usually take a month's rent as a fee. There are lots of agents, and many of them advertise in the expat magazines. When you move in you must register with the local PSB office.

Teaching and other work opportunities

There are plenty of jobs available for foreigners in Shanghai, with a whole strata of expat workers surviving as actors, cocktail bar staff, "Chinglish" correctors, models, freelance writers and so on. But to really make any money here, you need to either be employed by a foreign company or start your own business.

Various schemes place **foreign teachers** in Chinese educational institutions – contact your nearest Chinese embassy (see p.31) for details, or the useful resources listed here (see p.34). Some employers ask for a TEFL (Teaching English as a

---

ROUGH GUIDES TRAVEL INSURANCE

Rough Guides has teamed up with WorldNomads.com to offer great travel insurance deals. Policies are available to residents of over 150 countries, with cover for a wide range of adventure sports, 24hr emergency assistance, high levels of medical and evacuation cover and a stream of travel safety information. Roughguides.com users can take advantage of their policies online 24/7, from anywhere in the world – even if you're already travelling. And since plans often change when you're on the road, you can extend your policy and even claim online. Roughguides.com users who buy travel insurance with WorldNomads.com can also leave a positive footprint and donate to a community development project. For more information, go to Ⓦroughguides.com/travel-insurance.

Foreign Language) qualification, though a degree, or simply the ability to speak the language as a native, can be enough.

Teaching at a **private school**, you'll earn about ¥14,000 a month, more than your Chinese counterparts, though your workload of around twenty hours a week is correspondingly heavier. The pay is less at a public school or university, but will be bolstered by on-campus accommodation. Contracts are generally for one year. Most teachers find their students keen, hardworking, curious and obedient. However, avoid talking about religion or politics in the classroom, as this could get you into trouble. Be aware, too, of the risk of being ripped off and check out the institution thoroughly before committing yourself.

Studying

Private schools aimed at teaching business people how to get by in **Chinese** include the Panda School (☎62376298, ⓦpandachinesetraining.com) and Mandarin House (☎61371987, ⓦmandarinhouse .cn). Both offer a wide range of courses and private tuition.

USEFUL RESOURCES

Chinatefl ⓦ chinatefl.com. A good overview of English-teaching opportunities in the Chinese public sector.

Council on International Educational Exchange ⓦ ciee.org. Exchange programmes for US students of Mandarin or Chinese studies, with placements in Shanghai.

Jobs in Shanghai ⓦ jobsinshanghai.com. Comprehensive site aimed at English-speaking professionals.

Smartshanghai ⓦ smartshanghai.com/jobs. Handy digital noticeboard advertising a wide range of jobs.

Teach Abroad ⓦ teachabroad.com. Website for peopole looking to teach English abroad, with an option to upload your CV.

Mail

Main **post offices** are usually open daily between 9am and 7pm; smaller offices may close for lunch or at weekends. Convenient post offices include the International Post Office at 276 Suzhou Bei Lu (daily 7am–10pm) and those inside the Shanghai Centre at 1376 Nanjing Xi Lu and on Huangpi Bei Lu at the intersection with Jiangyin Lu.

The Chinese **postal service** is fairly reliable, with letters and parcels taking a couple of weeks to reach Europe or the US. Overseas postage rates are becoming expensive; a postcard costs ¥4.50, while a standard letter is ¥6. As well as at post offices, you can post letters in green **postboxes** or at tourist hotels, which usually have a postbox at the front desk. Envelopes can be frustratingly scarce; try the stationery sections of department stores. Stamps can be bought at post offices.

An **Express Mail Service** (EMS) to most countries and to most destinations within China is available from all post offices. Besides cutting delivery times, the service ensures the letter or parcel is sent registered – though note that the DHL courier service (38 Huaxiang Lu; ☎52277770) is rather faster, and costs about the same.

To send **parcels**, turn up at any post office with the goods you want to send and the staff will sell you a box to pack them in for ¥15 or so. Once packed, but before the parcel is sealed, it must be checked at the customs window in the post office. A 1kg parcel should cost upwards of ¥70 to send surface mail, or ¥120 by airmail to Europe. If you are sending valuable goods bought in China, put the receipt or a photocopy of it in with the parcel, as it may be opened for customs inspection further down the line.

Maps

While we've mapped the city extensively in this Guide, a large foldout **map** can be handy. In general, the free tourist maps – available in large hotels and printed inside tourist magazines – don't show enough detail. A wide variety of city maps are available at all transport hubs and from street vendors, hotels and bookshops, with the best selection available from the Foreign Language Bookstore on Fuzhou Lu (see p.163). With the city changing so fast, it's important to check that your map is up to date.

Money

Chinese **currency** is formally called the **yuan** (¥), more colloquially known as renminbi (RMB) or kuai; a yuan breaks down into units of ten jiao. Paper money was invented in China and is still the main form of exchange, available in ¥100, ¥50, ¥20, ¥10, ¥5 and ¥1 notes. Unlike in the rest of China, you'll receive a lot of ¥1 coins in Shanghai – this is because China's Mint is here. At the time of writing, exchange rates were around ¥7 to $1, ¥8.5 to £1 and ¥7.5 to €1.

China is suffering from a rash of **counterfeiting**. Check your change carefully, as the locals do – hold ¥50 and ¥100 notes up to the light and rub them; fakes have no watermarks and the paper feels different.

Banks and ATMs

Banks are usually open daily (9am–noon & 2–5pm), though foreign exchange (there's generally a particular counter for this, marked in English) is sometimes only available from Monday to Friday. All banks are closed on New Year's Day, National Day and the first three days of the Chinese New Year, with reduced hours for the following eleven days.

Visa and MasterCard can be used to make cash withdrawals from **ATMs** operated by the Bank of China, the Industrial and Commercial Bank of China, China Construction Bank, HSBC and Agricultural Bank of China. All ATMs with this capability have an English-language option. Note that most ATMs are located inside banks or shopping centres, and are therefore not available when the main buildings are closed; there are **24-hour ATMs** in the Hong Kong Plaza on Huaihai Zhong Lu and next to Citibank on the Bund. Your bank back home will probably charge a fee on each withdrawal, with a minimum of around US$3, so it's best to get large amounts out – the maximum for each withdrawal is ¥2000.

Keep your exchange receipts so that when you leave you can change your yuan into dollars or sterling at any branch of the Bank of China.

Credit cards and wiring money

Credit cards, such as Visa, American Express and MasterCard, are only accepted at big tourist hotels and the fancier restaurants, and by some tourist-oriented shops; there is usually a four percent handling charge. It's straightforward to obtain cash advances on a Visa or MasterCard at many Chinese banks (with a commission charge of three percent). For **lost or stolen cards**, call ☎12 7369 6933 (Amex), ☎108001107309 (MasterCard) or ☎10 800 110 2911 (Visa).

It's possible to **wire money** to Shanghai through Western Union (Ⓦwesternunion.com); funds can be collected from one of their agents in the city, in post offices and at the Agricultural Bank of China.

Opening hours

Offices and **government agencies** are open Monday to Friday, usually from 8am to noon and then from 1pm to 5pm; some open on Saturday and Sunday mornings too. **Museums** are either open all week or are shut on one day, usually Monday. The best time to sightsee is during the week, as all attractions are swamped with local tourists at weekends.

Further details on opening hours can be found in the relevant sections: post offices (see p.34), banks (see opposite), restaurants (see p.125), bars (see p.143) and shops (see p.156).

Phones

Local calls are free from landlines, and long-distance **China-wide calls** cost ¥0.3 a minute. Note that everywhere in China has an **area code** which must be used when phoning from outside that locality. The area code for Shanghai (☎021) has been excluded from listings in this Guide but must be added if you're dialling from outside the city. **International calls** cost from ¥3.5 a minute, or much less than that if you use an IP card (see below).

Public phones tend to be located outside small convenience stores – you won't have to look long to find one. Simply pick up, dial and pay, in cash, the amount shown on the meter afterwards. Most of these however, will not handle international calls.

The cheapest way to call overseas on any phone is to use an **IP (internet phone) card**, which come in ¥100 units. You dial a local number, then a PIN, then the number you're calling. Rates are as low as ¥2.4 per minute to the US and Canada, ¥3.2 to Europe. IP cards are sold from corner stores, mobile-phone shops and from street hawkers (usually outside the mobile-phone shops).

Note that calling from tourist hotels, whether from your room or from their business centres, will attract a surcharge that may well be extortionate.

Mobile phones

Your home **cellular phone** may already be compatible with the Chinese network (visitors from North America should ensure their phones are GSM/Triband), though note that you will pay a premium to use it abroad, and that callers within China have to make an international call to reach you. A cheaper option is to get an **international SIM card** before you go – try Ⓦonesimcard.com.

Alternatively, once in Shanghai you can buy a **GSM SIM card** (SIM卡, SIM kǎ or 手机卡,

> ## CALLING MAINLAND CHINA FROM ABROAD
>
> To **call mainland China from abroad**, dial your international access code, then 86 (China's country code), then the area code, minus the initial zero of the regional code (so for Shanghai call 21, not 021), then the rest of the number.

CALLING HOME FROM SHANGHAI

To **call abroad from Shanghai** and the rest of mainland China dial ☎00, then the destination's country code, then the area code, omitting the initial zero (if any), then the number.

COUNTRY CODES

Australia ☎61
New Zealand ☎64
Republic of Ireland ☎353
South Africa ☎27
UK ☎44
US & Canada ☎1

shǒujīkǎ) from any China Mobile or China Unicom shop – both have 24-hour English-speaking hotlines for enquiries (China Mobile ☎10086, China Unicom ☎10010) but we recommend China Mobile, as they have more stores. You'll need an unlocked phone, of course, and will have to show your passport; you'll then receive a new, local number. Pay-as-you-go deals are good value – for ¥100 or so you will get the SIM plus around 300MB of data and 100 minutes. Note that you won't be able to call overseas. You can **top up** anytime at store machines – just feed in the money and tap in your number (on-screen instructions are in Chinese only, but fortunately staff are generally on hand to help) – or buy prepaid top-up cards (充值卡, **chōngzhí kǎ**) from the same outlets. Making and receiving domestic calls using a local SIM costs ¥0.2 per minute, and texts ¥0.1; you can usually only send texts overseas, not call.

It's more convenient, but a bit more expensive, to get a prepaid pay-as-you-go SIM delivered to your hotel for when you arrive. Packages from ⓦ3gsolutions.com.cn/page/simcard and ⓦloyomobile.com start at US$20 or so. You can opt for a SIM that runs a **VPN**, so you can access blocked websites such as Google Maps (see p.25).

If you don't have a Chinese number, but are toting a smartphone, you can make calls and send messages using the **Wechat** app (see p.37) if you're on wi-fi. You can also **rent smartphones**, which is most conveniently arranged online at ⓦchina-mobile-phones.com or ⓦpandaphone.com. The phone can be picked up at your hotel and left there when you leave. Phones cost around ¥200 a week, and calls are charged at the local rate.

The cheapest **phones to buy** will cost around ¥250; make sure the staff change the operating language into English for you. You'll need to register with your passport.

Photography

The Chinese are pretty relaxed about having their picture taken, and the staff at museums and attractions surprisingly accommodating. Photographic **equipment** can be cheaper in Shanghai than in the West (see p.162).

Time

Shanghai, like the rest of China, is **eight hours ahead of GMT**, thirteen hours ahead of Eastern Standard Time (North American), sixteen hours ahead of Pacific Time and two hours behind Australian Eastern Standard Time. It does not have daylight saving time.

Tourist information

The official **China Tourist Service**, CITS, at 1227 Beijing Xi Lu (Mon–Fri 9am–6pm; ☎62898899) is pretty useless at supplying information, being geared mainly towards getting you to buy a tour; you'll probably just be handed a few leaflets. Things aren't much better at the tourist information outlets – there are a few around town, the most central being under the Bund Promenade (daily 9.30am–8pm; ☎63573718). The free 24-hour tourist hotline on ☎962020 can help with general enquiries.

You can pick up free leaflets, containing basic tourist information, at the upmarket hotels and at the airport. Much more useful, however, are the free **magazines** aimed at the expat community – such as *City Weekend*, *Time Out Shanghai* and *That's Shanghai* – and their associated websites (see p.25). These include restaurant, club and art listings, with addresses written in *pinyin* and Chinese, but no maps. You can pick them up at expat-oriented bars, hotels and restaurants; a reliable place to look is at any branch of *Wagas* (see p.127).

There's plenty of **online information** about China in general and Shanghai specifically (see p.25), though as a general rule, avoid websites run by official agencies such as CITS – they're dry as dust.

Travellers with disabilities

In China the disabled are generally hidden away, so attitudes are not very sympathetic and little special

ESSENTIAL APPS

Make your trip easier with some handy smartphone apps: all of the below are free.

Baidu maps Ⓦ map.baidu.com. Accurate Chinese-language take on Google Maps – which is blocked in China anyway, unless you're running a VPN (see p.25). Works in a limited way with *pinyin*, but you'll need to input Chinese characters for best results.

Ctrip and Elong Ⓦ english.ctrip.com, Ⓦ elong.net. Useful for booking flights and accommodation; use Travel China Guide (see below) for trains.

Didi Ⓦ xiaojukeji.com. Uber-like Chinese app for taxis; you offer a pickup fee and wait for drivers to respond. Drivers will take cash too, so there's no need for a domestic bank card. Chinese-language only, but not too hard to get to grips with.

ExploreMetro Ⓦ exploremetro.com. Searchable Shanghai metro map, allowing you to check departures and plan your route.

Pandabus Ⓦ pandabus.cn. Uses your phone's GPS to show public bus timetables for your location. Also works with English and Chinese text searches, though results will be in Chinese.

Pleco and Dianhua Ⓦ pleco.com, Ⓦ dianhuadictionary.com. Comprehensive dictionaries where you can input words in English,

pinyin or Chinese characters and get a translation. They both come in free and pay-for versions; Pleco scores higher here with optical character recognition.

Travel China Guide Ⓦ travelchinaguide.com. The best way to book train tickets online (see p.92).

Waygo Ⓦ waygoapp.com. Use your phone's camera to scan a Chinese-language menu, museum caption or transport timetable and get a basic translation of text. Limited but surprisingly useful.

WeChat Ⓦ wechat.com. Astonishingly, around thirty percent of the average Chinese netizen's internet time is spent on Wechat – called "weixin" in Chinese. It's a versatile digital platform that operates as journal and address book (rather like Facebook), messaging, VOIPing and calling. Its great digital wallet function can only be used if you have a Chinese bank account, sadly. The QR reader is handy, though – you'll see people using it instead of exchanging namecards. There's also a function for hooking you up with people nearby, which is good for finding new friends or dating.

provision is made. As its economic boom continues apace, Shanghai resembles a building site, with uneven, obstacle-strewn paving, intense crowds and traffic and few access ramps. Commendably, a huge effort has been made to make pavements and metro stations friendly to **the blind**.

Wheelchair users will generally find public transport inaccessible – there are lifts at metro stations but you can't count on them working. A

few of the upmarket hotels have experience in assisting disabled visitors; in particular, Shanghai's several *Holiday Inns* (☎63538008) and *Hilton*s (☎62480000) have rooms designed for wheelchair users.

Given the situation, it may be worth considering an **organized tour**. The official representative of the disabled in Shanghai is the Disabled Person's Federation at 189 Longyang Lu (☎58733212).

TAI JI ON THE BUND

The Bund and Nanjing Dong Lu

Shanghai's signature skyline, and the first stop for any visitor, is the Bund, a strip of grand colonial edifices on the west bank of the Huangpu River, facing the flashy skyscrapers of Pudong on the opposite side. The product of the city's commercial frenzy at the beginning of the twentieth century, this was where the great trading houses and banks built their headquarters, each trying to outdo the last in the pomp of their edifices. Today it's the most exclusive chunk of real estate in China, with pretensions to becoming the nation's Champs-Elysées; the world's most luxurious brands have set up shop here, and there are a clutch of celebrity restaurants and some iconic hotels. Visitors can get a first taste of the frantic pace of Shanghai's modern consumerism on the roads that lead from it back towards People's Square – Nanjing Dong Lu and Fuzhou Lu.

The Bund

外滩，wàitān • Ⓜ Nanjing Dong Lu

1

Though the row of European buildings along the Huangpu River has since 1949 been known officially as **Zhongshan Dong Yi Lu** – and locals know it better as Wai Tan (literally "outside beach") – to foreigners it will always be **the Bund**. The northern end starts from the confluence of the Huangpu and Suzhou Creek, by **Waibaidu Bridge**, and runs south for 1.5km to Jinling Dong Lu, formerly Rue du Consulat.

Named after the Anglo-Indian term for the embankment of a muddy foreshore, the Bund was old Shanghai's commercial heart, with the river quays on one side, the offices of the leading banks and **trading houses** on the other. These sturdy marble-and-granite structures, built in a mongrel mix of Anglo-Oriental styles ranging from Italian Renaissance and neo-Grecian to Moorish, were both a celebration of Western commercial enterprise and a declaration of dominance. During Shanghai's riotous heyday this was also a hectic working **harbour**, where vessels from tiny sailing junks to ocean-going freighters unloaded under the watch of British (and later American and Japanese) warships. Everything arrived here, from silk and tea to heavy industrial

■ ACCOMMODATION		● EATING		The Press by Inno Coffee	4	● SHOPPING	
24K Hotel	7	Mingtown	8½ Otto e Mezzo Bombana	1	The Stage, Westin	9	Apple Store	1
Blue Mountain Bund		Hikers Hostel 2	El Willy	11	Treats Deli	10	Foreign Language Bookstore	4
Youth Hostel	3	Mingtown	EQ	3	Wang Baohe	8	Nantai Costume Company	5
Dock Bund Hostel	1	Nanjing Lu 4	Je Me Souviens	6	Xin Guang Jiu Jia	2	Raffles City Mall	6
Jinjiang Inn	6	Westin 8	Lao Beijing	12	Yelixiali	5	Shanghai First Food Store	3
Le Royal Méridien	5		Lao Zhengxing	7			Silk King	2

THE BUND AND NANJING DONG LU

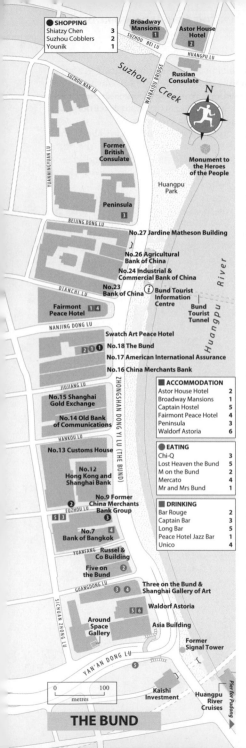

SHOPPING

Shiatzy Chen	3
Suzhou Cobblers	2
Younik	1

Broadway Mansions 1

Astor House Hotel 2

SUZHOU BEI LU

HUANGPU LU

Russian Consulate

SUZHOU WAN LU

Suzhou Creek

WAIBAIDU BRIDGE

N

Former British Consulate

Monument to the Heroes of the People

YUANMINGYUAN LU

Huangpu Park

Peninsula 3

BEIJING DONG LU

No.27 Jardine Matheson Building

No.26 Agricultural Bank of China

No.24 Industrial & Commercial Bank of China

Huangpu River

No.23 Bank of China

Bund Tourist Information Centre

DIANCHI LU

Fairmont Peace Hotel 14

Bund Tourist Tunnel

NANJING DONG LU

Swatch Art Peace Hotel

No.18 The Bund 2 1

No.17 American International Assurance

No.16 China Merchants Bank

JIUJIANG LU

No.15 Shanghai Gold Exchange

No.14 Old Bank of Communications

ZHONGSHAN DONG YI LU (THE BUND)

ACCOMMODATION

Astor House Hotel	2
Broadway Mansions	1
Captain Hostel	5
Fairmont Peace Hotel	4
Peninsula	3
Waldorf Astoria	6

HANKOU LU

No.13 Customs House

No.12 Hong Kong and Shanghai Bank

No.9 Former China Merchants Bank Group

EATING

Chi-Q	3
Lost Heaven the Bund	5
M on the Bund	2
Mercato	4
Mr and Mrs Bund	1

FUZHOU LU 2

No.7 Bank of Bangkok 4

DRINKING

Bar Rouge	2
Captain Bar	3
Long Bar	5
Peace Hotel Jazz Bar	1
Unico	4

YUANFANG LU

Russel & Co Building

Five on the Bund 2

GUANGDONG LU 3 4

Three on the Bund & Shanghai Gallery of Art

SICHUAN ZHONG LU

Waldorf Astoria 5 6

Around Space Gallery

Asia Building

Former Signal Tower

YAN'AN DONG LU 5

0   100
metres

Kaishi Investment

Huangpu River Cruises

Pier for Pudong

THE BUND

machinery. So too did wealthy foreigners, ready to pick their way to one of the grand hotels through crowds of beggars, hawkers, black marketeers, shoeshine boys and overladen coolies.

When the Communists took over in 1949 the buildings were abandoned, and though nothing was done to preserve these symbols of foreign imperialism, surprisingly little was destroyed. Now, as Shanghai rises, the street is once again a hub of commerce, though of the decidedly upmarket kind. As well as the city's ritziest luxury brand shops, the structures house some of Shanghai's fanciest **restaurants** (see p.130) – that said, if you just want to eat, rather than have a life- (and wallet-) transforming culinary experience, choice is much more limited.

Broadway Mansions

上海大厦, shànghǎi dàshà · 20 Suzhou Bei Lu · ☏ 63246260, ⓦ broadwaymansions.com

You can't miss the hulking **Broadway Mansions**, at the far north end of the Bund, though you may wish you could – this classic example of the po-faced stolidity of the Chicago School would make a good Orwellian Ministry of Truth. When it was built in 1933, it was the highest building in Asia. During World War II the building was taken over by the Japanese; it is now a half-decent **hotel** (see p.116). Its most illustrious resident was Jiang Qing (wife of Mao Zedong), who issued a decree during the Cultural Revolution banning barges and sampans from travelling up the Huangpu or Suzhou while she was asleep. If you're not staying here, you can appreciate the views by taking the lift to the eighteenth floor.

Russian Consulate

俄罗斯领事馆, éluósī lǐngshìguǎn · 20 Huangpu Lu

Over the road from *Broadway Mansions*, the **Russian Consulate** is one of the few Bund buildings that is used for its original purpose. The iron grilles on the windows came in useful on those occasions in the 1920s when this bastion of "Red" Soviet Russia was attacked by White Russians. In 1960, during one of the frostier periods of Sino-Soviet relations, it suffered the indignity of being turned into a bar for seamen; it returned to being a consulate in 1987.

Astor House Hotel

浦江饭店, pǔjiāng fàndiàn • 15 Huangpu Lu • ☎ 63246388, ⓦ pujianghotel.com

The grand **Astor House Hotel**, just north of Waibaidu Bridge, was built in 1846 and
enlarged in 1910, and was the city's glitziest venue until the *Peace Hotel* usurped that
status. It was also one of the few places where polite foreign and Chinese society
mingled, when "tea dances" were held – with rather more whisky than tea serving as
social lubricant. The original manager, a retired seaman, had the corridors painted with
portholes and the rooms decorated like cabins. Today, with its endless wooden
corridors, high ceilings and slightly eccentric air of batty gentility, the hotel has
something of the feel of a Victorian public school about it. It remains worth a snoop
for its grand lobby, renovated ballroom and a few relics of its past glories on display.

Shanghai Post Museum

上海邮政博物馆, shànghǎi yóuzhèng bówùguǎn • 276 Suzhou Bei Lu • Wed, Thurs, Sat & Sun 9am–4pm • Free •
☎ 63936666, ⓦ shpost.com.cn • Ⓜ Tiantong Lu

The Main Post Office was built in 1931, and is easily recognizable by its clocktower. It's
the only Bund building that has never been used for anything but its original function.
The third floor now houses the **Shanghai Post Museum**, which is more interesting than
it sounds. The collection of letters and stamps is only mildly diverting, but the
examples of postal transport, including a train carriage, and the old, rather stately
post-boxes are striking. The new atrium is very impressive. The roof terrace was being
renovated at the time of writing; the view from here is superb.

Waibaidu Bridge

外白渡桥, wàibáidùqiáo

Waibaidu Bridge, whose arched metal frame spans Suzhou Creek, marks the Bund's
northern edge. Built by the British in 1908, it was China's first steel truss bridge. At the
outbreak of the Sino-Japanese War in 1937 it represented the frontier between the
Japanese-occupied areas north of Suzhou Creek and the **International Settlement** to the
south – itself a no-man's-land, guarded at each end by Japanese and British sentries.
Though only built to last forty years, today it's as much a permanent feature as
anything in this city. It's a popular spot for wedding photographs, and you'll see
brides-to-be braving the traffic in order to be briefly framed by its striking girders.

Former British Consulate

英国驻上海总领事馆, yīngguó zhù shànghǎi zǒnglǐngg shì guǎn • 33 Zhongshan Dong Yi Lu

South of Waibaidu Bridge you'll come to the **former British Consulate**, set back from the
road in a neat garden. Built in 1852, it is one of the oldest Bund buildings. Lavishly
restored, it is today used for government functions and posh dos, so you won't get in
without an invite. It was once ostentatiously guarded by magnificently dressed Sikh
soldiers; nowadays, black-clad security guards will let you know where you're not allowed.

Peninsula hotel

上海半岛酒店, shànghǎi bàndǎo jiǔdiàn • 32 Zhongshan Dong Yi Lu • ☎ 23272888, ⓦ pensinsula.com/shanghai

In keeping with the area, the ritzy **Peninsula hotel** (see p.117), part of the Hong Kong
luxury hotel group, has gone for a traditional, **Art Deco** look. Head through the doors
into the windowless black marble interior and it's hard not to be reminded of some
great emperor's tomb. The ambience improves when you get to the lobby, where a
string quartet plays; it's a great spot for afternoon tea (see p.132).

Huangpu Park

黄浦公园, huángpǔ gōngyuán • Zhongshan Dong Yi Lu • Free

On the corner of Suzhou Creek and the Huangpu River, on the east side of the road,
Huangpu Park was a British creation, established in 1886 as the British Public Gardens

1

on a patch of land formed when mud and silt gathered around a wrecked ship. Sikh troops here enforced the rules that forbade Chinese from entering unless they were servants accompanying their employer. After protests, the regulations were relaxed in 1928 to admit "well-dressed" Chinese, who had to apply for a special entry permit. Though it's firmly established in the Chinese popular imagination as a symbol of Western racism, there's no evidence that there ever was a sign here reading "No dogs or Chinese allowed". These days the park contains a rather unattractive stone obelisk commemorating the **"Heroes of the People"**, and is also a popular spot for citizens to practise their early-morning *tai ji*.

In contrast to the snooty pretensions of the buildings over the road, the riverside **promenade** remains stoutly proletarian, full of out-of-towners taking the obligatory Shanghai shot of the Oriental Pearl Tower (see p.78). As well as affordable places to eat (including a *Costa* and a *Subway*) you'll find the entrance to the **Bund Tourist Tunnel** (外滩观光隧道, wàitān guānguāng suìdào), a psychedelic gateway to Pudong (see p.77).

Rockbund Art Museum

外滩美术馆, wàitān měishùguǎn · 20 Huqiu Lu · Tues–Sun 10am–6pm · ¥30 · ☎ 33109985, ⓦ rockbundartmusem.org

The narrow streets leading back from the Bund hold some fine Art Deco buildings, and the **Rockbund Art Museum**, an elegant monolith tucked behind the *Peninsula* hotel, is one of the most striking. Dating back to the 1930s, when it was the headquarters of the Royal Asiatic Society, it has been skilfully restored and converted into an achingly cool four-storey gallery of contemporary art, hosting shows that usually mix China's biggest hitters with international artists. There's no permanent exhibition, so check the website for what's on, and for the programme of events and lectures.

Jardine Matheson Building

外滩27号, wàitān èrshíqī hào · 27 Zhongshan Dong Yi Lu · ⓦ bund27.com

As you head south from the *Peninsula* hotel, the next grand edifice is at no. 27. This was the former base of **Jardine Matheson**, founded by William Jardine – the man who did more than any other individual to precipitate the Opium Wars and open Shanghai up to foreign trade (see p.166) – and the first foreign concern to buy land in Shanghai. It's seen a lot of different nationalities come and go: in 1941 the British Embassy occupied the top floor (facing the German Embassy, just across the road), shortly after which it was requisitioned by the Japanese navy, before doing service as the American consulate. Today it's known as the **House of Roosevelt**, and houses a Rolex shop, some stuffy, upscale restaurants that are worth sampling for afternoon tea (see p.132) and the city's biggest wine cellar.

Bank of China and around

中国银行, zhōngguó yínháng · 23 Zhongshan Dong Yi Lu

One of the Bund's more modern structures is the **Bank of China**, built in 1937 in the Chicago style with a Chinese hat as concession to local sensibilities. No. 24, which was originally the **Yokohama Bank**, is rather more successful in its blend of Eastern and neo-Grecian styles. Unfortunately (but hardly surprisingly) only a couple of the Japanese martial sculptures that once ornamented the facade have survived; look above the first-floor windows.

Fairmont Peace Hotel

和平饭店, hépíng fàndiàn · 20 Nanjing Dong Lu, by the Bund · Tours 10.30am & 2.30pm; 1hr · Tours ¥100 · ☎ 63216888, ⓦ fairmont.com/peacehotel

Straddling the eastern end of Nanjing Dong Lu is the **Fairmont Peace Hotel**, a handsome edifice that began its days as the notorious *Cathay Hotel* (1926). The

VICTOR SASSOON

"There is only one race finer than the Jews, and that's the Derby."

More than anyone, it was **Victor Sassoon** (1881–1961), infamous tycoon and bon vivant, who shaped Shanghai's prewar character. The Sassoons were Sephardic Jews from Iraq, whose family fortune was built by trading in India. Victor, one of the fourth generation (which included the writer Siegfried Sassoon) astonished the family by moving the company assets out of India and into China – largely, it is said, to dodge the British taxman. "Sir Victor", as he liked to be known, began pouring millions of dollars into Shanghai in the 1920s, virtually single-handedly setting off a high-rise real estate boom that was to last almost a decade. His **Art Deco** constructions include what have become many of the city's most distinctive landmarks, among them: Hamilton House and the *Metropole Hotel* (see p.47), at the intersection of Fuzhou Lu and Jiangxi Lu; the Cathay Theatre on Huaihai Zhong Lu; the *Orient Hotel* on Xizang Zhong Lu near People's Square; the Embarkment Building on Suzhou Bei Lu; Cathay Mansions – now the *Jinjiang* hotel (see p.65) – and the enduring landmark of the Bund, the *Cathay Hotel*, now the *Fairmont Peace Hotel* (see p.42).

At the *Cathay*, Victor lived in a penthouse with a 360-degree view over the city, and indulged his tastes for the finest of everything – including women. His suite had two bathtubs because, he said, he liked to share his bed but never his bath. As described by Stella Dong in *Shanghai, the Rise and Fall of a Decadent City*, his parties sound dazzling. At his shipwreck party, guests came dressed as if they were abandoning ship; the prize for best costume was awarded to a couple who were naked except for a shower curtain. At his circus parties, guests would dress up as clowns or acrobats while he, of course, played ringmaster, in top hat and tails and wielding a riding crop. Victor's world came crashing down with the Japanese invasion, though he was able to spirit most of his fortune away to the Bahamas, where he died in 1961.

hotel's main building (on the north side of Nanjing Dong Lu) is a relic of another great trading house, **Sassoon's**, and was originally known as Sassoon House. Like Jardine's, the Sassoon business empire was built on opium trading, but by the early years of the twentieth century the family fortune had mostly been sunk into Shanghai real estate, including the *Cathay* (see box, above). Nicknamed "The Claridges of the Far East" it was the place to be seen in prewar Shanghai: Douglas Fairbanks and Charlie Chaplin were among its celebrity guests and Noël Coward is supposed to have written *Private Lives* here while laid up with flu. It boasted innovations such as telephones in the rooms in advance of any European hotels, and had such luxuries as a private spring-fed plumbing system, marble baths with silver taps and vitreous china lavatories imported from Britain.

The *Peace* today is well worth a visit for the bar, with its legendary jazz band (see p.144), and for a walk around the lobby. On the first floor, a little **museum** of the hotel's history (daily 10am–7pm; ☎63216888, ext 6751) displays relics such as room keys and lampshades from the Thirties, and plenty of old photographs, including one of Mao meeting Monty. Letters from foreigners interred here as children during the Japanese occupation describe their enforced stay as a big adventure; they would treat the empty ballrooms as a playpark, oblivious to the warring outside. Contact the museum to join one of the daily **tours**, which include the grander guest rooms, themed after different nations, if they're not booked. There's a good **view** of the Bund from the balcony of the seventh-floor bar – staff will tolerate curious visitors popping in for a quick look, or you could buy an orange juice for around ¥50.

The smaller wing on the south side of Nanjing Dong Lu was originally the *Palace Hotel*, built around 1906. It was restored – like so much of the city – in time for the 2010 Expo and is now called the *Swatch Art Peace Hotel*, with a Swatch showroom and ritzy boutiques, and an extensive artists-in-residence programme.

1

No. 18 The Bund

外滩18号, wàitān shíbāhào · 18 Zhongshan Dong Yi Lu · **Art gallery** Tues–Sun 11am–9pm · ☎ 63238099, ⓦ www.bund18 .com/art-culture/18gallery

No. 18 The Bund was originally the Chartered Bank of India and Australia, but today is home to the city's most la-di-da shops, given gravitas by the building's Italian marble columns. As well as high-end stores such as Zegna and Cartier, the building houses a **contemporary art gallery** on the fourth floor, the swanky *Mr and Mrs Bund* restaurant (see p.130) and louche *Bar Rouge* (see p.143), which has a fantastic roof terrace with views of Pudong.

American International Assurance

外滩17号, wàitān shíqīhào · 17 Zhongshan Dong Yi Lu

At no. 17 The Bund, **American International Assurance** has returned to reoccupy the building it left in 1949. Back then it shared its tenancy with "the old lady of the Bund" – the English-language *North China Daily News*, whose motto is engraved over the ground-floor windows – "Journalism, Art, Science, Literature, Commerce, Truth, Printing". The Communists banned the paper from printing news in 1949, so the very last issue was given over to articles on the philosopher Lao Tzu and Hittite hieroglyphics.

Customs House

海关楼, hǎiguān lóu · 13 Zhongshan Dong Yi Lu

Continuing south down the Bund from no. 17, past neo-Grecian, Italian Renaissance and Art Deco edifices, brings you to the magnificent **Customs House** at no. 13, one of just a scattering of Bund buildings to have retained its original function. The clocktower was modelled on the tower that houses Big Ben in London, and after its completion in 1927, local legend had it that the chimes, which struck every fifteen minutes, confused the God of Fire: believing the chimes were a fire bell, the god felt Shanghai was suffering from too many conflagrations, and decided not to send any more. During the Cultural Revolution, loudspeakers in the clocktower played *The East is Red* at 6am and 6pm daily. You can step into the downstairs lobby for a peek at the ceiling mosaics and their maritime motifs.

Hong Kong and Shanghai Bank

汇丰中国, huìfēng zhōngguó · 12 Zhongshan Dong Yi Lu

Right next to the Customs House, and also with an easily recognizable domed roofline, the former headquarters of the **Hong Kong and Shanghai Bank**, built in 1921, has one of the most imposing of the Bund facades. It's now owned by the Pudong Development Bank, who allow visitors to poke around the entrance hall. Today, HSBC is one of Britain's biggest banks, though few of its customers can be aware of its original purpose – to finance trade between Europe and China. Each wall of the marble octagonal entrance originally boasted a mural depicting the bank's eight primary locations (Bangkok, Kolkata, Hong Kong, London, New York, Paris, Shanghai and Tokyo), and the eight words of its motto: "Within the four seas all men are brothers". The four huge marble columns in the **banking hall** are among the largest pieces of solid marble in the world. In the far left corner was a separate bank for Chinese customers, who entered using the entrance on Fuzhou Lu – the massive door, inscribed with the initials HSBC, still stands. The Chinese character *fu* (prosperity) can be seen on the walls and in the trim, and Chinese-style abstract designs decorate the cornices and ceilings.

It's considered lucky to rub the noses or paws of the **bronze lions** that stand guard outside the Corinthian columns of the entranceway. These are replacements for the two originals, which were removed by the Japanese; one stands today in the history museum (see p.78). They were officially named "Prudence" and "Security" but nicknamed "Stephen" and "Stitt", after the bank's general managers. One lion looks belligerent, the other smiles knowingly. There are similar pairs outside the HSBC headquarters in Hong Kong and London. Locals used to joke that the lions roared when a virgin passed – so their incessant silence said something about the relaxed morals of the Shanghainese.

Five on the Bund

外滩5号, wàitān wǔhào • 5 Zhongshan Dong Yi Lu

Most of no. 5 (officially known as **Five on the Bund**) is home to the Huaxia Bank. Head to Guangdong Lu, however, and you'll find the entrance to the building's upscale restaurant, *M on the Bund* (see p.130), which kicked off the area's renaissance when it opened in 1999.

Three on the Bund

外滩3号, wàitān sānhào • 3 Zhongshan Dong Yi Lu • ⓦ threeonthebund.com

Three on the Bund opened in 2004 and, with its mix of high-end shops, swanky restaurants – and a sprinkling of contemporary art to add cultural legitimacy – set the tone for the new developments that followed. Check out the Armani flagship store on the ground floor, before heading to the third floor for the Shanghai Gallery of Art, which is free to enter (see p.154).

Waldorf Astoria

华尔道夫大酒店, huá'ěrdàofū jiǔdiàn • 2 Zhongshan Dong Yi Lu • ☏ 63229988, ⓦ waldorfastoriashanghai.com

No. 2 The Bund, which opened in 1910 as the "The Shanghai Club", a private members' club for well-heeled Brits, closed its doors with the arrival of the Japanese in 1941 and then languished for decades. In 1988 Shanghai's first *KFC* took up residence, and trashed the period fittings. Happily, it has since been restored to its full glory as the

HUANGPU RIVER CRUISES

In addition to its major freeway projects and sophisticated metro system, Shanghai still uses the **Huangpu** as a vital resource – one-third of all China's trade passes through along this waterway. The river is also the city's chief source of drinking water – even though, thick and brown, it contains large quantities of untreated waste, including sewage and high levels of mercury and phenol. At least it no longer serves as a burial ground – until the 1930s Shanghainese too poor to pay to bury their relatives would launch the bodies into the river in boxes decked with paper flowers.

One highlight of a visit to Shanghai – and the easiest way to view the edifices of the Bund – is to take a **Huangpu River cruise** (黄浦江旅游, huángpǔjiāng lǚyóu). You'll be able to observe the paraphernalia of the shipping industry, from sampans and rusty old Panamanian-registered freighters to sparkling Chinese navy vessels, and get an idea of the colossal construction that is taking place on the eastern shore. Evening cruises offer spectacular views, the skyline shimmering with neon against the inky sky.

Cruises leave from a wharf at the south end of the Bund, opposite Jinling Dong Lu, and from bigger Shiliupu Wharf (十六浦码头, shí liù pǔ mǎtóu), ten minutes' walk further south. You can buy tickets at the wharves or at the **Bund Tourist Information Centre**, on the riverbank beside the entrance to the Bund Tourist Tunnel. Departure times vary depending on season and weather; as a rough idea, ninety-minute cruises (¥128) depart at least twice an hour between 11am and 9.30pm in shoulder season; they are much more frequent in high season. Boats travel south to Yangpu Bridge, then north towards Wusongkou before finally returning to the wharf. Hour-long cruises (¥100) are less frequent, usually hourly, and there is one daily three-hour cruise (¥150) in the afternoon, which goes all the way to the mouth of the Yangzi and back. Evening cruises include a buffet dinner (¥200).

You can also take a short cruise from **Pudong**, from the Pearl Dock (明珠码头, míngzhū mǎtóu; 10am–1.30pm every 30min; 30min; ¥100).

1

Waldorf Astoria. As with the other heritage hotels in the area, it is expensive to stay here (see p.117), but worth a visit to check out the stylish interior – in this case, a feast of Neoclassical opulence. Don't miss the *Long Bar*, rebuilt from photos of the club's original bar, and a fine evocation of 1930s Shanghai. The eastern end of the original 33m-long bar commanded a view of the Huangpu, and only the club's elite members were allowed to sit there (see p.144).

The Bund to People's Square

Two kilometres west of the Bund lies another hotspot for tourists, People's Square (see p.48). Connecting them is the consumer cornucopia of pedestrianized **Nanjing Dong Lu**, with its two major parallel arteries, dull Yan'an Dong Lu and quirky **Fuzhou Lu**. In the days of the foreign concessions, expatriates described Nanjing Dong Lu as a cross between New York's Broadway and London's Oxford Street. But it was also at this time that Nanjing Dong Lu and Fuzhou Lu were lined with **teahouses** that functioned as the city's most exclusive brothels, whose courtesans were expected, among their other duties, to be able to perform classical plays and scenes from operas, and to host banquets. In a juxtaposition symbolic of prewar Shanghai's extremes, strings of the lowest form of brothel, nicknamed "nail sheds", lay just two blocks north of Nanjing Dong Lu, along Suzhou Creek. The street was dubbed "Blood Alley" because of the nightly fights between sailors on leave who congregated here.

Nanjing Dong Lu

南京东路, nánjīng dōnglù • ⑩ Nanjing Dong Lu

On its eastern stretch, **Nanjing Dong Lu**'s garish neon lights and window displays are iconic; come here in the evening (before things start closing up at 9pm) to appreciate the lightshow in its full dazzling splendour. If you don't want to explore on foot, you could hop on the daft little **electric train** (¥5) that tootles up and down. The shopping is not what it once was, with the emphasis now on cheap rather than chic, but the authorities, aware of this, have started to boot out the more low-rent locals and get some international brands in, including Asia's biggest Apple Store at no. 300 (see p.162).

No. 635 was once the glorious **Wing On** emporium, and diagonally opposite was the **Sincere**. These were not just places to shop: inside were restaurants, rooftop gardens, cabarets and even hotels. Off the circular overhead walkway at the junction between Nanjing and Xizang Zhong Lu is the grandest of the district's department stores, the venerable **Shanghai No. 1 Department Store**; it's still a place of pilgrimage for out-of-towners, but there's nothing much of interest to a foreign visitor.

If you're looking for cheap clothes, you'll be spoilt for choice, but for something distinctly Chinese you'll have to look a bit harder. Your best bet for curiosities is to head to the **Shanghai First Food Store**, at no. 720 (see p.157). The Chinese often buy food as a souvenir, and this busy shop sells all kinds of locally made gift-wrapped sweets, cakes and preserves, as well as tea and tasty pastries. Nearby **Taikang Foods** at

---

SCAMMERS ON NANJING DONG LU

Foreign faces on Nanjing Dong Lu will be incessantly approached by pesky pimps, street vendors and "art students", but the most common **scam** is for one or two young guys or girls to befriend you, perhaps asking to practise their English or to help them take photos. They'll suggest you go to a bar for a coffee or a beer, which, when the bill comes, will cost hundreds of yuan. On a single stroll up the street, this will be tried a dozen times. There are plenty of places in Shanghai where a friendly approach is genuine, but this is not one of them. For more on scams, check our Basics chapter (see p.30).

no. 768 is another example, with a dried meat section at the back selling rather macabre flattened pig heads.

Fuzhou Lu
福州路, fúzhōu lù

Heading west from the Bund along **Fuzhou Lu**, you'll first come to the nautically themed *Captain Hostel* (see p.122), where taking the creaky lift to the sixth-floor *Captain Bar* (see p.143) will reward you with excellent views of Pudong. Continue west until you reach Jiangxi Nan Lu, and you'll see Shanghai at its most gloomily Gothamesque, thanks to twin Art Deco edifices, the **Metropole Hotel** and **Hamilton House**, once an apartment complex, on the south corner; both were built by British architects Palmer and Turner. The building at the northwest corner lodged the Shanghai Municipal Council, the governing body of the International Settlement.

Fifty metres further east, the court building at no. 209 used to be the **American Club**. Georgian-style, with marble columns, it was built in 1924 with bricks shipped in from the States. Crossing Henan Zhong Lu brings you to a brighter commercial area, with a medley of small stores selling art supplies, stationery, trophies, medical equipment and books, including the **Foreign Language Bookstore** at no. 390 (see p.163). Finally, at the end of the road, **Raffles City Mall** (see p.157) is one of Shanghai's best (and busiest) malls, with a juice bar and plenty of cheap, clean places to eat in the basement, clothes stores for pampered millennials on the floors above and a food court at the very top.

SHANGHAI MUSEUM

People's Square

The area around People's Square, or Renmin Square (Renmin Guangchang; 人民广场, rénmín guǎngchǎng) is the modern heart of Shanghai. It functions both as a transport hub (its perimeters are defined by the city's main arteries: Xizang, Nanjing and Yan'an roads) and as home to the grand temples of culture, history and government. There's an impressive clutch of sights here, all within walking distance of each other; few places in China have such a concentration of great sights, and you'll need a full day to do them justice. The pot-shaped Shanghai Museum is world class, and one of the city's highlights, while the nearby Shanghai Urban Planning Exhibition Hall looks to the future both in its design and its content. Just north is the unexpectedly peaceful Renmin Park, with its little Museum of Contemporary Art; overall, you have one of Shanghai's most rewarding districts.

In contrast to the dour totalitarianism of its Beijing counterpart at Tian'anmen, **People's Square** possesses a much more human feel. Instead of a concrete plain lined with po-faced edifices, Shanghai's urban centre comprises a rather haphazardly arranged park and a plaza dotted with a hotchpotch of modernist and colonial buildings (with, of course, a huge shopping mall underneath).

The easiest way to get here is on the **metro**; the People's Square station is at the interchange of lines #1 and #2. More than twenty exits cover a vast area, so work out which exit you want from the wall maps in the station, then navigate your way through the shopping mall – the low numbers bring you out in the southeast corner of the square near the museum, the high ones in the northwest near the park. There aren't many places to eat, so if you're here for the day you'll have to plan where you're having lunch (see p.131).

Shanghai Museum

上海博物馆, shànghǎi bówùguǎn • 201 Renmin Dadao • Daily 9am–5pm, last entry 4pm • Free; audio-guide ¥40 plus ¥400 deposit • ☎ 63723500, Ⓦ shanghaimuseum.net/en • Ⓜ People's Square

People's Square metro station can get fearsomely busy, but fortunately as you head west onto Renmin Dadao the crowds thin out dramatically. On the south side of this giant boulevard, People's Square is a pleasant plaza with a fountain where you might catch a few skateboarders, and tourists feeding the pigeons. At the back stands the unmistakeable showpiece **Shanghai Museum**.

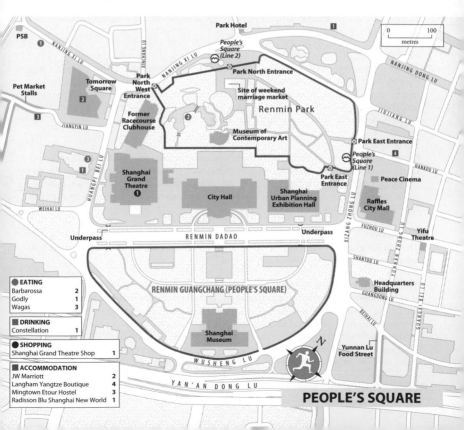

The building's form is based on a *ding*, an ancient Chinese pot, and its layout, like many Chinese buildings, is inspired by traditional cosmogony, with a square base to represent Earth and a rounded roof to represent Heaven. Inside, there are eleven galleries, with well-displayed pieces and plenty of explanation in English. You'll need several hours for a comprehensive tour, though some galleries can be safely skipped; the **best** work, on the whole, is on the ground and top floors. Informative leaflets are available from a desk on the ground floor.

Ground floor

One of the museum's major highlights is its **ground-floor gallery** of **bronzes**, most of which are more than two thousand years old yet appear strikingly modern in their simple lines and bold imagery. The cooking vessels, containers and weapons on display were used for ritual rather than everyday purposes, and are beautifully made. Many are covered with intricate geometric designs that reference animal shapes, while others reveal startlingly naturalistic touches – check out the cowrie container from the Western Han dynasty, with handles shaped like stalking tigers and lid surmounted by eight bronze yaks. There's also a charming wine urn with a dragon spout and another shaped like an ox. A display near the entrance shows how these were made, using an early form of the "lost wax" method – the original is made in wax, then covered in plaster, after which the wax is heated and poured away to create a mould.

A crowd-pleasing pottery dog guards the entrance to the **sculpture** gallery next door. Most of the exhibits are religious figures – boggle-eyed temple guardians, serene Buddhas and the like. Look out for the row of huge, fearsome Tang-dynasty heads and the figurines of dancers in flowing robes, which resemble Brancusi sculptures in their simplicity.

First floor

The Tang dynasty steals the show once again in the **ceramics** gallery, which takes over the **first floor**. The spiky, multicoloured tomb guardians, in the shape of imaginary beasts, make the delicate glazed pots look reserved in comparison. The accompanying text reminds you that the delicate art of porcelain was invented in China; some fine examples from the Song and Ming dynasties are on display.

Second floor

On the **second floor**, skip the calligraphy and carved seals unless you have a special interest and check out the **painting** gallery instead. The winning dynasty here has to be the Ming, as the amazingly naturalistic images of animals from this time are much easier to respond to than the interminable idealized landscapes. Look out in particular for Bian Wenzhi's lively images of birds.

Top floor

The **top floor** contains the most colourful gallery, dedicated to the many **Chinese minority peoples**. To anyone who thinks of China as a monoculture, this striking assembly will come as a shock. One wall is lined with spooky lacquered masks from Tibet and Guizhou (in southwest China), while nearby are colourfully decorated boats from the Taiwanese minority, the Gaoshan. The silver ceremonial headdresses of southwest China's Miao people are breathtaking in their intricacy, if rather impractical to wear; elsewhere, elaborate abstract designs turn the Dai lacquered tableware into art. In the section on traditional costumes, look out for the fish-skin suit made by the Hezhen people of Dongbei, in the far north. The explanation might insist on the "Chineseness" of all this but it's quite clear from their artefacts that these civilizations at the furthest edges of the Chinese Empire, many of them animist in their beliefs, are culturally very distant from the Han mainstream, and those from southwest China have more in common with their Thai or Laotian coreligionists.

The Ming- and Qing-dynasty **furniture** next door is more interesting than it sounds. The Ming pieces are elegant and reserved while those from the Qing, as illustrated in the diorama of a study room, swarm with intricate detail. They may look a little old-fashioned compared to, say, the bronzes downstairs, but there is a similar aesthetic on display – everyday objects raised to high art.

Along Renmin Dadao

人民大道, rénmín dàdào • ⓜ People's Square

2

Head from the Shanghai Museum to the north side of **Renmin Dadao**, and you are faced with some fine modern buildings, all worthy of exploration. Keep going north and you'll find some lovely old ones too, notably the **Former Racecourse Clubhouse** and the *Park* hotel.

Shanghai Urban Planning Exhibition Hall

城市规划展示馆, chéngshì guīhuà zhǎnshìguǎn • 100 Renmin Dadao • Tues–Sun 9am–5pm, last entry 4pm • ¥30 • ☎ 63722077, ⓦ supec.org

It's surely revealing that one of Shanghai's grandest museums is dedicated not to the past but the future: the **Shanghai Urban Planning Exhibition Hall** is interesting for its insight into the grand ambitions and the vision of the city planners. Most worthy of note is the 1:500 scale, tennis court-sized **model** of the city on the second floor, showing what Shanghai will (if all goes to plan) look like in 2020. There's no room in this brave new world for shabby little alleyways: it's a parade ground of skyscrapers and apartment blocks in which, according to this model, the whole of the Old City (see p.53) is doomed. In a video room next door you get taken on a virtual helicopter trip around this plan, which is liable to make you giddy. Back on the first floor, there's a collection of **old photographs** of Shanghai from colonial times – most interesting if you've already grown somewhat familiar with the new look of these streets. Avoid the tacky "olde-worlde" cafés in the basement.

Shanghai Grand Theatre

上海大剧院, shànghǎi dàjùyuàn • 300 Renmin Dadao • ☎ 63273094, ⓦ shgtheatre.com

West of the frumpy City Hall you come to the impressive **Shanghai Grand Theatre**, distinguished by its convex roof and transparent walls and pillars – a different take on the same cosmological principles that influenced the designers of the Shanghai Museum (see opposite). Created by the architectural agency responsible for the Bastille Opera House in Paris, it has ambitions of being a truly world-class theatre (see p.150). Pop into the on-site café or the **shop**, a good source of reasonably priced DVDs and CDs (see p.163).

Former Racecourse Clubhouse

You'll spot the **Former Racecourse Clubhouse** by its distinctive clocktower, which was modelled on the tower that holds Big Ben. It was until recently an art museum, and at

THE SHANGHAI RACECOURSE

The area now covered by People's Square was originally the site of the **Shanghai racecourse**, built by the British in 1862. The races became so popular among the foreign population that most businesses closed for the ten-day periods of the twice-yearly meets. They soon caught on with the Chinese too, so that by the 1920s the **Shanghai Race Club** was the third-wealthiest foreign corporation in China. When not used for racing the course was the venue for polo and cricket matches. During World War II it served as a holding camp for prisoners and as a temporary mortuary; afterwards most of it was levelled, and while the north part was landscaped to create Renmin Park, the rest was paved to form a dusty concrete parade ground for political rallies. The former paved area has now been turned over to green grass, bamboo groves and fountains, while the bomb shelters beneath have become shopping malls.

the time of writing was being renovated for a new role as (yet another) exclusive club. Head inside, if they'll let you; you'll see hints of its former use in the equestrian detailing on the balustrades.

Renmin Park

人民公园, rénmín gōngyuán · Daily 24hr (but only the north gate is open after 7pm) · Free · Ⓜ People's Square

Just east of the Former Racecourse Clubhouse is the north gate to lovely **Renmin Park**. It's surprisingly quiet, with rocky paths winding between shady groves and alongside ponds – the only sign that you are in the heart of a modern city are the skyscrapers looming above the treetops. In the morning, the park is host to *tai ji* practitioners and joggers, while old folk arrive to camp out all day playing cards.

Bearing left brings you to a small square. At the weekend, this is the venue for an extraordinary **marriage market**. Hundreds of middle-aged parents mill round with printouts, some hung from trees or umbrellas, displaying the statistics of their children – height, education, salary, astrological sign – in order to arrange dates. Interestingly, few show photos – looks aren't high on the list of relevant attributes, unlike birthplace, which determines where you can live and work. Quite often the kids either don't know or don't approve of their elders meddling in their love lives, and the parents will have to make the subsequent "dates" look accidental. It's an ancient practice that dies hard. Chinese weddings are still essentially family unions, and with the one-child policy leaving so many families pinning their hopes on one individual, the stakes are high. Parents of boys are particularly anxious, as the same policy has helped create a worrying gender imbalance: Shanghai girls are in short supply. It is estimated that by 2030, 25 percent of Chinese men in their 30s will be unmarried.

Museum of Contemporary Art

上海当代艺术馆, shànghǎi dāngdài yìshùguǎn · Daily 10am–6pm, last admission 5pm · ¥50 · ☎ 63279000, Ⓦ mocashanghai.org

The attractive, glass-walled **Museum of Contemporary Art** (**MoCA**) is a privately funded museum (with no permanent collection) whose temporary shows are invariably interesting and imaginatively curated – its three storeys make an excellent exhibition space. There's a lot of video and installation art, with a roughly equal balance between Chinese and foreign artists, and the museum holds regular talks and tours.

Tomorrow Square

明天广场, míngtiān guǎngchǎng · Ⓜ People's Square

Exit via the north entrance of Renmin Park, turn left and cross back over Huangpi Bei Lu – that claw-roofed monolith towering over you, with a striking resemblance to Saruman's castle from the *Lord of the Rings* films, is **Tomorrow Square** (2002). The top floors house the *JW Marriott* hotel (see p.117); take the lift to the lobby on the 38th floor for great views over People's Square – you can see how much prettier it would be without the City Hall. If you want to linger you'll have to buy a drink (a coffee will set you back ¥60).

Jiangyin Lu

江阴路, jiāngyīn lù · Ⓜ People's Square

Just behind Tomorrow Square, and in stark contrast to its corporate sheen, is an area of ramshackle low rise, **Jiangyin Lu**. Heading west along here for a hundred metres or so, past the excellent *Mingtown Etour Hostel* at no. 55 – the cute bar is a good place for a cheap drink – brings you to a little pet market, where you can buy a noisy cricket in a bamboo cage for ¥5 or a snake for a lot more.

YUYUAN BAZAAR

The Old City and around

The Old City (老城, lǎochéng) is a rough oval circumscribed by two roads,
Renmin Lu and Zhonghua Lu, which follow the old path of the city walls. This
district never formed part of the International Settlement and was known by
the foreigners who lived in Shanghai, rather patronizingly, as the Chinese City.
Based on the original walled city of Shanghai, which dated back to the
eleventh century, the area was reserved in the nineteenth and early twentieth
centuries as a ghetto for vast numbers of Chinese who lived in conditions of
appalling squalor, while the foreigners carved out their living space around
them. It's an area of about four square kilometres, and at its northern edge is
not half a kilometre from the Bund – though a great distance in spirit.

Although tree-lined ring roads replaced the original walls and moats as early as 1912, and sanitation has obviously improved vastly since, to cross the boundaries into the **Old City** is still, for now, to enter a different world. The twisting alleyways are a haven of free enterprise, bursting with makeshift markets selling fish, vegetables, cheap trinkets, clothing and food. Ironically, for a tourist entering the area, the feeling is like entering a Chinatown in a Western city. It probably won't stay that way for long, though; as **prime real estate**, the area is squarely in the sights of developers and city planners and many of the lanes are in the process of being demolished.

In modern times the area has been slashed down the middle by the main north–south artery, **Henan Nan Lu** (河南南路, hénán nán lù). The easiest approach from Nanjing Dong Lu is to walk due south along Henan Lu or Sichuan Zhong Lu; you could also simply take the metro to Yuyuan Garden.

Visitor activity centres on the tourist **Yuyuan Bazaar** and the neighbouring **Yu Gardens**, but there are also a few charming **temples** sunk into the **alleyways**. Head west from here and you'll hit the swanky **Cool Docks** development at the riverside; a twenty-minute walk west brings you to Huaihai Zhong Lu (淮海东路, huáihǎi zhōng lù), Xintiandi and Tianzifang, all of which are in the Old French Concession district (see p.58).

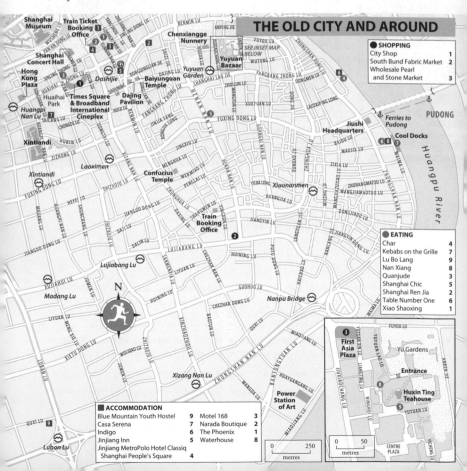

Yu Gardens

豫园, yùyuán · Daily 8.30am–5.30pm, last entry 5pm · April–Oct ¥40; Nov–March ¥30 · ☎ 63260830 · Ⓜ Yuyuan Garden

A classical Chinese garden featuring pools, walkways, bridges and rockeries, the **Yu Gardens** (Yu Yuan or Jade Garden) were created in the sixteenth century by a high-ranking official in the imperial court in honour of his father. Despite fluctuating fortunes, the gardens have surprisingly survived the passage of the centuries. They were spared from their greatest crisis – the Cultural Revolution – apparently because the anti-imperialist "Small Sword Society" had used them as their headquarters in 1853 during the Taiping Uprising (see p.168).

Though firmly on all tourist itineraries, the gardens are less impressive than those in nearby Suzhou (see p.98), and most foreign visitors leave underwhelmed – but the Shanghainese are proud of them, as they predate foreign Shanghai by three centuries. During the **lantern festival** on the fifteenth day of the traditional New Year, they are brightened up by thousands of lanterns and an even larger number of spectators.

Garden connoisseurs will appreciate the whitewashed walls topped by undulating dragons made of tiles, the lotus ponds full of koi and the paths winding round hillocks. The first building you come to is the **Cuixiu Hall** (Hall of Gathering Grace), built as a venue for the appreciation of an impressive 12m-high **rockery**; Chinese gardens are meant to be landscapes in miniature, so the rockery is something of a mini-Himalaya. The **Yuhua Tang** (Hall of Jade Magnificence) behind it has some lovely wooden screens on the doors and inside is full of Ming-dynasty rosewood furniture. The huge, craggy, indented rock in front of the hall was intended for the Summer Palace in Beijing, but the boat carrying it sank in the Huangpu, so it was recovered and installed here. Chinese guides demonstrate that a coin dropped in the hole at the top can emerge from several different exits – according, so they say, to your astrological sign. The southeast section of the gardens is a self-contained **miniature garden** within a garden and tends to be rather less busy, so it's a good place to head for a sit-down.

Huxin Ting teahouse

湖心亭茶馆, húxīntíng cháguǎn · 257 Yuyuan Lu · Daily 8am–9pm · ☎ 63736950 · Ⓜ Yuyuan Garden

The charming (if touristy) **Huxin Ting** (Heart of Lake Pavilion) is a two-storey teahouse on an island at the centre of an ornamental lake, reached by a zigzagging bridge. The Queen of England and Bill Clinton, among other illustrious guests, have dropped in for tea here; these days it's pricey (¥60 for limitless tea), and service is brusque. Rely on the waiter's recommendation and you'll be given the most expensive option, so insist on seeing the menu. Vendors on the bridge sell fish food for ¥5 so you can feed the carp.

Yuyuan Bazaar

豫园商城, yùyuán shāngchéng · Ⓜ Yuyuan Garden

Surrounding the Yu Gardens is the touristy **Yuyuan Bazaar**, a tangle of narrow lanes lined with souvenir shops, all new but built in a style of architectural chinoiserie. Some might complain that it looks tacky but it's very popular with Chinese tourists, and it gets fearsomely busy. If you need to get some souvenir **shopping** done in a hurry, this is the place to come, though watch out for scam artists (see p.30). You'll have to bargain hard, except at the large jewellery shops, where gold and platinum pieces are sold by weight, and the price per gram – lower than in the West – is marked on the wall. Wooden signs point to the more famous shops.

Chenxiangge Nunnery

沉香阁, chénxiāng gé · 29 Chenxiangge Lu · Daily 8am–4pm · ¥10 · Ⓜ Yuyuan Garden

A short walk west from the Yu Gardens, the **Chenxiangge Nunnery** is one of the more active of Shanghai's temples. This tranquil complex is enlivened by the presence of a few dozen resident nuns, who gather twice daily to pray and chant in the Daxiongbao Hall, under the gaze of the Sakyamuni Buddha. His gilded statue is flanked by images of 384 disciples, all supposedly the work of a single recent, still living, craftsman.

The alleyways

If you head west out of the Yuyuan Bazaar (past all the construction work) you will soon find yourself in some gritty **alleyways** – the real old town, if you like. It's being torn down at a fearsome rate, but hopefully there will still be a few streets left by the time you read this.

Dajing Lu

大镜路, dàjìng lù · Ⓜ Yuyuan Garden

Crossing Henan Nan Lu brings you to the most interestingly ramshackle street, **Dajing Lu**, where you'll likely come across ducks being killed and plucked, laundry and cured meat hung up on the same lines, and plenty of hole-in-the-wall restaurants with their fare – crabs, toads, shrimps and the like – crawling around plastic tubs outside. Look behind you for a great Shanghai snapshot, the Pudong skyscrapers rising over the shabby street like a mirage – very *Blade Runner*.

Baiyunguan Temple

白云观, báiyún guān · 239 Dajing Lu · Daily 9am–5pm · ¥5 · ☎ 63287236 · Ⓜ Dashijie

At the end of Dajing Lu is the pretty Taoist **Baiyunguan Temple**. Worshippers light incense and burn "silver ingots" made of paper in the central courtyard – some burn paper cars and houses too – while Taoist priests wander round in yellow robes with their long hair tied in a bun. In the main hall there's a huge effigy of the Jade Emperor looking judgemental. Taoism is the most esoteric of China's three big religions, and there are some striking figures of Taoist Immortals on display at the side of the hall – look for the fellow with arms coming out of his eyes.

Dajing Pavilion

大镜阁, dàjìng gé · 237 Dajing Lu · Daily 9am–4pm · ¥5 · Ⓜ Dashijie

Next door to the Baiyunguan Temple, the **Dajing Pavilion** is a new structure built over the last surviving slice of a Ming-dynasty wall. Brick markings on the wall bear the names of the two emperors, Tongzhi and Xianfeng, who commissioned it as protection against Japanese pirates. The pavilion today contains a small exhibition on the history of the Old City.

Confucius Temple

文庙, wén miào · Wenmiao Lu · Daily 9am–5pm · ¥10 · Ⓜ Laoximen

Sunk deep into the southwestern corner of the Old City is the **Confucius Temple**. Confucius was a philosopher who, around 500 BC, lectured on ethics and statecraft, emphasizing the importance of study and obedience. He was deified after his death and his theories provided the ideological underpinnings to the feudal Chinese state. Though Confucianism is no longer an active religion, its ideological influence on Chinese culture is obvious in the general Chinese respect for education and patriarchal authority.

Like most such temples across China, the Confucius Temple has been transformed into a park and museum. Shanghai has had a temple dedicated to Confucius since the Yuan dynasty but most of the present buildings date back to 1855, when the Small Sword Society (see p.168) made the temple a base. The only original Yuan building left is the elegant three-storey **Kuixing Pavilion**, near the entrance, which is dedicated to the god of artistic and intellectual endeavour. An appealing atmosphere of scholarly introspection infuses the complex – students wishing for good exam results tie red ribbons to the branches of the pine trees, and there's a statue of Confucius himself looking professorial (though it's not the recently approved "official" likeness).

In the **study hall** is an exhibition of teapots, more interesting than it sounds, as some display a great deal of effort and ingenuity. One, appropriately for the venue, is in the shape of a scholar, with the spout being his book, while another is nearly a metre high – it must have been hell to pour.

Note that **fake students and guides** hang out here and offer to show visitors around. They are pretty low key and helpful, and they will arrange a free tea-tasting in the shop, but their aim is to get you to buy ridiculously overpriced souvenirs or teas – don't believe the spiel that your money will go to the temple. Enjoy the tea if you think it's worth the hard sell, but make it clear you won't be buying anything or making any donations if that is the case.

The temple is never busy except on Sundays, when there is a secondhand **book fair** in the main courtyard. Outside, vendors sell kitschy trinkets and street food.

3

Cool Docks

老码头, lǎo mǎ tóu · 479 Zhongshan Nan Lu · Ⓜ Xiaonanmen, then a 15min walk

Keep heading east from the Old City till you hit the river, continue south past the ferry to Pudong, and suddenly things get startlingly salubrious: you've hit the **Cool Docks**, a strip of renovated warehouses just off the waterfront, filling up with fancy restaurants. Clearly this is envisioned as the new Xintiandi (see p.59), though you have to wonder if the lack of transport connections is going to stymie the plan – and of course anything that has to name itself "cool", by definition, usually isn't. Still, it's a pleasant place for a meal if you sit outside by the artificial pond – check out *Kebabs on the Grille* (see p.131) or *Table Number One* (see p.132). If you're wondering where the bars are, go east down any alley towards the river and you'll find to a slew of identikit riverside places where you can sit outside and admire Pudong's light show. Alternately, head to the excellent rooftop bar of the *Waterhouse* hotel (see p.118). In summer, an **artificial beach** sets up at the northern edge of the area, by the river (10am–10pm; admission varies, around ¥50). There's little more here than deckchairs and a shallow strip of sand, but there are regular events – check online – and you can bring your own food and drink.

Power Station of Art

上海当代艺术博物馆, shànghǎi dāngdài yìshù bówùguǎn · 200 Huayuangang Lu, near Miaojiang Lu · Daily 9am–5pm · Free · ☎ 31108550, ⓦ powerstationofart.com · Ⓜ Xizang Nan Lu, then a 15min walk

A couple of kilometres south of the Old City, on the site of the 2010 Expo, the huge **Power Station of Art** is a state-run contemporary art museum in a repurposed power station. Perhaps an attempt by the city fathers – aware that nothing confers prestige like a bright new gallery – to replicate the success of London's Tate Modern, the building, with its sturdy industrial fixtures and vast halls, is certainly striking. With no permanent display, there are generally three or four shows on the go at a time, including international touring exhibitions; it's also home to the **Shanghai Biennale** (see p.26). Check out the rooftop café for great views, and the shop for cool artsy trinkets. The area is a little **isolated**; if you're planning on getting a cab back into the centre, you'll probably have to walk some way back towards the metro. For more art, follow the river south for a couple of kilometres to the West Bund art strip (see p.87).

The Old French Concession

Shanghai might be changing at a furious rate but one thing stays the same: the Old French Concession (法租界, fǎzūjiè) is its most charming area, and one that has retained its historic feel. The neighbourhood is predominantly low rise, thanks to a colonial ruling that no building be more than one and a half times taller than the road is wide, and lined with glorious old mansions – many of which have been converted to restaurants, boutiques, embassies and galleries. Certain Gallic characteristics linger here, in the local chic and in a taste for bread and sweet cakes, and even in the many old plane trees that provide shade. The district invites leisurely strolling, with a little shopping, people-watching, a good meal and lots of coffee the order of the day.

Less crowded than Nanjing Dong Lu and more upmarket, **Huaihai Zhong Lu** (淮海中路, huáihǎi zhōng lù) is the main road through the heart of the area; more interesting are the quieter streets leading off it. To the east you'll find the **Xintiandi** development, a zone of rebuilt traditional houses (*shikumen*) that even critics of its yuppie ambience admit has charm, and, just south of here, the busy **Tianzifang** area, where alleys of *shikumen* have been converted to artsy boutiques and coffee shops; both are well worth exploring. To the west, there are plenty of former residences and boutiques to poke around in the area of Ruijin Er Lu, Maoming Nan Lu and Fenyang Lu (汾阳路, fēnyáng lù). As the street heads towards Hengshan Lu (衡山路, héngshān lù), embassies, bars and restaurants start to predominate. The apex of sophistication, with a smartly international feel, is further west, around Fuxing Xi Lu, **Wukang Lu** and Anfu Lu.

Metro stations are scattered sparsely throughout the Old French Concession, so you should expect to do a lot of walking – cycling is a good option, too, though note that bikes are not allowed on Huaihai Zhong Lu.

Brief history
Established in the mid-nineteenth century, the former French Concession lay to the south and west of the International Settlement, abutting the Chinese City (see p.53). Despite its name, its population was never particularly **French**. Before 1949, in fact, it was a shabby district mainly inhabited by Chinese and White Russians – what is now Huaihai Zhong Lu was then Avenue Joffre, after the French general, but it was nicknamed "Little Moscow". Other Westerners looked down on the White Russians as they were obliged to take jobs that, it was felt, should have been left to the Chinese (see box, p.66).

It's hard to imagine it now, but the French Concession was notorious for being low rent, for its lawlessness and for the ease with which police and French officials could be bribed – in contrast to the well-governed areas dominated by the British. This made it ideal territory for **gangsters**, including the king of all Shanghai mobsters, **Du Yuesheng**. For similar reasons, political activists also operated in this sector – the first meeting of the Chinese Communist Party took place here in 1921, and both Zhou Enlai and Sun Yatsen, the first provisional president of the Republic of China after the overthrow of the Qing dynasty, lived here. The preserved former homes of these two in particular (see p.64 & p.63) are worth visiting simply because, better than anywhere else in modern Shanghai, they give a sense of how the Westerners, and the Westernized, once lived.

4

Xintiandi
新天地, xīntiāndì • ⓂHuangpi Nan Lu, then walk south for 5min; alternatively, walk north from Ⓜ Xintiandi

Although it might seem like an obvious idea, the **Xintiandi** development, which comprises two blocks of renovated and rebuilt *shikumen* (see box, p.62) converted into a genteel open-air mall, was the first of its kind in China. It actually owes its form to the presence within it of the house where the Chinese Communist Party was formed (see p.62) – that meant that the developers couldn't just level the area and throw up something brand new. Their solution, a kind of mock heritage zone, has met with such success that town planners all over the country are now following suit.

Detractors may call it a working-class neighbourhood reimagined as a yuppie playground, but architecturally the area is a triumph – its stone buildings have retained their charm without being chintzy and the attention to detail is fantastic. Paved and pedestrianized, with *longtang* opening out onto a central plaza, Xintiandi is a great place to wind down or to linger over a coffee, with upscale restaurants and shops and plenty of alfresco seating for people-watching. Access is subtly but strictly controlled, with security guards keeping the riffraff out, so there aren't even any "art students" (see p.30) to hassle you.

THE OLD FRENCH CONCESSION

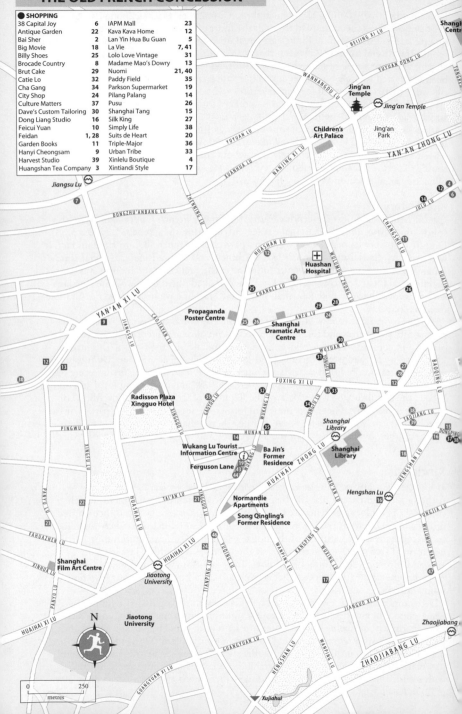

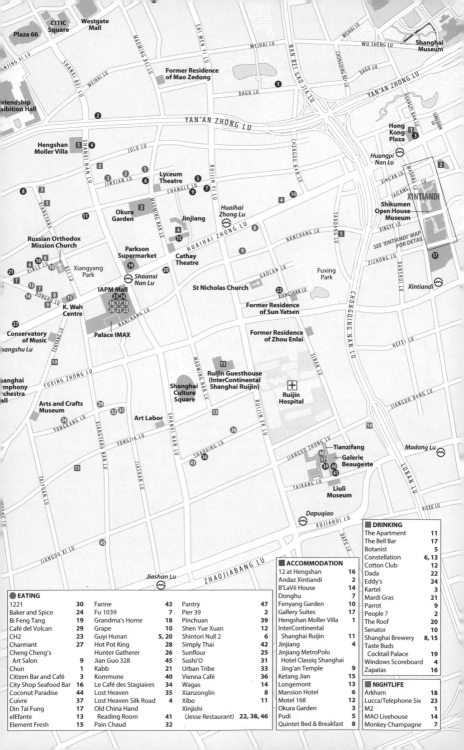

Plaza 66 · **CITIC Square** · **Westgate Mall**

Shanghai Museum

Friendship Exhibition Hall

Former Residence of Mao Zedong

Hengshan Moller Villa

Hong Kong Plaza

Huangpi Nan Lu

XINTIANDI

Shikumen Open House Museum

SEE 'XINTIANDI' MAP FOR DETAIL

Lyceum Theatre

Okura Garden

Jinjiang

Huaihai Zhong Lu

Russian Orthodox Mission Church

Parkson Supermarket

Cathay Theatre

Xiangyang Park

Shaanxi Nan Lu

IAPM Mall

St Nicholas Church

Fuxing Park

Xintiandi

K. Wah Centre

Conservatory of Music

Palace IMAX

Former Residence of Sun Yatsen

Former Residence of Zhou Enlai

Ruijin Guesthouse (InterContinental Shanghai Ruijin)

Ruijin Hospital

Arts and Crafts Museum

Shanghai Culture Square

Shanghai Symphony Orchestra Hall

Art Labor

Tianzifang

Galerie Beaugeste

Madang Lu

Liuli Museum

Dapuqiao

Jiashan Lu

● EATING

1221	30	Farine	43	Pantry	47
Baker and Spice	24	Fu 1039	7	Pier 39	2
Bi Feng Tang	19	Grandma's Home	18	Pinchuan	39
Café del Volcan	29	Grape	10	Shen Yue Xuan	12
CH2	23	Guyi Hunan	5, 20	Shintori Null 2	6
Charmant	27	Hot Pot King	28	Simply Thai	42
Cheng Cheng's		Hunter Gatherer	26	Sunflour	25
Art Salon	1	Jian Guo 328	45	Sushi'O	31
Chun	1	Kabb	21	Urban Tribe	33
Citizen Bar and Café	3	Kommune	40	Vienna Café	36
City Shop Seafood Bar	16	Le Café des Stagiaires	34	Wagas	14
Coconut Paradise	44	Lost Heaven	35	Xianzonglin	8
Cuivre	37	Lost Heaven Silk Road	4	Xibo	11
Din Tai Fung	17	Old China Hand		Xinjishi	
elEfante	13	Reading Room	41	(Jesse Restaurant)	22, 38, 46
Element Fresh	15	Pain Chaud	32		

■ ACCOMMODATION

12 at Hengshan	16
Andaz Xintiandi	2
B'LaVii House	7
Donghu	7
Fenyang Garden	9
Gallery Suites	17
Hengshan Moller Villa	1
InterContinental	
Shanghai Ruijin	11
Jinjiang	4
Jinjiang MetroPolo	
Hotel Classiq Shanghai	
Jing'an Temple	9
Ketang Jian	15
Longemont	13
Mansion Hotel	6
Motel 168	12
Okura Garden	3
Pudi	5
Quintet Bed & Breakfast	8

■ DRINKING

The Apartment	11
The Bell Bar	17
Botanist	5
Constellation	6, 13
Cotton Club	12
Dada	22
Eddy's	24
Kartel	3
Mardi Gras	21
Parrot	9
People 7	2
The Roof	20
Senator	10
Shanghai Brewery	8, 15
Taste Buds	
Cocktail Palace	19
Windows Scoreboard	4
Zapatas	16

■ NIGHTLIFE

Arkham	18
Lucca/Telephone Six	23
M2	1
MAO Livehouse	14
Monkey Champagne	7

SHIKUMEN

The **shikumen**, or stone-gated house, was developed in the late nineteenth century as an adaption of Western-style terrace housing to Chinese conditions. By the 1930s, such residences were ubiquitous across Shanghai, and housed eighty percent of the population. Crammed together in south-facing rows, with a narrow alley or *longtang* in between, they were all built to a similar design, with a stone gate at the front leading into a small walled yard. Some were very salubrious, others little more than slum dwellings. Those aimed at the middle classes had five rooms upstairs, five down. The least desirable room was the north-facing *tingzijian*, at the bend in the staircase; these were generally let out to impecunious lodgers such as students and writers. Many classics of Chinese literature were composed in these poky spaces.

As the city's population mushroomed in the twentieth century, *shikumen* were partitioned into four or five houses. In the rush to develop, most *shikumen* neighbourhoods have now been demolished; those that remain tend to be cramped and badly maintained, with archaic plumbing. Xintiandi is the sole example of stylish renovation – perhaps pastiche would be a more accurate word, as there's not much left of the original houses. The *longtangs* at Taikang Lu (see p.64) and Duolun Lu (see p.83) have, however, been well preserved.

North Block

Heading into the **North Block**, you'll pass the city's most popular *Starbucks* and an *Element Fresh* (see p.127). The branch of the popular Shanghai Tang boutique on the left is lovely (see p.159), with a great tiled floor, but the prices for their distinctive clothes and accessories are mind-boggling; you'll find crude knock-offs at any fake market (see p.158). It's also worth having a jaunt down the narrow lane on the northeast side: that impressive mansion is 1 Xintiandi, where its Hong Kong owners, of the Shui On Group, hang out and count their money.

Shikumen Open House Museum

石库门民居陈列馆, shíkùmén mínjū chénlièguǎn • 25 North Block • Daily 10am–10pm • ¥20 • ☎ 33070337

The **Shikumen Open House Museum**, at the south end of Xintiandi North Block, does an excellent job of evoking early twentieth-century Chinese gentility. This reconstruction of a typical *shikumen* is filled with everyday objects – typewriters, toys, a four-poster bed and the like – so it doesn't look as bare as the "Former Residences" elsewhere in the city. A top-floor display details how Xintiandi came about, admitting that most of it was built from scratch. A quote on the wall is perhaps more revealing than was intended: "Foreigners find it Chinese and Chinese find it foreign."

Site of the First National Congress of the Chinese Communist Party

中国一大会址纪念馆, zhōngguó yīdàhuìzhǐ jìniànguǎn • 76 Xingye Lu, at junction with Huangpi Nan Lu • Daily 9am–5pm, last admission 4pm • Free (bring ID)

On the east side of Xintiandi you'll find one of the shrines of Maoist China, the **Site of the First National Congress of the Chinese Communist Party**. The official story of this house is that on July 23, 1921, thirteen representatives of the communist cells that had developed all over China, including its most famous junior participant **Mao Zedong**, met here to discuss the formation of a national party. The meeting was discovered by a French police agent (it was illegal to hold political meetings in the French Concession), and on July 30 the delegates fled. Quite how much of this really happened is unclear, but it seems probable that there were in fact more delegates than the record remembers – the missing names would have been expunged according to subsequent political circumstances.

There's a little **exhibition hall** downstairs, where the period relics – such as maps, money and a British policeman's uniform and truncheon – are more interesting than the outdated propaganda tracts. The last room has a waxwork diorama of Mao and his fellow delegates.

South Block

Xintiandi's **South Block** is rather anticlimactic, with a modern glass mall at the end that rather spoils the olde-worlde effect. Inside you'll find the good Hong Kong restaurant, *Crystal Jade* (see p.133), as well as the UME International Cineplex (see p.153) and a host of luxury brands.

Fuxing Park

复兴公园, Fùxīnggōngyuán · 105 Fuxing Zhong Lu · Daily 6am–6pm · Free · Ⓜ Xintiandi

Fuxing Park was laid out by the French in 1909, and remains rather European in feel, so the bronze statue of Marx and Engels in the northwest corner seems rather incongruous. You'll see middle-aged locals performing *tai ji*, ballroom dancing and opera singing, or snoozing on the many benches.

Former Residence of Sun Yatsen

孙中山故居, sūnzhōngshān gùjū · 7 Xiangshan Lu · Daily 9am–4.30pm · ¥20 · ☎ 64372954 · Ⓜ Xintiandi

Just outside the western exit of Fuxing Park stands the **Former Residence of Sun Yatsen**, the first president of the Chinese Republic, and his wife, Song Qingling. The first building you enter is a rather dry museum, with an exhibition of the man's books and artefacts, and not much in English. Much more interesting is the building next door, his actual house, which, just as an example of an elegantly furnished period house, is worth a wander round.

St Nicholas Church

圣尼古拉斯教堂, shěng nígǔlāsī jiàotáng · 16 Gaolan Lu · Ⓜ Xintiandi

The lovely Russian Orthodox **St Nicholas Church** was built in 1933 by White Russian exiles. It was abandoned in 1941, and then did service as a laundry and a washing-machine factory. An image of Mao was hung from the roof during the Cultural Revolution, to prevent it being sacked. In recent years, it has been used as a restaurant and nightclub; these closed when the Russians complained that was sacrilegious, and during the 2010 Expo it was reconsecrated to allow services. It is presently empty and though there are plans to return it to its original purpose the government is cautious, aware that it would set an awkward precedent for the many other old religious buildings in Shanghai.

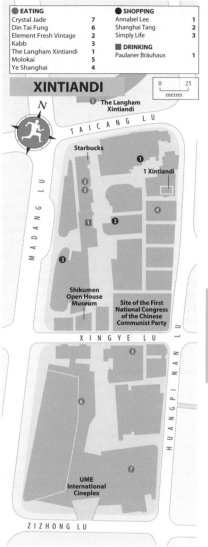

● EATING		● SHOPPING	
Crystal Jade	7	Annabel Lee	1
Din Tai Fung	6	Shanghai Tang	2
Element Fresh Vintage	2	Simply Life	3
Kabb	3	■ DRINKING	
The Langham Xintiandi	1	Paulaner Bräuhaus	1
Molokai	5		
Ye Shanghai	4		

XINTIANDI

0   25
metres

The Langham Xintiandi

TAICANG LU

Starbucks

1 Xintiandi

MADANG LU

Shikumen Open House Museum

Site of the First National Congress of the Chinese Communist Party

XINGYE LU

HUANGPI NAN LU

UME International Cineplex

ZIZHONG LU

Former Residence of Zhou Enlai

周恩来故居, zhōuēnlái gùjū • 73 Sinan Lu • Daily 9am–4pm • Free • ☎ 64730420 • Ⓜ Xintiandi

Tucked away in a very smart neighbourhood of old houses lies the **Former Residence of Zhou Enlai**. Zhou was Mao's right-hand man, but, as a much more urbane character than the Chairman, he has always been looked on with rather more affection. He was head of the Shanghai Communist Party when he lived here, and as such was kept under surveillance from a secret outpost over the road. There's not, in truth, a great deal to see, beyond a lot of hard beds in bare rooms; the garden, oddly, with its hedges and ivy-covered walls, is vaguely reminiscent of the English suburbs of the 1930s.

Tianzifang

田子坊, tiánzǐfāng • Main entrance 210 Taikang Lu • ☎ 54657531 • Ⓜ Dapuqiao

Tianzifang is a fashionably artsy shopping and lunching quarter. Head to Taikang Lu and take any of the alleys that head north, and you'll enter the **Taikang Lu Art Area** (泰康路田子坊, tàikānglù tiánzǐfāng), a web of alleys full of tiny boutiques, souvenir stalls, coffee shops, handmade jewellery stores, art galleries, interior design consultancies and the like, all housed in converted *shikumen* houses. Its northern boundary is Sinan Lu, but don't try to come in from there, as the entrance is tough to find.

Inevitably, the place gets compared with Xintiandi; but whereas the architecture there is modern pastiche, this is a set of real, warts-and-all *longtangs*, with the result that it's quainter, shabbier and more charming. If you're looking for cool knick-knacks, quirky souvenirs, tasteful homewares or a designer original, this is the place. Sadly most of the newer arrivals are selling tourist tat, but they haven't yet pushed out the better stores. For gorgeous **clothes** by local designers, head to La Vie (see p.159) or Nuomi (see p.159). For a **coffee** stop, the centrally located *Kommune* (see p.137) is a local institution, while for **food**, there are a plethora of tiny but pricey restaurants.

There's a **map** just inside the entrance – take careful note, though you'll likely get lost anyway as the alleys are something of a warren. And if you can, avoid the weekend, when the narrow lanes get fearsomely busy.

Liuli Museum

琉璃艺术博物馆, liúli yìshù bówùguǎn • 25 Taikang Lu • Tues–Sun 10am–5pm • ☎ 64672268, Ⓦ liulichinamuseum.com • Ⓜ Dapuqiao

The small and elegant **Liuli Museum**, dedicated to glasswork, is worth a visit if you're in the area. Temporary glass art shows, usually by foreign artists, are held above the ground-level shop, while the top floor is dedicated to Loretta Yang's striking, if kitschy, Buddhist glass sculptures – check out the thousand-armed Guanyin and the masks that seem to be floating in glass blocks. Whatever her worth as an artist, Loretta is not exactly humble – she set up the museum, and there are rather too many signs telling you what a wonderful person she is. Avoid those and give your attention to the charming display of antique glass jewellery.

Ruijin Guesthouse (InterContinental Shanghai Ruijin)

瑞金宾馆, ruijīn bīnguǎn • 118 Ruijin Er Lu • ☎ 64725222, Ⓦ ruijinhotelsh.com • Ⓜ Shaanxi Nan Lu

The south section of **Ruijin Er Lu** (瑞金二路, ruijīn èr lù) is busy and cramped, but there's a wonderful escape in the form of the stately **Ruijin Guesthouse**, just south of Fuxing Zhong Lu. This Tudor-style country manor was home in the early twentieth century to the Morris family, owners of the *North China Daily News*; Mr Morris raised greyhounds for the Shanghai Race Club and the former Canidrome dog track across the street. The house, having miraculously escaped severe damage during the Cultural Revolution because certain high-ranking officials used it as their private residence, has now been turned into the exclusive **InterContienantal Shanghai Ruijin** hotel (see opposite). Even if you're not a guest, you're free to walk around the spacious, quiet grounds, where it's hard to believe you're in the middle of one of the world's most hectic cities.

Maoming Nan Lu

茂名南路, màomíng nánlù • Ⓜ Shaanxi Nan Lu

Maoming Nan Lu is the artery for one of the city's most prestigious districts. There is a plethora of boutiques, and it's a good place to pick up a tailored suit or *qipao* (see p.160). Two plush **hotels**, the *Okura Garden* and the *Jinjiang*, are both worth a visit for glimpses of former glories.

Okura Garden hotel

上海花园饭店, huāyuán fàndiàn • 58 Maoming Nan Lu • ☎ 64151111, Ⓦ gardenhotelshanghai.com

The **Okura Garden hotel**, originally the French Club, or Cercle Sportif Français, was taken over by the Americans during World War II and converted by the egalitarian Communists into the People's Cultural Palace. It's a swanky place to stay (see p.120), but anyone can wander round the lovely gardens and look at the sumptuous stained-glass ceiling in the ballroom.

Jinjiang hotel

锦江之星, jǐnjiāngzhīxīng • 59 Maoming Nan Lu • ☎ 62582582, Ⓦ jinjianghotels.com

The **Jinjiang hotel** compound includes the former **Grosvenor Residence** complex, the most fashionable and pricey address in pre-World War II Shanghai. The hotel has been modernized (see p.119), but the *VIP Club* still retains much of its 1920s architecture and *Great Gatsby* ambience. Non-guests might be able to take a peek by taking the lift to the top floor of the old wing of the *Jinjiang*, where the club is located, although gaining entrance to one of the twenty astonishingly beautiful, refurbished Art Deco VIP mansion rooms on the floors directly below might prove more difficult.

Around Shanxi Nan Lu

陕西南路, shǎnxī nánlù

The area **around Shanxi Nan Lu** is rather busier with traffic than elsewhere in the French Concession, but it's still good for walking, with shade provided by the plane trees, and plenty of quirky little shops to explore.

Hengshan Moller Villa

衡山马勒别墅饭店, héngshān mǎlèbiéshù fàndiàn • 30 Shanxi Nan Lu • ☎ 62478881, Ⓦ mollervilla.com • Ⓜ Shaanxi Nan Lu

The **Hengshan Moller Villa** is a Gothic fantasy of turrets and crenellations so incongruous that if you glimpse it from a moving vehicle it's easy to think you've imagined it. It was built in 1936 by Eric Moller, and – rumour has it – designed by his 12-year-old daughter; there's certainly something appealingly childlike about the tapering spires and striped brickwork. It's like a castle made of cake – perhaps she should have been allowed a hand in more of Shanghai's buildings. These days it's a pricey hotel (see p.119).

Russian Orthodox Mission Church

圣母大堂, shèngmǔ dàtáng • 55 Xinle Lu • Ⓜ Shaanxi Nan Lu

With its unmistakeable proud blue dome, the **Russian Orthodox Mission Church** provides evidence of the area's strong Russian connection. It's been used as a factory, a disco and a teahouse, but today it's empty. You can nose around outside, but the interior is not open to the public.

WHITE RUSSIANS

After the **Bolsheviks** took power in 1917, czarist loyalists, known as **White Russians** to distinguish themselves from the "Red" Communists, first fought and then, when defeated, fled into exile. Many came to Shanghai. As stateless peoples without extraterritorial protection they were subject to Chinese laws, and suffered harsh Chinese punishments. Some had brought their family jewels and heirlooms, but most arrived with little.

The girls, ex-ballerinas and opera singers among them, could at least rely on their feminine charms; many became "taxi girls", dancing for a small gratuity at nightclubs, or the mistresses of established Westerners – the divorce rates shot up as a result, particularly among the British. Other girls (as many as one in four, according to a League of Nations report), drifted into prostitution.

The lives of the men were even more precarious. Destitution forced many to earn their living in ways no other foreigner would consider, as rickshaw pullers or beggars. Ex-soldiers found work as bodyguards for Chinese gangsters. This was all terribly embarrassing to other foreigners, as it punctured a carefully constructed facade of superiority, and a scheme was mooted to have them all packed off to Australia, though it came to naught.

But the influence of the Russians was by no means all negative; as well as a certain élan, they brought a wealth of skills. Cultivated sophisticates became teachers, exposing the children of boorish merchants to cultured pastimes such as fencing and horseriding, and it was Russian musicians, ballerinas and singers who, more than anyone, created the city's unique cultural scene.

Arts and Crafts Museum

工艺美术博物馆, gōngyì měishù bówùguǎn • 79 Fenyang Lu • Daily 9am–4pm • ¥8 • ☎ 64314074 • Ⓜ Changshu Lu

A grand French mansion from 1905, designed by the master architect Ladislav Hudec (see p.169), has been rather haphazardly converted into the **Arts and Crafts Museum**. Visitors are first confronted with a gamut of overpriced craft shops; ignore these and head upstairs to find an intriguing collection of jade, ivory, wood and embroidery. A lot of the objects are very well made but seem rather fussy. The most striking exhibits are the ivories, carved in the Sixties, that depict communist subjects, political meetings and the like; they're brilliantly done but look very kitsch now. You'll also see craftspeople practising their trades – jade being worked at a lathe, a seamstress embroidering and so on.

West of Changshu Lu

West of Changshu Lu metro station you really get a good idea of what the French Concession is all about. Many of the villas here have been converted to **embassy** properties (the more sensitive are guarded by soldiers with fixed bayonets) and there are plenty of smart places to eat and a fair few beauty salons – but, oddly, not that many shops. It's more a place to soak up atmosphere on a sunny day or people-watch over a cappuccino than to take in sights.

Propaganda Poster Centre

宣传画年画艺术中心, xuānchuánhuàniánhuà yìshùzhōngxīn • Basement flat, building 4, 868 Huashan Lu; the security guard at the entrance will give you a name card with a map on the back showing you the way • Daily 9.30am–4.30pm • ¥25 • ☎ 62111845, Ⓦ shanghaipropagandaart.com • Ⓜ Changshu Lu

A ten-minute stroll northwest of Changshu Lu metro station on Huashan Lu, the **Propaganda Poster Centre** is an abrupt change of tone, providing a fascinating glimpse into communist China. The walls are covered with more than three thousand Chinese **Socialist Realist posters**, arranged chronologically from the 1950s to the 1970s – the curator will talk you round, whether or not you understand his Chinese. There are, fortunately, English captions. Slogans like "The Soviet Union is the stronghold of world peace" and "Hail the over-fulfilment of steel production by ten million tons", and images of sturdy, lantern-jawed peasants and soldiers defeating green-skinned imperialists or riding tractors into a glorious future, offer a dramatic portrayal of the communist dream.

Surprisingly, the style of this dry communist art owes much to images with a very different message – **popular prewar calendar posters** – and the exhibition concludes with a room of these. These images, once disseminated all over China, show fetching Chinese girls in fashionable dress and make-up, surrounded by the accoutrements of modernity. They served once to introduce the Chinese to the delights of consumer culture, such as cigarettes and hair curlers, and daring new fashions such as the slim-cut *qipao* and bobbed hair.

Take a look at the knick-knacks in the **gift shop** – an image of an ack-ack gunner on a teapot, perhaps, or a silk painting of Mao playing ping pong. Postcards are good value at ¥10 each.

Wukang Lu and around

武康路, wǔkāng lù • Ⓜ Jiaotong University

As Rue Ferguson, **Wukang Lu** was one of the chicest strips of real estate in old Shanghai, and today this quiet tree-lined strip of mansions feels quintessentially French Concession.

Song Qingling's Former Residence

宋庆龄故居, sòngqìnglíng gùjū • 1843 Huaihai Xi Lu • Daily 9–11am & 1–4.30pm • ¥20 • ☎ 64747183

As the wife of Sun Yatsen, Song Qingling was part of a bizarre family coterie – her sister Song Meiling was married to Chiang Kai-shek and her brother, known as T.V. Soong, was finance minister to Chiang. She lived in Shanghai on and off from 1948 until her death in 1981; today **Song Qingling's Former Residence** serves as a charming step back into a residential Shanghai of the recent past. The trappings on display – including her enormous official limousines parked in the garage – are largely post-1949. Inside, note the lovely wood panelling and lacquerwork.

Normandie Apartments

武康大楼, wǔkāng dàlóu • 1850 Huaihai Zhong Lu

Heading north from Huaihai Xi Lu, you'll pass one of Shanghai's most distinctive Art Deco buildings, Ladislav Hudec's **Normandie Apartments**, built in 1926. Though its battleship shape echoes New York's Flatiron building, it's built in French Renaissance style, with elegant cantilevered balconies. During the Cultural Revolution it was nicknamed "the Shanghai Diving Pool", as it was a favoured suicide spot. A few minutes' walk north brings you to *Farine* (see p.137), where you can join well-heeled locals for a cappuccino before exploring the boutiques and galleries of Ferguson Lane.

Wukang Lu Tourist Information Centre

武康路 旅游资讯中心, wǔkānglù zīxùn zhōngxīn • 393 Wukang Lu • Daily 9am–5pm • ☎ 64335000

The **Wukang Lu Tourist Information Centre** hosts a slick display of scale models of the French Concession's standout historical buildings, including many that are a short walk from here. The models are well made, but unfortunately there is little information giving their context or history – you'll have to find that elsewhere. Nonetheless, it's a good place to drop into; unlike almost every other official tourist information site in Shanghai it's actually useful, providing maps for self-guided walking tours and a bike-sharing scheme (see p.23).

Ba Jin's Former Residence

巴金故居·千景旅游网, bājīn gùjū – qiānjǐng lǚyóu wǎng • 113 Wukang Lu • Tues–Sat 10am–4pm • Free, bring ID

Ba Jin was one of China's greatest novelists, who did his best work in Shanghai in the 1930s. He was known for smart social critiques – his most famous novel, *The Family* (1933), was written to shed light on the uncomfortable realities of the traditional Chinese family. After being hounded during the Cultural Revolution the author was rehabilitated when it was over, and lived the rest of his days in this mansion. Today **Ba Jin's Former Residence** feels cosy, if rather tweely decorated, full of displays of his manuscripts and books. There's also a rather lovely garden.

Jing'an

Jing'an (静安, jìng'ān), west of People's Square, has always been one of the smartest areas in the city; in the colonial era, it was a popular place for the "Shanghailanders" – Europeans who settled here – to build their mock-Tudor mansions behind high walls. Today Jing'an is notable for its grand, exclusive hotels and ultramodern malls. Unexpectedly, and as a counterpoint to the rampant commercialism that surrounds them, the area is also home to two of the city's few notable places of worship: Jing'an and Yufo temples, both of which are surprisingly busy with devotees. The impressive new Natural History Museum, in a quirky sculpture park, is a pleasing addition to the local scene, while in the north, close to Suzhou Creek, the Moganshan Arts District has dozens of art galleries and boutiques to explore.

Nanjing Xi Lu

南京西路, nánjīng xī lù • Ⓜ People's Sqaure, Ⓜ Nanjing Xi Lu and Ⓜ Jing'an Temple; bus #20 runs the length of the road

The main artery of Jing'an, **Nanjing Xi Lu** was once known as Bubbling Well Road after a spring that used to gush at the far end of the street. It's now one of Shanghai's busiest shopping boulevards, though with a parade of giant malls it's rather less intimate than some of the city's other shopping areas; after all the unrelenting materialism you may be ready for the attractive **Jing'an Temple** at the street's western end.

Han City

假货市场, jiǎhuò shìchǎng • 580 Nanjing Xi Lu • Daily 10am–8pm • Ⓜ People's Square

Starting from People's Square and heading west along Nanjing Xi Lu, first stop for most visitors is **Han City** on the north side of the street. The sign by the entrance declaring "protect intellectual property" must have been put up by someone with a well-developed sense of irony, as the entire mall, all three storeys, is devoted to stalls selling fake goods – clothes, watches, software, bags and shoes (see p.158). Not everyone enjoys the experience, as the place is shabby, the vendors are pushy and hard bargaining is essential. If you're dead-set on getting your hand on knock-offs, the mall under the Science Museum (see p.158) is much bigger, but this place is undoubtedly convenient. Rumours that Han City will soon be closing down have persisted for years.

Upscale malls

West of Han City, the north side of the street is given over to a string of malls – **Westgate** (梅龙镇广场, méilóngzhèn guǎngchǎng), **CITIC Square** (中信泰富广场, zhōngxìntàifù guǎngchǎng) and **Plaza 66** (恒隆广场, hénglóng guǎngchǎng) – kitschy buildings arranged in a row like souvenirs on a mantelpiece. They're all rather heavily weighted towards luxury brands, with the result that there are generally more staff than shoppers. The last of the giants is the **Shanghai Centre** (上海商城, shànghǎi shāngchéng) at 1376 Nanjing Xi Lu, which despite an underwhelming entrance through a car park, is one of the more interesting luxury places, home to the decent *Element Fresh* café (see p.127), a tiny branch of Garden Books (see p.163) and the five-star *Portman Ritz-Carlton* hotel (see p.121). The Shanghai Centre Theatre here has nightly acrobatics shows (see p.150).

Shanghai Friendship Exhibition Hall

展览馆, zhǎnlǎnguǎn • 1000 Yan'an Zhong Lu • ☎ 62790279 • Ⓜ Jing'an Temple

The **Shanghai Friendship Exhibition Hall**, a Stalinist wedding cake built to celebrate communism, must surely be in a permanent sulk at the behemoths of capitalism that hem it in. It's worth examining for its colossal ornate entrance, decorated with columns patterned with red stars and capped by a gilded spire. Constructed by the Russians in 1954, it was originally known as the Palace of Sino-Soviet Friendship and housed a permanent exhibition of industrial machinery from the Shanghai area – proof of the advances achieved after 1949. These days it's used as a vast and vulgar hall for trade fairs and art shows.

Jing'an Temple

静安寺, jìng'ān sì • 1686 Nanjing Xi Lu • Daily 7.30am–5pm • ¥50 • Ⓜ Jing'an Temple

It may be hemmed in by skyscrapers, but **Jing'an Temple** refuses to be outdone; this recently rebuilt complex is religious architecture Shanghai style – lavish and shiny, designed to impress, and expensive to get into. Building work began on the temple in the third century, and its apparent obscurity today belies its past as the richest Buddhist foundation in the city. In the late nineteenth century it was headed by legendary abbot Khi Vehdu, who combined his religious duties with a gangster lifestyle; the abbot and his seven concubines were shadowed by White Russian bodyguards, each carrying a leather briefcase lined with bulletproof steel, to be used as a shield in case of attack.

The **central hall** is constructed of Burmese teak and features flying eaves and sturdy *dougongs*. The last pillar on the right as you face the hall has been left deliberately

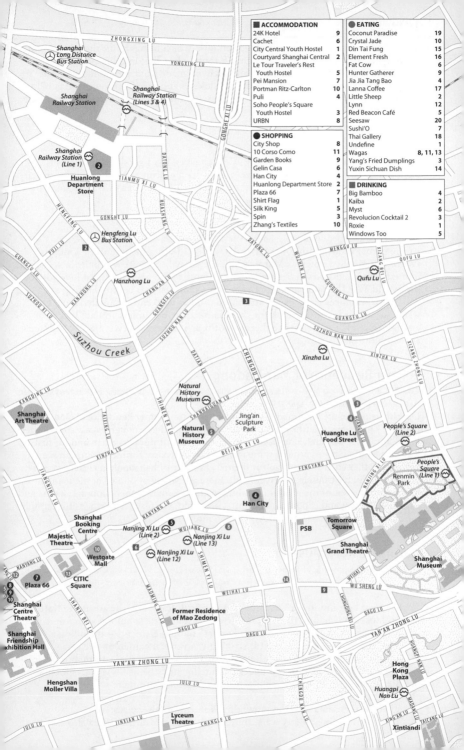

5

unfinished, retaining knots and a truncated fork, which brings home the huge size of the original trees. Inside, an 8.8m-high, 15-tonne silver Buddha glimmers in the gloom. A side hall holds an elegant slim Guanyin, made from a thousand-year-old camphor tree. Head round the back, to the cloisters and meeting rooms, and you'll see that no expense has been spared in the fittings; even the lift doors have been engraved with guardian Bodhisattvas.

Jing'an Park

静安公园, jìng'ān gōngyuán • Ⓜ Jing'an Temple

Attractive **Jing'an Park**, once Bubbling Well cemetery, has a good lunch-stop in the form of the *Thai Gallery* restaurant (see p.139). It's a welcome oasis in a part of the city where peace and quiet are rarely found. A pleasant walled garden (¥3) has a small photo exhibition on the history of the area.

Children's Palace

上海市少年宫, shànghǎishì shàoniángōng • 64 Yan'an Xi Lu • Wed–Fri 9am-4pm • ¥10 • ☎ 62481850 • Ⓜ Jing'an Temple

At the corner of Wulumuqi Bei Lu and Yan'an Xi Lu lies the grandiose **Children's Palace**. Originally known as Marble Hall, the sprawling estate was built in 1918 as a home for the Kadoories, a Sephardic Jewish family who were principal investors in pre-World War II Shanghai. It now serves as a children's art centre, hosting song and dance performances on weekday afternoons and at weekends. Casual visitors are welcome, and it is worth a look for the architecture; but unless you are lucky enough to catch a performance there is not much to peruse beyond a few children's art exhibitions.

Former Residence of Mao Zedong

毛泽东故居, máozédōng gùjū • 5–9 Lane 120, Maoming Bei Lu • Tues–Sun 9–11am & 1–4pm; you need to show your passport, or a valid mobile phone number • Free • ☎ 62723656 • Ⓜ Nanjing Xi Lu

Despite its name, the Chairman didn't live long at the **Former Residence of Mao Zedong** – just a few months in 1924 – but that's more than enough excuse for another Party shrine. Downstairs, along with waxworks of a youthful Chairman and his first wife and children posed around some elegant Qing-dynasty furniture, you can see a battered leather chair where Mao ruminated, a couple of half-smoked cigars preserved in perspex and his trousers, neatly folded. There are plenty of photos of the man and his friends; the rest of the exhibit is mainly made up of newspaper clippings, letters and hagiographic text and is not that engaging. That said, the place is worth visiting simply for being a well-preserved typical *shikumen* house (see box, p.62).

Natural History Museum

上海自然博物馆, shànghǎi zìrán bówùguǎn • Jing'an Sculpture Park, 399 Shanhaiguan Lu, near Datian Lu • Tues–Sun 9am–5.15pm, last admission 4.30pm • ¥30; cinema screenings ¥40 • ☎ 68622000, Ⓦ www.snhm.org.cn • Ⓜ Shanghai Natural History Museum

With a great location in the charming **Jing'an Sculpture Park**, the attractive **Natural History Museum** is bound to impress. First, the design: its spiralling structure echoes a nautilus shell, and the external walls emulate natural elements – including a stone wall inspired by tectonic plates and, strikingly, a vertical garden on the east wall. Secondly, the sheer volume of stuffed, plastinated or animatronic animals on display is quite astonishing. Exhibition spaces are intelligently themed – subjects include the Big Bang, evolution, early civilization, and so on – and there are plenty of captions in English.

As ever, the **dinosaurs** steal the show: there's an enormous skeleton of a Mamenchisaurus, and a pretty scary animatronic Tyrannosaurus. There's also a lifelike recreation of the African savannah, cutesy dioramas of early Chinese villages and some gory Damien Hirst-style cross-sections – most strikingly, of an ocean sunfish. It would take several hours to do the place justice, more if you take in one of the regular documentary screenings in the **4D cinema**.

The museum is a big hit with locals, so be prepared to queue for ten minutes or so to get in, or even longer on weekends and holidays.

Yufo Temple

玉佛寺, yùfó sì • 170 Anyuan Lu • Daily 8am–5pm • ¥20 • ☎ 62663668, Ⓦ yufotemple.com • Ⓜ Changshou Lu

Some 1.5km north of the Jing'an Temple, the **Yufo Temple** (Jade Buddha Temple), offers a less grand but rather more authentic experience. The pretty temple buildings have flying eaves, complicated brackets and intricate roof and ceiling decorations, and hold huge statues of Buddhas and Bodhisattvas. It's a lively place of worship, with great gusts of incense billowing from the central burner and worshippers kowtowing before effigies and tying red ribbons to branches, bells and the stone lions on the railings.

The star attractions, though, are the relics. Two **jade Buddhas** were brought here from Myanmar (Burma) in 1882 and the temple was built to house them. The larger, at nearly 2m tall, sits upstairs in a separate building at the back of the temple (follow the signs) – you will be expected to join the devotees in paying ¥15 for a bottle of oil that is used to keep the lanterns by the statue burning. Carved from a single block of milky white jade, it is encrusted with agate and emerald. The second statue, in the western hall, is a little smaller, at around 1m long, but easier to respond to. It shows a recumbent Buddha at the point of dying (or rather, entering nirvana), with a languid expression like a man dropping off for a nap.

The central **Great Treasure Hall** holds three huge figures of the past, present and future Buddhas, as well as the temple drum and bell. The gods of the twenty heavens, decorated with gold leaf, line the hall like guests at a celestial cocktail party, and a curvaceous copper Guanyin stands at the back. It's all something of a retreat from the material obsessions outside, but it's still Shanghai: religious trinkets, such as fake money for burning and Buddhas festooned with flashing lights, are for sale everywhere and the monks do a roaring trade flogging blessings. If you're peckish, check out the attached vegetarian restaurant: ignore the fancy dining hall and head past it to the little canteen, where a bowl of noodles costs around ¥15 – go for the mushrooms.

Moganshan Arts District

莫干山路50号, mògānshānlù wǔshíhào • 50 Moganshan Lu • Most galleries, though not all, are closed Mon • Ⓜ Shanghai Zhan is a 20min walk away; it's best to take a taxi

The **Moganshan Arts District** (M50) is a complex of studios and galleries in a former industrial zone beside Suzhou Creek, 1km northeast of the Yufo Temple. In the early 1990s, attracted by cheap rents, artists began to take over the abandoned warehouse buildings here and to use them as studios. Then the art spaces moved in, and now the design studios and cafés and more commercial galleries are arriving as the district gentrifies. What makes the area interesting for the moment is the way it is both shabby and sophisticated, jumbling together paint-spattered artists, slick dealers and pretentious fashionistas, and terrible kitsch with pretty decent work. Most of the smaller galleries double as studios and there's something for all tastes, from cutting-edge video installations to chintzy souvenirs. It's a good place to dip your toe into the thriving Shanghai art scene, though it's not comprehensive.

Entrance is through a gate signed **50 Moganshan Lu** (there's a map on the wall near here). There are dozens of galleries, many of them small concerns selling work that's frankly rather derivative – lots of McStruggle (see p.153) and brightly coloured

5

caricatures. You'll need to hunt around for good places; we've detailed a couple below. When you've had your fill of art, flop into a beanbag at hipster hangout *Undefine* (see p.140), at the back of the complex, which does excellent coffee.

Island 6 Art Centre

六岛艺术中心, liùdǎo yìshù zhōngxīn • Building 6, 1F • Daily 10am–7pm • Free • ☎ 62277856, ⓦ island6.org

The not-for-profit arts collective **Island 6 Art Centre** has noble motives, prides itself on its technological nous and puts together varied multimedia and cross-cultural shows. The space doubles as a high-tech studio, so it's possible to meet the artists themselves.

Art Scene Warehouse

艺术景仓库, yìshùjǐng cāngkù • Building 4, 1F • Tues–Sun 10.30am–6.30pm • ☎ 62774940, ⓦ artscenewarehouse.com

To see the best of Chinese art, you need to seek out the big hitters, who represent some true innovators. The best place to start is the cavernous **Art Scene Warehouse**, just beyond the main gate and on the left. Not only will you find a representative selection of contemporary paintings, but also the work is sympathetically displayed (which you can't say about all the galleries) in a minimalist white space.

CENTURY PARK

Pudong

Pudong (浦东, pǔdōng), the eastern bank of the Huangpu River, opposite the Bund, was transformed in just a couple of decades from paddy fields into a glittering cityscape of giant boulevards and architectural showpieces. The maze of skyscrapers now stretches east as far as the eye can see. In fact there may be too many: the weight of all those buildings is causing Pudong to sink at the rate of 1.5cm a year. Some might also say that the iconic skyline is only interesting from a distance. The bustling street life that so animates the rest of Shanghai is striking for its absence – there are too many windy boulevards between those fancy monoliths – and it's the only part of the city that does not reward aimless wandering. That said, if you know where you're going, a visit to Pudong can be very worthwhile.

6

Historically, the area was known as the wrong side of the Huangpu. Before 1949, it was populated by unemployed migrants and prostitutes, and characterized by murders and the most appalling living conditions in the city. It was here that bankrupt gamblers would *tiao huangpu* – commit suicide by drowning themselves in the river. Shanghai's top gangster, Du Yuesheng, more commonly known as "Big-eared Du", learned his trade growing up in this rough section of town. Under communist rule it continued its slide into shabby decay until in 1990, fifteen years after China's economic reforms started, it was finally decided to grant Pudong the status of Special Economic Zone (SEZ). This decision, more than any other, is fuelling Shanghai's dizzying economic advance.

There are two areas that reward exploration. First is **Lujiazui**, the battery of skyscrapers just across the water from the Bund, home to the giant **Shanghai Tower**, the **Shanghai World Financial Centre** and the **Jinmao** and **Oriental Pearl** towers – all with viewing platforms – as well as a decent **history museum**. Also worthwhile is spacious **Century Park**, 4km to the southwest; successful architectural experiments here include the **Science and Technology Museum** and the **Oriental Arts Centre**.

In 2010 the south end of Pudong was the site of the **World Expo**, which was a great fillip for Shanghai, the spur for dozens of infrastructure, renovation and regeneration projects. The majority of weird and wonderful national pavilions were dismantled after

■ ACCOMMODATION		● EATING		Jade on 36	7	■ DRINKING		■ NIGHTLIFE	
Eton	1	Blue Frog	9	The Kitchen Salvatore Cuomo	1	100 Century Avenue	3	Mercedes Benz Arena	6
Grand Hyatt	3	Din Tai Fung	3	Qian Xiang Ge	11	The Camel	5	● SHOPPING	
Park Hyatt	4	Element Fresh	10	Sproutworks	2	Cloud Nine	2	Shanghai Tang	2
Pudong Shangri-La	1	Farine	4	Xinjishi (Jesse Restaurant)	6	Flair	1	Super Brand Mall	1
		Haiku by Hatsune	5	Yi Café	8	Paulaner Bräuhaus	4		

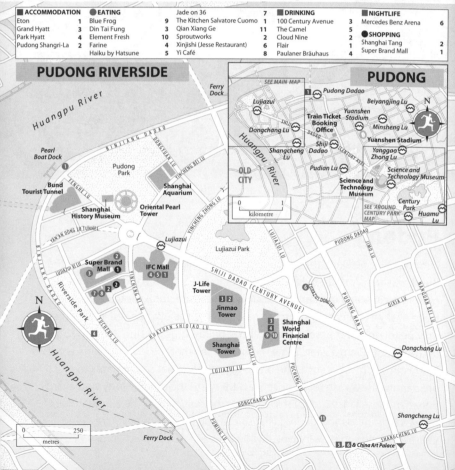

the show, but a couple of buildings have been left on the Pudong site as a legacy – the eighteen-thousand-seat Mercedes Benz Arena (1200 Expo Ave; ⓦ mercedes-benzarena .com) and the **China Art Palace**, which makes the long trip down here worthwhile.

Another long trip, deep into Pudong's suburbs, will take you to the **Long Museum**; a new private museum with big ambitions, it's an essential destination for the artily inclined.

ARRIVAL AND DEPARTURE   PUDONG

By Bund Tourist Tunnel The oddest way to cross from the west bank of the Huangpu to Pudong is to take the Bund Tourist Tunnel (外滩观光隧道, wàitān guānguāng suìdào) under the river to emerge near the Oriental Pearl Tower. Capsules (daily 8am–10.30pm; every 1min; ¥50 one way, ¥70 return) take a couple of minutes to chug creakily past psychedelic light displays, which have names such as "Heaven" and "Meteor Shower". It's something of a kitsch throwback and not what you'd expect in sophisticated Shanghai. The entrance is in the underpass at the north end of the Bund, opposite Beijing Dong Lu.

By ferry Ferries (daily 7am–10pm; every 15min; ¥2) run from Jinling Wharf at the end of Jinling Dong Lu to the south end of Binjiang Dadao (see below), a 5min walk to the Super Brand Mall. There's another ferry from just north of the Cool Docks, at the end of Fuxing Dong Lu, which takes you to the far southern end of Binjiang Dadao.

By metro Metro line #2 runs from People's Square to Lujiazui in less than 5min, and all the way to the Science and Technology Museum in 10min; lines #4, #6 and #9 also have stops in Pudong.

By bus Bus #3 runs from in front of the Shanghai Museum (see p.49) to the Jinmao Tower, but avoid rush hour when the traffic in the tunnel gets badly snarled up.

Lujiazui

陆家嘴, lùjiāzuǐ • ⓜ Lujiazui

In Lujiazui you'll find not just Shanghai's daftest edifice, the bulbous **Oriental Pearl Tower**, but also its most elegant, the **Jinmao Tower**, and its highest, the **Shanghai Tower** – all of them offer sublime views across the city, so pick a clear day to visit. In order to take advantage of the crowds of Chinese visitors who flock to the Pearl Tower a rash of **attractions** have opened nearby; among the touristy tack, the **history museum** and the **aquarium** are worth a look. This is an area where it helps to plan where you're going to eat, as there aren't too many options. For **cheap eats** head to the Super Brand Mall (正 大广场, zhèngdà guǎngchǎng), the Jinmao Tower's basement food court or the *Element Fresh* café in the Shanghai World Financial Centre (see p.79); for a pricier, more memorable experience you can't beat the *Pudong Shangri-La* (see p.121).

Binjiang Dadao

滨江大道, bīnjiāng dàdào

The riverside promenade, **Binjiang Dadao**, is a pleasant place for a stroll, close enough to the river to hear the slap of the water and much less crowded than the other side. There is outside seating at each of the name-brand **bars and cafés** (*Starbucks, Paulaner Bräuhaus, Häagen-Dazs*) at the north end of the strip, from where you can appreciate the glorious views of the full length of the Bund.

It's a short walk from here to the **Pearl Dock** (明珠码头, míngzhū mǎtóu) where you can get a half-hour boat tour down the Huangpu (see p.45); alternatively you can walk the riverbank south for another pleasant, leafy 2km to the dock opposite Zhangyang Lu, for ferries back to Puxi (every 15min 7am–10pm; ¥2); you'll be dropped just north of the Cool Docks (see p.57).

Shanghai Aquarium

上海海洋水族馆, shànghǎi hǎiyáng shuǐzúguǎn • 1388 Liujiazui Lu • Daily 9am–6pm • ¥160 • ☎ 58779988, ⓦ aquarium.sh.cn

The decent **Shanghai Aquarium** is a stone's throw from the Pearl Tower. On display are sharks, penguins and seals as well as endemic species such as the Chinese alligator; particularly impressive is the aquarium's 150m-long viewing tunnel. Other than the species names you won't find much English information.

6

Oriental Pearl Tower

东方明珠广播电视塔, dōngfāngmíngzhū guǎngbō diànshìtǎ • 1 Shiji Dadao • Daily 8am–9.30pm • ¥180 for access to highest level; ¥150 for the level below • ☎ 58791888, ⓦ orientalpearltower.com

The 457m-high **Oriental Pearl Tower** is a gaudy eyesore stuck in the toe end of Pudong and surrounded by tacky attractions, a throwback to less sophisticated times. Still it remains a must do for Chinese tourists, so there's often a very long queue to get in: don't bother trying to come here on the weekend or during a holiday. The observation decks in the Jinmao, Shanghai and Shanghai World Financial Centre towers are higher, much classier and far less busy – though, of course, viewing the city from inside the Pearl Tower does have one major advantage: for once, you can't see the ugly thing. There are fifteen viewing platforms in all, and the pricing system is ridiculously complex, with tickets including entry to the Shanghai History Museum (see below). The highest bauble is the "Space Module" at 350m – but this has the longest queues and the windows are dirty. Better is the smaller bauble underneath, which has a reinforced glass floor for proper, all-round views, though it's not for the faint-hearted. The revolving restaurant in the middle globe is best avoided, as is the "space show" exhibition.

Shanghai History Museum

上海城市历史发展馆, shànghǎi chéngshì lìshǐ fāzhǎnguǎn • Daily 8am–9.30pm • ¥35

The **Shanghai History Museum**, at the base of the Oriental Pearl Tower, is far better than you might expect. The majority of exhibits, which focus on the nineteenth century onwards, do a good job of evoking the glory days, with waxwork figures in dioramas of pharmacies, teahouses and the like. One of the old bronze lions from outside the HSBC building (see p.45) is on display, as well as a boundary stone from the International Settlement, and there's a detailed model of the Bund as it would have looked in the 1930s.

Jinmao Tower

金茂大厦, jīnmào dàshà • 88 Shiji Dadao; enter on the north side • Observation deck (金茂大厦88层观光厅, jīnmào dàshà bāshíbācéng guānguāngtīng) daily 8.30am–10pm • ¥120 • ☎ 50476688, ⓦ www.jinmao88.com

Shanghai's most attractive modern building, **Jinmao Tower**, is an elegantly tapering postmodern take on Art Deco, built by the Chicago office of Skidmore, Owings & Merrill in 1998. All the proportions are based on the lucky number 8 – the 88 floors are divided into sixteen segments, each of which is one-eighth shorter than the sixteen-storey base – but never mind the mathematics, the harmony is obvious at first glance. The roof wittily references a pagoda and, for once, doesn't look like a tacked-on afterthought. What look from a distance like filigree are actually decorative metal struts – they make the building appear eminently climbable, and indeed it has been scaled pretty frequently, hence the "no climbing" signs around the base. The tower's first 53 floors are offices; from there on up is the spectacular *Grand Hyatt* hotel (see p.121).

The **observation deck** on the 88th floor is accessible from the basement, via an entrance on the building's north side. An ear-popping lift whisks you up 340m in a matter of seconds. The spectacle before you is of course sublime, but turn round for a giddying view down the building's galleried atrium. There are plans to open an outdoor viewing platform, accessible from here – daredevil visitors will be roped to the building and escorted along a barrierless walkway.

Alternatively, and more sedately, for great views for free, go in the front door (on the eastern side) and up to the hotel lobby on the 54th floor where you can take advantage of the *Hyatt's* comfy, window-side chairs.

Shanghai Tower

上海中心大厦, shànghǎi zhōngxīn dàshà • 501 Yincheng Zhong Lu • Observation deck daily 9am–9pm • ¥160 • ☎ 33831088, ⓦ shanghaitower.com.cn

The **Shanghai Tower**, 632m high and with 121 storeys, is currently the second-tallest building in the world. Built in 2015, this is a skyscraper with a twist, literally; the

6

building corkscrews 120 degrees as it rises. In fact, that elegant curl is an outer layer of glass; between the inner and outer layers are atriums that are open to the public. Plans are also under way for the tower to host the world's highest hotel, which should open in 2018. The top-floor **observation deck** is not cheap, but it's the best in the area – and, at 561m, the highest in the world. Enter through the west side, and check out the time-lapse film of Pudong from 1840 up to the present day as you queue for your ticket. There follows an impressive multimedia exhibition about skyscrapers with some fascinating designs and models, before good-looking if slightly robotic staff usher you into the world's fastest lift. They'll announce it when you hit the top speed of 64km per hour – but your popping ears will already be giving you the news. The 360-degree viewing platform is pleasingly free of commerce, with full-length windows for maximum vertigo; it's pretty stunning to be able to look down on the world's third-tallest building, the Shanghai World Financial Centre, just next door, while the swathes of bright-roofed housing developments to the east and the sights of Puxi and the Huangpu to the west look like toys.

Shanghai World Financial Centre

环球金融中心, huánqiú jīnróng zhōngxīn • 100 Shiji Dadao • Observation decks daily 8am–11pm, last admission 10pm • Little deck (423m) ¥120, larger deck (439m) ¥150, top deck (474m) ¥180 • ☏ 4001100555, ⊛ swfc-observatory.com

The **Shanghai World Financial Centre** (2007) might have lost its crown as China's tallest building to the neighbouring Shanghai Tower, but at 492m it is no shrinking violet. Locally known as "the bottle opener", this structure is all about simple lines; a tapering slab whose most distinctive feature is the hole in the top. That hole was originally meant to be circular, but was redesigned as an oblong when the mayor complained that it would look like the Japanese flag hovering over the city. Most of the 101 floors house offices, but the *Park Hyatt* hotel, currently the highest in the world (see p.121), takes up floors 79 to 93. Of most interest to visitors are the **observation decks** above that, which offer, on a clear day or after dark, fantastic views – the top level, naturally, is the most impressive. Polite, well-groomed and unnecessary button-pressing staff escort you into a lift where the floors flicker past and lights softly glow – all in all, an experience rather more *2001* than the usual *Blade Runner*. At the top level, the strip above the hole, you'll be greeted by a magnificent 360-degree view across the city. Hardened glass tiles in the floor even allow you to look right down between your feet; a sign nearby asks you not to jump on them – as this seems to imply there's a chance they'll break, it's pretty unnerving. Landmarks are pointed out in the booklet that comes with your ticket, and you can get a photo printed for ¥50. Heading back down, you'll pass an *Element Fresh* café (see p.127) and a *Costa* coffee bar on the second floor.

Century Park and around

From Lujiazui, the eight-lane **Shiji Dadao** (**Century Avenue**; 世纪大道, shìjì dàdào) zooms west for 4km to one of the city's largest green expanses, **Century Park**. The area was spruced up heavily for the 2010 Expo, which is perhaps why there's an odd feeling here of being on a stage set that's waiting for its actors. Indeed, the futurist yet generic look to the streetscapes round here make them a favourite for sci-fi filmmakers (see p.152). It is, however, a pleasant place to pass some time, with wide pavements and priority

6

given to pedestrians over traffic, stretches of unbroken lawn and low-rise buildings conferring a great sense of space – and making you realize how cramped the rest of the city is. Skaters and kite-flyers congregate here, as both activities are banned in the city centre, and it's one of the few places you'll see joggers.

There are also some striking new buildings – not high-rises, for once – foremost among which are the **Science and Technology Museum** and the **Oriental Arts Centre**. There's no shopping to speak of, apart from a giant fake market (see p.158), and not many places to eat – the cheap canteen in the Science and Technology Museum metro station is one option.

Century Park

世纪公园, shìjì gōngyuán • Huama Lu • Daily 7am–6pm • ¥10; tandem bike rental ¥50/hr, pedalo rental ¥60/hr • Ⓜ Century Park

Century Park, designed by a British firm, is spacious, the air is clean (well, cleaner) and it's possible to feel that you have escaped the city, at least on weekdays when it's not too crowded. You can rent a tandem bike – sadly you're not allowed to ride your own bicycle – and pedalos are available on the big central lake.

Science and Technology Museum

上海科技馆, shànghǎi kējìguǎn • 2000 Shiji Dadao • Tues–Sun 9am–5pm • ¥60; space theatre screenings (every 40min) ¥40; IMAX (10.30am–4.30pm; hourly) ¥30/¥40; IWERKS (every 40min) ¥30 • Ⓦ www.sstm.org.cn • Ⓜ Science and Technology Museum

The **Science and Technology Museum** is an absolutely enormous building. Of the two wings, you can safely ignore the one on nature, which is mostly filled with stuffed animals, in favour of the diverting science wing, which scores well for interactivity and has lots of English captions. The section on space exploration is great – a big topic in China right now, with the nation fully intending to get to the moon as soon as possible – featuring spacesuits, models of spacecraft and the like, and a gyroscope to make you queasy. In the section on robots you can take on a robotic arm at archery and play a computer at Go, then watch a virtual endoscopy (which might also make you feel queasy).

The **cinemas** provide the most interest. The space theatre shows astronomical films; the two IMAX domes in the basement show cartoons; and the IWERKS dome on the first floor is an attempt to take the concept of immersive realism even further. The seats move, and there are water and wind effects – no Smell-O-Vision yet, but surely it's only a matter of time.

The only distinctly Chinese example of science on display is a fantastic Ming-dynasty **azimuth** in the courtyard. Held up by sculpted dragons, it's a more successful blend of science and aesthetics than anything inside.

Oriental Arts Centre

上海东方艺术中心, shànghǎi dōngfāng yìshù zhōngxīn • 425 Dingxiang Lu • ☎ 68547759, Ⓦ shoac.com.cn • Ⓜ Science and Technology Museum

Just north of the Science and Technology Museum, the **Oriental Arts Centre** (2004) is a magnificent, glass-faced, flower-shaped building that houses a concert hall, opera theatre, exhibition space and performance hall – they form the petals. It was designed by French architect Paul Andreu, who also created the new opera house in Beijing. If you happen to be in the area, it's worth a visit just to appreciate the elegant curves, to puzzle at why they made the interior walls to resemble snakeskin, and to check out the charming fourth-floor exhibition of European music boxes (daily 10am–5pm; ¥50), which includes automata that can blink, draw and sing.

China Art Palace

中华艺术宫, zhōnghuá yìshù gōng · 161 Shangnan Lu, near Guozhen Lu · Tues–Sun 9am–5pm · Free; audio-guide ¥20, ¥200 deposit · ☎ 63272425, ⓦ sh-artmuseum.org.cn · Ⓜ China Art Museum

It may be a long way from anything else, but the huge **China Art Palace** is worth a diversion to see – and it's right by the metro. The enormous red crown-like building, home of the China pavilion at the 2010 Expo site, is meant to look like a *dougong*, or roof bracket, with four legs like a *ding* pot.

There are five floors; the lift starts you at the top and you work your way down. First you'll find an exhibition of early twentieth-century Chinese art, which shows home-grown artists who returned from abroad grappling with exciting foreign ideas such as Impressionism. The intricate animation based on the classic scroll painting, **Along the River During Qingming Festival**, which was the most popular exhibit at the Expo, is displayed here, though you have to pay ¥60 to see it.

The fourth floor is dedicated to the **Shanghai Film Animation studio**, which churned out children's stories from the 1950s to the 1980s. There are plenty of cells and cut-outs – and it might just inpsire you to dig up more about the underappreciated art of Chinese animation, which was a big influence on the rather more famous Japanese tradition.

The third and second floors hold temporary shows, usually big names from abroad, while the ground floor is the realm of dull works by academic artists and Socialist Realist pictures celebrating achievements such as the Chinese conquering Mount Everest and the opening of the Maglev.

Long Museum (Pudong)

龙美术馆, lóng měishùguǎn · 2255 Luoshan Lu · Daily 9.30am–5pm · ¥50 · ☎ 68778787, ⓦ thelongmuseum.org/en · Ⓜ Huamu Lu, then a 15min walk

The odd, rather forbidding-looking **Long Museum (Pudong)** – a minimalist brick with tiny windows – holds treasures from the collection of billionaires Wang Wei and Liu Yiqian. This is a permanent exhibition – their second, more popular and accessible museum at West Bund (see p.88) holds temporary shows. But although this place is long way out – 45 minutes on the metro from the centre of town, then a fifteen-minute walk – it is worth the trip, a tremendously ambitious attempt to introduce the entire span of Chinese art. All exhibits are well captioned and displayed, with lights that brighten as you approach.

Exhibits are arranged chronologically across three floors; the earliest art is on the top floor, so it's best to start here. Avoid the interminable calligraphy in the painting gallery and seek out the meticulous, lively animal and bird studies, most from the Ming dynasty, and the lovely wooden screens in the furniture gallery. The gallery on revolutionary art is full of official, Soviet-influenced Socialist Realist paintings – images of Mao inspecting factories and the like. The ground-floor collection of twentieth-century and contemporary art is a mixed bag, but there's usually something to respond to, perhaps the gaudy satires of postmodernists Fang Lijun and Zhou Chunya.

LU XUN MEMORIAL

Hongkou

North of the Bund, you enter Hongkou (虹口, hóng kǒu) an area that, before World War II, was the Japanese quarter of the International Settlement. Since 1949 it has been largely taken over by housing developments, but though it may seem undistinguished – you certainly won't find any celebrity restaurants – it's a charming, rather homely neighbourhood, with plenty of unsung architectural gems. Two obvious areas of interest are the pretty Duolun Culture Street and Lu Xun Park, around which are scattered several memorials dedicated to the political novelist Lu Xun. Both are within easy walking distance of each other, making a good focus for a stroll, a mooch around the shops and a coffee. Tourists don't get out here much, but it's popular with locals and lively at weekends.

Another Hongkou highlight is **1933 Millfun**, a huge old abattoir that resembles an Expressionist movie set and now hosts arty businesses and bizarre themed cafés. The surrounding area is rapidly gentrifying, filling up with design businesses and other hipsterish concerns attracted by the cheap rents, and transforming into a cool, creative hub.

Duolun Culture Street

多伦文化名人街, duōlún wénhuà míngrén jiē • Ⓜ Dongbaoxing Lu, then a 5min walk; or bus #21 from Sichuan Zhong Lu, behind the Bund

Duolun Culture Street is a pedestrianized strip lined with *shikumen* houses (see box, p.62) that have been converted into genteel teahouses and little shops selling antiques, curios, coins and art equipment. The street was once home to some of China's greatest writers, including Mao Dun, Guo Moruo and Lu Xun (see box, p.85), to whom so many statues have been dedicated that he seems almost to have been deified. One bronze effigy has Lu in conversation with Guo; beside them is an empty seat where you can sit and join the debate, which has inevitably become a favourite photo spot.

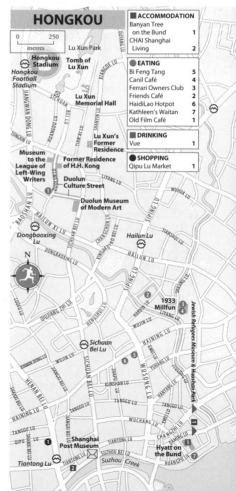

Museum to the League of Left-Wing Writers

中国左翼作家联盟会址纪念馆, zhōngguó zuǒyìzuòjiā liánméng huìzhǐ jìniànguǎn • 201 Lane 2, Duolun Lu • Tues–Sun 9am–4pm • ¥5

The small **Museum to the League of Left-Wing Writers** was set up in 1930. Writers, sadly, don't make for compelling museums and the collection of oddments, books and photos is less interesting than the building itself, a fine example of a well-preserved *shikumen* house.

Former Residence of H.H. Kong

孔祥熙公寓, kǒngxiángxī gōngyù • 250 Duolun Lu • Not open to the public

The grand **Former Residence of H.H. Kong**, built for the Guomindang politician in 1924, is the grandest example of Spanish-style architecture in Shanghai. You can still see the columns copied from the Alhambra and, if you peek in, the lovely tiles of the interior.

Duolun Museum of Modern Art

多伦现代美术馆, duōlún xiàndài měishùguǎn • 27 Duolun Lu • Tues–Sun 10am–6pm • ¥10 • ☎ 65872530, Ⓦ duolunmoma.org

An unattractive seven-storey monolith brooding at the end of Duolun Lu, **Duolun Museum of Modern Art** is a state-run gallery, so you won't see anything remotely contentious here; still, the place does pull in some big-name shows, often featuring visiting overseas artists. Artists in residence have studios on the fifth floor, and visitors are welcome to come and chat. There's a good, if pricey, bookshop and regular performances and lectures.

Jewish Refugees Museum

犹太难民纪念馆, yóutài nànmín jìniànguǎn • 62 Changyang Lu • Daily 9am–5pm • ¥20 • ☎ 65126669 • Ⓜ Dalian Lu

The site of the old Ohel Moishe Synagogue, just east of **Huashan Park** (华山公园, huáshān gōngyuán), is now home to the **Jewish Refugees Museum**. Built in 1927, the building has been heavily restored – only the wooden floors are original – but it remains an atmospheric and thought-provoking place, focusing on the lives of the twenty-thousand-odd Jews who fled to Shanghai in World War II (see box, below). There are plenty of old photos and images of Victor Sassoon's many buildings (see box, p.43), and lots of archive footage. An informative thirty-minute guided tour is included in the admission fee, though you are free to walk around by yourself.

Lu Xun Park

鲁迅公园, lǔxùn gōngyuán • 146 Jiangwan Dong Lu • Daily 6am–7pm • Free • Ⓜ Hongkou Football Stadium

Lu Xun Park is one of the best places in the city to observe Shanghainese at their leisure. Mornings see mass *tai ji* workouts, while later in the day, amorous couples frolic on paddle boats in the lagoon, old men teach their grandkids how to fly kites, and middle-aged women while away their time with games of badminton and cards. You might even catch some open-air ballroom dancing or an impromptu musical performance.

Tomb of Lu Xun

The park is home to the pompous **Tomb of Lu Xun**, complete with a seated statue and an inscription in Mao's calligraphy, which was erected here in 1956 to commemorate the fact that Lu Xun (see box, opposite) spent the last ten years of his life in this part of Shanghai. The building of the tomb went against the writer's own wishes to be buried simply in a small grave in a western Shanghai cemetery.

Lu Xun Memorial Hall

鲁迅纪念馆, lǔxùn jìniànguǎn • Daily 9–11am & 1.30–4pm • Free

The great Chinese author is further commemorated in the **Lu Xun Memorial Hall**, also in the park, to the right of the main entrance. Exhibits include original correspondence, among which you'll see letters and photographs from George Bernard Shaw.

JEWISH SHANGHAI

Many of the founders of international Shanghai were **Sephardic Jews** who fled the Middle East in the nineteenth century, with families such as the Kadoories and the Sassoons (see box, p.43) amassing vast fortunes and empires. The Jewish presence increased during World War II, when more than twenty thousand refugees from Europe arrived. As stateless persons, they were forced to live in a special enclosure in Hongkou, centred on Huashan Park and nicknamed Little Vienna, where they lived cheek by jowl with the local Chinese.

After the war, most Jews left Shanghai, and the only records of their presence today are touches only the sharpest observer will pick up: a Star of David on an old window grille or nail holes where the *mezuzoth* once hung. In the middle of Huashan Park is a small memorial in Chinese, Hebrew and English, and just to its north a plaque marks the site of the American Jewish Joint Distribution Committee, which cared for the refugees. Regular English-language **tours** of Jewish Shanghai are run by Dvir Bar-Gal (4hr; ¥400; Ⓦ shanghai-jews.com).

LU XUN

Lu Xun (1881–1936) is regarded as the father of modern Chinese literature. Coming from humble origins in the nearby city of Shaoxing, he gave up a promising career in medicine to write books with the intention, he claimed, of curing the nation's social ills. He used the demotic of the day, eschewing the sophisticated and obscure language of the literati so that ordinary people could read his work. And his stories are certainly short and punchy, something that can't be said about all Chinese classics.

The writer's first significant work was *Diary of a Madman*, published in 1918. Taking its name from Gogol's short story of the same name, it was a satire on Confucian society. Three years later followed his most appealing and accessible book, *The True Story of Ah Q*, a tragicomic tale of a peasant who stumbles from disaster to disaster and justifies each to himself as a triumph – an allegory for the Confucian state. Ah Q ends up embracing the cause of revolution and is executed, as ignorant at the end as he was at the beginning.

Lu Xun's writing earned him the wrath of the ruling Guomindang and in 1926 he took refuge in Shanghai's International Settlement. The last ten years of his life were spent in his simple quarters in Hongkou. Since his death, the fact that Lu Xun never joined the Communist Party has not stopped the authorities from glorifying him as an icon of the Revolution.

7

Lu Xun's Former Residence

鲁迅故居, lǔxùn gùjū • Shanyin Lu, Lane 132, House 9 • Daily 9am–4pm • ¥8 • ☎ 56662608 • Ⓜ Hongkou Football Stadium

A block southeast of Lu Xun Park, **Lu Xun's Former Residence** is worth a look if you are in the area. The humble and sparsely furnished house, where the writer and his wife and son lived from 1933 until his death in 1936, offers an intriguing glimpse into typical Japanese-influenced housing of the period – small, neat and tasteful.

Hongkou Stadium

虹口足球场, hóngkǒu zúqiúchǎng • Ⓜ Hongkou Football Stadium

You can't miss the hulking thirty-thousand-seat **Hongkou Stadium** on the west side of Lu Xun Park, which has its own metro station on line #3. Shanghai Shenhua football team plays here, with matches held on Saturdays between March and November (see p.27).

1933 Millfun

一九三三老场坊, yījiǔsānsān lǎochǎngfāng • Ⓜ Hailun Lu, then a 10min walk

Shanghai's jumbled streetscapes often look Gothamesque – it's easy to look up and imagine Batman flapping around. But the caped crusader's final showdown with the villain would definitely happen at **1933 Millfun** – this place is extraordinary. The brooding hulk squatting by the river was built in 1933 by British architect Balfours as an abattoir, the largest in east Asia. Roofless, with six storeys and made entirely of concrete, it has 26 freestanding "air bridges" radiating from a central atrium and connecting kinking walkways. Oddly angled ramps, staircases and struts add to the impression of a monochrome stage set, something like an Escher drawing.

Today the complex is home to an eccentric clutch of businesses serving the area's hipsters, including cafés themed around Ferraris (see p.141), teddy bears and dogs (see p.141). The biggest business is a wedding photographer, and the sight of couples posing in rented finery adds another incongruous element to the scene. There aren't any distinguished restaurants, so come after lunch, and bear in mind that it's liveliest at the weekend. Finish your afternoon of oddity by checking out the nearby *Friends Café* (see p.141) – based on a certain sitcom and eerily familiar.

LONGHUA TEMPLE

Xujiahui and beyond

Shanghai stretches to the west for a considerable distance, all the way to Hongqiao and beyond; the best sights are at the edge of the Old French Concession. At the riverside, you'll find the West Bund, a laidback new cultural zone book-ended by two impressive galleries, the Long Museum and the West Bund Art Centre. Further south near the river are the Botanical Gardens, while to the west lie an intriguing Jesuit cathedral, the city's most active Buddhist temple and the thought-provoking Longhua Cemetery of Martyrs. Most visitors only head west of Xujiahui to get to Hongqiao Airport, but if you have time it's worth a trip to the Wanguo Cemetery and Shanghai Zoo, particularly if you have kids in tow.

West Bund

西岸, xīʾàn • Ⓜ Damuqiao or Ⓜ Yunjin Lu

The riverside strip stretching from Lupu Bridge to Longyao Lu, once known for aircraft manufacture, has been imaginatively remodelled as the **West Bund**, a leafy, 2km-long promenade and arts district. This is one of the few public places in Shanghai where you can find space and quiet, with plenty of spots to sit and watch tankers glide past on the Huangpu. You may well see herons fishing in the shallows – a sight that would have been unthinkable twenty years ago, and testament to the success of the city's clean-up efforts. There's also a climbing wall, a jogging trail and a skate park, for more active pursuits.

Two contemporary galleries sit at either end of the strip: the **Long Museum** to the north and the **Yuz Museum** to the south. The **West Bund Art Centre** also sits at the southern end, with the impressive **ShanghART** gallery next door (see p.154). If you only have time or inclination for one gallery, pick the Long – it's better and cheaper than the others.

There are no cafés along the riverside, just a few vending machines and a couple of uninspiring Japanese restaurants. Your best bet for a caffeine stop is the café at the Long Museum – you don't need to be visiting the gallery to enter. Note that it's only a ten minute walk upriver from the north end of the West Bund to Lupu Bridge (see p.88).

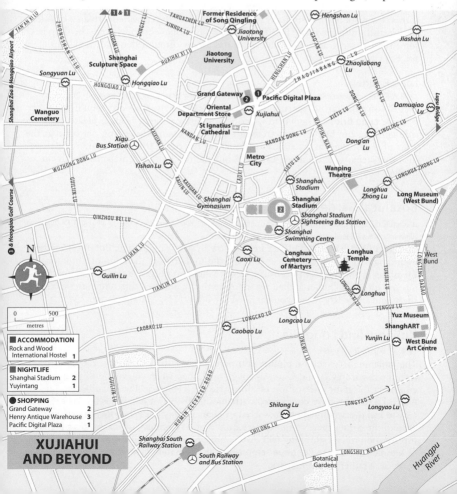

Long Museum (West Bund)

龙美术馆西岸, lóng měishùguǎn xī'àn · 3398 Longteng Dadao, near Ruining Lu · Tues–Sun 10am–5.30pm, last admission 4.30pm · ¥50 · ☎ 64227636, ⓦ thelongmuseum.org · Ⓜ Longhu Zhong Lu, then a 10min walk

Rather more successful than its older sister in Pudong (see p.81), the **Long Museum (West Bund)**, built by local firm Atelier Deshaus, is rated by architects as one of the most striking museums in Asia. This riverside site was once used to unload coal, and the museum has been built around the old coal hopper – a massive udder-like hulk – and an angular unloader; stripped of function, they look as sculpturally distinctive as anything inside. The museum itself is a pristine, concrete space built around a repeated arch motif. With no permanent collection, it has three storeys displaying contemporary art, a basement for shows of older art, and a pleasant **café**.

Yuz Museum

余德耀美术馆, yú dé yào měishùguǎn · 35 Fenggu Lu, near Longteng Dadao · Prices vary; around ¥100 · ☎ 62105207, ⓦ www.yuzmshanghai.org · Ⓜ Yunjin Lu, then a 10min walk

The **Yuz Museum** is another huge private gallery designed to show off a billionaire's collection – in this case, that of Chinese Indonesian Budi Tek. The building, an old aircraft hangar remodelled by Japanese architect Sou Fujimoto, is truly vast, and the shows that work best are similarly grandiose – such as the entwined airplanes of Adel Abdessemed, displayed here in 2016. There is no permanent collection. The shop has some striking artist-designed homeware, and the airy ground-floor café is elegant, if pricey (a coffee costs ¥60).

8

Lupu Bridge

卢浦大桥, lúpǔdàqiáo · 909 Luban Lu · Viewing platform daily 9am–4pm (closed during high winds) · ¥80 · Ⓜ Luban Lu

Just beyond the far northern end of the West Bund riverside area you'll find massive **Lupu Bridge**, the world's second-longest steel-arch bridge. Head to the west side and you can buy a ticket to climb up to the open-air viewing platform at the apex of the bridge's arch, about 100m above the river. There are more than three hundred steps, so it's bracing exercise, but the top is a great place to watch the passing boats.

Botanical Gardens

上海植物园, shànghǎi zhíwùyuán · 111 Longwu Lu · Daily 7am–4pm · ¥40 · ☎ 54363369, ⓦ shbg.org · Ⓜ Shilong Lu, then a 20min walk; or bus #56 south down Longwu Lu

More than nine thousand plants are on show in the vast, 240-acre **Botanical Gardens**, including two pomegranate trees that are said to date from the reign of Emperor Qianlong in the eighteenth century; despite their antiquity they still bear fruit. Look out too for the orchid chamber, where more than a hundred different varieties are on show, and the aviary where you can feed the doves (¥1).

Xujiahui and Longhua

徐家汇, xújiāhuì · Ⓜ Xujiahui

The **Xujiahui** metro station pitches you right into the thick of things. You come out into the five-storey Grand Gateway mega-mall, then when you've found your way out, emerge at the giant intersection of Hongqiao Lu, Hengshan Lu, Zhaojiabang Lu and Caoxi Lu, where you're confronted with another five giant malls (see box, p.156). It's easy to feel overwhelmed by the surfeit of neon and concrete, but fortunately just around the corner there's a rather nice cathedral, **St Ignatius'**, which makes a pleasant interruption to any shopping trip. Afterwards, hop into a taxi (or take a bus) a couple of kilometres south to **Longhua Temple** and the **Cemetery of Martyrs** – which also works as a rather charming park.

St Ignatius' Cathedral

圣依纳爵主教坐堂, shèngyīnàjué zhǔjiào zuòtáng • 158 Puxi Lu • Mon–Sat services 6.30am, Sun services 8am • ⓘ 64382595

It may be hard to imagine today, but Xujiahui is actually the site of Shanghai's oldest Western settlement: the Jesuits set up here in the seventeenth century. The only significant remnant from their sojourn is the red-brick, Gothic-style **St Ignatius' Cathedral**, built in 1910 on the grave of Paul Xu Guangqi, Matteo Ricci's personal assistant and first Jesuit convert. The cathedral was vandalized during the Cultural Revolution, its stained-glass windows smashed, and eventually used as a granary. It reopened in 1979, when the spires were renovated; the new windows marry Christian and Chinese motifs. St Ignatius' is one of the many places of public worship to have received a new lease of life as China's Christian population has boomed.

Longhua Cemetery of Martyrs

龙华烈士陵园, lónghuá lièshì língyuán • 180 Longhua Xi Lu • Daily 6.30am–4pm • ¥1, exhibition hall ¥5 • Ⓜ Longhua

A couple of kilometres southeast of St Ignatius' Cathedral, **Longhua Cemetery of Martyrs** memorializes those who died fighting for the cause of Chinese communism in the decades leading up to the final victory of 1949. Commemorative stone sculptures, most in a bombastic, Soviet style and many bearing a photo and a name, dot the park; the fresh flowers brought daily testify to the resonance these events still hold. Particularly remembered are those workers, activists and students massacred on this site by Chiang Kai-shek in the 1920s; a chilling underground hallway leads from the old prison to the execution ground. In the centre of the park is a pyramid-shaped **exhibition hall** with a rather random show of paintings and relics.

Longhua Temple

龙华寺, lónghuá sì • 2853 Longhua Lu • Daily 5.30am–4pm • ¥10 • ⓘ 64566085 • Ⓜ Longhua

The **Longhua Temple** is the most active Buddhist site in Shanghai and a centre for training monks. There has been a temple on the site (or at least in the area) since the third century, and though the present buildings are only around a century old, the design and layout are true to the original, comprising a complex of elegant multi-eaved halls. Pleasantly laidback, the temple sees many more devotees than day-trippers; visiting is a must during Spring Festival (see p.27), when it hosts a huge and boisterous fair. At this time, the temple bell, in the tower to the right of the entrance, is banged 108 times, supposedly to ease the 108 "mundane worries" of Buddhist thought. You can whack it yourself, any time, for ¥10; three hits is considered most auspicious.

The temple's standout feature is its tenth-century **pagoda**, an octagonal, 40m-high structure with seven brick storeys each embellished with wooden balconies and red-lacquer pillars. Until the feverish construction of bank buildings along the Bund in the 1910s, it was the tallest edifice in Shanghai. After a long period of neglect (Red Guards saw it as a convenient structure to plaster with banners), an ambitious rezoning project has spruced up the pagoda and created the tea gardens, greenery and shop stalls that now huddle around it.

A pleasant **vegetarian restaurant** at the back of the complex serves simple noodle dishes (¥10–25) – head through the canteen and behind it you'll find a charming teahouse.

Wanguo Cemetery

万国烈士陵园, wànguó lièshì língyuán • Songyuan Lu • Ⓜ Songyuan Lu

There were once ten cemeteries for foreigners in Shanghai, but most of the tombstones of those interred in the city suffered ignoble fates – destroyed, used as foundation stones for buildings or sold in antique stores. Those that remain have been collected in the **Wanguo Cemetery**. More than six hundred people are buried here, from nearly thirty nations, though many of the tombstones have been removed. The great Jewish families, the Kadoories and the Sassoons (see box, p.43), are memorialized, as is "Friend of China" Talitha Gerlach, whose tomb bears her photograph. Gerlach worked to improve the conditions of Chinese labourers and set up a night school for women; in 1987, she was awarded the first green card given by the Communists to a foreigner in Shanghai. The cemetery's most celebrated occupant, however, is local: Song Qingling (see p.67) has her own mausoleum here and, next to it, a small exhibition on her life.

Shanghai Zoo

上海动物园, shànghǎi dòngwùyuán • 2381 Hongqiao Lu • Daily: April–Sept 6.30am–5.30pm; Oct–March 7am–5pm • ¥40 • ☎ 62687775, ⓦ shanghaizoo.cn • Ⓜ Shanghai Zoo

A couple of kilometres west of Wanguo Cemetery along Hongqiao Lu, shortly before the airport, is **Shanghai Zoo**, the grounds of which were one of Shanghai's most exclusive golf courses until 1949. The zoo is massive, so you might want to consider being shuttled around on a tourist cart (¥15). More than two thousand animals and birds are caged in conditions rather better than most Chinese zoos, though that is not saying much. The stars, inevitably, are the ten giant pandas. Children will enjoy the petting zoo and the twice-hourly elephant show. Check out the animal-shaped topiary in the lovely grounds. The zoo is overrun at weekends, so try to come during the week.

8

Around Shanghai

Shanghai being the polluted, hectic, crowded urban jungle it is, it would be a rare visitor who never felt the urge at some point to escape to fresh air, trees and a bit of peace and quiet. Though you'll find no wilderness in the flat, wet and heavily populated outskirts, the nearby cities of Suzhou and Hangzhou are two of the most appealing in China, and their landscaped gardens and parks will restore stretched nerves; both are ideal for a two- or three-day break. A bus ride north of Hangzhou will bring you to the hill resort of Moganshan, which despite being just a couple of hours from Shanghai feels a world away in spirit. A few worthwhile attractions closer to the city make for ideal day-trips – and handily, as they are all accessible by metro, they can be easily combined.

9

Thames Town is an odd pastiche of England with plenty of quirky photo opportunities; Qibao is a little historical theme park; and She Shan, the biggest hill in the area at 100m high, features some interesting historic buildings. Also accessible by metro are attractive Nanxiang, with its lovely garden, and the new Disneyland.

Further afield, the canal towns of Zhouzhuang, Tongli, Wuzhen and Xitang are attractive places to wander, though they are firmly on the tourist circuit: if possible, visit them on a weekday; they can get crowded at weekends (and don't even consider heading there on a Chinese national holiday).

GETTING AROUND   AROUND SHANGHAI

BY TRAIN

Trains are the most efficient way of getting to the larger cities near Shanghai. Most leave from Shanghai Railway Station in the north of the city (on metro lines #1, #3 and #4), though some for Hangzhou also leave from Shanghai South Station (on metro lines #1 and #3). Super-fast G-class trains to Beijing, Suzhou and Hangzhou leave from Hongqiao Station in the west (on subway lines #2 and #10).

BUYING TICKETS

Note that you'll need your passport to collect a ticket, even if you pay for it online. Usually, tickets can be bought sixty days in advance, and advance bookings are certainly worthwhile at peak times, such as over the Spring Festival (see p.27) or during the public holidays

that begin on May 1 (Labour Day) and Oct 1 (National Day). Most hotels will sort tickets out for you for a small fee, and of course you could always just turn up at the station and queue, but the best way to book is online, through ⓦtravelchinaguide.com or ⓦenglish.ctrip .com; you'll pay a fee of about US$5. You receive a booking number – turn up at the station and use that and your passport to pick up your ticket from any ticket booth. At busy times you can expect to queue for half an hour. Note that foreigners cannot use the stations' automatic machines (which require a Chinese ID card to use).

BOOKING OFFICES

Though they are slowly being phased out, it is still possible to book tickets from a number of offices around

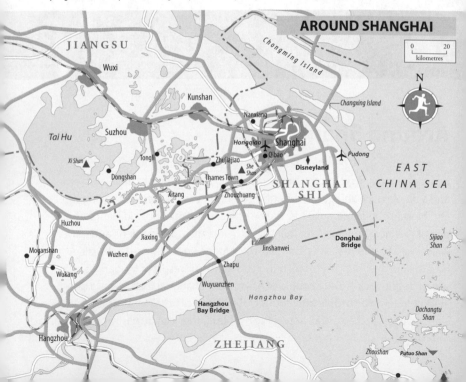

town, for a ¥5 fee – you almost certainly won't have to queue, but no English will be spoken by the usually rather brusque staff. Handy booking offices (daily 8am–noon & 1–5pm) are at 1057 Zhonghua Lu near the Old City; 77 Wanhangdu Lu (near Jing'an Temple) in Jing'an; 627 Nanjing Dong Lu; 124 Guizhou Lu and 1071 Zhangyang Lu in Pudong.

BY BUS AND TAXI
The most convenient way to get to the canal towns is by public bus, tour bus or taxi (see p.97).

BY METRO
The metro has an impressive spread: handily, it can get you to Qibao, She Shan, Thames Town, Disneyland and Nanxiang.

Qibao

七宝, qībǎo · Attractions Daily 8.30am–4.30pm; Shadow-puppet Museum performances 1pm & 3pm · ¥30, all-inclusive ticket, or ¥10 at each attraction · Ⓜ Qibao; take exit two, turn right, then follow the brown signs

Qibao is a historical theme park in the western suburbs – essentially alleyways and a canal, lined with renovated buildings which serve as olde-worlde souvenir shops, snack stalls and museums. It's worth a look if you aren't visiting one of the larger water towns (see p.95), if you like the idea of getting out of the city centre without any transport hassles (it's just an hour on metro) or if you're hoping to get all your souvenir shopping done at once. The all-in ticket gives you access to nine tourist sights (all of them historical buildings with small exhibitions), or you can pay to see them individually. The most rewarding are the cute old **Bell Tower** (钟楼, zhōnglóu) and the **Shadow-puppet Museum** (皮影艺术馆, píyǐng yìshùguǎn). There are plenty of stalls and little eateries, with the biggest concentration along Nan Dajie (南大街, nándàjiē) – local specialities include smoked toad (熏癞蛤蟆, xūn làiháma) and red-braised pork (红烧肉, hóng shāo ròu) as well as horrific *Eraserhead*-esque nude birds on a stick, and rotten dofu, which looks and smells like fried gymsock. A thirty-minute **boat trip** from the wharf (游船码头, yóuchuán mǎtóu) costs just ¥20.

She Shan

余山, shéshān · Ⓜ She Shan

Such is the flatness of the surrounding land 30km southwest of Shanghai that **She Shan**, a low range which only rises about 100m, is visible for many kilometres around. The park is divided into **West Hill** and **East Hill**; the more attractive West Hill offers some historical sights and the adjacent Happy Valley amusement park, while East Hill has a forest park popular with families.

West Hill

西山, xīshān · Daily 8.30am–4.30pm · Free · Bike rental ¥1/hr, deposit ¥200, ID required · **Observatory** Daily 8am–5pm · ¥12 · **Happy Valley** Daily 9am–6pm · ¥200, ¥100 for kids under 1.4m, free for kids under 1.2m · A free shuttle bus from Ⓜ She Shan stops at West Hill and Happy Valley (9am–3pm every 20min); the cable car costs ¥10

It's a pleasant walk up West Hill at any time of year, along paved paths through dense bamboo forest; you could also rent a bike at the entrance, or take a **cable car**. The peak here is crowned by an impressive **basilica**, a legacy of nineteenth-century European missionary work – She Shan has been owned by a Catholic community since the 1850s – though the present church was not built until 1925. Also on the hill are a meteorological station and an old **observatory**, the latter with a small exhibition displaying an ingenious earthquake-measuring device – dragon heads, with balls in their mouths, circle a pendulum; when the pendulum swings due to an earthquake, it knocks a ball out, thus indicating the earthquake's direction. Just behind West Hill, the enormous **Happy Valley** amusement park boasts six rollercoasters, including a 1km-long wooden boneshaker. This place is a little ramshackle, but clean, and gets really busy at weekends and school holidays. Kids love it.

9

East Hill

东山, dōngshān · Daily 8am–6pm · ¥45; sculpture park ¥120; rowing boats ¥60/hr · Ⓜ She Shan, then 10min walk

East Hill has been redeveloped as a woodland park, including the artificial Moon Lake. A ten-minute walk west from the entrance brings you to a **sculpture park**; the road curves south to get around the hill itself. There's nothing particularly distinguished about the thirty or so works of art, but they serve as handy way-stations on a nice walk. With a long artificial **beach** around a **lake**, manicured lawns and plenty of playgrounds, this makes a good retreat to take the kids, and is busy with families at the weekend. Rowing boats can be rented, or if you want to escape the crowds, just head uphill into the woods.

Disneyland

上海迪士尼乐园, shàng hǎi dí shì ní lè yuán · 360 Shendi Xi Lu, Chuansha · Daily 9am–9pm · One-day ticket ¥500, children ¥375; buy tickets online · Ⓦ shanghaidisneyresort.com · Ⓜ Shanghai Disney, line #11

Love it or loathe it, **Disneyland** is here – and it's huge. It feels a bit different, though, with no shows in English, and none of that "Main Street USA" shtick – this Disneyland is designed to be "distinctly Chinese", and the majority shareholder is not Disney but the Chinese government.

Though its soft opening met with teething troubles – long queues, the ire of Chinese nationalists, sky-high food prices, a ban on selfie sticks, ¥60 for a souvenir balloon that was confiscated when you tried to take it on the metro – the park will no doubt be running smoothly, and with fearsome crowds, by the time you read this. It's centred around Disney's largest ever theme-park **castle**, at the end of Mickey Avenue; crowd favourites so far have included the Pirates of the Caribbean boatride, the Tarzan live show and the very fast TRON rollercoaster.

You will need to plan if you don't want to get caught up in the queues. The best advice is buy your ticket online in advance, download the Shanghai Disney app to check on waiting times, and get there early – it's an hour on the metro. When the rope drops, hurry to get a fast pass (free) for the popular rides; you can ride the less busy attractions while waiting for your allotted slot. Oddly enough, things are likely to be quiet in the Star Wars Launch Pad exhibition, as the Lucas magnum opus has never been a big deal in China.

Thames Town

泰晤士小镇, tài wù shì xiǎo zhèn · 30km southwest of Shanghai · Ⓜ Songjiang University, then take a cab (¥25)

The satellite town of **THAMES TOWN** was conceived as a copy of an English village, and as such has a weird charm for lovers of urban oddities. It was built in 2001 as one of nine satellite towns, each pastiching a European architectural style. Thames Town is meant to house ten thousand, but about half of the flats are empty, having been bought as investments, which leaves it feeling a little deserted. Red phone boxes and postboxes and Victorian lampposts are dotted around streets with names including High Street and Prince Street; look out for cherub ornaments and the odd garden gnome, and the generic statues supposed to represent famous Britons – Shakespeare, Churchill and Harry Potter among them. Other details of small-town British life are inadvertently authentic: many of the little gardens have been paved over for parking, the shopping centre is shuttered and the beautiful church is empty. By far the most attractive area is the central **village green**, where brides- and grooms-to-be pose for their pre-wedding photos. **Food** and drink options are limited, but for a British(ish) lunch – fish and chips or chicken tikka – seek out *GLO London* on Sanqin Bei Lu (daily 11.30am–3pm & 5–10pm; ☎67817566, Ⓦglolondon.com).

Nanxiang

The extension to metro line #11 has brought the sleepy suburban district of **Nanxiang** into easy visiting distance, and it's well worth checking out. Wander around the lovely classical **Guyi Garden**, then explore the **old town** nearby – though it's easy to get to, this area has yet to feature on any tourist trails, and has an authenticity that is lacking at other, more striking destinations.

Guyi Garden

古猗园, gǔyī yuán · 218 Huyi Gong Lu, near Guyi Yuan Lu · Daily 7am–6pm · ¥12 · Ⓜ Nanxiang, then a cab (¥15)

It may not have the historical pedigree of Yu Yuan or anything in Suzhou, but the huge classical **Guyi Garden** is actually (whisper it) more interesting to visit. Guyi performs a Chinese garden's function – of being a tranquil, contemplative space – far better than its rivals by virtue of being beautiful, big enough to get lost in and pretty empty. There are no tour groups here, only locals playing cards or practising *tai ji* among the pavilions, roofed corridors, kinking walkways, flowerbeds and groves of osmanthus and bamboo. There is also plenty of birdlife, including mallard ducks on the central Frolicking Goose Pond and a couple of tame black swans in the waterway behind it.

The garden was created by Magistrate Min Shiji, who came to a sticky end: a plaque marks the spot where he was killed by his own servants. The garden was adapted and expanded during the Qing dynasty, until in 1789 it was bought by local merchants who turned it into a public park, and put up a temple to the City God. You can walk around it in a couple of hours; there are signs in English as well as Chinese, and a map by the entrance. Highlights include the raised **Tranquil Pavilion**, which gives an overview of the site; the **Fragrance Veranda**, constructed for the sniffing of nearby plum trees, orchids and chrysanthemum; and the **Nine Zigzag Bridge**, from which you can feed the carp.

The park is also home to a couple of eighth-century stele in the east, carved with Buddhist symbols; they must be some of the oldest things in Shanghai. There's a small **teahouse** in the northwest corner.

Nanxiang Old Town

南翔老街, nán xiáng lǎo jiē

Take the north exit from the Guyi Garden and cross the road, and you will see the entrance to a zone of narrow stone alleys crisscrossed with canals. This is **Nanxiang Old Town**, lined with rickety wooden buildings, most of them shops. You'll see more striking architecture at any canal town, but unlike at those places, here you will find authenticity. Behind the restored storefronts are ordinary businesses serving the famous local Nanxiang dumplings, grilled kebabs, radish cakes, alfafa pancakes and the like. There is even a dog-meat restaurant, though you'll need to read Chinese to spot it: dog is a popular winter dish in the Shanghai countryside but you'd never see it served anywhere foreigners might be expected to visit. The area's small-town charm is at its best in the evenings, when it's busy with promenaders. At the rough centre of the area stand the brick **Twin Towers** (双塔, shuāng tǎ) – all that remains of a Song-dynasty temple.

The water towns

An extensive canal system once transported goods all around imperial China, and the attractive water towns that grew up around them – notably **Zhujiajiao**, **Zhouzhuang**, **Xitang**, **Wuzhen** and **Tongli** – present some of eastern China's most distinctive urban environments. Whitewashed Ming and Qing timber buildings back onto the narrow waterways, which are crossed by charming humpback stone bridges; travel is by foot or punt as the alleys are too narrow for cars. Today, these sleepy towns are a popular escape from the city, each one a nostalgia theme park for the urban sophisticate. They're

9

fine as day-trips but don't expect much authenticity – there are far more souvenir shops than dwellings – and avoid the weekends, when they're overrun. You'll usually be charged an **entrance fee**, which gets you into the historical buildings – mostly the grand old houses of wealthy merchants – although in Zhujiajiao the attractions are ticketed individually.

Zhujiajiao

朱家角, Zhūjiājiǎo • 30km west of Shanghai • **Attractions** Daily 8am–4pm • ¥10–30; combination ticket for all nine attractions ¥80 • **Boat trips** ¥60 for a six-person boat up the main canal; longer trips ¥120 • Pink tour buses travel here direct from Pu'an Lu bus stop (普安路, pǔ'ān lù), just south of Renmin Square (6am–10pm every 20min; 1hr; ¥12); otherwise, you can catch a cab (¥50) from ⑩ Xujing, at the end of metro line #2, or from the centre of town (around ¥2000), or take a bus from the Shanghai Stadium Sightseeing Bus Station

ZHUJIAJIAO is the most easily accessible of the water towns. The cluster of rickety old residences, stone alleys and humped bridges can easily be explored in a couple of hours, and there are nine ticketed **attractions** – old houses or small exhibition spaces. The best-preserved street is Bei Dajie, which has some elegant Qing-dynasty buildings as well as a plethora of snack vendors. In the peaceful **Kezhi Garden** (课植园, kè zhí yuán) at its northern end, you'll find a well-proportioned five-storey pavilion built in 1912. The standout sight is five-arched **Fangsheng Bridge** (放生桥, fàng shēng qiáo), the largest stone bridge in Shanghai, built in 1812. You can appreciate it from the water by taking a trip with one of the many boatmen.

Zhouzhuang

周庄, zhōuzhuāng • 60km southwest of Shanghai, just across the border in Jiangsu province • ¥100, includes all attractions • **Boat trips** ¥100 • Regular buses from Shanghai South bus station (1hr30min), plus tour buses (see opposite)

Lying astride the large Jinghang Canal connecting Suzhou and Shanghai, ZHOUZHUANG grew prosperous from the area's brisk grain, silk and pottery trade during the Ming dynasty. Many rich government officials, scholars and artisans moved here and built beautiful villas, investing money into developing the stately stone bridges and tree-lined canals that now provide the city's main attractions.

Zhouzhuang's most highly rated views are of the pretty sixteenth-century twin **stone bridges** in the northeast of town. Also firmly on the itinerary are a **boat ride** round the canals – you'll have to be firm if you don't want to be serenaded – and **lunch**. There is no shortage of restaurants offering set meals based around the local specialities of pig's thigh, meatballs and clams (around ¥60/head).

Shen House

沈厅, shěntīng • South side of Fuan Bridge • Daily 8.30am–4.30pm

Zhouzhuang's biggest mansion is the **Shen House** in the east of town, built in 1742. More than a hundred rooms (not all open) are connected by covered colonnades, with grand public halls at the front and the more intimate family chambers at the back. Period furnishings help evoke a lost age of opulence, though it is all rather dark; the neat gardens offer a pleasant contrast.

An exhibition of **folk instruments** in the Xiaotong Tower at the rear is worth seeking out, as is the nearby statue of the mansion's founder, Shen, looking rather pleased with himself.

Xitang

西塘, xītáng • 60km southwest of Shanghai in Jiangsu province • **Attractions** Daily 9am–5pm • ¥50; free on Fri morning & Sun afternoon • Regular buses from Shanghai South bus station (2hr), plus tour buses (see opposite)

XITANG featured in *Mission Impossible III*, and you won't forget the fact – posters of Tom Cruise adorn most of the businesses. Though short on specific sights, the lanes, canals and bridges are undeniably picturesque. And if it rains, at least you'll be dry: the locals, tired of the wet climate, built roofs over the main alleyways – the biggest is more than 1km long, running alongside the central canal. Many of the buildings are now restaurants serving up local specialities such as pork with sweet potatoes. If you tire of walking, consider a cycle rickshaw (¥100 for forty minutes).

Tongli

同里, tónglǐ · 80km southwest of Shanghai · Daily 9am–5pm · ¥100, includes all attractions except the Sex Museum · Regular buses from Shanghai South bus station (1hr 30min), plus tour buses (see below)

Of all the water towns, **TONGLI** has the best sights, and with more than forty humpback bridges (some over 1000 years old) and fifteen canals it offers plenty of photo ops.

Tuisi Garden

退思园, tuìsī yuán · Beitu Lu · Daily 8am–6pm

Tongli's highlight is the UNESCO-listed **Tuisi Garden**, built by disillusioned retired official Ren Lansheng in 1886 as a place to retreat and meditate – though you'll have to come in the early morning, before the tour groups arrive, to appreciate the peacefulness of the place. With its harmonious arrangements of rockeries, pavilions and bridges, zigzagging over carp-filled ponds, it is comparable to anything in Suzhou.

Sex Museum

中华性文化博物馆, zhōnghuá xìngwénhuà bówùguǎn · Daily 9am–5.30pm · ¥20

The passion project of anthropologist Liu Dalin, and designed to be educational rather than salacious, the **Sex Museum** has some intriguing exhibits – figurines of Tang-dynasty prostitutes, special coins for use in brothels and a wide range of dildos. Some of the sex toys are more than 2000 years old.

Wuzhen

乌镇, wūzhèn · 120km southwest of Shanghai · West side ¥150 (¥80 after 6pm); east side ¥80 · Regular buses from Shanghai South bus station (2hr), plus tour buses (see below)

A little further out than the other water towns, **WUZHEN** is less busy and has also benefited from recent restoration. It was once a wealthy place, and many of its grand residences now act as museums or studios where local crafts such as silk painting or tea-leaf-dye printing are demonstrated. It's especially nice at **night**, when most visitors have left and the town is bathed in a romantic glow of lantern light – if you're planning to stay overnight in a water town, this is a good one to pick.

The town is divided into two areas, twenty minutes apart; the western section is the larger and more interesting, and home to all the attractions described here. Prime draw is the little **Xiuzhen Taoist Temple** and its collection of folk art, including intricate wood-carvings and leather shadow-puppets which you can watch in action at the nearby **playhouse** (hourly shows 10am–5pm). The **Xu Family Hall** on Dongzha Jie paints a vivid picture of genteel nineteenth-century Chinese country life with its darkly furnished, creaking interior and tables bearing tea cups as if the owners have just left. The **Bed Museum** (江南 百床馆, jiāngnán bǎichuángguǎn), also in a grand old house on Dongzha Jie, displays four-poster, enclosed antique beds – extravagantly decorated, if not very comfortable looking. The most lavish is the hyperbolic Qing-dynasty "bed of a thousand workers", which took dozens of craftsmen three years to make. Most of the carvings feature motifs that signify health and longevity – bats, turtles and double-happiness symbols.

The **Fanglu Pavilion** (访卢阁, fǎnglúgé), at 143 Changfeng Jie near the centre of town just to the south of Ying Bridge, is a teahouse with picturesque views over the canal. It's a good place for a rest, though as ever in these places, you won't find it cheap (¥48 a pot).

ARRIVAL AND DEPARTURE   THE WATER TOWNS

By tour bus The cheapest option (¥130–150, including the entrance fee) is to take a day-trip bus from the Shanghai Stadium Sightseeing Bus Station (上海体育馆 旅游集散中心, shànghǎi tǐyùguǎn lǚyóu jísàn zhōngxīn; ☎ 24095555) at 666 Tianyaoqiao Lu, on the south side of the Shanghai Stadium in the southwest of the

9

city, a 10min walk from the Shanghai Stadium metro station. There are two other convenient sightseeing bus stops: one at the South Railway Station, 666 Shilong Lu, on metro lines #1 and #3 (☎54363617) and another at Hongkou Stadium; take metro line #3 or # 8, and the station is outside exit 2 (☎56963248). Services run from 7am till around 10am, with a couple of buses afterwards till noon; they all return in the afternoon. Often a

(non-English-speaking) guide is provided, though you're free to wander off on your own. You can order tickets up to three days in advance on the phone and they'll deliver them to your hotel for a fee (¥10–30).

By bus There are public buses to the water towns from the Shanghai South bus station.

By taxi A day-trip will cost in the region of ¥500, about half that for Zhujiajiao.

ACCOMMODATION

ZHOUZHUANG

International Youth Hostel 周庄国际青年旅馆, zhōuzhuāng guójì qīngnián lǚguǎn 86 Beishi Jie ☎0512 57204566, ⓦwww.yhachina.com. Cosy establishment with quite spacious rooms – even the dorms. Staff are helpful and there's a café. Rates rise by fifty percent or more at weekends. Dorms **¥75**, doubles **¥200**

XITANG

Jinshui Lou Ge 近水楼阁客栈, jìnshuǐ loúgé kèzhàn 10 Chaonan Dai ☎133 75731700. Simple place with whitewashed walls and exposed wooden beams. The small rooms are attractively decorated with reproduction Ming-dynasty furniture, including four-poster beds. **¥220**
Xitang Youth Hostel 西塘忆水阑庭国际青年旅舍,

xītáng yìshuǐ lántíng guójì qīngnián lǚshè 6 Tangjia Lane, off Xi Xia Jie on the west side of town ☎0512 65218885, ⓦwww.yhachina.com. Traditional white walls and black tiles on the outside; inside there's a pleasant courtyard with bamboos overlooked by balconies, a small café and simple, clean rooms, some with wooden floors. Dorms **¥75**, doubles **¥170**

WUZHEN

Wuzhen Guesthouse 乌镇民宿, wūzhèn mínsù 137 Xizha Jie ☎0573 88731230, ⓦwuzhen.com.cn. Not a single guesthouse, but a cooperative of quaint B&B-style properties all over town, run by local families who will cook your meals for you. It's worth paying extra for a riverside view; rates can reach ¥600. **¥130**

Suzhou

苏州, sūzhōu

SUZHOU, about 90km west of Shanghai, is famous for its **gardens**, its **canals** and its **silk**. He Lu, semimythical ruler of the Kingdom of Wu, is said to have founded Suzhou in 600 BC as his capital, but it was the arrival of the **Grand Canal** more than a thousand years later that marked the beginning of the city's prosperity. In the late thirteenth century, Marco Polo reported "six thousand bridges, clever merchants, cunning men of all crafts, very wise men called Sages and great natural physicians". This moneyed, educated elite was responsible for carving out the intricate gardens that are now Suzhou's chief attractions.

The most famous gardens – **Zhuozheng Yuan**, **Shizi Lin** and **Wangshi Yuan** – attract a stream of visitors year-round, but many equally beautiful yet lesser-known alternatives, notably **Canglang Ting** and **Ou Yuan**, are comparatively serene and crowd-free. The gardens can be appreciated at any time of year, but spring brings the most blossom and brightest colours. Suzhou also boasts some rather charming **temples** and **pagodas**, and a couple of decent **museums**.

CHINESE GARDENS

The famed **gardens of Suzhou** have been laid out here since the Song dynasty, a thousand years ago, and in their Ming and Qing heyday it is said that the city had two hundred of them.

Chinese gardens do not set out to improve upon a slice of nature or to look natural. As with painting, sculpture and poetry, the aim is to produce for contemplation the **balance**, **harmony**, **proportion** and **variety** that the Chinese seek in life. Little pavilions and terraces are used to suggest a larger scale, undulating covered walkways and galleries to give a downward view, and intricate interlocking groups of rock and bamboo to hint at, and half conceal, what lies beyond. Almost everything you see has some symbolic significance – the pine tree and the crane for long life, mandarin ducks for married bliss, for example.

9

It's easy enough to get your bearings here. **Renmin Lu**, the main street, zooms south through the centre from the train station. The traditional commercial centre, **Guang Chedao**, lies around **Guanqian Jie**, halfway down Renmin Lu, the centre of an area of cramped, animated streets thronged with small shops, teahouses and restaurants.

Beisi Ta

北寺塔, běisì tǎ · Renmin Lu · Daily 7.45am–5pm · ¥25

Just south of the train station, the sixteenth-century **Beisi Ta** (North Temple Pagoda) looms up unmistakably. The pagoda is, at 76m, the tallest Chinese pagoda south of the Yangzi, though it retains only nine of its original eleven storeys. Climbing it gives an excellent view over some of Suzhou's more conspicuous features – the Shuang Ta, the Xuanmiao Guan and, in the far southwest corner, the Ruiguang Ta. There's also a pleasant teahouse on site.

Suzhou Silk Museum

丝绸博物馆, sīzhōu bówùguǎn · 2001 Renmin Lu · Daily 9am–5pm · Free · ☎ 0512 82112636, ⓦ szsilkmuseum

The **Suzhou Silk Museum** is one of China's better-presented museums, labelled in English throughout. Starting from the legendary inventor of silk, Lei Zu, the concubine of the equally legendary emperor Huang Di, it traces the history of silk production and its use from 4000 BC to the present day. There are displays of looms and weaving machines, and reproductions of early silk patterns, but the most riveting display – and something of a shock – is the room full of silkworms munching mulberry leaves and spinning cocoons, and copulating moths.

Suzhou Museum

苏州博物馆, sūzhōu bówùguǎn · 204 Dongbei Jie · Tues–Sun 9am–4pm · Free · ☎ 0512 67575666, ⓦ szmuseum.com

Designed by I.M. Pei, the **Suzhou Museum** is a successful update of Suzhou's characteristic white-wall and black-beam building style. The collection itself is small but choice, with plenty of English captions. You'll see some exquisitely delicate China and jade pieces in the first two galleries – look out for the ugly jasper-carved toad – but the highlight is the craft gallery and its fantastically elaborate bamboo-root carvings of Buddhist scenes. There are temporary displays in the modern art gallery.

The **Prince Zhong Residence**, adjacent to the museum and included on the same ticket, is a traditional courtyard house turned exhibition hall. The small rooms show Ming and Qing furniture, rare books and a display on the Taiping Rebellion, in which the house's original owner was involved. The most engrossing display is on Chinese opera, and includes a little theatre and costumes.

Zhuozheng Yuan

拙政园, zhuózhèng yuán · Dongbei Jie · Daily 7.30am–5.30pm · April–Oct ¥70; Nov–March ¥50 · ☎ 0512 67537002, ⓦ szzy.cn

At forty thousand square metres, the **Zhuozheng Yuan** (Humble Administrator's Garden) is the largest garden in the city. Based on water, it's set out in three linked sections: the eastern part (just inside the entrance) consists of a small lotus pond and pavilions; the centre is largely water, with two small islands connected by zigzag bridges; and the western part has unusually open green spaces. Built at the time of the Ming by an imperial censor, Wang Xianchen, who had just resigned his post, the garden was named by its creator as an ironic lament on the fact that this was now all he could administer.

Shizi Lin

狮子林, shīzi lín · 23 Yuanlin Lu · Daily 7.30am–5.30pm · April–Oct ¥30; Nov–March ¥20

One of Suzhou's must-see gardens, **Shizi Lin** (Lion Grove) was laid out by monk Tian Ru in 1342 and largely consists of rocks that are supposed to resemble lions. Part of the rockery takes the form of a convoluted labyrinth, from the top of which you emerge occasionally to gaze down at the water reflecting the trees and stones.

Xuanmiao Guan

玄妙观, xuánmiàoguān • Guanqian Jie • Mon–Fri 7.30am–4.30pm • ¥20 • Bus #1, #2, #20 or #101 to Guanqian Jie, from where it's a short walk

The **Xuanmiao Guan** (Taoist Temple of Mystery) stands rather incongruously at the heart of the modern city's consumer zone. Founded during the Jin dynasty in the third century AD, the temple has been destroyed, rebuilt, burnt down and put back together many times. Nowadays the attractive complex basically consists of a vast entrance court full of resting locals with, at its far end, a hall of Taoist deities and symbols – the whole thing encircled by a newly constructed park.

Yi Yuan

怡园, yíyuán • 1265 Renmin Lu • Daily 7.30am–midnight • ¥4 • Bus #1, #8, #32, #38 or #502

A few minutes south of Guanqian Jie is one of the lesser gardens, **Yi Yuan** (Joyous Garden), laid out in the late Qing dynasty by official Gu Wenbin. Considerably newer than the others, it is supposed to encompass all the key features of a Chinese garden; unusually, it also has formal flowerbeds and arrangements of coloured pebbles.

Museum of Opera and Theatre

戏曲博物馆, xìqǔ bówùguǎn • 14 Zhongzhangjia Xiang • Daily 8.30am–4.30pm; performances Sun 2pm • Free; performances ¥30 • ☎ 0512 67275338 • Bus #202 or #204

A ten-minute walk along narrow lanes east from the end of Guanqian Jie, the **Museum of Opera and Theatre** stands on Zhongzhangjia Xiang. The rooms are filled with costumes, masks and musical instruments – even a model orchestra, complete with cups of tea – but it's the building itself that's the star, a Ming-dynasty theatre made of latticed wood. The Suzhou area is the birthplace of the 5000-year-old **Kun opera** style, China's oldest operatic form. Kun is distinguished by storytelling and ballad singing but, as it is performed in the obscure Suzhou dialect, can be hard to follow even if you speak Chinese. They stage a ninety-minute performance here every Sunday; just turn up and buy a ticket before the show.

Ou Yuan

耦园, ǒuyuán • 5–9 Xiaoxinqiao Chedao, off Cang Jie • Daily 8am–5pm • ¥20 • Bus #301, #305 or #701

Abutting the outer moat and set along a canal, the **Ou Yuan** is a quiet garden, free from tour groups. Here a series of hallways and corridors opens onto an intimate courtyard, with a pond in the middle surrounded by abstract rock formations and relaxing teahouses.

Shuang Ta

双塔, shuāng tǎ • 22 Dingshui Chedao • Daily 7am–4.30pm • ¥4 • Bus #2, #5, #27 or #68

Several blocks east of Renmin Lu and immediately south of Ganjiang Dong Lu, the **Shuang Ta** (Twin Pagodas) are matching slender towers built during the Song dynasty by a group of successful candidates in the imperial examinations who wanted to honour their teacher. The teahouse here is crowded in summer with old folk fanning themselves against the heat.

Canglang Ting

沧浪亭, cānglàng tíng • 3 Canglangting Jie • Daily 7.30am–5.30pm • ¥20 • ☎ 0512 65293190 • Bus #1, #14, #28 or #701

South of Shiquan Jie, the intriguing **Canglang Ting** (Dark Blue Wave Pavilion) is the oldest of the major surviving gardens. Built by scholar Su Zimei around 1044 AD, it's approached through a grand stone bridge and ceremonial marble archway. The curious Five Hundred Sage Temple in the south of the garden is lined with stone tablets recording the names and achievements of Suzhou's statesmen, heroes and poets.

9

Wangshi Yuan

网师园, wǎngshī yuán • 11 Touxiang Chedao • Daily: March–Nov 7am–10pm; Dec–Feb 7.30am–5.30pm • March–Nov ¥30, ¥80 in the evening including performance; Dec–Feb ¥20 • ☎ 051 265293190 • Bus #2, #4 or #14

The intimate **Wangshi Yuan** (Master of the Nets Garden) lies down a narrow alleyway on the south side of Shiquan Jie. The garden, so named because the owner, a retired official, decided he wanted to become a fisherman, was started in 1140, but was later abandoned and not restored to its present layout until 1770. Considered by garden connoisseurs to be the finest of them all, it boasts an attractive central lake, minuscule connecting halls, pavilions with pocket-handkerchief courtyards and carved wooden doors – and rather more visitors than it can cope with. The garden is said to be best seen on moonlit nights, when the moon can be seen three times over from the Moon-watching Pavilion – in the sky, in the water and in a mirror. Other features include its delicate latticework and fretted windows. Between March and November, Wangshui Yuan also plays host to nightly **performances** of Chinese performing arts, from Beijing opera to folk dancing and storytelling – performances run from 7.30 to 10pm, with last entry at 9pm.

Pan Men and around

盘门, pánmén • 1 Dong Dajie • Daily 8am–4.45pm • ¥25 • Bus #7 from the train station passes the southern edge of the moat

One of the city's most pleasant districts centres on **Pan Men** (Coiled Gate) and a stretch of the southern part of original city wall, built in 514 BC; the gate is the only survivor of eight that once surrounded Suzhou. The best approach is from the south, via **Wumen Qiao** (吴门桥, wúmén qiáo), a delightful high-arched bridge (the tallest in Suzhou) with in-built steps; it's a great vantage point for watching the canal traffic. Just inside Pan Men sits the dramatic **Ruiguang Ta** (瑞光塔, ruìguāng tǎ), a 1000-year-old pagoda now rebuilt from ruins, once housing a rare Buddhist pearl stupa (since moved to the Suzhou Museum).

ARRIVAL AND DEPARTURE
SUZHOU

By train There are frequent fast D- and G-class trains to Suzhou from both Shanghai and Hongqiao stations (30min); try to avoid getting a train that drops you at Suzhou North, which is 6km from the centre (if you do wind up here, take metro line #2 into town). From the main train station, you can get into town on buses #1 and #20, or on the metro.

By bus Buses to Suzhou leave from Shanghai South Bus Station and Hengfeng Lu Bus Station by the main train station (every 20min; 1hr30min); there is also a service from both of Shanghai's airports. In Suzhou, buses from Hengfeng Lu arrive at the train station; all other Shanghai buses pull in at the North Bus Station (北公共汽车站, běi gōnggòng qìchēzhàn) directly east of the train station. The South Bus Station (南公共汽车站, nán gōnggòng qìchēzhàn), which sees arrivals from points south including Hangzhou and Zhouzhuang, is at the junction between Nanyuan Dong Lu and Yingchun Lu – buses #29 and #101 run into town from the station, or it's ¥11 in a cab.

GETTING AROUND

By bus Buses are a cheap way to get around, though as ever watch your pockets. There are no English announcements or signs. Note the *pinyin* for your stop – written on the timetable at the bus stop – and listen out for the on-board announcement.

By bike The best way to get around is by rented bike, which will cost around ¥30 for a day with a deposit of a few hundred yuan. There are many bike rental places along Shiquan Jie and a couple on Renmin Lu.

By metro Suzhou's metro has two lines; for visitors they're most useful for getting into town from the stations.

By taxi Taxis are plentiful, but it's not easy to find an empty one at the weekend; flag fall is ¥10.

INFORMATION AND TOURS

Tourist office The tourist office at 345 Shiquan Jie (Mon–Sat 8.30am–5.30pm; ☎0512 65305887, ⓦ www.visitsz .com) can help arrange city tours.

Boat trips Frequent canal boats leave from a dock by Renmin Bridge, near the train station, taking 45 minutes to make a circuit of the city. There are many different operators – expect to pay around ¥100.

ACCOMMODATION

The main hotel area, and the heaviest concentration of gardens and historic buildings, is in the **south** of the city, around Shiquan Jie. We've quoted high-season (June–Sept) rates; out of season (Oct–May), you should be able to get a discount of at least twenty percent if you ask.

Archi Garden 筑园, zhùyuán 31 Pingjiang Lu ☎0512 65810618, ⓦarchi-garden.com. An arty spot, with just four spartan, immaculate rooms – sliding doors, white linen and an atmosphere so quiet you could hear a pin drop. The lobby also functions as a café, gallery and style-book library. **¥650**

Bamboo Grove 竹辉饭店, zhúhuī fàndiàn 168 Zhuhui Lu ☎0512 65205601, ⓦbg-hotel.com. A tour-group favourite, this efficient if rather old-fashioned Japanese-run four-star imitates local style with black-and-white walls and abundant bamboo in the garden. There are a couple of good restaurants on site. **¥1300**

Mingtown Suzhou Youth Hostel 28 Pingjiang Lu ☎0512 65816869. An attractive courtyard and local-style buildings make this the most appealing budget option in town. Doubles (with shared bathrooms) are very stylish for the price, though the dorms can be stuffy. Bike rental ¥30/day. Dorms **¥85**, doubles **¥230**

Pan Pacific 吴宫喜来登酒店, wúgōng xīláidēng jiǔdiàn 259 Xinshi Lu, near Pan Men ☎0512 65103388, ⓦpanpacific.com. This pastiche Chinese mansion sprawls over two city blocks and, though the building is old, it is still the most attractive choice in its range thanks to the large rooms and charming gardens. Indoor and outdoor swimming pools are a plus. Heavy discounts available online. **¥986**

Pingjiang Lodge 平江客栈, píngjiāng kèzhàn 33 Pingjiang Lu ☎0512 65233888, ⓦthe-silk-road.com. This appealingly rustic venue seeks to re-create the charm of old Suzhou, with traditionally styled rooms. It's popular with Chinese families. **¥530**

EATING

The town is well stocked with restaurants for all budgets. Suzhou cooking, with its emphasis on **fish** from the nearby lakes and rivers, is justly renowned; specialities include *yinyu* ("silver fish") and *kaobing* (grilled pancakes with sweet filling). A number of restaurants of repute on **Taijian Lane**, each claiming more than one hundred years of history, are good for a splurge on local dishes – *Songhelou Caiguan* is the best.

Bookworm 老书虫, lǎoshū chóng 77 Gunxiu Fang ☎0512 50074471, ⓦsuzhoubookworm.com. A relaxed, stylish café that attracts a diverse crowd. Pop in for coffee or an evening drink, or take part in the many events that they organize – art and literary festivals, open mics, pub quizzes. Daily 9am–midnight.

Finland Home Café 芬兰之家, fēnlán zhījiā 99 Shilin Si Jie, at the junction with Pingliang Lu ☎0512 67773994, ⓦfinlandhomecafe.com. An eclectic menu and a warm welcome make this relaxed restaurant, run by an Iranian and Finnish couple, a local favourite. The decor, with its reindeer-hide hangings, might be pure Lapland, but the menu is, for the most part, straight out of Tehran – try the tzatziki and mutton kebabs. Live music most nights. Daily 11am–10pm.

Mingtown 明堂, míngtáng 28 Pingjiang Lu ☎0512 65816869. Right next door to the youth hostel, *Mingtown* is popular with backpackers on account of its tasty food, decent coffee and only slightly wonky pool table. Good for a Western breakfast (¥20–28), it transforms into a bar of sorts in the evening. Daily 8am–11pm.

Songhelou Caiguan 松鹤楼菜馆, sōnghèlóu càiguǎn Taijian Lane ☎0512 67700688. The most famous restaurant in town, claiming to be old enough to have served Qing Emperor Qianlong, who reigned 1736–95, and presumably got rather better service than they manage these days. The menu is elaborate and long on fish and seafood (crab, eel, squirrel fish and the like), though not cheap at around ¥150 a head. Daily 11am–2pm & 5–8.30pm.

Xinjiang Yakexi 新疆亚克西酒楼, xīnjiāng yǎkèxī jiǔlóu 768 Shiquan Jie ☎0512 65291798, ⓦszyakexi.com. Xinjiang comfort food – pulled noodles with vegetables (*latiaozi*) and *naan* bread, among others – in a bright dining room bustling with local Uyghurs and tourists (mains ¥20–30). Also sells lamb kebabs cooked on a grill outside for just ¥4. Daily 9am–midnight.

DRINKING AND NIGHTLIFE

Suzhou has a vibrant nightlife scene. The oldest **bars** (as well as the oldest profession) are along Shiquan Jie, but the Ligong Di area (especially **1912 Bar Street**) on the southeastern corner of Jinji Lake is fast overtaking it as the place to head after dark – particularly with the expat community, due to its many new bars, clubs and international restaurants. Note too that the *Bookworm* and *Mingtown* (see above) are good places for a drink, while between March and Nov there's a nightly **opera** extravaganza at Wangshi Yuan (see opposite).

9

Goodfellas 菲拉主题吧 fēilā zhǔtíbā A9, 1912 Bar Street ☎ 0512 62962789, ⓦ southerncrosssz.com. The best of the foreigner-friendly bars in this area, *Goodfellas* has live music (Tues–Sat 9pm–1am) on its ample stage, as well as pool and darts, and dancing later in the night. They serve a good range of foreign draughts as well as some fine cocktails. Daily 6.30pm–2am.

SHOPPING

There are numerous opportunities to shop for **silk**, paintings and embroidery in Suzhou, although be aware of outrageous prices, especially in the boutiques along Shiquan Jie and Guanyin Jie, and the night market on Shi Lu. Bargain hard, as these sellers can quote prices up to ten times the going rate.

The Antique Store 1208 Renmin Lu ☎ 0512 65233851. Jade, jewellery and reproduction antique furniture; there's some room for bargaining. Daily 9am–5pm.
King Silk Store 丝绸博物馆, sīchóu bówùguǎn

2001 Renmin Lu. This silk shop next to the Silk Museum has a good selection, including great duvets starting at just over ¥300. Daily 9am–5pm.

DIRECTORY

Banks and exchange The Bank of China head office, 1450 Renmin Lu, in the centre of town, just north of Guanqian Jie, has money exchange and international ATMs (daily 8.15am–5.15pm).
Hospital The best hospital in the city for foreigners is the Suzhou Kowloon Hospital (上海交通大学医学院苏州九龙医院, shànghǎi jiāotōng dàxué yīxuéyuàn sūzhōu jiǔlóng yīyuàn) at 118 Wangsheng Jie about a ¥60 taxi-ride from the centre in the Suzhou Industrial Park Zone.
Post office Suzhou's main post office (daily 9am–6pm) is at the corner of Renmin Lu and Jingde Lu.
Visa extensions 201 Renmin Lu, at the junction with the small lane Dashitou Xiang.

Hangzhou
杭州, hángzhōu

HANGZHOU, one of China's most established tourist attractions, lies in the north of Zhejiang province at the head of Hangzhou Bay, an hour or so by train from Shanghai's Hongqiao Station. The modern city is not of much interest – people are here for **Xi Hu** (the **lake** around which Hangzhou curls) and its shores, a picturesque ensemble of hills, trees, flowers, causeways, fishing boats, pavilions and pagodas.

Broadly, the city has two halves; to the east and north of the lake is **downtown**, while to the west and south you'll find greenery and scenic spots. The commercial centre lies around the **Jiefang Lu/Yan'an Lu** intersection, with accommodation, restaurants and shops; buses around the lake also leave from here.

On the lake are various **islands** and causeways, while the shores are home to many **parks** holding Hangzhou's most famous sights. These range from the extravagant and historic **Yuefei Mu** (Tomb of Yuefei) to the ancient hillside Buddhist carvings of **Feilai Feng** and the associated **Lingyin Temple**, one of China's largest and most renowned. Farther afield, beautiful tea plantations nestle around the village of **Longjing**, while south down to the **Qiantang River** are excellent walking opportunities.

Brief history

With the building of the Grand Canal at the end of the sixth century, Hangzhou became the centre for trade between north and south China, and the Yellow and Yangzi river basins. During the **Song dynasty**, it was made the **imperial capital**, setting off a boom in all the trades that waited upon the court, particularly silk. Marco Polo, writing of Hangzhou towards the end of the thirteenth century, spoke of "the City of Heaven, the most beautiful and magnificent in the world". Though its role as imperial capital ceased when the Southern Song dynasty was overthrown by the Mongols in 1279, it remained an important centre of commerce. **Ming** rulers repaired the city walls and deepened the Grand Canal so that large ships could go all the way from

CLOCKWISE FROM TOP SUZHOU MUSEUM (P.100); WUZHEN (P.97); BUDDHIST SCULPTURES, FEILAI FENG (P.108) >

9 Hangzhou to Beijing, and two great **Qing** emperors, Kangxi and Qianlong, built villas, temples and gardens by the lake. Although largely destroyed in the Taiping Rebellion (see p.168), it recovered quickly, and the **foreign concessions** that were established towards the end of the century – followed by the building of rail lines from Shanghai and Ningbo – stimulated the growth of new industries alongside traditional silk and brocade manufacturing.

Xi Hu

西湖, xīhú

Xi Hu forms a series of landscapes with rocks, trees, grass and lakeside buildings reflected in the water and backed by luxuriant wooded hills. The **lake** itself stretches just over 3km from north to south and just under 3km from east to west, though the surrounding parks and associated sights spread far beyond this. On a sunny day the

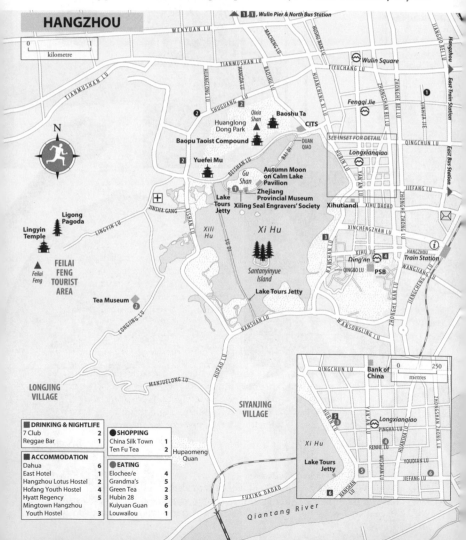

HANGZHOU

■ DRINKING & NIGHTLIFE	
7 Club	2
Reggae Bar	1

■ ACCOMMODATION	
Dahua	6
East Hotel	1
Hangzhou Lotus Hostel	2
Hofang Youth Hostel	4
Hyatt Regency	5
Mingtown Hangzhou Youth Hostel	3

● SHOPPING	
China Silk Town	1
Ten Fu Tea	2

● EATING	
Elochee/e	4
Grandma's	5
Green Tea	2
Hubin 28	3
Kuiyuan Guan	6
Louwailou	1

colours are brilliant, but even with grey skies and choppy waters, the views are soothing and tranquil; for the Chinese they are also laden with literary and historic associations. Although the crowds and hawkers are sometimes distracting, the area is so large that you can usually find places to escape the hubbub.

As early as the Tang dynasty, efforts were made to control the waters of the lake using dykes and locks; the two **causeways** that now cross sections of the lake, **Bai Di** across the north and **Su Di** across the west, originated in these ancient embankments. Mainly used by pedestrians and cyclists, the causeways offer instant escape from the noise and smog of the built-up area to the east.

Bai Di

白堤, báidī
Bai Di, about 1500m long, is the shorter and more popular of the two causeways. Starting in the north of the lake near the *Shangri-La* hotel, it runs along the outer edge of Gu Shan before crossing back to the shore, enclosing a small strip known as Beili Hu (North Inner Lake). The low stone **Duan Qiao** (Broken Bridge), at the far eastern end of the causeway, gets its name because winter snow melts first on the hump of the bridge, creating the illusion of a gap.

Gu Shan

孤山, gūshān
The little island of **Gu Shan** is one of Hangzhou's highlights, a great place to relax under a shady tree. Dotted with pavilions and pagodas, this tiny area was originally landscaped under the Tang, but the present style dates from the Qing, when Emperor Qianlong built himself a palace here. Occupying part of the palace, facing south to the centre of the lake, is the **Zhejiang Provincial Museum** (浙江博物馆, zhèjiāng bówùguǎn; 25 Gushan Lu; Tues–Sun 8.30am–4.30pm; free; ☎0571 87980281, ⓦzhejiangmuseum.com), a huge place with English captions throughout. The main building in front of the entrance houses historical relics, including superb bronzes from the eleventh to the eighth century BC. Another hall centres on coin collections and has specimens of the world's first banknotes, dating to the Northern Song; you'll get an appreciation of the deep conservatism of Chinese society from its coinage, which remained fundamentally unchanged for two thousand years from the Han to the Qing dynasties. Other galleries outside hold displays of painting and Tibetan Buddha statues.

The curious **Xiling Seal Engravers' Society** (西泠印社, xīlíng yìnshè; Gushan Lu; daily 9am–5pm; ¥5), founded in 1904, occupies the western side of Gu Shan, next to the *Louwailou* restaurant. Its tiny park encloses a pavilion with a pleasant blend of steps, carved stone tablets, shrubbery and nearby a small early Buddhist stupa.

Su Di

苏堤, sūdī
The longer causeway, **Su Di**, named after the Song-dynasty poet-official Su Dong Po, who was governor of Hangzhou, starts from the southwest corner of the lake and runs its full length to the northern shore close to Yuefei Mu. Consisting of embankments planted with banana trees, weeping willows and plum trees, linked by six stone arch bridges, the causeway encloses a narrow stretch of water, **Xili Hu** (West Inner Lake).

Santanyinyue Island

三潭印月, sāntán yìnyuè • ¥20 (included in tourist boat fees)
In the southern part of the lake, just east of Su Di, is the largest of the islands, Xiaoying, built up in 1607. It's better known as **Santanyinyue** (Three Flags Reflecting the Moon) **Island** after the three "flags" in the water – actually stone pagodas, said to

9

control the evil spirits lurking in the deepest spots of the lake. Bridges link across from north to south and east to west so that the whole thing seems like a wheel with four spokes; the central hub has a shop and a restaurant.

North of the lake
栖霞山, qīxiá shān

The seven-storey **Baoshu Ta** (保淑塔, bǎoshū tǎ) is a 1933 reconstruction of a Song-dynasty tower, and a nice place to walk to along hillside paths. From Beishan Lu a small lane leads up behind some buildings to the pagoda. Tracks continue beyond, and you can climb right up to **Qixia Shan** (Mountain Where Rosy Clouds Linger) above the lake.

Yuefei Mu
岳飞墓, yuèfēi mù • 80 Beishan Lu • Daily 7.30am–5.30pm • ¥25 • ☎ 0571 8798 6653 • Buses #K7, #Y1, #Y2 or #Y3 from the train station

The twelfth-century Song general Yuefei is considered a hero in modern China thanks to his unquestioning patriotism, and his tomb, **Yuefei Mu**, is one of Hangzhou's big draws. Having emerged victorious from a war against barbarian invaders from the north, Yuefei was falsely charged with treason by a jealous prime minister, and executed at the age of 39. Twenty years later, the subsequent emperor annulled all charges against him and had him reburied here with full honours. Walk through the temple to reach the tomb itself – a tiny bridge over water, a small double row of stone men and animals, steles, a mound with old pine trees and four cast-iron statues of the villains, kneeling in shame with their hands behind their backs. The calligraphy on the front wall of the tomb reads, "Be loyal to your country".

Baopu Taoist Compound
包朴道院, bāopǔ dàoyuàn • Daily 7am–5pm • ¥5

About halfway along the path up from Baoshu Ta you'll see a yellow-roofed monastery, the **Baopu Taoist Compound**, lurking below to your left. It's well worth a stop, especially in the late afternoon, if only because you might be able to watch discreetly one of the ancestral worship ceremonies that are held here, with priests clad in colourful garb and widows clutching long black necklaces. If you climb the stairs, you will find several smaller halls where old men practise their calligraphy and young women play the *pipa*.

Huanglong Dong Park
黄龙洞公园, huánglóngdòng gōngyuán • Daily 6.30am–4pm • ¥15 • Bus #Y3

A short uphill walk north from the Baopu Taoist Compound brings you to the charmingly secluded **Huanglong Dong Park** (Yellow Dragon Cave Park). It is sunk between sharply rising hills with a pond, teahouses, a shrine to Yue Lao (the Chinese god of arranged marriages) and a pavilion where musicians perform traditional music.

Feilai Feng
飞来峰, fēilái fēng • Daily 5.30am–5.30pm • ¥45 • Buses #Y1, #Y2, #Y4, #7 or #807

Three kilometres west of the lake, some of Hangzhou's most famous sights are scattered around **Feilai Feng**, "The Hill that Flew Here". The name derives from the tale of an Indian Buddhist named Hui Li who, upon arrival in Hangzhou, thought he recognized the hill as one from back home, and asked when it had flown here. Near the entrance is the **Ligong Pagoda**, constructed for that same monk. To the right of the entrance is a snack bar and beautiful views over the neighbouring tea plantations up the hill.

The main feature of Feilai Feng is the hundreds of **Buddhist sculptures** carved into its limestone rocks. These date from between the tenth and fourteenth centuries and are the most important examples of their type to be found south of the Yangzi. Today the little Buddhas and other figurines are dotted about everywhere, moss-covered and laughing among the foliage. It's possible to follow trails right up to the top of the hill to escape the tourist hubbub.

Lingyin Temple

灵隐寺, língyǐn sì · Daily 7am–5.30pm · ¥65 · ☎ 0571 87968665

Deep inside the Feilai Feng tourist area you'll eventually arrive at **Lingyin Temple** (Temple of the Soul's Retreat), one of the biggest temple complexes in China. Founded in 326 AD by Hui Li, who is buried nearby, it was the largest and most important monastery in Hangzhou and once had three thousand monks, nine towers, eighteen pavilions and 75 halls and rooms. Today it is an attractive working temple with daily services, usually in the early morning or after 3pm.

The temple was so badly riddled with woodworm that in the 1940s the main crossbeams collapsed onto the statues; the 18m-high Tang statue of Sakyamuni is a replica, carved in 1956 from 24 pieces of camphorwood. Elsewhere in the temple, the old frequently brushes against the new – the **Hall of the Heavenly King** contains four large and highly painted Guardians of the Four Directions made in the 1930s, while the Guardian of the Buddhist Law and Order, who shields the Maitreya, was carved from a single piece of wood eight hundred years ago.

Tea Museum

茶博物馆, chá bówùguǎn · 88 Longjing Lu · Tues–Sun 8.30am–4.30pm · Free · ☎ 0571 87964221 · Bus #27 or #Y3 from Pinghai Lu in the town centre to the former Zhejiang Hotel, where both buses stop, then walk southwest to the museum along a small lane just to the north of, and parallel to, the main road

Down in the southwestern quarter of the city, in the direction of the village of Longjing, the dominant theme is tea production: gleaming green tea bushes sweep up and down the land, and old ladies pester tourists into buying fresh tea leaves. Fittingly, this is where you'll find the **Tea Museum**, a smart place with lots of captions in English, covering themes such as the history of tea and the etiquette of tea drinking. There are displays on different varieties of tea, cultivation techniques, the development of special teaware and finally, reconstructed tearooms in various ethnic styles, such as Tibetan and Yunnanese.

Longjing

龙井, lóngjǐng · Bus #K27 from the northwestern lakeshore near the Tomb of Yuefei, or #Y3

The village of **Longjing** (Dragon Well), with tea terraces rising on all sides behind the houses, is famous as the origin of **Longjing tea**, perhaps the finest variety of green tea produced in China. Depending on the season, a stroll around here affords glimpses of leaves in different stages of processing – being cut, sorted or dried. You'll be hassled to sit at an overpriced teahouse or to buy leaves when you get off the bus – have a good look around first, as there is a very complex grading system and a huge range in quality and price. The **Dragon Well** itself is at the end of the village, a group of buildings around a spring, done up in a rather touristy fashion.

Hupaomeng Quan

虎跑梦泉, hǔpǎomèng quán · Daily 8am–5pm · ¥15 · Bus #504 or #Y5 from the city centre, down the eastern shore of the lake; bus #Y3 from Longjing passes close by

East of Longjing and south of Xi Hu, the area extending down to the Qiantang River is full of trees and gentle slopes. Of all the parks in this part of the city, perhaps the most attractive is the **Hupaomeng Quan** (Tiger Running Dream Spring). The spring here – according to legend, found by a ninth-century Zen Buddhist monk with the help of two tigers – is said to produce the purest water around, which serious connoisseurs use for brewing the best Longjing teas. For centuries, this has been a popular site for hermits to settle; now largely forested, it is dotted with teahouses, shrines, waterfalls and pagodas.

ARRIVAL AND DEPARTURE   HANGZHOU

BY TRAIN

The easiest way to get to Hangzhou is by fast G- and D-class train from Shanghai's Hongqiao Station (frequent; 1hr–1hr 30min; around ¥80 one way).

Hangzhou East Station (杭州东站, hángzhōu dōngzhàn) Most fast trains stop at this high-speed

9

hub, 5km out of the centre. The easiest way to get to the northeastern lakefront from here is on the metro or by bus #K28. The last fast train back to Shanghai is at 10.31pm.

Hangzhou Station (杭州火车站, hángzhōu huǒchēzhàn) This station is more convenient, just 2km east of Xi Hu. D-class trains that terminate here leave from Shanghai's Hongqiao Station every hour. Reaching the lake on foot takes about 20min; otherwise, take bus #7, #K7 or #Y2. The last fast train back to Shanghai from here is at 8.25pm.

BY BUS
Buses from Shanghai take just over two hours.

Public bus from Shanghai Most services leave from the Shanghai South Bus Station and pull in at the North Bus Station (汽车北站, qìchē běizhàn) – buses #K15, #K67 and #K290 run the 9km to the centre – or at the East (Jiubao) Bus Station (九堡汽车站, jiǔbǎo qìchēzhàn) in the northeast of town at 3339 Desheng Dong Lu. The East Bus Station is connected by metro to the centre of town.

Private bus from Shanghai Private buses from outside Shanghai Railway Station drop off at the square in front of Hangzhou main station.

From Suzhou Buses drop off at the square in front of the main train station.

GETTING AROUND

By bus There are some useful "Y" tourist bus routes around the lakeshore; ask for information at any of the many tourist booths.

By metro The metro system has three lines, but is of little use to casual visitors except to connect the train stations with the lake area; journeys cost ¥2–8 (daily 5.30am–11pm).

By boat It would be a shame to leave Hangzhou without taking a boat ride on Xi Hu. Tourist boats (¥45) depart from jetties all around the lake; trips take 90min and include a jaunt around Santanyinyue (entrance fees included in the ticket price). You can also rent a four-person boat for ¥80/hr.

By bike All hostels and most hotels rent bikes out for around ¥50/day, and there is a comprehensive public bike scheme – with more than two thousand stations, it's the biggest such scheme in the world. Show your passport and leave a ¥300 deposit at one of the many booths around West Lake; you'll be issued with a card that allows you to take bikes from any station. Bikes are free for the first hour, then cost ¥3/hour.

By taxi Taxis are a convenient way to get around town with the meter starting at ¥11 for the first 3km.

INFORMATION

Hangzhou Tourist Centre In front of the train station (daily 8am–8pm; ☎0571 87961729, ⊛gotohz.gov.cn), the tourist centre runs one-day tours of Hangzhou and surrounding canal towns and cities, as well as shuttles to Shanghai's Pudong airport. Pick up a free, annually updated city guide in English which contains many maps and useful information. There are also offices at the airport and on Yan'an Lu, and several visitor information booths dotted around town.

More Hangzhou ⊛morehangzhou.com. Expat listings magazine with handy restaurant and nightlife recommendations. You'll find the print edition in expat-oriented restaurants.

ACCOMMODATION

There are some excellent hotels in Hangzhou, particularly on the **lakefront**, and a handful of **hostels**. Rooms fill quickly in the spring and autumn, so you would be wise to book in advance.

Dahua 大华饭店, dàhuá fàndiàn 171 Nanshan Lu ☎0571 87181888, ⊛dh-hotel.com. On the lakeside, several blocks south of Jiefang Lu. It's an old-fashioned government hotel and though that's usually a red flag this place isn't bad: spacious grounds with comfortable rooms and attentive service justify the prices. Mao Zedong and Zhou Enlai stayed here whenever they were in town. It also has a good and reasonably priced restaurant overlooking the lake. **¥1550**

East Hotel 杭州逸酒店, háng zhōu yì jiǔ diàn 198 Nan Hushu Lu ☎0571 88099999, ⊛easthotelhangzhou .com. It might be fashionably dark, but this well-located, comfortable new hotel offers good value, with big online discounts. The breakfast buffet is lavish and there's a free morning shuttle bus to the local tourist sites. **¥950**

Hangzhou Lotus Hostel 杭州市西湖区曙, hángzhōu shìxīhú qūshǔ 174 Shuguang Lu ☎0571 85831772. Despite the name, this is more of a hotel, though it does have dorms (four- and six-bed). It's clean, smart and pleasantly secluded, a little far from town but just 5min from the west side of West Lake. There aren't many dining options in the area but the on-site café is serviceable. They'll rent you a bike for ¥30 a day. Dorms **¥85**, doubles **¥400**

Hofang Youth Hostel 荷方青年旅舍荷, hé fāng qīng nián lǚ shè 67 Hefang Jie ☎0571 87063299. This homely hostel, a renovated old house in a quiet pedestrian alleyway, scores for being clean and central and having friendly staff, making it one of the best of the cheapies. Dorms **¥95**, doubles **¥240**

9

Hyatt Regency 凯悦酒店, kǎiyuè jiǔdiàn 28 Hubin Lu ☎0571 87121234, ⓦhangzhou.regency.hyatt.com. This hotel offers lake views, with excellent restaurants on site (see below) and a good swimming pool. **¥1566**
Mingtown Hangzhou Youth Hostel 明堂国际青年旅舍, míngtáng guójì qīngnián lǚshè 101 Nanshan Lu ☎0571 87918948, ⓔmingtown@

foxmail.com. A nice range of rooms, including a few with a view of the lake or a private bathroom. It has all the hostel facilities you'd expect, plus a good bar/restaurant and a very pleasant rooftop overlooking the lake. Discounts for YHA members. It's about 1km southwest of Dingban Lu metro stop, on the #Y2 bus from the train station. Dorms **¥85**, doubles **¥395**

EATING

Hangzhou has plenty of good places to eat. The wedge-shaped neighbourhood between Hubin Lu and Yan'an Lu is home to a number of Chinese restaurants and fast-food joints, while touristy **Hefang Jie** is also a good spot for Chinese restaurants and snacks. Lastly, the area between Shuguang Lu and the park has its own little cultural microclimate – downmarket and sometimes seedy, but fascinating nonetheless.

Elochee/e 路吃, lù chī 120–3 Wushan Lu ☎0571 86496090. Hangzhou cuisine served in a smart but relaxed diner; try the veggie goose (beancurd) or the Longjing shrimp. You're much less likely to have to queue than at the more reputed establishments, and a meal won't cost more that ¥150. Daily 10am–10pm.
Grandma's 外婆家, wài pó jiā 3 Hubin Lu ☎0571 85101939; 61 Macheng Lu ☎0571 88051987. Tasty local food at decent prices means these places are always busy. They're hot and noisy, too – the way the Chinese like it. Go for the signature dishes such as claypot chicken, stinky tofu or crystal prawns. There is a no-reservations policy, so get there early if you don't want to wait. Daily 11am–10pm.
Green Tea 绿茶, lǜchá 83 Longjing Lu ☎0571 87888022. Sitting amid tea plantations, next door to the Tea Museum itself, this out-of-the-way yet very popular restaurant – a rickety pine structure sitting lakeside above the lily pads – is quite a treat. Its collection of dishes is extensive (there's no English menu, but there are plenty of pictures; mains from around ¥40); the barbecued beef deserves a special mention. There are no reservations, and it's very busy, so arrive at 11.30am for lunch and 5.30pm for dinner to be close to the head of the queue. Daily 11am–10pm.

Hubin 28 湖滨28, húbīn èrshíbā hào GF, Hyatt Regency, 28 Hubin Lu ☎0571 87791234, ⓦhangzhou.regency.hyatt.com. This highly rated restaurant is certain to impress, so dress up. It's all local food, given the fine-dining treatment; try the hot and sour mandarin fish or the signature *dongpo* pork, served shaped into a pyramid. Expect to pay at least ¥500/person. Daily 11am–11pm.
Kuiyuan Guan 奎元馆, kuíyuán guǎn 154 Jiefang Lu, just west of Zhongshan Zhong Lu ☎0571 87029012. Specializing in more than forty noodle dishes for all tastes, from the mundane (beef noodle soup) to the acquired (pig intestines and kidneys). It also offers a range of local seafood delicacies. A little tricky to find – go through the entrance with Chinese lanterns hanging outside, and it's on the left, upstairs. Daily 8am–9pm.
Louwailou 楼外楼, lóuwài lóu Gu Shan Island ☎0571 87969023. The best-known restaurant in Hangzhou and on every Chinese tourist's bucket list. Specialities include *dongpo* pork, fish-shred soup and beggar's chicken (a whole chicken cooked inside a ball of mud, which is broken and removed at your table). Lu Xun and Zhou Enlai, among others, have dined here. Pricey at around ¥200/person. Daily 11am–11pm.

DRINKING AND NIGHTLIFE

For nightlife, **Shuguang Lu** and the north end of **Nanshan Lu** are the best bar strips in the Xi Hu area, but they tend to be a bit touristy; the local hangouts are to be found slightly outside the centre, especially in the area north of Shuguang Lu. For up-to-date **information**, check ⓦmorehangzhou.com.

7 Club 7号酒吧, qīhàojiǔbā 43 Shuguang Lu (behind the florist) ☎0571 86431517. Intimate and friendly basement bar with mostly local, but some expat customers. An outstanding selection of Belgian and British bottled beers, as well as cocktails and single-malt scotch; prices start at ¥50. It's very laid back, and the eclectic mix of music is kept at a reasonable volume. Some English spoken. Daily 6pm–2am.
Reggae Bar 黑根酒吧, hēigēn jiǔbā 131 Xue Yuan Lu ☎0571 86575749. About 3km north of Shuguang

Lu, this happy, three-storey bar is a favourite among local and foreign students, and sees plenty of action at the weekend; it's also a good place to find out about the best events. The decor is arty/squat-party style, but drinks are top quality, with many imported beers at reasonable prices (bottles ¥20–45). The track selection goes beyond reggae, with DJs working to get the dancefloor moving and student bands playing live Tues–Sun 8.30–10pm. Daily 6pm–5am (or later).

SHOPPING

The most touristy concentration of souvenir outlets – selling silk, tea and crafts – is along **Hefang Jie**. An L-shaped **night market** bends around the western end of Renhe Lu, with street sellers peddling a proletarian jumble of wares from watches to DVDs to Little Red Books. The ritziest brand names are all on **Hubin Lu**, right on the waterfront.

China Silk Town 中国丝绸城, zhōngguó sīchóu chéng 127 Xinhua Jie ☎ 0571 85100192. Maybe avoid the clothes, which are a little gaudy, and go for pyjamas, umbrellas and fans at this venerable store. Daily 10am–5pm.

Ten Fu Tea 天福茗茶, tiānfú míngchá B1 132 Shuguang Lu ☎ 0571 8763063. Handy branch of a chain that sells tea and tea-related souvenirs; stock up on local varieties, Longjing and chrysanthemum. Daily 10am–5pm.

DIRECTORY

Banks and exchange The Bank of China head office is at 140 Yan'an Bei Lu (daily 8am–5pm), immediately north of Qingchun Lu.
Hospital Sir Run Run Shaw Hospital, 3 Qingchun Dong Lu (☎ 0571 86006613, ⓦ english-srrsh.com), is the best

equipped and has English-speaking staff.
Visa extensions Ask at the PSB in the centre of town, just south of Dingban Lu metro stop at 35 Huaguang Lu (Mon–Fri 8.30am–noon & 2.30–5pm; ☎ 0571 87280561).

Moganshan

莫干山, mògān shān • ¥80/day; ticket office (daily 8am–6.30pm) is at the gate to the village

The hill station of **MOGANSHAN**, 60km north of Hangzhou, was popular before World War II with the foreign set and has recently reprised its role as a rugged resort to escape the muggy summer. The old European-style villas, po-faced communist-style sanatoriums and local farmhouses are being restored and turned into guesthouses. There's little to do here but wander the incongruously European-looking village, **hike** in the bamboo forest and enjoy the views. It's lovely, but it can be expensive – accommodation prices rise in summer and almost double at the weekend. The centre of the village is over-developed, but a thirty-minute walk in any direction will take you into peace and quiet. Spring is the best time to come, before the summer hordes arrive, and avoid the weekend if possible. The place pretty much shuts down in winter.

ARRIVAL AND DEPARTURE

MOGANSHAN

The resort is not really geared up for independent travel, and the majority of visitors are on a **package** of some sort, with hotels picking guests up and often ferrying them around during their stay. You will be charged ¥80 for an **entry ticket** – retain it, as you have to keep showing it – and you may be turned away if you don't have accommodation booked. There is no direct route to Moganshan – you have first to head either to **Deqing** (德清, déqīng) or **Wukang** (武康, wǔkāng) at the bottom of the mountain. Once you're there, a taxi or minivan the rest of the way costs ¥120 or so. Don't get one of the three-wheelers – they're slow and often cheat tourists. It will probably be cheaper, and certainly easier, to prearrange a ride through your accommodation. Note that there are no **ATMs** in Moganshan, so arrive with enough money to last your stay.

FROM SHANGHAI
By train There is a daily train from Hongqiao station to Deqing at 7.30am (2hr).

FROM HANGZHOU
By train Regular trains depart from Hangzhou's central

train station day and night for the trip to Deqing (40min–1hr).
By bus Buses leave hourly from Hangzhou's North Bus Station for the run to Wukang (1hr).
By taxi A taxi all the way from Hangzhou to Moganshan will cost around ¥250.

ACCOMMODATION

The prices quoted below are for summer **high season**, during the week; at high-season weekends add thirty percent, or take thirty percent off if you're travelling in spring or autumn. Moganshan has a surfeit of faded, Chinese-style two-star accommodation (from ¥350); fine if you just want a bed, but a slightly more expensive room in one of the old villas listed below is more atmospheric. For a real retreat, stay in one of the **forest villas** (from ¥650 for a room on a weekday; cottages start at ¥1500) managed by the *Moganshan Lodge* (see below).

House 23, 24 and 25 ☏0572 8033822, ⓦmoganshanhousé3.com. Converted 1930s villas towards the top of the hill, offering self-catering accommodation. House 24, the newest, is the best. House 25 is a cottage retreat a 15min walk away in the woods. The hotelier will arrange transport from Shanghai or Hangzhou. ¥1800

Howoo Life Hostel 莫干山后坞生活度假酒店, mògānshān hòuwù shēnghuó dùjià jiǔdiàn 52 Xiwu Lu, Houwu village ☏0572 8041966. This woodland lodge is far from anywhere, so arrange for a taxi to pick you up from the station. It's a 30min walk to the nearest village, so you'll end up eating at the average on-site Chinese restaurant unless you've brought your own food. The family

rooms in the freestanding cabins are pricey and all that dark wood is terribly creaky; stay in the main hostel, on the top floor if possible, for minimal noise. Dorms ¥120, rooms ¥1000

Naked Retreats 62 Gao'an Lu, Shanghai ☏021 64318901, ⓦnakedretreats.cn. Rustic ecolodges tucked away in bamboo forest. Despite the name, there's no naturism involved, and the lodges are civilized (although a 20min drive from the nearest shop), with wood fires, jacuzzis and fitted kitchens, and a maid to do your cooking. Mountain-biking, horseriding, fishing and of course plenty of hiking, guided if you like, are also on offer. They'll arrange for you to be picked up from Deqing/Wukang or Hangzhou (from ¥350). ¥2000

EATING

Moganshan Lodge 莫干山旅馆, mògānshān lǚguǎn 343 Yin Shan Jie ☏0572 8033011, ⓦmoganshanlodge.com. Foreign-owned bar/café/restaurant in an old lodge – the *Songliang Shanzhuang Hotel* (松梁山庄, sōngliáng shānzhuāng) – at the southern end of the main street, with great views from the patio. The food is decent, though unless you order in

advance you don't get any choice (call or email enquiries@moganshanlodge.com; set dinners ¥178). It's also the best place for a drink in the evening. The helpful owners will point you in the right direction for walks; check out their website before you arrive for accommodation options and to get a feel for the town.

FAIRMONT PEACE HOTEL

Accommodation

Accommodation in Shanghai is plentiful, and often stylish. The grand old-world hotels might not quite offer the comfort and elegance of newer arrivals, but make up for it with heaps of faded character. A new breed of boutique establishments, popular with tourists, is cropping up in the Old French Concession, where the grand old properties can be converted into chic hotels, and there is a respectable amount of budget accommodation throughout the city. Hostels generally have decently priced rooms as well as dorms, so are worth considering even if you're not a backpacker. The Chinese hospitality industry is experiencing a steep learning curve, which means that the staff and services in newer places, and those that are foreign owned, are generally much better than the alternatives.

ESSENTIALS

BOOKING, COSTS AND CHECKING IN

Booking It is always best to book online. If you approach a hotel desk without a reservation to book a room, you'll probably pay more than if you sit in the lobby with a laptop and do the same on the net. In addition to its detailed user reviews, tips and photos, TripAdvisor (Ⓦtripadvisor.com) links to a number of booking engines; Ⓦtrivago.com also has plenty of choices. There's no booking fee at Asia Hotels (Ⓦasiahotels.com), though they do require that you pay a percentage of the room rate up front by credit card. The most useful websites for the budget places, with lots of reviews, are Ⓦhostelbookers.com and Ⓦhostelworld.com.

Costs Room rates tend to be higher than elsewhere in China but are still cheaper than you'll find in a large Western city. Prices will vary according to the time of year; the rates that we quote in this Guide are for a double room in high season (late March to mid-Sept). Off season, in winter, you will commonly find rooms a third cheaper, or even half this price; during Chinese national holidays they may be more expensive (see p.26). Fierce competition and the arrival of Airbnb and its local equivalents have depressed prices in recent years, and the ritzier places are currently locked in something of a price war: booking online, it's possible to get discounts of up to 70 percent at the mid- to high-end establishments. There are fewer discounts in the lower ranges, so if you want to spend between ¥600 and ¥1000 you should start by searching for discounted rooms at places you'd normally consider way above your usual price level.

Checking in Except at the budget business hotels and the smallest B&Bs, which don't see much foreign custom, reception staff will always speak passable English – or will fetch someone who does. Checking in involves filling in a form, showing your passport and visa and paying a deposit. Specify if you want a smoking or non-smoking room, as most hotels have both – that said, in cheaper places it's hard not to suspect that a non-smoking room is just one you haven't smoked in, with the ashtray removed. Wherever you're staying, remember to grab a few hotel business cards – these are vital when you want to let taxi drivers know how to get you back to your accommodation. And don't just show them the matchbox from the hotel bar – an apocryphal American tourist who did that was taken to a suburban match factory.

HOTELS

Upmarket There are plenty of upmarket places in Shanghai, where rooms cost upward of ¥1600, and more are being thrown up all the time. In terms of facilities, these hotels are comparable to their counterparts elsewhere in the world, offering gyms, saunas and swimming pools and lavish buffet breakfasts with plenty of choice. Locked in a space-race to achieve total frictionless guest comfort, they've started deploying Japanese loos with heated seats and bidet attachments, flatscreen TVs in the bathrooms and sensors that switch the lights on and off as you move around the room: exciting times. The choice in this category comes down to whether you want to be right in the heart of the neon jungle or if you want views of it from your window – few places manage both. An annoyance at this level is the high extra charges for services that are free in cheaper places, such as wi-fi (sometimes as much as ¥100 a day); hoick your laptop to a nearby café instead. Even if a room in one of these establishments is beyond your budget, you can still avail yourself of their lavish facilities, including restaurants that are often pretty good and, by Western standards, not expensive.

Mid-range The 2010 Expo left Shanghai with a decent supply of hotels boasting rooms at less than ¥1200. All are well equipped and comfortable, though they tend to be rather anonymous. An exception are those housed in converted French Concession mansions, where you'll get a characterful room but few, if any, extra facilities. Otherwise, you can expect an en-suite bathroom, a business centre, wi-fi (for which you may have to pay a small surcharge) and a booking service for onward transport – and the larger

10

WHICH AREA?

If you want to be near the centre of the action, go for somewhere between **People's Square** and the **Bund**, where there are options for all budgets. It might be noisy, but as soon as you walk out of the front door you'll know you're in the real Shanghai. There are a few options in the **Old City**, an area that is of little interest by itself but is rapidly gentrifying; you could say the same about **Hongkou**, in the north. For style and panache, head to the more genteel **Old French Concession**, where there are a number of mid-range hotels – including some good boutique properties – housed in attractive buildings and grounds. Close to upmarket dining and nightlife, these places are relatively quiet, but aren't generally close to a metro station. To the north, the upscale accommodation in the commercial district of **Jing'an** puts you at the heart of modern, international Shanghai, with plenty of places to eat, drink and shop nearby. For the latest in corporate chic, **Pudong** has the fanciest options, and rooms are generally much bigger than elsewhere, but really the area is pretty dull. You'll get value for money in the outskirts, but you'll be a long way from the action – make sure, at least, that you're close to a metro station.

10

ones will have a gym and sauna, too. Hotel food at this level is never much good, so meals are better eaten out than in the hotel restaurant. Breakfast – Chinese or Western – will be included, but it generally won't be anything to write home about. Mid-range hotels don't always offer non-smoking rooms; if there's a lingering stale smell, courtesy of a previous puffing tenant, demand another room.

Budget chains Budget hotel chains – good value at less than ¥500 a night – are presently blasting the much-loathed dingy two-star Chinese hotel of yore into deserved oblivion (at last budget travellers no longer have to tolerate cigarette burns on the carpets and mould on the walls). Not much English will be spoken, the hotel restaurant won't be up to much and you'll have to go out for breakfast, and there are no extras such as health centres or pools, but rooms are at least clean and bright, and wi-fi is free.

HOSTELS
Shanghai has a good set of decent, cheap accommodation options. In the youth hostels you can expect free internet,

some level of free wi-fi (perhaps only in the lounge or bar, or one particular spot by the lift), a self-service laundry, a/c rooms, a cheap bar that does a Western(ish) breakfast – and, probably, a resident cat, a pile of tatty expat magazines to leaf through and maybe even a pool or ping-pong table. Though you might find some aspects of your stay a little rough around the edges, standards in Shanghai hostels are higher than elsewhere in China and if the staff aren't always completely professional they usually make up for it with friendliness. They provide towels but you'll have to buy soap and shampoo. Anywhere calling itself a hostel will offer a discount (¥10 or so) with a Hostelling International card; you can usually pick up a card on the premises (¥50). The hostels we review in this Guide offer more rooms than dorms, so even if you don't identify with the backpacking hordes they're still worth considering. Note that dorm beds are comparatively poor value; you'd generally be better off finding someone to share a twin with.

APARTMENTS
If you plan to stay for an extended period, you'll need to make special arrangements and probably employ an agent to help you find a place – unless your employer has sorted everything out for you (see p.33). One good place to start looking for long-term rentals is ⓦ smartshanghai .com/housing, while ⓦ airbnb.com offers plenty of short-term options; you'll get great value for upmarket properties on the local equivalent, ⓦ tujia.com, but their website is only in Chinese.

HOTELS

THE BUND AND NANJING DONG LU
Astor House Hotel 浦江饭店, pǔjiāng fàndiàn 15 Huangpu Lu ☎63246388, ⓦpujianghotel.com; ⓜNanjing Dong Lu; map p.40. Formerly the *Astor Hotel* and dating back to 1846, this old-fashioned building (see p.41), just north of the Bund across Waibaidu Bridge, has the feel of a Victorian school, with creaky wooden floors, enormous rooms, rambling corridors and chunky brass fixtures. Portraits of past guests such as Einstein and Charlie Chaplin line the walls; they too may have wondered why the lift was so slow – never mind, the staircase is magnificent. Rooms vary so ask to see a few – basically it's a choice between the atmospheric old rooms or new and better-appointed executive suites. The views aren't great and the restaurant should be avoided – and as with all government-owned Chinese businesses, the finer points of service are lacking – but it's reasonably priced, and with heritage that has been preserved rather than reinvented. Think of it as a batty maiden aunt with some good stories and forgive its eccentricities. **¥1200**

Broadway Mansions 上海大厦, shànghǎi dàshà 20 Suzhou Bei Lu ☎63246260, ⓦbroadwaymansions.com; ⓜNanjing Dong Lu; map p.40. This hulking bruiser of a

1930s building, on the north bank of Suzhou Creek, was originally a residential block (see p.40). Today it seems aimed at Chinese business travellers, but it does offer superb views along the length of the Bund (room rates increase the higher you go). Some rooms are drab, others have been renovated, so check out a few – ask for a river view and specify a non-smoking room. It can leave something to be desired in terms of style and service, and the breakfast isn't up to much, but recent improvements mean this is one to consider if you can't get into one of the pricier neighbours. **¥1337**

★**Fairmont Peace Hotel** 和平饭店, hépíng fàndiàn 20 Nanjing Dong Lu, by the Bund ☎63216888, ⓦfairmont.com/peacehotel; ⓜNanjing Dong Lu; map p.40. As the *Cathay Hotel*, this was the most famous hotel in Shanghai, with a list of illustrious guests including Charlie Chaplin and Noël Coward (see p.42). Its star faded in the modern era thanks to bad management, but its fortunes have been turned around by the Fairmont group, who bought the place in 2007, and refurbished it completely. The place certainly looks grand, and the famous Art Deco lobby and *Jazz Bar* have been restored to their former glory. A low-rise extension at the rear contains modern luxuries such as a spa and sky-lit swimming pool, and there's a very civilized afternoon tea (see p.132). **¥2730**

Le Royal Méridien 世贸皇家艾美酒店, shìmào huángjiā àiměi jiǔdiàn 789 Nanjing Dong Lu ☎33189999, ⊛starwoodhotels.com; ⓜPeople's Square; map p.39. With its excellent location, smart services and discreet style, this high-end business-oriented venue at the Renmin Park end of Nanjing Dong Lu holds its own. The building is one of the city centre's landmarks, with 66 floors and what look like antennae on the roof. The rather cavernous reception, which has something of a Bond villain's lair about it, is on the eleventh floor. Ask for a room as high up as possible to take full advantage of the views from the floor-to-ceiling windows. **¥1634**

Peninsula 上海半岛酒店, shànghǎi bàndǎo jiǔdiàn 32 Zhongshan Dong Yi Lu ☎23272888, ⊛peninsula.com/shanghai; ⓜNanjing Dong Lu; map p.40. An impressive incarnation of the exclusive Hong Kong brand. It's an Art Deco delight, and the tone is set nicely by the white-columned lobby, where the local elite drink afternoon tea to the accompaniment of a string quartet (see p.132). Most rooms have a Bund view, and all feature TVs in the bathroom, walk-in closets and phones that offer free international calls. **¥3948**

★**Waldorf Astoria** 外滩华尔道夫酒店, wàitān huáěr dàofū jiǔdiàn 2 Zhongshan Dong Yi Lu ☎63229988, ⊛waldorfastoriashanghai.com; ⓜNanjing Dong Lu; map p.40. Shanghai's grandest old gentlemen's club (see p.45) has been restored to its former Baroque-Revival glory, with a glut of crystal chandeliers, marble floors and columns, and wrought-iron and brass fittings. There are attractive period details throughout, from the antique lift to the Art Deco-style sofas, but the highlight for heritage fans has to be the famous *Long Bar* (see p.144). The original 1910 building has the classiest suites, which boast Bund-view balconies – most rooms, though, are in the New Tower just behind, where the emphasis is on understated luxury; the spacious suites have internet-enabled flatscreen TVs, sunken baths and dressing rooms. The *Salon de Ville* restaurant has a rather good afternoon tea (see p.132). **¥3247**

Westin 威斯汀大酒店, wèisītīng dàjiǔdiàn 88 Henan Zhong Lu ☎63351888, ⊛westin.com/shanghai; ⓜNanjing Dong Lu; map p.39. Chinese fancy hotels usually try to impress with either a water feature or palm trees in the lobby; the over-the-top *Westin* goes for both. So is it the best? Well no, it's been superceded by ritzier new arrivals, but it's not bad for the price. It scores for having good on-site restaurants, such as *The Stage* (see p.130), and a nice little bakery (see p.131), for the Banyan Tree Spa (see p.28), and for its location behind the Bund, but loses a few points for the Vegas ambience and the lack of views from most of the rooms. Decor is modern with a few flash touches such as rainforest showerheads and mood lighting. **¥1588**

PEOPLE'S SQUARE

★**JW Marriott** 明天广场JW万怡酒店, míngtiān guǎngchǎng JW wànyí jiǔdiàn Tomorrow Square, 399 Nanjing Xi Lu ☎53594969, ⊛marriott.com; ⓜPeople's Square; map p.49. Occupying the top floors of one of Shanghai's most uncompromising landmarks (something like an upraised claw), this swanky venue boasts more than two hundred serviced apartments for stressed executives, who will at least always be able to find their way home. With its excellent location and magnificent views it's one of the best of the top-end destinations, though not if you suffer vertigo or dislike ear-popping elevators – the lobby is on the 38th floor. Request an east-facing room for views of the liveliest scenes; the windows are huge and have deep sills for sitting and gazing. The indoor and outdoor pools, both a good size, are recommended. **¥1640**

Langham Yangtze Boutique 上海朗廷扬子精品酒店, shànghǎi lǎngtíngyángzǐ jīngpǐn jiǔdiàn 740 Hankou Lu ☎60800800, ⊛yangtzeboutique.langhamhotels.com; ⓜPeople's Square; map p.49. Though not as "boutique" as it bills itself – it's too big and corporate – the Art Deco building and retro styling give this monolith a heritage feel. Rooms are spacious, with TVs in the bathroom; many have balconies. Front-facing rooms on the higher floors are the best. **¥1200**

Radisson Blu Shanghai New World 新世界丽笙大酒店, xīnshìjiè lìshēng dàjiǔdiàn 88 Nanjing Xi Lu ☎63599999, ⊛radisson.com; ⓜPeople's Square; map p.49. This swish business hotel offers a slick and upscale experience, though the lobby, with its gold lighting, is a bit over the top. It has all the facilities you could expect, including spa, gym and pool, and a great location at the end of Nanjing Xi Lu, though its eclectic design features give the distinct impression that it hasn't yet worked out an identity. That UFO on the roof is actually a revolving restaurant; the view is more distinguished than the food. **¥1221**

THE OLD CITY AND AROUND

Casa Serena 巴越风大酒店, bāyuèfēng dàjiǔdiàn 68 Taicang Lu ☎53821600, ⊛casaserenahotel.com; ⓜHuangpi Nan Lu; map p.54. Whether you'll like this place will most likely depend on how keen you are on imitation period furniture – the stuff is everywhere – while incense in the corridors, big wooden doors and lots of pale stone give it an oddly monastic feel. There are only eighteen rooms; ask to see a few, as all are different and some are rather worn or chintzy, though each has an appealing glass-walled bathroom with a big tub. Though it might not be as stylish as it thinks it is, it's still more personal than the chains and is well located right next to Xintiandi for plenty of dining options – the on-site *Bellagio's* is well regarded, too. **¥1260**

★**Indigo** 外滩英迪格酒店, wàitān yīngdígé jiǔdiàn 585 Zhongshan Dong Er Lu ☎33029999, ⊛shanghai.hotelindigo.com; ⓜYuyuan Garden; map p.54. This funky

10

10

luxury hotel, at the far south end of the Bund – and a little far from the metro – is right on the river, so the best rooms have fantastic views. The design stands out, with quirky detailing everywhere – in the lobby a pod for relaxing sits next to a fire-engine-red rickshaw, and in the bathrooms you'll find Japanese-style electric toilets and rubber ducks. Rooms are big and comfortable and service is attentive. The steakhouse, *Char*, gets great reviews (see p.131), and don't miss the thirtieth-floor *Sky Bar* for the views. Big discounts online. **¥2725**

★**Jinjiang MetroPolo Hotel Classiq Shanghai People's Square** 锦江都城上海青年会经典酒店, jǐnjiāng dūchéng shànghǎi qīngnián huì jīng diǎn jiǔdiàn 123 Xizang Nan Lu ☎ 63261040; Ⓜ Dashijie; map p.54. Lovers of the English language bristling at the ridiculous name (the "o"s! That q! Why?) will be further annoyed to learn that this this was once the nicely monikered *Marvel Hotel*. Fortunately the name is all that's changed, and this long-running and well-respected travellers' staple remains worth considering. You won't get excited by the anonymous decor, but the big brick lump offers a great location, in the thick of the action just off People's Square, right next to the metro, at a reasonable price. Rooms are clean, spacious and well soundproofed (as they need to be, on such a busy road). Ask for an upper floor, for the views. **¥780**

Narada Boutique 中星君亭酒店, zhōngxīng jūntíng jiǔdiàn 839 Renmin Lu ☎ 63265666, Ⓦ naradaboutiquehotel.com; Ⓜ Dashijie; map p.54. Well located, a few minutes from the metro and a short walk from People's Square, this place may look like just another slick corporate monolith from the outside, but it does at least make a bold stab at character. Oriental-style styling is splashed all over the interior – carved wood panelling, Southeast Asian statuary and, if you haven't yet got the point, bamboo birdcages lining the corridors and net-shrouded canopy beds in the rooms. There's a good choice at breakfast, both Western and local, and a terrace to eat on when the weather is fine. They don't have a pool, though, nor much of a gym. **¥1640**

Waterhouse 水舍时尚设计酒店, shuǐ shè shí shàng shè jì jiǔdiàn 1–3 Maojiayuan Jie ☎ 60802988, Ⓦ waterhouseshanghai.com; Ⓜ Xiaonanmen; map p.54. Fans of the first *Zoolander* film will remember the absurd "Derelicte" fashion show, which took inspiration from the homeless. This "boutique property" seems to apply a similar principle to interior design, as the industrial chic lobby resembles a crack den with nice furniture: holes in the exposed brick walls, pitted concrete floor, mysterious stains. The smartly dressed staff at reception look like detectives at a crime scene. Fortunately, bar the odd bare brick wall, the aesthetic stops there, and the nineteen rooms are smart and comfortable – you're right on the water, so the higher ones have a Pudong view. The on-site restaurant, *Table Number One*, has a good reputation (see p.132), as does the rooftop cocktail bar. It's in the Cool Docks area (see p.57), a 20min

walk to the metro and a long way from anything interesting except more fancy restaurants. **¥1780**

THE OLD FRENCH CONCESSION

12 at Hengshan 十二号豪华精选酒店, shí èr hào háo huá jīng xuǎn jiǔ diàn 12 Hengshan Lu ☎ 33383888, Ⓦ theluxurycollection.com/12hengshan; Ⓜ Hengshan Lu; map pp.60–61. This may not be quite the luxury experience that's touted in the hotel bumf, but it is worth it if you can get one of their hefty discounts. The sprawling property is usefully located right by the metro, with just a short walk to plenty of bars and restaurants, and although it's on the main street most rooms overlook the courtyard garden, so there's some quiet. The Japanese-style robo-loos and automatic nightlights in the rooms are a nice touch, and the pool, sauna and gym are all decent. **¥2384**

★**Andaz Xintiandi** 新天地安达仕酒店, xīntiāndì āndáshì jiǔdiàn 88 Songshan Lu ☎ 23101234, Ⓦ shanghai.andaz.hyatt.com; Ⓜ Xintiandi; map pp.60–61. This Hyatt-run property is, supposedly, "design led": for that read lots of carved wooden screens, statement lighting and quirky art. There are some fancy touches, too: loos are Japanese style, with heated seats and bidet attachments, and you can control the room lights, a/c and TV from an in-room iPad. Afternoon tea in the lobby is an elegant treat (see p.132). The hotel is in a great location, convenient for the metro and pretty central; it's at the edge of the Xintiandi complex, so there are plenty of restaurants on your doorstep, but the area can be noisy at weekends. Pricey, but worth it, and you may find tempting discounts online. **¥2000**

★**B'LaVii House** 宝丽会馆, bǎolì huìguǎn 285 Hunan Lu ☎ 64677171; Ⓜ Huangpi Nan Lu; map pp.60–61. This elegant, well-appointed mansion has fourteen sleek rooms arranged around a courtyard; they're all individually decorated, but dark wood furniture and red lacquer are common to all. The surrounding area is quiet and civilized, and there are plenty of dining options nearby; that said, it's no trial eating in, either, as the on-site restaurant *Lapis Thai* is very good. Note that the staff's English is generally patchy. Booking is essential; decent discounts online. **¥1757**

Donghu 东湖宾馆, dōnghú bīnguǎn 70 Donghu Lu, one block north of Huaihai Zhong Lu ☎ 64158158, Ⓦ donghuhotel.com; Ⓜ Changshu Lu; map pp.60–61. Seven buildings in total make up the *Donghu*, in a sprawling complex on either side of Donghu Lu. The villas on the south side have a chequered past; they served as an opium warehouse and the centre of gangland operations in the 1920s and 1930s (see p.170). Today, rooms in this section are sedate and spacious with big bathrooms – the best are in Building One, where all the furniture is in traditional Chinese style. The rooms in the annexe on the north side of the street are much less interesting, and a bit rundown, but cheaper. Unusually for a hotel in this range, there's a good-sized indoor pool. Food is mediocre, so you should eat out, even for

TOP 5 STYLISH STAYS
Andaz Xintiiandi See opposite
Cachet See p.120
CHAI Shanghai Living See p.122
Pudi See p.120
URBN See p.121

breakfast; there are plenty of great places in the area. Overall, its good location, smattering of heritage and pleasant gardens make this one worth considering. **¥750**

★**Fenyang Garden** 汾阳花园酒店, fényáng huāyuán jiǔdiàn 45 Fenyang Lu ☎54569888, ⊛fenyanggardenhotel.com; ⓜChangshu Lu; map pp.60–61. This elegant and discreet converted villa is set back from the road in well-maintained grounds. You won't hear traffic, just music from the students practising at the Conservatory next door. It's grand, featuring a fine clutch of chandeliers, and rooms are spacious and refined, though perhaps the place is not as slick as it could be – there's no business centre, service is only OK and wi-fi is patchy, and breakfast is a little too Chinese for most foreign tastes. Still, overall it's a good, civilized option for the French Concession, and there are plenty of great places to eat in the area. **¥1107**

Gallery Suites 联艺凯文公寓, liányì kǎiwén gōngyù 525 Hengshan Lu ☎51795000, ⊛artgalleryhotels.com; ⓜHengshan Lu; map pp.60–61. This artsy, forty-room hotel – entirely non-smoking – is well located a short walk from Hengshan Lu metro station. There isn't much to the lobby, but the Art Deco-styled rooms are spacious, with big desks and elegant fittings, and freestanding, claw-foot tubs in the bathrooms – to which, weirdly, there's no door, only a bead curtain. Ask for a room away from the busy road, and ideally get one overlooking the courtyard. There's no restaurant, but it's no problem finding a good place to eat nearby. A good pick in this price range. **¥980**

Hengshan Moller Villa 衡山马勒别墅饭店, héngshān mǎlèbiéshù fàndiàn 30 Shanxi Nan Lu ☎62478881, ⊛mollervilla.com; ⓜShaanxi Nan Lu; map pp.60–61. Describing itself as a "boutique heritage hotel", the main villa here is a gorgeous Scandinavian-Gothic fantasy (see p.65), built in the 1930s and set in lovely, quiet grounds. The couple of rooms in the main villa (¥3250) have balconies, wood panelling and fireplaces, but you'll need to book those way in advance. Rooms in the new three-storey block just behind are clean and modern, of much less interest but considerably cheaper. Stay for the building only; service is so-so and the restaurant is to be avoided. **¥1580**

InterContinental Shanghai Ruijin 瑞金宾馆, ruìjīn bīnguǎn 118 Ruijin Er Lu (main entrance on Fuxing Lu) ☎64725222, ⊛ruijinhotelsh.com; ⓜShaanxi Nan Lu; map pp.60–61. Tudor-style villa complex set in manicured gardens complete with lawn tennis courts. It's a city landmark (see p.64); in the 1920s, it was home to the editor of the *North China Daily News*, and in the 60s and 70s the hotel hosted Ho Chi Minh and Nixon. The villas, none higher than four storeys, are cosy and exclusive; Mao used to stay in Building One, which has the finest Art Deco touches in the lampshades, balustrades and window decorations. Today, the largest and best-appointed rooms, with the best facilities, are in the new club building. **¥2400**

Jinjiang 锦江之星, jǐnjiāngzhīxīng 59 Maoming Nan Lu ☎62582582, ⊛jinjianghotels.com; ⓜShaanxi Nan Lu; map pp.60–61. This vast place with many wings, built in the 1930s, is one of Shanghai's most historic addresses (see p.65). Perhaps it's a trifle old-fashioned, and has been overtaken by slick new competitors, but it has a nice location in sedate gardens, just north of Shaanxi Nan Lu metro, off busy Huaihai Zhong Lu. Try to get a room in the renovated Georgian-style Cathay Building at the north end of the complex. Non-smoking rooms are limited to the seventh floor. Look for big online discounts. **¥1100**

Jinjiang MetroPolo Hotel Classiq Shanghai Jing'an Temple 锦江都城达华经典酒店, jǐnjiāng dūchéng dáhuá jīngdiàn jiǔdiàn 918 Yan'an Xi Lu ☎35645165; ⊛Jiangsu Lu; map pp.60–61. An intriguing prospect, this: a 1930s apartment building, designed by Art Deco maestro Ladislav Hudec (see p.169), that's been sympathetically renovated and given a mid-range price tag. The elegant building, with its simple horizontal lines, exudes class, and works well as a hotel, though it lacks facilities – there's no pool, and the small gym is in a separate building, for example. It's a bit out of the way, next to an elevated highway and a 15min walk to the metro, which may be why it's a little less expensive than you might expect. Try to get a room at the back, away from the noisy street. The very cheapest rooms don't have windows; it's worth paying a bit more for one of the upper-level suites (¥1630), which have a balcony. **¥1100**

★**Ketang Jian** 客堂间璞堤克酒店, kètáng jiānpú dīkè jiǔdiàn 335 Yongjia Lu ☎54666335, ⊛ketangjian.com; ⓜShaanxi Nan Lu; map pp.60–61. There aren't enough of this type of hotel in Shanghai – small, well located, characterful, not too pricey. You're right at the heart of the French Concession here, and the half-dozen or so guestrooms are spacious and charming, given an appealingly vintage look with a mix of old and new furniture and decor. On the downside, there are no facilities, the free breakfast is terrible (don't even bother), the attached restaurant can be noisy (go for a high room) and the service could be friendlier – you're pretty much left to your own devices by the non-English-speaking staff. Overall though, it's still decent value. **¥989**

Longemont 龙之梦大酒店, lóng zhī mèng dà jiǔ diàn 1116 Yan'an Xi Lu ☎61159888, ⊛thelongemonthotels.com; ⓜJiangsu Lu; map

10

10

pp.60–61. The chic, comfortable and spacious rooms boast great views, so aim for the highest floor you can get. Breakfast is so-so and English-speaking skills rather poor for an international business hotel, but it's centrally located, and not far from the metro. The pool and spa are good, and there are a couple of on-site restaurants. Look for online discounts. **¥1650**

Mansion Hotel 上海首席公馆酒店, shànghǎi shǒuxí gōngguǎn jiǔdiàn 82 Xinle Lu ☎ 54039888, ⓦ chinamansionhotel.com; ⓜ Shaanxi Nan Lu; map pp.60–61. This painstakingly reconstructed 1920s mansion, discreetly tucked away from the street among manicured gardens, has the feel of a stuffy private members' club – in fact it was once home to notorious gangster Du Yuesheng (see p.170). The building is magnificent but they've tried a little too hard with the lobby and corridor furnishings, cramming repro antiques and memorabilia into every corner. Still, the thirty guestrooms are impressive, if perhaps a little dark and chintzy – all rooms have two-person jacuzzi tubs – and the rooftop terrace is a great venue for a drink. One downside is the lack of facilities – there's no gym or lounge, for example. Big discounts available online. **¥3260**

Okura Garden 花园饭店, huāyuán fàndiàn 58 Maoming Nan Lu ☎ 64151111, ⓦ gardenhotelshanghai .com; ⓜ Shaanxi Nan Lu; map pp.60–61. The grounds are lovely at this Japanese-run mansion, and the lobby, which used to be the Cercle Sportif Français (see p.65), has some great Art Deco detailing. Rooms, though, are in a nondescript monolith looming at the back, and they are rather outdated and kitschy. Still, service and cleanliness is at Japanese levels, and bathrooms boast that staple of Japanese luxury, the multifunction toilet with bidet attachment and seat warmer. There's also an *onsen* for Japanese-style communal bathing, and a Japanese breakfast. Be sure to ask for a non-smoking room. **¥1224**

Pudi 璞邸精品酒店, púdǐ jīngpǐn jiǔdiàn 99 Yandang Lu ☎ 51585888, ⓦ boutiquehotel.cc; ⓜ Huangpi Nan Lu; map pp.60–61. This small boutique hotel has stylish and unusual touches such as aquariums in the lobby and copper sinks, kitchenettes and big desks in the rooms – not to mention what is reputed to be the only hotel room in China for pets. Some people, however, may find it all a little too fashionably dark. It's well located right next to Fuxing Park in the French Concession, but as it's built over a nightclub you might want to avoid the lower floors; also, don't bother with the restaurant or the breakfast. Note that the entrance is round the side of the building, and not too easy to spot. **¥1579**

★Quintet Bed & Breakfast 五重奏旅店, wǔchóngzòu lǚdiàn 808 Changle Lu, near Changshu Lu ☎ 62499088, ⓦ quintet-shanghai.com; ⓜ Changshu Lu; map pp.60–61. A three-storey courtyard house converted into a snug guesthouse, *Quintet* scores high on style, with each of the six split-level rooms designed around

a theme. It's small and intimate, staff are knowledgeable, and the whole place is non-smoking. There aren't many business facilities, but it's ideal for tourists looking for something a little different. Reservations are essential – check out the rooms on the website. **¥1200**

JING'AN

★Cachet 凯世精品酒店, kǎi shì jīng pǐn jiǔ diàn 931 Nanjing Xi Lu ☎ 33024990, ⓦ cachethotels.com; ⓜ Nanjing Xi Lu; map pp.70–71. When it was the *JIA* hotel it was all style and no substance, but having been refreshed under new management, this fancy property – 45 rooms adapted from an old apartment block – is worth considering. It's smart, friendly and fashionable, and right next to the metro in a busy area. Service is good, and rooms are big for this part of the city, though you won't find a pool or much of a gym. Ask to be put on a high floor, as lower rooms can be noisy – it's worth investigating the larger, pricier suites, as they have balconies. Breakfast is in an annexe off the lobby that doesn't feel very private. **¥1866**

Courtyard Shanghai Central 浦西万怡酒店, pǔ xī wàn yí jiǔ diàn 338 Hengfeng Lu ☎ 22153888, ⓦ marriott.co.uk/hotels/travel/shapx-courtyard-shanghai-central; ⓜ Hanzhong Lu; map pp.70–71. You just know that a hotel with the word "Central" in the name is going to be anything but, and so it proves here. Never mind; this is a good-value, clean, crisp and modern property run by Marriott, offering big rooms with great views and all mod cons. It's in a bland part of Hongkou, north of Suzhou Creek, but you're only a couple of minutes' walk from the metro. Bear in mind that there is a lot of construction going on around here, so you'll need a room on a higher floor to avoid the noise. Wi-fi is only free in the lobby. Good discounts available online. **¥1160**

Pei Mansion 贝轩大公馆, bèi xuān dà gōng guǎn 170 Nanyang Lu ☎ 62897878, ⓦ peimansionhotel.com; ⓜ Jing'an Temple; map pp.70–71. This three-storey 1930s mansion has been converted into a little guesthouse and while there are no facilities to speak of it will certainly appeal to fans of old Shanghai and anyone bored with slickly anonymous lodgings. Much of the original Art Deco styling remains, including a magnificent spiralling "dragon" staircase; even the creaky elevator, the city's oldest, is original. Furniture and fittings are period or retro; by the time you've discovered the wireless on your bedside cabinet you'll want to crank it up and start dancing a charleston. That said, keeping in period is not necessarily entirely a good thing, of course; rooms can look a little dingy, and modern conveniences like the shower stall start to look out of place. The garden's decent, though, so try to get a room with a balcony that overlooks it; and the area, though quiet, is pretty central – it's a 10min walk to the metro. Staff aren't that friendly or well trained, and don't speak much English, and the breakfast is not worth bothering with. **¥1600**

Portman Ritz-Carlton 波特曼丽嘉酒店, bōtèmànlìjiā jiǔdiàn 1376 Nanjing Xi Lu ☎62798888, ⓦritzcarlton.com; ⓜNanjing Xi Lu; map pp.70–71. With six hundred rooms on fifty floors and a location bang in the middle of town, this was once the mother ship of Shanghai's business hotels – it is in danger of being superseded by newer, hungrier rivals, however, and there is talk of the government taking the building back. Beyond the underwhelming entrance and the luxurious foyer, rooms are crisply modern with Chinese motifs and wooden sliding-panel doors. There's a health club, two swimming pools, tennis and squash courts and a gym, and the Shanghai Centre expat complex next door has good cafés – including a branch of *Element Fresh* (see p.127) – bars and restaurants. It's a reliable staple if you want to be at the centre of the action and don't need a view. Big discounts are sometimes available online. **¥1785**

★**Puli** 璞丽酒店, púlì jiǔdiàn 1 Changde Lu ☎32039999, ⓦthepuli.com; ⓜJing'an Temple; map pp.70–71. This elegant, attractive hotel is coolly minimal; "designer" without being too gimmicky or hip. The tone is set by the multipurpose 32m-long bar in the lobby, and the chic reception staff. Rooms have wooden floors and grey slate walls and stylish, if rather impractical, sinks. There's a great spa (see p.28) and a sizeable pool, too. The *Puli* has a reputation for smart service, and staff speak good English. Ask for a view of Jing'an Park. **¥2600**

URBN 雅悦酒店, yǎyuè jiǔdiàn 183 Jiaozhou Lu ☎51534600, ⓦurbnhotels.com; ⓜJing'an Temple; map pp.70–71. Though it doesn't quite live up to the hype it has generated, this hip little hotel is still pretty good value for an upmarket place. The low lighting and rough grey brick are leavened with quirky touches, such as a wall made of leather suitcases behind reception, and rooms are elegant with sunken baths, flatscreen TV and a view of the garden. On the downside, the much-trumpeted eco-credentials seem to be little more than a marketing gimmick, and the neighbourhood is rather anonymous, though it's just a 10min walk to the metro. Breakfast, not included in the room rate, is rather pricey – luckily there is a branch of *Wagas* (see p.127) down the road. **¥1600**

PUDONG

Eton 裕景大饭店, yùjǐng dàfàndiàn 69 Dongfang Lu ☎38789888, ⓦtheetonhotel.com; ⓜPudong Dadao; map p.76. Perhaps a little far out in Pudong, but right next to the metro, this luxury Singaporean venue offers a certain style (think corporate boutique chic) and offers lavish facilities – flatscreen TVs in the bathroom, for example – at cheaper rates than its competitors. Ask for a room with a view of the Huangpu. Look out for big discounts online. **¥1820**

Grand Hyatt 上海金茂凯悦大酒店, shànghǎi jīnmào kǎiyuè dàjiǔdiàn Jinmao Tower, 88 Shiji Dadao

---

TOP 5 ROOMS WITH A VIEW
Banyan Tree on the Bund See below
Grand Hyatt See below
Indigo See p.117
JW Marriott See p.117
Park Hyatt See below

10

☎50491234, ⓦshanghai.grand.hyatt.com; ⓜLujiazui; map p.76. Taking up the top floors of the magnificent Jinmao Tower, this is one of the world's highest hotels. Rooms are largely undistinguished but, with their floor-to-ceiling windows, are all about the view, so it's worth paying a little extra (and reserving well in advance) to go as high as you can – if possible, get one overlooking the Bund, preferably on a corner. Spacious bathrooms, all glass and mirrors, are designed so that you can even get your cloud fix from the tub, and they have Japanese heated seat toilets too. Great design, lots of lucky numbers (see p.78) and awesome views – but, it has to be said, the area is hardly interesting. **¥2064**

★**Park Hyatt** 柏悦酒店, bóyuè jiǔdiàn Shanghai World Financial Centre, 100 Shiji Dadao ☎68881234, ⓦshanghai.park.hyatt.com; ⓜLujiazui; map pp.70–71. This ultramodern business hotel, spread across floors 79 to 93 of the Shanghai World Financial Centre, has stolen the "world's highest hotel" crown from its sister establishment, the *Grand Hyatt* in the Jinmao Tower, and just might have the edge for service, too. The surprisingly large, high-ceilinged rooms offer amazing views, of course, while facilities include an infinity pool and a spa, a good afternoon tea (see p.132) – and the world's highest bar (see p.146). **¥3215**

Pudong Shangri-La 浦东香格里拉大酒店, pǔdōng xiānggélǐlā dàjiǔdiàn 33 Fucheng Lu ☎68828888, ⓦshangri-la.com/shanghai; ⓜLujiazui; map p.76. One of Pudong's monster hotels, with almost a thousand rooms, the *Shangri-La* is popular with upscale business travellers for comfort, convenience and, of course, the views through its huge windows. Classy, with discreet Chinese motifs in the decor, it's not overly corporate, which makes up for the time it takes to get across the river. It's worth upgrading for a Bund view. The hotel is also home to two well-regarded restaurants, *Jade on 36* (see p.140) and *Yi Café* (see p.141). **¥3115**

HONGKOU

Banyan Tree on the Bund 外滩悦榕庄酒店, wài tān yuè róng zhuāng jiǔ diàn 19 Gongping Lu ☎25091188, ⓦbanyantree.com/en/cn-china-shanghai-on-the-bund; ⓜTianqiao; map p.83. This luxury hotel is not on the Bund, or even all that near: it's on the river, yes, but a fair distance north of any colonial charm, next to the International Ferry Terminal (which, granted, would have made for a less evocative moniker). No matter: there are great views of Pudong, the grounds are extensive and there is a free shuttle bus to the Bund. Rooms are cosy, with bathtubs by the

10

windows so you can gaze and bathe at the same time. Get a room on as high a floor as you can, and expect to catch a lot of cabs. All in all it's only really worth considering if you get a good deal online. **¥3600**

★**CHAI Shanghai Living** 上海灿客栈, shànghǎi càn kèzhàn 400 Suzhou Bei Lu ☎63561812, ⊛chailiving .com; Ⓜ Tiantong Lu; map p.83. One of the city's more unusual accommodation options, but well worth seeking out. Basically, it's luxury serviced apartments in an Art Deco apartment block that's seen better days. There's no lobby or reception to speak of – you'll be met on arrival and shown around. Your neighbours will be locals who hang their washing and practise *tai ji* in the corridors. The apartments are wonderful, though. Each is thoughtfully and quirkily designed, with wooden floors, underfloor heating and fully equipped kitchens – go for one with a view of Pudong. Obviously there's no gym or business centre, but you do get free wi-fi. It's a little far from the action, just north of Suzhou Creek, though only a few minutes' walk from the metro. You have to book for a minimum of three nights **¥1650**

BUDGET CHAINS

24K Hotel 24K国际连锁酒店, èrshísì kèi guójì liánsuǒ jiǔdiàn 155 Weihai Lu ☎51181222, Ⓜ Nanjing Xi Lu, map p.39; 555 Fuzhou Lu ☎5150358, Ⓜ People's Square, map p.49; ⊛24khotels.com. This business hotel chain has a winning formula: chirpy design, spacious no-frills rooms and cheaper prices than the competition. Most branches are a little too far out to be convenient, but these two are very central, located on busy roads not far from People's Square, and walkable from the metro. It's wise to pay a little extra for a window and a bathroom. You'll have to go out to eat, but if you're just looking for somewhere comfortable to crash, this is one to consider. Little English is spoken. **¥288**

Jinjiang Inn 锦江饭店, jǐnjiāng fàndiàn 33 Fujian Nan Lu ☎65979188, Ⓜ People's Square, map p.49; 293 Yunnan Lu ☎63262200, Ⓜ Dashijie, map p.54; reservations ☎4008209999, ⊛jinjianginns.com. This sober, no-frills budget business-hotel chain has dozens of branches in Shanghai; we've listed the two most central, both of which can be booked from their website (you'll have to register, but you also then get a small discount) or from the reservation hotline. They certainly do the job if all you need is a comfortable, clean room and free wi-fi, and they also offer non-smoking rooms and cable TV. Staff won't speak much English though. **¥422**

Motel 168 莫泰连锁旅店, mòtài liánsuǒ lǔdiàn 531 Jingling Dong Lu, Ⓜ Dashijie, map p.54; 1119 Yan'an Xi Lu, by Fanyu Lu, Ⓜ Jiangsu Lu, map pp.70–71; ⊛motel168.com. There are two dozen or so branches of this functional American-style business hotel all over Shanghai – we've listed the two most convenient locations. Services are basic but the rooms are clean, with bright, breezy decor. Just don't expect much character, or English-language skills from the staff. **¥288**

HOSTELS

THE BUND AND NANJING DONG LU

Blue Mountain Bund Youth Hostel 蓝山外滩国际青年旅舍, lánshān wàitān guójì qīngnián lüshè 6F, 350 Shanxi Lu ☎33661561, ⊛bmhostel.com; Ⓜ Nanjing Dong Lu; map p.39. This hostel is clean, friendly and well located – just south of Suzhou Creek, a 10min walk from the Bund. Note that it occupies the sixth floor of an office building, and the lifts are slow. It can feel a bit crowded, as communal areas are small, and wi-fi is only available in the bar (which kills the atmosphere there). There are four-, six- and eight-bed dorms, all of them same-sex, plus en-suite doubles. Dorms **¥126**, doubles **¥398**

Captain Hostel 船长青年酒店, chuánzhǎng qīngnián jiǔdiàn 37 Fuzhou Lu ☎63235053, ⊛captainhostel.com.cn; Ⓜ Nanjing Dong Lu; map p.40. This well-located hostel, right on the Bund, has a nautical theme – rooms are made up to look like cabins, with portholes for windows, and staff are dressed in sailor suits (though it hasn't made them any jollier). It also has a good bar – the *Captain Bar* (see p.143) – on the sixth floor, with great views of Pudong – though two beers will cost as much as a bed for the night. On the downside, communal areas are a bit grotty, wi-fi is only available in the lobby and the general atmosphere is of a place getting by on its reputation. The double rooms are not good value, so you'd be better off heading elsewhere for those, but the dorms (eight- and ten-bed, same-sex) are cheap – note that the cleaning staff will barge in and get on with it whether you're in bed or not. Bike rental is ¥2/hr (guests only), and there's free use of a washing machine. Dorms **¥100**, doubles **¥950**

Dock Bund Hostel 外滩源青年旅舍, wàitānyuán qīngnián lüshè 55 Xianggang Lu ☎53500077, ⊛bmhostel.com/en/gyls-dock.html; Ⓜ Tiantong Lu; map p.39. This little cheapie is just behind the Bund – you could pretty much throw rocks at the *Peninsula*. There's virtually no lobby, communal areas are small and corridors are shabby, but there's a great deal of variety among the rooms; some are much bigger than others, a few are smelly and those overlooking the street are a bit noisy. Be firm if you don't like where you've been put and they'll move you. Dorms are mixed, with ten beds. Patchy wi-fi means you'll probably encounter the other guests sitting in the corridor with their laptops. Dorms **¥100**, doubles **¥320**

★Mingtown Hikers Hostel 明堂上海旅行者国际青年旅馆, míngtáng shànghǎi Lǚxíngzhě guójì qīngnián lǚguǎn 450 Jiangxi Zhong Lu ☏63297889; ⓜNanjing Dong Lu; map p.39. Very well located just west of the Bund, this cheap and cheerful hostel gets booked up quickly. It's sociable, so can be noisy, and the dark en-suite doubles (¥380) are not a good deal – but all the other options are reasonable for the price. The dorms are same-sex, with four, six or eight beds. Pretty good wi-fi, too. Dorms **¥100**, doubles **¥320**

Mingtown Nanjing Lu 南京路青年旅舍, nánjīng lù qīngnián lǚshè 258 Tianjin Lu, near Shanxi Nan Lu ☏63220939; ⓜNanjing Dong Lu; map p.39. Clean, friendly and very well located, the newest *Mingtown* hostel is another smart addition to their backpacker brand, offering double rooms and eight-bed same-sex dorms in a sympathetically converted apartment building with brass fittings and tiled and wooden floors. Ask for a high floor for quiet and a view, a lower one if you don't fancy trudging up and down the steep stairs. Wi-fi is patchy, but the lobby and bar (where it works) are pleasant, so hanging out there is no hardship. There's a kitchen too, and a pool table. Dorms **¥140**, doubles **¥390**

PEOPLE'S SQUARE

★Mingtown Etour Hostel 上海明堂新易途国际青年旅馆, shànghǎi míngtáng xīnyìtú guójì qīngnián lǚguǎn 55 Jiangyin Lu ☏63277766; ⓜPeople's Square; map p.49. In an old Shanghai building, this is the best of the cheapies, being very well located – tucked in the alleyway behind Tomorrow Square, right beside Renmin Park – yet quiet and surprisingly affordable. A dark corridor opens into a relaxing courtyard featuring a pond with goldfish and a decent bar. Bathrooms are shared between two or three rooms, all of which vary in size – one or two of the doubles have balconies – so ask to see a few before you commit. All dorms are same-sex and have eight beds. There's a self-service laundry and kitchen, and wi-fi throughout. Dorms **¥120**, doubles **¥280**

THE OLD CITY AND AROUND

Blue Mountain Youth Hostel 蓝山国际青年旅舍, lánshān guójì qīngnián lǚshè Bldg 1, 1072 Nong, Quxi Lu ☏63043938, ⦿bmhostel.com; ⓜLuban Lu; map p.54. Though it's a long way from the centre, in the southwest of the city, this hostel is next to the metro station – you'll see the triangular YH sign as soon as you exit. Offering good value in this price range, it's a large and well-run place, deservedly popular with young Chinese backpackers, offering double rooms and eight- and ten-bed same-sex dorms. All rooms are clean, with wooden floors, but ask to see a few, as some don't have windows (and are no cheaper than those that do). There are a few en-suite doubles (¥390), but otherwise all bathrooms are

TOP 5 CHEAPIES

Jinjiang MetroPolo Hotel Classiq Shanghai People's Square See p.118
LeTour Traveler's Rest Youth Hostel See below
Mingtown Etour Hostel See opposite
Mingtown Hikers Hostel See above
Rock and Wood International Hostel See p.124

10

shared. Facilities include good wi-fi coverage, bike rental, a kitchen and a washer-dryer (¥15), as well as the obligatory bar, pool table and skinny cat. Dorms **¥120**, doubles **¥280**

The Phoenix 老陕客栈, lǎoshān kèzhàn 17 Yunnan Nan Lu ☏62886803; ⓜDashijie; map p.54. In a good location close to People's Square and a short walk from Dashijie metro station, this is clearly a converted hotel: it takes more than a little graffiti and resident pets to create an authentic hostel vibe. Well, they are trying, and the staff are decent. The big ten-bed mixed dorms are good value, but the otherwise rather ordinary double rooms have glass-walled bathrooms, so if you don't already know your roommate's most intimate details, you soon will. The rooftop bar is a nice idea but prices are a little steep for its clientele. It tends to be popular with the partying crowd, who like to crash close to the action. Wi-fi is patchy. Dorms **¥140**, doubles **¥550**

JING'AN AND AROUND

City Central Youth Hostel 万里路国际青年旅舍, wànlǐlù guójì qīngnián lǚshè 300 Wuning Lu, near Zhongshan Bei Lu ☏52905577; ⓜCaoyang Lu; map pp.70–71. Despite the name – it's rather far out, in the west of town, though only about 300m north of the metro station – this giant, no-nonsense hostel, painted a striking blue and orange, boasts some of the city's cheapest rooms and dorms (mixed or female-only; eight and ten beds). It's clean, and staff are efficient, but wi-fi is only available in the lobby and you needn't bother with the bar-cum-restaurant. It can be tricky to find: follow the metro line north until you reach the crossroads with Wuning Lu, cross over and on your right you'll see an archway. Walk through it and you'll see the hostel sign. Dorms **¥85**, doubles **¥298**

★ Le Tour Traveler's Rest Youth Hostel 乐途国际青年旅舍, lètú guójì qīngnián lǚshè Lane 36, 319 Jiaozhou Lu ☏62671912, ⦿letourshanghai.com; ⓜJing'an Temple; map pp.70–71. This huge hostel was once a textile factory and though it's been livened up with a lick of green paint, murals and graffiti, the concrete floors in the hallways and ceiling ducts reveal its industrial origins. Though the doubles are comparatively pricey for what you get, the eight- and ten-bed dorms are good value – and the facilities are great. As well as a

10

rooftop bar and bike rental, there's a DVD room, a mini-gym and a ping-pong table, which is perhaps why it's so popular with European school groups. There's no kitchen, though, and wi-fi is only available in the lobby. It's a 10min walk north from Jing'an Temple metro station, and can be hard to find, as it's down a narrow alley just off busy Bai Lan Lu. Look out for the big green building; if you reach Wuding Lu you've gone too far. Dorms ¥120, doubles ¥390

Soho People's Square Youth Hostel 苏州河畔国际青年旅舍, sūzhōu hépàn guójì qīngnián lǔshè 1307 Suzhou Nan Lu ☎58888817; ⓜXinzha Lu; map pp.70–71. A hostel that's big, efficient and, while a little far from the action, just a few minutes' walk from the metro. Rooms vary widely; some are stuffy and others are windowless, and that doesn't seem to be reflected in the price, so ask to see a few before you choose. Like many accommodation options aimed at young Chinese, the decor is pretty chintzy. The segregated six-bed dorms are acceptable. Dorms ¥120, doubles ¥328

XUJIAHUI AND BEYOND

★**Rock and Wood International Hostel** 老木国际青年旅舍, lǎomù guójì qīngnián lüshè Lane 615, 278 Zhaohua Lu ☎33602361, ⓦrockwood .hostel.com; ⓜYan'an Xi Lu; map p.87. One of those places that, being a little far from the centre, tries harder than its competitors. It scores highly for being clean, spacious and attractive, with big, comfortable communal areas – home to a few pets and a lot of potted plants and bamboo. There are six- and eight-bed female-only and mixed dorms, but the best options are the well-designed, good-value doubles. Dorms ¥140, doubles ¥360

LOST HEAVEN THE BUND

Eating

Food is one of the great attractions of China; eating might not be the reason you came, but it will be one thing you remember. And Shanghai can make a convincing claim to be China's culinary hotspot. Upmarket restaurants helmed by starry celebrity chefs are opening every few months – these are great places for splashing out, but what any visitor, on any budget, can really appreciate is the diversity and quality of everyday places to eat. It's all a little more expensive than in the rest of China, but still a bargain – it's not difficult to get a good meal for around ¥80 a head. Note that a lot of the best places are chains, with several locations, many of them inside plazas and malls.

You'll be able to find all of China's many excellent regional **cuisines** (see box, p.128) in Shanghai – Sichuan and Cantonese are perennially popular. Japanese and Korean food are widely available, and Thai and Taiwanese places are also in vogue right now. If you're looking for Western food, you've come to the right Chinese city; a great number of restaurants cater for expats, and all the big internationals are here too.

Finally, remember that **street food** is sadly just no longer worth the risk, certainly if it's fried – the oil is too often dodgy. Try to avoid drinking tap **water**, too, as it's laced with heavy metals.

ESSENTIALS

REVIEWS

For the latest in dining – and bitchy user reviews of over-hyped restaurants – check the following sites:

ⓦ **cityweekend.com.cn/shanghai** A useful, if rather arbitrary, ranking system. Lots of user reviews.

ⓦ **smartshanghai.com** Expat-oriented listings site with reviews that include Chinese addresses and maps.

ⓦ **timeoutshanghai.com** Good in-depth reviews, including Chinese addresses, though they do tend to big up whatever is currently fashionable.

ⓦ **viamichelin** Michelin recently handed out 31 stars to Shanghai restaurants. Their benediction fell mostly on chains, tourist traps and Cantonese fine diners, leaving the city's discerning foodies scratching their heads in bemusement. However, rather more interesting than the capricious star sprinkling is their bib gourmand list of great cheap eats: restaurants where you can get a good dinner for less than ¥200. All the details, including maps, are on the website.

RESTAURANTS

Cost Restaurants are more expensive in Shanghai than elsewhere in the country, although they remain reasonable by international standards; most dishes at Chinese places will cost around ¥60, and many upmarket Western restaurants have meal specials that come to less than ¥90 (¥88 is a popular set-menu price, 8s being lucky). Even the city's plethora of stylish destination restaurants are relatively competitively priced, especially if you go for their lunch deals. Where we've quoted prices/head in the reviews below these will cover a couple of dishes and tea. Tipping is never expected, but some of the swankier places, and most hotel restaurants, add a 15 percent service charge.

Meal times The Chinese like to eat early, sitting down for lunch at noon and dinner at 6pm; you'll find the popular Chinese places packed in the early evening, empty at 9pm and closed by 10pm. On the other hand, anywhere with a bar, or any expat-oriented place, will usually be open much later.

DINING ETIQUETTE

Cold appetizers are served first, main courses arrive a few minutes later, then the meal is finished off with soup and perhaps some fruit. Note that **rice** generally arrives about halfway through the meal, and is eaten to fill you up rather than be mixed with your dishes. If you want it brought earlier, you have to ask for it – say **mǐ fàn**. **Tea** is free at old-fashioned places; if you want your teapot refilled, upend the lid. It's common at **business banquets** to drink **báijiǔ**, the pungent Chinese booze that tastes like lighter fluid, in toasts, during which you are expected to **gān bēi** – swallow it all in one ghastly, throat-searing gulp. You won't get away with saying that you just like a little in moderation, so it might be a good idea on such occasions to pretend that you don't drink at all.

As for **table manners**, well, earthy peasant values are out of fashion, so don't spit on the floor; apart from that, pretty much anything goes. It's impolite to show your teeth, so if you want to use a toothpick, cover your mouth with the other hand. Slurping your soup is normal, and even considered rather polite. You don't have to eat with chopsticks; all restaurants have knives (**dāozi**) and forks (**chāzi**). Tofu dishes are eaten with a spoon.

Service standards can leave something to be desired. The Chinese way of dealing with staff can take some getting used to, as it can seem very forward: diners are expected to wave and shout for attention. If you want the waitress, call **fúwùyuán**, and if you want the bill yell for the **mǎidán**.

In restaurants, Chinese diners don't usually share the **bill**. Instead, they contest for the honour of paying it, with the most respected person winning. If you are dining with Chinese friends or colleagues you should make some effort to stake your claim but, as a visiting guest, you can pretty much guarantee that you won't get to pay a jiao. If it makes you uncomfortable, insist that next time dinner is on you. Equally, if you're the most senior or respected figure – or a guy taking a Chinese girl on a date – be prepared to stump up for everything.

Menus Almost every restaurant has a picture menu, some of them the size of coffee-table books. Only the cheapest places won't have any English.

Smoking Only the fancier restaurants will have a no-smoking section as a matter of course.

CAFÉS AND QUICK BITES

Fast food For fast food, *McDonald's*, *KFC* and their ilk are everywhere like a rash. Malls and shopping centre can be relied on to have a cluster of fast-food restaurants in the basement and a food court on the top floor, or both; recommended malls with both are Raffles City near People's Square, IAPM on Huaihai Lu and the Super Brand in Pudong.

Pastry shops Unlike many other Chinese, the Shanghainese are famous for their sweet tooth, a tradition that dates back to the period of the International Settlement. They are indulged by bakeries and pastry shops across the city; try Nanjing Dong Lu, the deli at the *Westin* (see p.131), *Sunflour* (see p.138), *Baker and Spice* (see p.137), *Farine* (see p.137) or *Pain Chaud* (see p.138).

Cafés Café culture has really taken off in Shanghai, and every mall and shopping street now boasts a *Starbucks* or a *Costa* – a British chain that is spreading fast, with ninety branches in Shanghai already (including a useful one on Nanjing Xi Lu, which is otherwise devoid of cafés). As any tourist itinerary here involves lots of fairly unstructured wandering around, visitors might find themselves spending more time than they thought people-watching over a cappuccino. All cafés have wi-fi unless otherwise noted – note that in some chains (including *Starbucks* and *Costa*) you have to provide a Chinese mobile phone number in order to receive by SMS a wi-fi access code: if you're not toting a phone, you'll have to ask a member of staff to help. You won't have that problem in independent cafés, where a password is all that is required. If you're looking for a pitstop in the afternoon, many of the best restaurants and hotels now serve afternoon tea (see box, p.132).

Breakfast places The typical Chinese breakfast of glutinous rice and fried dough sticks appeals to few foreigners; steamed buns and dumplings are a tastier local alternative (see p.128). Fortunately, there are plenty of places for a good Western breakfast – best are *Wagas* (see below) and *Element Fresh* (see below). If you're clucking for a fresh croissant and a coffee, the bakeries and pastry shops (see above) will serve you well.

DELIVERY

Scooter-borne delivery is popular, especially for busy workers at lunchtimes. Note that *Element Fresh* (see below) and *Sushi'O* (see p.136 & p.139) will deliver for free.

Sherpa's ☎62096209, ⓦ sherpa.com.cn. Sherpa's will deliver from a host of different restaurants around town – you pay more (and wait longer), the further you are from the restaurant. Delivery fees are reasonable, starting at ¥15.

SUPERMARKETS

With so many affordable restaurants around, self-catering is hardly necessary, but if you do want to give the kitchen a workout you'll find it easy to get ingredients. Every neighbourhood has a wet market, but for Western goods you'll have to head to an international supermarket. We've reviewed the major supermarkets in our Shopping chapter (see p.157).

11

CITY-WIDE CHAINS

Element Fresh 新元素, xīnyuánsù 4F, K. Wah Centre, 1028 Huaihai Zhong Lu (Old French Concession) ☎54038865, ⓜ Shaanxi Nan Lu, map pp.60–61; 2 North Block, 181 Taicang Lu (Xintiandi) ☎63260950, ⓜ Xintiandi, map p.63; Shanghai Centre (east side), 1376 Nanjing Xi Lu (Jing'an) ☎62798682, ⓜ Jing'an Temple, map pp.70–71; 2F, Shanghai World Financial Centre, 100 Shiji Dadao (Pudong) ☎68774001, ⓜ Lujiazui, map p.76; ⓦ elementfresh.com. This airy, informal bistro is the best place in town for a Western breakfast, with plenty of options both hearty and healthy – you'll pay ¥80 for breakfast and limitless coffee. It's also well liked for its deli-style sandwiches, smoothies and health drinks. The branch at the World Financial Centre is particularly useful, as affordable options are few and far between in Pudong. The branch in Xintiandi, called Element Fresh *Vintage*, is more upmarket. Free delivery. Old French Concession Mon–Thurs & Sun 8am–11pm, Fri & Sat 8am–midnight; Xintiandi daily 8am–2am; Jing'an daily 7am–11pm; Pudong daily 10am–10pm.

Wagas 沃歌斯, wògēsī 277 Huangpi Bei Lu, near Weihai Lu (People's Square) ☎53752758, ⓜ People's Square, map p.49; 7 Donghu Lu, near Xinle Lu (Old French Concession) ☎54661488, ⓜ Changshu Lu, map p.54; 169 Wujiang Lu (Jing'an) ☎62670339, ⓜ Nanjing Xi Lu, map p.39; 265 Jiaozhou Lu (Jing'an) ☎62720353, ⓜ Jing'an Temple, map pp.70–71; LGF, 11A, CITIC Square, 1168 Nanjing Xi Lu (Jing'an) ☎52925228, ⓜ Jing'an Temple, map pp.70–71; ⓦ wagas.com.cn. This relatively new, bright and breezy New York-style deli brand is everywhere – you're almost bound to eat here at least once. Order the breakfast sandwich before 11am on a weekday and it's half-price – just ¥29. Wraps, sandwiches, pasta dishes and the Thai curry offer good value, too, all at around ¥60. A good range of juices and smoothies are on offer, though these are comparatively pricey at ¥40 or so. Daily 7.30am–10pm.

THE BUND AND NANJING DONG LU

The strip of real estate along the Bund must have the world's densest concentration of **destination restaurants**. All boast great views of the Bund, have been lavishly designed and feature food that's meant to be talked about. They're great for a splurge and not always as pricey as they look. Many offer a comparatively inexpensive afternoon tea (¥150 or so), as do the fancy hotels (see p.132), usually between 2pm and 5pm.

RESTAURANTS

8½ Otto e Mezzo Bombana Rockbund, 169 Yuanmingyuan Lu, near Beijing Dong Lu ☎60872890, ⓦottoemezzobombana.com/shanghai; ⓜNanjing Dong Lu; map p.39. Chef Umberto Bombana has created a menu of Italian cuisine – home-made pastas, raviolis and ragout, all wonderfully done and served in a dining room that's classy without being too grand. Great views of the Pearl Tower from the balcony. It has recently been granted two Michelin stars, so will get busy: you'd better reserve. ¥600/person. Daily 4pm–late.

Chi-Q 2F, Three on the Bund, 3 Zhongshan Dong Yi Lu ☎63216622, ⓦjean-georges.com/restaurants/china/shanghai/chi-q; ⓜNanjing Dong Lu; map p.40. This new restaurant from Jean Georges Vongerichten, offering something a little different, is a big hit with the glitterati. It serves Korean standards, such as chicken wings and scallion pancakes, and each table has its own charcoal barbecue over which diners cook a basket of meat (traditionally beef) or seafood. There are also a few fusion dishes, such as *bibimbap* with wagyu. It's a good-looking venue but will hit the wallet hard; ¥700/person. Daily 6–10.30pm.

★ **El Willy** 5F, 22 Zhongshan Dong Lu, near Xinyong'an Lu, South Bund ☎54045757, ⓦelwillygroup.com; ⓜYuyuan Garden; map p.39. Modern Spanish fine dining, mostly tapas, in a quirkily decorated dining hall with a great view of the river. Recommended dishes include gazpacho, goose-liver pate, suckling pig and prawn paella, and marrowbone with mushrooms. Portions are small considering the prices, but there's a reasonable lunch/brunch deal for ¥198. You'll certainly have to reserve. Mon–Fri 11.30am–2.30pm & 6–11.30pm, Sat & Sun 11.30am–3pm & 6–11.30pm.

EQ 1F, Shen Bao Bldg, 309 Hankou Lu ☎51690815, ⓦeqfoods.com.cn; ⓜNanjing Dong Lu; map p.39. A

CHINA'S REGIONAL CUISINES – AND WHERE TO EAT THEM

The Chinese obsess about food: the Mandarin for "how are you?" – ni chi fan ma – literally translates as "have you eaten yet?" Accordingly, they have created one of the world's great **cuisines**. It's much more complex than you might suspect from its manifestations overseas, with each region boasting its own delicious specialities. All kinds of Chinese food are available somewhere in the city, including of course the city's own distinctive Shanghai cuisine.

SHANGHAI CUISINE

Shanghai cuisine is sweet, light and oily. Much of the cooking involves adding ginger, sugar and sweet rice wine, but spice is used sparingly. Fish and shrimp are considered basics in any respectable meal; eel and crab may appear too. **Fish and seafood** are often lightly cooked (steamed mandarin fish is especially good), or even served raw; "drunken shrimps", for instance, are simply live shrimps drowning in wine. Crawfish is a popular comfort food; the critters are cooked with chilli, served whole, and eaten with the fingers (plastic gloves are usually provided). Between October and December look out for the local speciality, **hairy crabs** (known as mitten crabs in the West), a grey freshwater crustacean that's harvested in its breeding season. Prise the shell off and you'll find delicious white meat inside, and, if it's a female, maybe the highly prized orange roe.

   Meat dishes are well represented too. Sweet and sour spareribs are given a zesty tang by their heavy sauce. One unmissable local treat is "beggars' chicken", in which the whole bird is wrapped in lotus leaves, sealed with clay and oven-cooked. Every meal will feature so-called "cold" dishes, eaten as appetizers at room temperature; try crispy eel or "drunken chicken" (chicken marinated in rice wine).

   The adventurous should try the **thousand-year-old egg** – preserved eggs flavoured with lime and ginger – or the fermented **stinky tofu**, which tastes better than it smells.

   Finally, don't overlook the humble staples. Shanghai-style fried **noodles** are ubiquitous, and make a great quick lunch. They're similar to chow mein, but the noodles are cut much thicker, and usually fried with pork. **Dumplings**, or xiǎolóngbāo, are delicious small buns filled with pork and a gelatinous soup – be careful though, as they're steaming hot inside – and served

fresh, cheerful Scandinavian diner, with healthy pasta and salad dishes, and speciality pulled pork sandwiches from free-range pigs, all priced at less than ¥60. A good range of smoothies, too. A handy place to know about in an area that has a dearth of good, casual places to eat. Daily 9am–9pm.

Je Me Souviens 意难忘, yì nán wàng 5F, 663 Jiujiang Lu ☎61207657; ⓜPeople's Square; map p.39. An odd kind of mash-up this – an attractive Hong Kong-style diner with a French name offering Cantonese and Western food. Signature dishes are Singapore-style ribs and sirloin steak, and they're both pretty good – the food is well presented and agreeably inexpensive at ¥200 a head or so. Decent service, but not much English. Daily 11am–10pm.

Lao Beijing 老北京, lǎobĕijīng 1 Henan Nan Lu ☎63734515; map p.39. This big, chintzy and well-regarded Peking duck restaurant is handy for the Bund. Arrive early, as the place starts winding down at 8pm. It's not expensive at ¥160/duck, which feeds two. Watch your duck being skilfully eviscerated at the table, wrap it up and slather it with bean sauce, and finish with duck soup. Just don't expect to be able to go jogging afterwards. Daily 11am–2.30pm & 5–10pm.

Lao Zhengxing 老振兴餐馆, lǎozhèngxīng cānguǎn 556 Fuzhou Lu ☎6322624, ⓦlaozhengxing-sh.com; ⓜYuyuan Garden; map p.39. This grand old Shanghai restaurant is popular for its light, non-greasy Shanghai cuisine, which they've been serving up since 1862. Gold doors lead to a dining hall glittering with gilt, but there's nothing too over the top about the menu, with most dishes costing around ¥50. The house special is the smoky red sauce that graces most of the seafood dishes, including the famous herring and the pork (¥42). Also consider the eight treasures rice, tofu stew and fried river prawns. A good introduction to local cuisine, and not pricey at around ¥150 a head; arrive early and don't expect great service, or any English. Daily 11am–11pm.

★**Lost Heaven the Bund** 花马天堂, huāmǎ tiāntáng 17 Yan'an Dong Lu, near Sichuan Nan Lu ☎63300967, ⓦlostheaven.com.cn; ⓜNanjing Dong Lu; map p.39. Specializing in the cuisine of Yunnan province, this is an expat favourite. The decor is as exotic as the food, though the lighting is on the dark side – perhaps to make it more conducive to dating couples. This is the biggest, but there are a couple of other branches (see p.136). The chicken with coriander and the lamb ribs are excellent. For pre- or post-dinner cocktails, head to the roof

11

with a sauce made with ginger and vinegar. You should also try **shēngjiānbāo**, a **steamed bun** with a crispy base and topped with chives and sesame.

In addition to the restaurants listed in our "top five" box (see p.137), the little restaurants lining Shanghai's **food streets** and markets are great places to eat Shanghai cuisine with the locals. You won't find many English menus, so just point at whatever your neighbour is having, or whichever critter slithering round the bucket that takes your fancy.

SICHUAN CUISINE

Sichuan, in China's far west, is renowned for its heavy use of **chillis** and lip-tingling **pepper**, though plenty of other flavours, such as orange peel, ginger and spring onions, are used. **Classic dishes** include hot spiced bean curd (**mápó doùfu**), stir-fried chicken with peanuts and chillis (**gōngbǎo jīdīng**) and fish with pickled vegetables (**suān cài yú**). **Good Sichuan restaurants** include *Yuxin Sichuan Dish* (see p.139) or, if you'd rather go easy on the spice, *Pinchuan* (see p.136).

CANTONESE CUISINE

Cantonese cuisine, from China's south, is the one most foreigners are already familiar with, featuring plenty of lightly seasoned fresh fish and vegetable dishes. A meal of *dim sum* (**diǎnxīn** in Mandarin) comprises tiny flavoured buns, dumplings and pancakes and is often eaten in Shanghai as lunch. There's no shortage of **dim sum restaurants** in Shanghai; try chic *Crystal Jade* (see p.133), cheap and cheerful *Bi Feng Tang* (see p.133 & p.141) or upscale *Shen Yue Xuan* (see p.136).

NORTHERN CUISINE

The cuisine of **northern China** is hearty, with steamed buns and noodles as staples. Dishes tend to be heavily seasoned, with liberal use of vinegar and garlic. **Peking duck** is the most famous dish, best sampled at *Lao Beijing* (see p.129). The classic winter warmer, **hotpot**, where diners dip raw ingredients into a heated stock, is the speciality of *Hot Pot King* (see p.134). **Xinjiang cuisine**, from the far northwest, is closely related to Central Asian food, with flatbreads, noodles and lashings of lamb, often grilled; it originates with the Muslim Uighur peoples, and is halal. Give it a go at *Yelixiali* (see p.130).

11

TOP 5 COFFEE STOPS

Barbarossa Central coffee shop with a great view. See opposite.

Café del Volcan Aussie-style coffee cool. See p.137.

Farine Where the classy set get their caffeine hit. See p.137.

Seesaw Quality coffee, roasted in house. See p.139.

Undefine Great coffee in arty surrounds. See p.140.

terrace. About ¥250/person; reservations advised. Daily noon–2pm & 5.30–10.30pm.

M on the Bund 米氏西餐厅, mǐshì xīcāntīng 7F, Five on the Bund, 5 Zhongshan Dong Yi Lu, entrance on Guangdong Lu ☎63509988, ⓦm-restaurantgroup .com/mbund; Ⓜ Nanjing Dong Lu; map p.40. Opened in 1999, *M on the Bund* is famous as the oldest of the Bund's destination restaurants. For years it rather sat on its laurels, but new chef Hamish Pollitt seems to have brightened things up with his mix of European, Australian and North African dishes. Suckling pig and roast lamb (both ¥288) are recommended for dinner, and the set lunch won't break the bank at ¥198/person for two courses. There's a good-value afternoon tea, too (see p.132). Views over the river are superb – reserve, and ask for a table by the window. Daily 11.30am–2.30pm & 6–10.30pm.

Mercato 6F, Three on the Bund, 3 Zhongshan Dong Yi Lu ☎63219922, ⓦthreeonthebund.com; Ⓜ Nanjing Dong Lu; map p.40. Celebrity chef Jean Georges Vongerichten serves up Italian home-style cooking in a comfortable rustic-chic environment. The signature dish is lobster with shrimp ravioli, while the pizzas are the best in the city – try the four cheese and arugula – and quirky delights include a strawberry and ricotta appetizer. The drinks list features plenty of Italian-inspired cocktails and grappas. The food – around ¥500/person – is undeniably great, but some diners find the seating a little too tight. Reserve, and ask for a seat with a view. Mon–Wed 5.30–11pm, Thurs–Sun 5.30pm–1am.

★**Mr and Mrs Bund** 6F, 18 Zhongshan Dong Yi Lu ☎63239898, ⓦmmbund.com; Ⓜ Nanjing Dong Lu; map p.40. Local celebrity chef Paul Pairet creates a wide range of imaginative French dishes with a twist – foie gras crumble, lemon tart served in a lemon and the like. There's a serve-yourself wine bar and a deck with an amazing view, and the ambience is lively and trendy. It's very hip, having made it into the San Pellegrino world's best restaurants list, so you'll have to reserve. A meal will set you back at least ¥600/person, but their late-night deals (Thurs, Fri & Sat 11pm–2am) get you a two-course set menu for ¥250. Mon & Sun 11.30am–2pm & 6–10.30pm, Tues–Thurs 11.30am–2pm & 6pm–2am, Fri & Sat 11.30am–2pm & 6pm–4am.

The Stage, Westin 威斯汀舞台餐厅, wēisītīng wǔtái cāntīng 88 Henan Zhong Lu ☎63350577, ⓦwestinshanghai.com/dining-the-stage-buffet-restaurant; Ⓜ Nanjing Dong Lu; map p.39. Upscale but casual buffet, given a theatrical feel by the open cooking stations where chefs prepare a good range of Western and Asian cuisine. Lunch is ¥258, dinner ¥328 – plus 15 percent service charge for both. It's *the* place for a buffet Sunday brunch – ¥588 (plus service charge) for as much as you can eat and drink, including champagne and caviar. Come hungry and not too hungover, and pig out while watching the acrobat show. Reservations necessary. Daily 6am–midnight; Sun brunch 11.30am–2.30pm.

Wang Baohe 王宝和酒家, wángbǎohé jiǔjiā 603 Fuzhou Lu ☎63223673; Ⓜ Nanjing Dong Lu; map p.39. Billing itself the "king of crabs and ancestor of wine", this local staple has been around for more than two hundred years and these days rests on its laurels somewhat. As its tagline suggests, it's famous for its crab dishes; eight-course crab set meals start at ¥350/person. Otherwise try tofu with crab (¥68), crab dumplings (¥35) and fried noodles with crab and fish (¥88). During hairy crab season (Oct–Dec) you'll have to reserve well in advance. Daily 11am–2pm & 5–9pm.

★**Xin Guang Jiu Jia** 新光酒家, xīn guāng jiǔ jiā 512 Tianjin Lu ☎63223978; Ⓜ Nanjing Dong Lu; map p.39. You would never guess it from the decor but this unassuming little place, in an alley off Nanjing Lu, is where in-the-know locals and Asian foodies go for crab: or at least the lazy ones do. For here they specialize in banquets of prepicked crab meat, so there's none of that fiddly deshelling with surgical implements. There's a minimum charge of ¥400/person: go for the ¥950 set menu for two. Note that they don't open very late, so arrive early, and make sure to reserve in hairy crab season (Oct–Dec). Daily 11am–9pm.

★**Yelixiali** 耶里夏丽新疆餐厅, yēlǐxiàlì xīnjiāng cāntīng 7F, 819 Nanjing Dong Lu ☎63338750; Ⓜ People's Square; map p.39. This is Shanghai's best Xinjiang restaurant, probably its biggest too, and very popular with natives from that region. To find the entrance, head south down Guizhou Lu, off Nanjing Dong Lu, and you'll see a poky corridor on the right, leading into the building – this leads to a shabby elevator that will take you up to the seventh floor and disgorge you into a huge, busy, noisy, Central Asian dining hall. The menu is huge but you can't go wrong with the spicy staples – lamb skewers, "big-plate" chicken, *lamian* noodles – all of which you can wash down with Xinjiang black beer. A meal won't set you back much more than ¥200/person. There's a stage with regular dancing shows, by girls in minority dress – you may get invited to join them for a quick turn (ideally before you've eaten). Daily 11am–late.

CAFÉS

The Press by Inno Coffee Shun Pao Plaza, 309 Hankou Lu ☎51690777; Ⓜ Nanjing Dong Lu; map p.39. This smart venue is worth checking out for the building alone – constructed in 1872, the vast, high-ceilinged space has some lovely plasterwork and huge windows. China's first daily newspaper, *Shen Bao*, was run from here; that's picked up in the modern decor, with quotes and framed newspages on the walls. The food is so-so but it's a great coffee-and-cheesecake pitstop,

which will set you back ¥60 or so. Daily 10.30am–9pm.

Treats Deli Westin hotel, 88 Henan Zhong Lu ☎63351888, ⓦwestinshanghai.com/dining-treats-deli; Ⓜ Nanjing Dong Lu; map p.39. Tucked at the back of the over-the-top *Westin* hotel lobby (see p.117), this good-value deli deserves a mention for being understated (in contrast to the hotel). Tasty cakes, tarts, sandwiches, snacks and coffees are served – treat yourself to a lychee vodka truffle (¥12). Daily 9am–7pm.

PEOPLE'S SQUARE

As well as the venues reviewed here, check out **Yunnan and Huanghe Lu food streets** (see box, p.139). If you're doing the sights and looking for a pitstop, it's good to know about *Barbarossa* (see below) and the food court on the top floor of Raffles City Mall – the mall also has a number of decent small eateries in the basement.

RESTAURANTS

Godly 功德林素食馆, gōngdélín sùshíguǎn 445 Nanjing Xi Lu ☎63270218; Ⓜ People's Square; map p.49. A venerable vegetarian restaurant with temple-themed decor, specializing in fake meat dishes. It's all rather hit and miss, so you need to take care when making your menu selections. Try the meatballs, roast duck, crab and ham, but avoid anything meant to taste like fish or pork, and be wary of ordering a meal consisting only of vegetables – it will probably turn out to be far too oily. The staff could be a little livelier, too. That said, it's undeniably cheap, at around ¥80/head. Daily 11am–2pm & 5–10pm.

CAFÉS

Barbarossa 芭芭露莎, bābālùshā 231 Nanjing Xi Lu, inside Renmin Park ☎63180220; Ⓜ People's Square; map p.49. This mellow, onion-domed Arabian fantasy is beautifully situated by the lotus pond in Renmin Park, and makes a great pitstop for anyone doing the sights in People's Square. There's a bar upstairs; downstairs also functions as a restaurant but we're calling it a café as that's what it does best. Relax over a drink, smoke a hookah and admire the view of the skyscrapers over the treetops – but don't eat here, as the food is overpriced. Note that after 7pm only the park's north gate will be open. Happy hour daily 5–8pm. Daily 11am–late.

THE OLD CITY AND AROUND

The **Yu Yuan** area was traditionally an excellent place for snacks – xiǎolóng bāo dumplings and the like – eaten in unpretentious surroundings, but now that the area is firmly on the Chinese-tourist trail places are beginning to get very busy and a little more expensive. For quick bites, check out the satay, noodle and corn-on-the-cob stands lining the street bordering the western side of **Yuyuan Bazaar**. And for something much more upmarket, head east (it's best to get a cab) to Xintiandi wannabe the **Cool Docks** (see p.57), a set of renovated warehouses filling up with pricey restaurants.

RESTAURANTS

Char 29–31F, Indigo hotel, 585 Zhongshan Dong Er Lu ☎33029995, ⓦwww.char-thebund.com; Ⓜ Yuyuan Garden; map p.54. This upmarket steakhouse atop a hip hotel (see p.117) is given a rustic feel by the dark-wood interior and copper pots on the wall. There are fantastic views over the river and because you're a little south of the main Bund area, it feels less touristy than other Bund fine dining options. Food, mostly steaks and seafood, is well regarded but pricey – 1.2kg of tomahawk beef, which serves two, costs ¥1188; it's put on a heated plate and you're given a selection of knives with which to attack it. The bar area is worth checking out while you're here; until 9pm they offer bottled beer or a glass of wine for ¥50. Daily 6pm till late.

Kebabs on the Grille 克比印度料理, kèbǐ yìndù liàolǐ Cool Docks, 505 Zhongshan Nan Lu, near

Maojiayuan Lu ☎61526567, ⓦkebabsonthegrille.com; Ⓜ Xiaonanmen; map p.54. One of the few places in Shanghai where you can get a good curry, and the view of the Cool Docks plaza is a bonus. Try the Kashmiri chicken and garlic *naan* and leave room for the eponymous meaty skewers. The all-you-can-eat Sunday brunch is ¥150. It's the least busy of all the restaurants around here, which says nothing about the food: the Chinese, on the whole, just aren't keen on the cuisine. Daily 11am–10.30pm.

Lu Bo Lang 绿波廊, lǜbōláng 115–131 Yuyuan Lu, just south of the Huxing Ting Teahouse ☎63280602; Ⓜ Yuyuan Garden; map p.54. Tourist-friendly venue, tricked out with chinoiserie and with decent, if pricey, *dim sum* and Shanghai dishes such as crab and cabbage; a meal will cost about ¥120 a head. Daily 11am–2pm & 5–8.30pm

Nan Xiang 南翔馒头店, nánxiáng mántóudiàn 85 Yuyuan Lu ☎63554206; Ⓜ Yuyuan Garden; map p.54. A

AFTERNOON TEA

Many of Shanghai's fanciest hotels and restaurants offer **afternoon tea**, a good way to sample luxurious locations without breaking the bank. It's particularly worth trying on the Bund, where the venues are glorious (and the only alternative pitstops in the area are the coffee chains). The following are all good options:

Andaz Xintiandi See p.118. This upscale hotel has a pleasingly affordable tea tag, at ¥193/person, which gets you a good mix of treats including tasty scones and quiches. You can take it in the lounge or, weather permitting, on the terrace. Daily 2.30–5.30pm.

elElefante See p.134. Photos of this whimsical, cute-as-a-button afternoon tea, which comes served on a mini-picnic table, will win you instant social-media chic. Savouries includes miniature brioche and panini, and there's a big array of colourful sweets, including churros, tiny trifles and "carrots" made of chocolate. ¥258 for two people. Tues–Sun 3–5pm.

Fairmont Peace Hotel See p.116. Head to the *Jasmine Lounge*, on the ground floor, for a fairly traditional afternoon tea of sandwiches, cakes, scones and the like, with a choice of English, Chinese or fruit tea, all beautifully presented on a tiered tray. ¥268/person (plus 15 percent service charge). Daily 2–6pm.

The Langham Xintiandi 天地朗廷酒店, tiān dì lǎng tíng jiǔ diàn 99 Madang Lu ☎23302288, ⓦlanghamhotels/shanghai; ⓜXintiandi; map p.63. A lavish meal including sandwiches, tarts and scones, all served on Wedgwood china, in an elegant hotel lobby. ¥368/person. Daily 2.30–5pm.

M on the Bund See p.40. Afternoon tea on the terrace at this destination restaurant is one of the great Bund bargains at just ¥150/head. Sat & Sun 3–5pm.

Park Hyatt See p.76. Ring and book a window seat – you'll be on the 87th floor with fantastic views. A good mix of sweets and savouries. ¥340/person. Daily 2–6pm.

Peninsula See p.40. Beautifully presented goodies in the city's most luxurious lobby, with live violin and cello accompaniment. ¥345/person. Daily 2–6pm.

Waldorf Astoria See p.40. Tasty eats include the signature red velvet cupcake. ¥388/person. Mon–Fri 2–6pm, Sat & Sun 1.30–6.30pm.

famous dumpling place that's on the "must-do" list for Chinese tourists, meaning that sometimes it's just too busy to bother with. The ground floor is for proles; the higher you go, the fancier the decor becomes, and the pricier the dumplings – though the staff don't get any less surly. Most customers are here for takeaway – eat in and there's a minimum spend of ¥60/person, which will get you a decent selection of dumplings, whichever floor you pick. Daily 7.30am–9pm.

Quanjude 全聚德烤鸭店, quánjùdé kǎoyādiàn 4F, 786 Huaihai Zhong Lu ☎54045799, ⓦquanjude.com.cn; ⓜDashijie; map p.54. Part of the Peking duck restaurant chain, with a whole duck (which will feed two) going for ¥160. Service is slow, so be prepared for a wait. Watch the bird carved at your table, then smear it with sauce and wrap it in a pancake, and finish with duck soup. You can even have a side order of duck tongues. It's rich and fatty, so not for weightwatchers, or as a start to a night out. Daily 11am–11pm.

Shanghai Chic 上海会馆, shànghǎi huìguǎn 5F, Metropolis Mall, 489 Henan Nan Lu, near Fuxing Dong Lu ☎63357779; ⓜYuyuan Garden; map p.54. This is a good new Shanghainese restaurant; OK, it's in a mall a little far from anywhere interesting, but it's worth the trip if you're looking for upscale, unpretentious local food. Ignore the pricey exotica on the huge menu – sea cucumber, ostrich and the like – and stick with staples such as mandarin fish, dumplings and *hongshaorou*. About ¥250/head. Daily 11am–9.30pm.

Shanghai Ren Jia 上海人家, shànghǎi rénjiā 141 Yunnan Nan Lu ☎63513060; ⓜDashijie; map p.54. Huge, bustling chain restaurant with a cheap and cheery atmosphere and interesting twists on standard Shanghainese cuisine. It's best to come in a large group so you can order and share multiple dishes. Roasted pig's trotter (¥58) is the house speciality, and they also serve "drunken shrimp"; the critters come to the table live and soaked in booze – you pull off their heads and eat them while they twitch. Daily 11am–2pm & 5–9pm.

★**Table Number One** Waterhouse hotel, Cool Docks, 1–3 Maojiayuan Lu, near Zhongshan Nan Lu ☎60802918, ⓦtableno-1.com; ⓜXiaonanmen; map p.54. Fine dining in a casual atmosphere from London chef Jason Atherton. The dining hall is simple to the point of being plain, but the food is lavishly presented on breadboards, in pots and the like. There are lots of small, tapas-like seafood dishes designed to share; the white crab with avocado sorbet (¥58) is especially good, while the suckling pork with apricot mustard is a solid main (¥258). Expect to pay about ¥400/person, which is good value: comparable Bund restaurants cost a lot more. Daily noon–10.30pm.

★**Xiao Shaoxing** 小绍兴饭店, xiǎoshàoxīng fàndiàn 118 Yunnan Nan Lu (east side), immediately north of Jinling Zhong Lu ☎68662270; ⓜDashijie; map p.54. Old-fashioned Chinese-style dining – bright and noisy, with big tables; the waitresses expect you to shout for their attention – that may not be suitable for a date but is fun for a group. It's famous in Shanghai for its "drunken chicken" (the meat is steeped in rice wine), which costs ¥80; other dishes are much cheaper. Adventurous diners might wish to sample the blood soup or chicken feet. Daily 11am–2pm & 5–8.30pm.

THE OLD FRENCH CONCESSION

The Old French Concession is where most **expatriates** eat and correspondingly where prices begin to approach international levels. Menus are in **English**, and English will likely be spoken, too. In **Xintiandi**, an olde-worlde complex of upscale bars, restaurants and cafés (see p.63), you're spoilt for choice but you won't see much change from ¥200. Note that this area is poorly served by public transport (you're generally at least a 10min walk from the nearest metro station) so you may want to take a cab.

RESTAURANTS

1221 1221餐馆, yī èr èr yī cānguǎn 1221 Yan'an Xi Lu, near Pan Yu Lu ☎62136585; Ⓜ Yan'an Xi Lu; map pp.60–61. It's a little out of the way, a 10min walk east of the metro, but this is a pretty decent, foreigner-friendly Shanghainese restaurant. Decor is modern and minimalist so don't expect an evocation of Old Shanghai in anything but the food. The drunken chicken and *xiang su ya* (fragrant crispy duck) are good, as are the onion cakes. It's a good choice for vegetarians too. About ¥120/person. Reserve. Daily 11.30am–11pm.

Bi Feng Tang 避风塘, bìfēngtáng 175 Changle Lu ☎64670628, Ⓦ bifengtang.com.cn; Ⓜ Changshu Lu; map pp.60–61. This chirpy Cantonese chain selling cheap and filling *dim sum* and a few Sichuan dishes comes into its own late at night; it's a popular place to fill up after an evening out. End your meal with the custard tarts. There's another branch in Hongkou (see p.141). Mon–Fri 10am–5am, Sat & Sun 8am–5am.

Charmant 小城故事, xiǎochéng gùshì 1414 Huaihai Zhong Lu ☎64318107; Ⓜ Changshu Lu; map pp.60–61. A good place to know about – convenient and cheap, *Charmant* functions as much as a café as a restaurant, and is open until the early hours, making it a handy last spot after a night on the tiles. Slip into a window booth and linger over a peanut smoothie, which is nicer than it sounds, or a hot chocolate. For meals (around ¥80/ head), the Taiwanese-style pork or tofu and the cold chicken noodles are recommended. Daily 11.30am–2am.

Cheng Cheng's Art Salon 屋里香私房菜, wūlǐxiāng sīfángcài 164 Nanchang Lu, near Sinan Lu ☎53065462; Ⓜ Changshu Lu; map pp.60–61. If you're bored with trendy minimalism, try this place, occupying a renovated colonial building quirkily decorated with all manner of paintings and bric-a-brac. It serves Shanghai home-style cooking, not too oily, and is pretty reasonably priced: try the chicken with shallots (¥30) or asparagus with crab (¥88). Daily 11.30am–2pm & 5–10pm.

Chun 春, chūn 124 Jinxian Lu, near Maoming Lu ☎62560301; Ⓜ Shaanxi Nan Lu; map pp.60–61. This is like having dinner in someone's front room: there's no sign outside, only four tables and no menu – you just turn up and eat whatever the robust lady boss puts in front of you.

Needless to say, the Shanghai dishes on offer are excellent and, don't worry, it's all very cheap – a meal for two will cost less than ¥100. You'll certainly have to reserve, and there's no English spoken, so get a Chinese-speaker to do it for you. Daily 6–9pm.

City Shop Seafood Bar City Shop, IAPM Mall, 999 Huaihai Zhong Lu ☎51758208; Ⓜ Shaanxi Nan Lu; map pp.60–61. This recommendation is a little left field: it is literally a counter in an upscale supermarket (see p.157), next to the fish section, and thus scores zero for ambience. But is actually a great cheap way to sample fresh seafood, plucked from the display and cooked in front of you – most people go for the tasting selection – prawns, oyster and half a lobster for ¥180. Daily 10am–6.30pm.

Coconut Paradise 椰香天堂, yē xiāng tiān táng Ferguson Lane, 378 Wukang Lu, near Tai'an Lu ☎54245886; Ⓦ lostheaven.com.cn; Ⓜ Shanghai Library; map pp.60–61. This softly lit Thai restaurant, which comes under the umbrella of the *Lost Heaven* chain (see p.129, p.136 & p.138), has a lavish interior, this time with a Southeast Asian theme – lots of trinkets and statues. All the Thai standards are on the menu, at affordable prices, though purists might find the dishes a little light on the spices. A good place for a date. Daily 11.30am–2pm & 5.30pm–10.30pm.

★**Crystal Jade** 翡翠酒家, fěicuì jiǔjiā Unit 12A–B, 2F, Bldg 7, South Block, Xintiandi ☎63858752, Ⓜ Xintiandi; map p.63. Good Cantonese food, sophisticated looks and down-to-earth prices (around ¥120/head) make this *the* place to eat in the area, and one of the best in town for *dim sum* and xiǎolóng bāo (it made Michelin's bib gourmand list). Even being tucked away at the back of the upper floor of a shopping centre doesn't dent its popularity – you'd be wise to reserve. Try the barbecued pork and leave room for mango pudding. Solitary diners are made to feel comfortable at the long central table. There's another branch in Jing'an (see p.138). Daily 11am–3pm & 5–11.30pm.

Cuivre 1502 Huaihai Zhong Lu ☎64374219, Ⓦ cuivre .cn; Ⓜ Changshu Lu; map pp.60–61. This glamorous, Michelin-starred French restaurant would be a great place for a date, as it's hip – menus are on iPads and the bar stools are made of bicycles – but not pretentious. The food

11

is decent, portions are generous and there's a good wine list (water is pricey, though). Try the port-marinated foie gras as a starter, then follow with the beef tenderloin. Around ¥350/person. Their Sunday brunch deal is popular (three courses for ¥198); try the French toast and poached egg. Reservations recommended. Wed–Fri 6–10.30pm, Sat & Sun noon–2pm & 6–10.30pm.

★**Din Tai Fung** 鼎泰丰, dīngtàifēng 3F, IAPM Mall, 999 Huaihai Zhong Lu (Old French Concession) ☎54668191, Ⓜ Shaanxi Nan Lu, map pp.60–61; 11A, 2F, Bldg 6, South Block, 123 Xingye Lu (Xintiandi) ☎63858378, Ⓜ Xintiandi, map p.63; Ⓦ dintaifung .com.tw. The winning formula at this Taiwanese chain (which also has branches in Jing'an and Pudong) is to offer Shanghai street food in upscale surroundings, with chefs cooking behind a glass wall. Its pork dumplings (xiǎolóng bāo) are excellent, but don't neglect the other varieties, particularly shrimp and crab roe. Eating here is a lot more expensive than eating in the street, of course, at around ¥100/person. Both daily 11am–3pm & 5–11pm.

★**elEfante** 20 Donghu Lu, near Huaihai Lu ☎54048085, Ⓦ el-efante.com; Ⓜ Changshu Lu; map pp.60–61. Chef Willy Trullas cooks up Mediterranean food in this stylish and upmarket venue that has elephants everywhere. Crab salad (¥98) and pork belly (¥78) are recommended, but you can't really go wrong choosing from the extensive tapas and seafood menu – or perhaps try the afternoon tea (see p.132). When it's sunny out, ask for a table on the patio. There's also a deli selling imported Spanish food. ¥400/person. Tues–Sun 11am–3pm & 6–10.30pm.

★**Fu 1039** 福一零三九, fú yīlíngsānjiǔ 1039 Yuyuan Lu ☎52371878; Ⓜ Jiangsu Lu; map pp.60–61. Located in a restored mansion, this place looks like it's going to be fearsomely expensive but isn't (you'll spend about ¥300/ head). It clearly doesn't feel the need to brag – you can't see it from the street and there's not even a sign; to find it, head up the lane at 1039 Yuyuan Lu (close to the metro station) for about 100m, then turn left. The cuisine is sweet and mild Shanghainese, with dishes such as steamed carp drizzled with Shaoxing wine and sautéed chicken with mango. Not much English is spoken, but there's a picture menu. Reservations are essential. There are two other *Fu* restaurants nearby – *Fu 1088* and *Fu 1015* – but they are much pricier, aimed at banqueting businessmen, and less good. Daily 11am–2pm & 5–11pm.

★**Grandma's Home** 外婆家, wài pó jiā Level LG1, IAPM Mall, 999 Huaihai Zhong Lu ☎87002008; Ⓜ Shaanxi Nan Lu; map pp.60–61. This chirpy, buzzy restaurant is a little cramped, with diners sharing long communal tables, but the Hangzhou food is cheap and delicious and service is speedy. You're handed a menu-sheet and a pencil and told to tick what you want – you can't go wrong by sticking with the marked house specials,

such as the excellent "grandma's chicken" – the whole bird, cooked in a broth, which arrives in the pot. Pair it with cauliflower and Ninghai-style potatoes. There's a no-reservation policy, so arrive early or expect to wait. Daily 10am–9.30pm.

Grape 葡萄园, pútáo yuán 55A Xinle Lu, near Xiangyang Bei Lu ☎54040486; Ⓜ Changshu Lu; map pp.60–61. Unchallenging decor and some English-speaking staff make this long-running Shanghainese place popular with expats, but it's good enough to draw the local crowd too. Try the lamb with leek or duck pancakes and make room for a few of their savoury cold dishes, or take the opportunity to give bullfrog and eel a go. Reasonably priced, at ¥100 a head, and well located for postprandial window-shopping. Daily 11am–midnight.

Guyi Hunan 古意湘味浓, gǔyì xiāngwèinóng 89 Fumin Lu, near Julu Lu ☎62495628, Ⓜ Changshu Lu; 5F, IAPM Mall, 999 Huaihai Zhong Lu ☎54668537, Ⓜ Shaanxi Nan Lu; both map pp.60–61. This popular institution is the best in the city to sample Hunan cuisine – known for being hot and spicy and for its liberal use of garlic, shallots and smoked meat. Reserve in advance and bring a few people to sample a good range of dishes. Go for the chilli-sprinkled spareribs, fish with beans and scallions, or tangerine-peel beef, which tastes better than you might expect. The chef's speciality, open face fish, is as tasty as it is ugly. About ¥140/head. No reservations after 6.30pm, so expect to wait. Both daily 11am–2pm & 5.30–10.30pm.

Hot Pot King 来福楼, láifú lóu 2F, 146 Huaihai Zhong Lu, near Fuxing Xi Lu ☎64736380; Ⓜ Changshu Lu; map pp.60–61. An accessible, friendly place to sample the local favourite, hotpot, with English menus, understanding staff and tasteful decor. Order lamb, glass noodles, mushrooms and tofu, and chuck them into the simmering pot in the middle of the table. Perfect for winter evenings, or to fill up after the bars – it's open very late, and much healthier than a kebab. ¥90/person. Daily 11am–4am.

Hunter Gatherer 106 Anfu Lu ☎54610552, Ⓦ behuntergatherer.com; Ⓜ Changshu Lu; map pp.60–61. Head through the attached shop and climb upstairs to this clean and crisp, Scandi-style health-food canteen, where most of the produce is from their own farms. Pick a base, protein, veg and garnish from the tubs (which sit there all day, so you're better off eating an early lunch than a late dinner). It functions well as a café too, with a good selection of drinks; try the coconut cold-brew latte (¥42). There's another useful branch in Jing'an (see p.138). Daily 10am–10pm.

Jian Guo 328 建国328小馆, jiànguó sān èr bā xiǎoguǎn 328 Jianguo Xi Lu ☎64713819; Ⓜ Jiashan Lu; map pp.60–61. This cramped neighbourhood restaurant is a great place to eat Shanghainese food. It's relaxed and inexpensive, there's no smoking and the

11

Taiwanese owner is attentive – they don't use MSG, either, and the food isn't too oily. The long menu features all the local classics – among the choice dishes are yellow croakers with scallions (¥58) and deep-fried duck leg (¥38). Eating here shouldn't cost more than ¥100/person, but you'll probably have to reserve and not much English is spoken. Daily 11am–9.30pm.

Kabb 凯博西餐厅, kǎibó xīcāntīng LG1, IAPM Mall, 999 Huaihai Zhong Lu (Old French Concession) ☎64483039, Ⓜ Shaanxi Nan Lu, map pp.60–61; 181 Taicang Lu, 5 Xintiandi Bei Lu (Xintiandi) ☎33070798, Ⓦ Xintiandi; map p.63; Ⓦ kabbsh.com. Relaxed and casual American-style bar and grill. Wraps, nachos, steaks, burgers and the like are huge, and it's especially good value at breakfast and lunchtime. About ¥150/person. Mon–Fri 11am–midnight, Sat & Sun 9.30am–midnight.

Lost Heaven 花马天堂云南餐厅, huāmǎtiāntáng yúnnán cāntīng 38 Gaoyou Lu ☎64335126, Ⓦ lostheaven.com.cn; Ⓜ Changshu Lu; map pp.60–61. This fashionable venue, one of a small chain (see p.129, p.136 & p.138), serves food from China's southwest, a cuisine that has Southeast Asian notes – try the stir-fried beef, goat's cheese and scallion chicken. With candlelit tables, dark-wood floors and stone-mask decorations, the ambience is wonderfully atmospheric, if a little dark. ¥250/head. Daily 11.30am–1.30pm & 5.30–10.30pm.

Lost Heaven Silk Road 花马天堂丝绸之路, huāmǎ tiāntáng sīchóuzhīlù 758 Julu Lu ☎62669816, Ⓦ lostheaven.com.cn; Ⓜ Changshu Lu; map pp.60–61. The new dining room here is painted to resemble the magnificent Buddhist caves at Dunhuang, a Silk Road stopping point: it's somewhat kitsch but you have to admire the effort. The food follows the theme too, with dishes from northwest China, India and Pakistan; think mutton skewers, *naan* bread and lots of lamb. The kitchen isn't quite up to the standards of the other *Lost Heavens* (see p.129 & above), though. Daily 5–10pm.

Molokai 摩罗街, móluó jiē 3F, Bldg 6, Xintiandi South Plaza, 123 Xingye Lu ☎53210881; Ⓜ Xintiandi; map p.63. Clean and smart Hong Kong-style diner that looks pricier than it is. The menu is erratically international, but for the best that the place has to offer, stick with Cantonese dishes such as shrimp wontons (¥28) and scrambled egg with shrimp (¥52). Finish with a chocolate brownie (¥38). Daily 11am–11pm.

Pinchuan 品川, pǐnchuān 47 Taojiang Lu ☎64379361; Ⓜ Shanghai Library; map pp.60–61. Sichuan cuisine, decent service, comfortable, upscale surroundings and reasonable prices (¥120 or so a head) make this an expat favourite. The spice quotient is tame for purists but will suit those who want a gentle introduction to the fiery cuisine. Try the mápó dòufu and "saliva chicken" (kǒu shuǐ jī). Daily 11am–2pm & 5–10pm.

Shen Yue Xuan 申粤轩, shēnyuè xuān 849 Huashan Lu ☎62511166; Ⓜ Shanghai Library; map pp.60–61. The best Cantonese place in Shanghai, situated in an old mansion and serving scrumptious *dim sum* at lunchtime; try the shrimp dumplings and thousand-year egg congee. In warmer weather you can dine alfresco in the garden, a rarity for a Cantonese restaurant. About ¥120 a head. Daily 11am–11pm.

Shintori Null 2 新都里无二店, xīndūlǐ wúèrdiàn 803 Julu Lu ☎54045252; Ⓜ Changshu Lu; map pp.60–61. This nouvelle Japanese trendsetter is easy to miss first time: push open an unmarked door, then head down the bamboo-lined path. First sight of the venue, with its clamorous open kitchens and industrial chic decor, is startling, but so are the prices; take someone you want to impress and be prepared to spend around ¥700/person (that's also the price of the tasting menu). Entertaining presentation will give you something to talk about, though you'd better order a lot or you'll be complaining about the small portions. Finish with green tea tiramisu. Mon–Fri 5.30–10.30pm, Sat & Sun 11.30am–10.30pm.

Simply Thai 天泰餐厅, tiāntài cāntīng 5-C Dongping Lu ☎64459551, Ⓦ simplythai.com.cn; Ⓜ Shanghai Library; map pp.60–61. A decent Thai joint, with an eclectic range of reasonably priced dishes (less than ¥100) and a smart but informal setting with a leafy courtyard. Try the stir-fried asparagus and fish cakes. There's another branch in Xintiandi, but that's not nearly as good. Daily 11am–11pm.

Sushi'O 21–23 Yongkang Lu ☎15000820420, Ⓦ sushi-o.cn; Ⓜ Shaanxi Nan Lu; map pp.60–61. California-style sushi served in a casual, bistro-style dining room; affordable and popular, if not completely authentic. It might be a bit less busy when you read this, as the party-pooping Party has just closed all the bars around it. A selection platter costs ¥160, and that might do it for two; the set lunch is ¥50. Free delivery available. There's a second, larger branch in Jing'an (see p.139). Daily 11am–11pm.

Xibo 锡伯新疆餐厅, xībó xīnjiāng cāntīng 3F, 83 Changshu Lu, near Julu Lu ☎54038330, Ⓦ xiboshanghai .com; Ⓜ Changshu Lu; map pp.60–61. Xinjiang cuisine, from China's far northwest, has always been popular in Shanghai but usually the speciality restaurants are loud and gaudy. This cosy venue is a winner for its understated, classy decor and for its well-presented dishes from Xinjiang's Xibo minority people. The flavours are spicy and Central Asian. "Big plate" chicken – a huge spicy stew to share – is a favourite, and make sure you order some lamb skewers on the side. Roasted aubergine with peppers is the best of the vegetable dishes. Pleasingly affordable at around ¥170 a head. Daily 11am–midnight.

★**Xinjishi (Jesse Restaurant)** 新吉士餐厅, xīnjíshì cāntīng 41 Tianping Lu, near Huaihai Xi Lu

ⓣ62829260, ⓜShanghai Library; 28 Taojiang Lu, near Wulumuqi Lu ⓣ64450068, ⓜChangshu Lu; L302, 3F, IAPM Mall, 999 Huaihai Zhong Lu ⓣ64229091, ⓜShaanxi Nan Lu; all map pp.60–61. The decor at the original Tianping Lu branch is a bit tatty but there's nothing wrong with the tasty and reasonably priced home-style cooking (most dishes are around ¥70). Dishes hail from around the country, but it's best to go for the soy-braised pork, pickled aubergine, crab-flavoured tofu and other local favourites. It's always packed, so reserve. It's spawned a chain, but the newer branches listed here – and the one in Pudong (see p.140) – aren't quite as good, though they certainly look flashier. All daily 11am–4pm & 5.30pm–midnight.

Ye Shanghai 夜上海, yè shànghǎi House 6, North Block, 338 Huangpi Nan Lu, Xintiandi ⓣ63112323, ⓦelite-concepts.com/yes; ⓜXintiandi; map p.63. Shanghai cuisine in an understated take on colonial chic. Tucked away down an alley, it's actually one of the best Xintiandi places, with a very good three-course lunch deal (¥88). Otherwise, go for drunken chicken, prawns with chilli sauce or one of the many crab dishes as a good introduction to local flavours. Around ¥200/person. Daily 11.30am–2.30pm & 6.30–10pm.

CAFÉS

Baker and Spice 195 Anfu Lu, near Wulumuqi Lu ⓣ54042733, ⓦbakerandspice.com.cn; ⓜShanghai Library; map pp.60–61. An attractive artisanal bakery from the people behind *Wagas* (see p.127). The quiches, pastries and breads are excellent, the carrot cake is the city's best, and they make a mean espresso. There's not much seating – just one big table – though that doesn't stop some customers from lingering half the day. Daily 7am–8.30pm.

Café del Volcan 80 Yongkang Lu ⓣ15618669291, ⓦcafevolcan.com; ⓜShaanxi Nan Lu; map pp.60–61. This tiny Australian-owned boutique makes great coffee, and though it isn't cheap at ¥36 for a latte, there's always a queue. All beans are roasted on the premises, and baristas are keen to chat about what makes their brew special. No wi-fi. Mon–Fri 8am–8pm, Sat & Sun 10am–6pm.

CH2 威斯忌, wēisījì 1250 Huaihai Zhong Lu ⓣ54047770; ⓜChangshu Lu; map pp.60–61. Minimalist decor and a cheese- and chocolate-themed menu. They do meals, but they're so-so – come for the speciality hot chocolate or one of the many varieties of cheesecake. Shame there's a minimum spend (¥40), a maximum time (2hr) and spotty service. Tues–Sun 10.30am–11.30pm.

★**Citizen Bar and Café** 天台餐厅, tiāntái cāntīng 222 Jinxian Lu ⓣ62581620, ⓦcitizenshanghai.com; ⓜShaanxi Nan Lu, map pp.60–61. A great Continental-style café tucked away in an elegantly gentrified neighbourhood. It's very popular with French expats – perhaps because of the good coffee, or the limitless potential for people-watching from the balcony. Food is a bit pricey, but there's a wide choice of bar snacks and it's a very civilized venue for a pre-dinner martini or a slice of apple pie. Daily 11am–1am.

★**Farine** Ferguson Lane, 378 Wukang Lu ⓣ64335798, ⓦfarine-bakery.com; ⓜShanghai Library; map pp.60–61. Artisanal bread and pastries, all baked on the premises. Excellent coffee too (though pricey at ¥38), and the outside seating is good for watching the smart set swagger by. Daily 7am–10pm.

Kommune 公社酒吧, gōngshè jiǔbā Bldg 7, Lane 210, Taikang Lu ⓣ64662416, ⓦkommune.me; ⓜDapuqiao; map pp.60–61. Hip café located at the heart of Tianzifang – head north up the easternmost of the north–south alleys, take the first left and it's just there. It's not cheap – nothing round here is – but it's perennially popular thanks to the courtyard seating. Deli sandwiches from ¥38, smoothies from ¥48. Daily 9am–midnight.

Le Café des Stagiaires 54–56 Yongkang Lu, near Xiangyang Lu ⓣ34250210, ⓦcafedesstagiaires.com; ⓜShaanxi Nan Lu; map pp.60–61. This artsy café and bar on buzzing Yongkang Lu has plenty of panache. It's attractively decorated with European memorabilia, and the loos are papered with CVs – the name is French for "intern". As well as coffee, there's a good wine list and simple French food and pizza on offer. At night it's one of the most popular places in the area for a drink, and looks likely to survive the Yongkang bar cull. Daily 9am–1am.

11

TOP 5 SHANGHAI CUISINE

Jian Guo 328 An intimate neighbourhood venue with a warm atmosphere. Stick with the fish dishes. See p.134.

Shanghai Ren Jia The Chinese like their restaurants rènào (hot and noisy), and this is a good example. Try the drunken shrimps – if you're brave enough. See p.132.

Wang Baohe Popular place for a crab banquet. See p.130.

Xiao Shaoxing Where locals get their drunken chicken. See p.132.

Xinjishi (Jesse Restaurant) Where the stylish set go for down-to-earth home-style cooking. See opposite & p.140.

Old China Hand Reading Room 汉源书屋, hànyuán shūwū 27 Shaoxing Lu, near Shanxi Nan Lu ☎ 64732526, ⓦ han-yuan.com; ⓜ Dapuqiao; map pp.60–61. Bookish but not fusty, this café owned by local photographer Deke Erh is the place to come for leisurely reflection. There's a huge collection of tomes to peruse or buy, many printed by the café press, which specializes in coffee-table books about French Concession architecture. Period furniture, big picture windows and – what's that eerie quality? Oh, silence. Afternoon coffee with a scoop of ice cream and biscuits is ¥45. No meals. Daily 10am–midnight.

★**Pain Chaud** 34 Yongkang Lu ☎ 34250210; ⓜ Shaanxi Nan Lu; map pp.60–61. Freshly baked breads and pastries at this smart, French-style upmarket bakery, which also does tasty sandwiches (¥60) in crusty bread and excellent baguettes. It's not cheap, but the ¥30 deal for coffee and a croissant makes it a good bet for breakfast if you're staying nearby. Daily 8am–10pm.

Pantry 205 Wulumuqi Nan Lu ☎ 13818719543; ⓜ Hengshan Lu; map pp.60–61. This co-op sells excellent baked goods, preserves and biscuits, and it's one of the few places you can get a good bagel. They do small set meals for breakfast, lunch and afternoon tea. Daily 8am–6pm.

Pier 39 39号码头, sānshíjiǔhào mǎtóu 172 Jinxian Lu ☎ 62581939; ⓜ Shaanxi Nan Lu; map pp.60–61. Bright and breezy little California-style café, popular with expats for its big salads and clam chowder,

which comes inside a sourdough loaf (¥58). Free delivery. Daily 11am–10pm.

Sunflour 阳光粮品 yángguāng liángpǐn 322 Anfu Lu ☎ 64737757, ⓦ sunflour.com.cn; ⓜ Changshu Lu; map pp.60–61. Popular, if pricey, bakery and café selling breads, pastries and sandwiches to take away or eat in. Decent breakfasts too, including a good full English (¥42). Daily 7am–10.30pm.

Urban Tribe 城市山民, chéngshì shānmín 133 Fuxing Xi Lu ☎ 64335366, ⓦ urbantribe.cn; ⓜ Shanghai Library; map pp.60–61. This is really a boutique selling ethnic knick-knacks, but there's a nice bamboo garden at the back with coffee served in cute handmade cups (¥25). Daily 9.30am–10pm.

Vienna Café 维也纳咖啡馆, wéiyěnà kāfēiguǎn 25 Shaoxing Lu, near Ruijin Er Lu ☎ 6445213; ⓜ Shaanxi Nan Lu; map pp.60–61. Popular and rather charming Austrian-style café, almost managing that fin-de-siècle vibe. You can't fault their strudel or *Kaiserschmarrn* – pancake served with apple sauce. Thurs night is movie night. Daily 8am–8pm.

Xianzonglin 仙踪林, xiānzōnglín 671 Huaihai Zhong Lu; ⓜ Shaanxi Nan Lu; map pp.60–61. A Taiwanese chain café that specializes in bubble tea – that's the sweet stuff with gooey balls in it. The huge drinks list includes plenty of oddities such as blueberry tea. Join the local teens and sip while you sit on a swing – kids will love it. Daily 10am–10pm.

JING'AN

Jing'an is a good area for **international cuisine**, and though you won't find any romantic converted villas there are some surprisingly intimate venues. For something more local, try **Huanghe Lu food street** (see box, opposite).

RESTAURANTS

Coconut Paradise 椰香天堂泰国料理, yēxiāng tiāntáng tàiguó liàolǐ 38 Fumin Lu, near Yan'an Zhong Lu ☎ 62481998, ⓦ lostheaven.com.cn; ⓜ Jing'an Temple; map pp.70–71. This renovated French-style villa hosts arguably the city's best Thai restaurant, one of the *Lost Heaven* group (see p.136); thanks to the many candles and the Buddhist theme, it's certainly the most atmospheric. Eat in the garden if the weather permits. At ¥150 a head, it's less pricey than it looks. Daily 11am–2pm & 5–11pm.

★**Crystal Jade** 翡翠酒家, fěicuì jiǔjiā 7F, Westgate Mall, 1038 Nanjing Xi Lu, near Jiangning Lu ☎ 52281133; ⓜ Najing Xi Lu; map pp.70–71. This sister branch to Xintiandi's popular *dim sum* restaurant (see p.133) is less swanky – and less busy; if it's a weekend night and you haven't booked, this is the one to go for. Daily 11am–3pm & 5–11.30pm.

★**Din Tai Fung** 鼎泰丰, dǐngtàifēng 1F, Shanghai Centre, 1376 Nanjing Xi Lu, near Xikang Lu ☎ 62899182, ⓦ dintaifung.com.tw; ⓜ Jing'an Temple; map pp.70–71. Excellent Taiwanese chain (see p.134) – with branches

in the Old French Concession, Xintiandi and Pudong – offering a classy take on Shanghai street food. Daily 11am–3pm & 5–11pm.

Fat Cow 135 Yanping Lu, by Wuding Lu ☎ 52282298, ⓦ fatcowshanghai.com; ⓜ Changping Lu; map pp.70–71. A casual, American-stlye place with a simple formula of burgers, steaks and booze. Set lunches start at ¥55. Happy hour Mon–Fri 4–8pm, with rotating daily food specials. Daily 11am–midnight.

Hunter Gatherer 105 Yanping Lu, near Wuding Lu ☎ 52281860, ⓦ behuntergather.com; ⓜ Changping Lu; map pp.70–71. The largest branch of the Scandi-style health-food canteen (see p.134) where the produce on offer is grown at their own farms. Daily 10am–10pm.

Jia Jia Tang Bao 佳家汤包, jiājiā tāngbāo 90 Huanghe Lu ☎ 63276878; ⓜ Changping Lu; map pp.70–71. This cheap and cheerful little place has a huge reputation for that Shanghai signature dish, *xiǎolóng bāo* (see box opposite), and other dumpling varieties. Crab dumplings are ¥99 for a steamer of a dozen, the normal varieties around ¥13. They whip out an English menu when

FOOD STREETS

Street food, so prevalent elsewhere in China, has pretty much disappeared from the city centre. Happily Shanghai still boasts some notable **food streets** lined with cheap restaurants, which come alive at night, turning into forests of neon – it's best to avoid any roadside stalls, though, as they're not particularly hygienic. The most popular foodie area with visitors is **around Yuyuan Bazaar** (see p.55), which has plenty of venerable dumpling shops, but for a more local experience, head to **Huanghe Lu** (黄河路, huánghé lù), north of Renmin Park – in particular the section north of Beijing Xi Lu – where you'll find lots of restaurants, many of them open 24 hours. *Yang's Fried Dumplings* (see p.139) and *Jia Jia Tang Bao* (see p.138) have great reputations for, respectively, dumplings and **xiǎolóng bāo**, though there's always a queue. Sit-down places offer Shanghai staples such as **hóngshāo ròu** and lion's head meatballs.

Yunnan Lu (云南路, yúnnán lù), a block east of Renmin Park, is the most established of the food streets, though these days it's more of a restaurant row, with ingredients, including snakes and toads, on display on the pavement.

Finally, for the complete opposite of a local experience: the bizarrely named **Foreigner Street 101**, an 0.5km strip in Gubei, in the far south, that is lined with expat-oriented restaurants, most of them established brands. It's safe and family-friendly, but probably not worth making the trip to unless you're really homesick.

11

they see a foreigner. There are big queues at meal times and some varieties of dumplings sell out quickly – best get there early. Daily 7.30am–7pm.

★**Little Sheep** 小肥羊火锅, xiǎoféiyáng huǒguō 777 Jiangning Lu ☎52891717, ⓦxfy.cn; ⓜJiangnin Lu; map pp.70–71. Cheap and cheerful Mongolian hotpot chain that's highly regarded, though pretty ordinary looking. There's a picture menu, so just pick a bunch of ingredients, including plenty of thinly sliced lamb, throw them into the pot, and work on steaming up the windows. ¥60/person. Daily 10.30am–4am.

Lynn 琳怡中餐厅, línyí zhōngcāntīng 99 Xikang Lu, near Nanjing Xi Lu ☎62470101; ⓜJing'an Lu; map pp.70–71. This demure, Art Deco-styled Shanghainese and Cantonese restaurant is popular with the trendy Chinese crowd, especially at weekends, when there's an ¥88 all-you-can-eat *dim sum* deal. It's noisy, so don't take a date, but it's hard to fault the food. Daily 11.30am–2.30pm & 6–10.30pm.

Sushi'O 155 Yanping Lu ☎62362619, ⓦsushi-o.cn; ⓜChangping Lu; map pp.70–71. This casual venue specializes in California-style sushi rolls, with a few rice and *tonkatsu* dishes. They also offer free delivery, and a daily happy hour on drinks (5–8pm). There's another branch in the Old French Concession (see p.136). Daily 11am–10pm.

Thai Gallery 189 Huashan Lu, inside Jing'an Park, near Yan'an Zhong Lu ☎62179717, ⓦthaigallery.cn; ⓜJing'an Temple; map pp.70–71. The food is just OK at this popular Thai restaurant, but the bright decor is great and the park location makes for a lovely ambience on a sunny day. There's lots of outdoor seating, which is another bonus. Daily 11.30am–2.30pm & 5.30–11.30pm.

Yang's Fried Dumplings 小杨生煎馆, xiǎoyáng shēngjiānguǎn 97 Huanghe Lu ☎5375179;

ⓜPeople's Square; map pp.70–71. This tiny shop has a reputation for serving the best *shēngjiānbāo*, or pan-fried pork dumplings, in the city, so there's always a queue. Most people buy to take away but there are a few seats. For ¥6 you get four fluffy steaming buns, sprinkled with sesame seeds and filled with a very hot broth. Daily 6.30am–8pm.

★**Yuxin Sichuan Dish** 渝信川菜, yúxìn chuāncài 3F, 333 Chengdu Bei Lu ☎52980438; ⓜNanjing Xi Lu; map pp.70–71. Shanghai's best Sichuan food, served in a huge, no-nonsense dining hall. It's very popular with families and the white-collar crowd, so reservations are recommended. Go for the *kou shui ji* (spicy chicken) and *sha guo yu* (fish pot), with which you can work on developing a face as red as the peppers. About ¥100/person. Little English is spoken, but there's a picture menu. Daily 11am–2pm & 5–9.30pm.

CAFÉS

Lanna Coffee 8 Yuyuan Dong Lu ☎180 17678867, ⓦlannacoffee.cn; ⓜJing'an Lu; map pp.70–71. This little bare-brick and dark-wood venue is very popular at lunchtime for its freshly roasted Yunnan coffee and bagels. The ¥48 sandwich and coffee deal is excellent value. Daily 10am–7pm.

Red Beacon Café Jing'an Sculpture Park, 500 Beijing Xi Lu, near Shimen Er Lu ☎52289562; ⓜNatural History Museum; map pp.70–71. This trendy monochrome café is decent, with a long, reasonably priced drinks list (coffee is ¥20) but it's the location that's the real draw here, in one of the city centre's rare green spaces. Head to the outdoor seating, beside a striking red pagoda-like structure, and enjoy a cappuccino. Daily 11.30am–6pm.

★**Seesaw** 433 Yuyuan Lu, inside the Jing'an Design Centre ☎52047828, ⓦseesawcoffee.com; ⓜJing'an

Temple; map pp.70–71. Go through the arch and the hipsterish café is on the right, in the atrium of a renovated house. This may be the best coffee in town – there's a huge range of beans, including some from their own plantation in Yunnan, all roasted in house. Nice selection of desserts, too. Daily 8.30am–10pm.

Undefine Room 105, Bldg 6, M50, 50 Moganshan Lu ☎ 62266020, ⊛ undefine.com.cn; Ⓜ Jiangning Lu; map pp.70–71. This gem in the Moganshan Arts District (see

p.73) is a warehouse space turned café that also displays art. The coffee is excellent (¥25, more for one of the craft varieties), and goes well with the home-made brownies (¥30). There is craft beer on sale too – ¥30 a glass, or ¥60 for as much as you can drink (!) – presumably the arty set is too reserved to take advantage of what appears to be the best drinks deal in the city. Head up the quirky if impractical staircases to find cosy spaces with beanbags and study tables. Daily 10.30am–6pm.

PUDONG

Pudong is rather soulless, and the best restaurants are those attached to the swanky **hotels**. For **cheap eats**, try the Super Brand Mall or the basement food court of the Jinmao Tower (see p.78), or head to the Shanghai World Financial Centre, where there's a branch of *Element Fresh* (see p.127), which provides one of the few opportunities for casual Western-style dining in the area.

RESTAURANTS

Blue Frog 蓝蛙, lán wā Basement, Shanghai World Financial Centre, 100 Shiji Dadao ☎ 68778668, ⊛ bluefrog.com.cn, Ⓜ Lujiazui; map p.76. Burgers, pasta, sandwiches and salads, washed down with a good selection of draught and bottled beers. Popular for rotating lunch deals and a long happy hour (daily 4–8pm). Daily 8am–2am.

★**Din Tai Fung** 鼎泰丰, dīngtàifēng 3F, Super Brand Mall, 168 Lujiazui Xi Lu, Pudong ☎ 50478883, ⊛ dintaifung.com.tw; Ⓜ Lujiazui; map p.76. The food is always good at this upmarket chain (which has branches in the Old French Concession, Xintiandi and Jing'an) specializing in dumplings and Shanghai street food. Daily 11am–3pm & 5–11pm.

Haiku by Hatsune Basement 1, IFC Mall, 8 Shiji Dadao ☎ 38820792, ⊛ haikushanghai.com; Ⓜ Lujiazui; map p.76. A stylish and upmarket California-style Japanese restaurant and sushi bar that has a reputation as one of the city's best. Reservations advisable. Around ¥250/person. Daily 11.30am–2pm & 5.30–10pm.

★**Jade on 36** 翡翠36餐厅, fěicuì sānshíliù cāntīng 36F, Tower 2, Pudong Shangri-La, 33 Fucheng Lu ☎ 68828888, ⊛ jadeon36.com;

Ⓜ Lujiazui; map p.76. A fashionable fine-dining experience with a diverse menu of quirky fusion dishes, such as foie gras lollipops or salmon poached in lemongrass. Expect to pay at least ¥600/head; the lavish Sunday brunch, including free-flowing champagne, is a reasonable ¥758. Views are sublime, and the attached bar is very swish. Mon–Sat 6–10.30pm, Sun 11.30am–2pm.

The Kitchen Salvatore Cuomo 2967 Binjiang Dadao, near Fenghe Lu ☎ 50541265, ⊛ ystable.co.jp; Ⓜ Lujiazui; map p.76. Upmarket dining in what is basically a glass box by the river – giving you plenty of opportunity to enjoy the view. The menu is simple – pizzas, pasta and steaks and the like – but it's reliably tasty (and should be at these prices). ¥500/person. Daily 11am–2.30pm & 6–10pm.

Qian Xiang Ge 黔香阁, qiánxiānggé 171 Pucheng Lu, near Shangcheng Lu ☎ 58871717; Ⓜ Lujiazui; map p.76. Big, busy and unpretentious dining hall serving spicy/sour Guizhou cuisine, with most patrons going for the excellent sour fish soup (*suantang yu*) or spicy chicken (*dao han ji*). Everything comes with pickled vegetables. ¥120/head. Daily 11am–2pm & 5–10pm.

Sproutworks Basement 2, Super Brand Mall, 168 Lujiazui Xi Lu ☎ 68905966, ⊛ sproutworks.com.cn; Ⓜ Lujiazui; map p.76. This casual health-food restaurant features flavourful and healthy salads and sides. ¥45 gets you four portions: favourites include cranberries and breadcrumbs, kale with almonds and spicy butternut squash. Panini, soups and desserts are also available, and there are plenty of smoothies, too. Daily 10am–10pm.

Xinjishi (Jesse Restaurant) 新吉士餐厅, xīnjíshì cāntīng 2F, Zhong Guo Mansion, 166 Lujiazui Dong Lu, near Yincheng Lu ☎ 68419719; Ⓜ Lujiazui; map p.76. A new *Jesse* restaurant (see p.137), rather bland in feel, that serves Shanghai classics such as red-braised

---

TOP 5 BUDGET EATS

Bi Feng Tang Tasty Cantonese comfort food served till late. See p.133 & opposite.

Grandma's Home Hugely popular for Hangzhou cuisine. See p.134.

Sproutworks Bright and wholesome health-food canteen. See above.

Xiao Shaoxing Great drunken chicken in this lively canteen. See p.132.

Yuxin Sichuan Dish Probably the best Sichuan in town. See p.139.

pork and drunken chicken. Daily 11am–4pm & 5.30–11pm.

Yi Café 一咖啡, yī kāfēi 2F, Tower 2, Pudong Shangri-La, 33 Fucheng Lu ☎ 68828888, ⦿ shangri-la .com/shanghai/pudongshangrila/dining/restaurants/ yi-cafe; Ⓜ Lujiazui; map p.76. Ten open kitchens dish up an enormous range of international cuisines at this all-day buffet. There's an appealing theatricality to the decor and staff: servers whizz around on rollerblades and the dessert trolley is manned by a clown. Weekday lunch is ¥238, the very popular weekend brunch is ¥298, and dinner is ¥308 (all plus 15 percent service charge). Daily 6am–10.30am & 11am–11pm.

CAFÉS

Farine LG 22, IFC Mall, 8 Shiji Dadao ⦿ farine-bakery.com; Ⓜ Lujiazui; map p.76. Artisan bakeries are thin on the ground in Pudong, so this branch of the Old French Concession favourite (see p.137) is welcome. They're open early, so it's a good bet for breakfast. Mon–Fri 7am–9pm, Sat & Sun 9am–10pm.

HONGKOU

Gritty working-class Hongkou is rapidly **gentrifying**, so although stand-out places to eat are currently thin on the ground, they are bound to increase. The hipsterish café and bar zone in and around **1933 Millfun** looks like a sign of things to come.

11

RESTAURANTS

Bi Feng Tang 避风塘, bìfēngtáng 358 Haining Lu, near Wusong Lu ☎ 63935568, ⦿ bifengtang.com.cn; Ⓜ Sichuan Bei Lu; map p.83. Relatively quiet branch of this reliable Cantonese chain (see p.133), serving tasty, filling food. Mon–Fri 10am–5am, Sat & Sun 8am–5am.

HaidiLao Hotpot 海底捞火锅, hǎidǐlāo huǒguō 269 Haining Lu ☎ 63097326, Ⓜ Sichuan Bei Lu; map p.83. This busy Sichuan-style hotpot chain is well regarded for service – free shoeshines while you wait for a table – and has excellent, good-value food. Order mushrooms, mutton and the house special, beef balls, and cook them yourself in the steaming, spicy broth. Unlike most local restaurants, it's open late, hotpot being popular for a post-bar binge. Daily 11am–1am.

Kathleen's Waitan 4F, 200 Huangpu Lu, near Qingpu Lu ☎ 66600989, ⦿ kwaitan.com; Ⓜ Nanjing Dong Lu; map p.83. This smart restaurant, near the Bund, is fairly new; it seems to try a little harder, and is a little more affordable, than its illustrious competitors. There are stunning views of Pudong from the terrace, so it's a good spot for afternoon tea (see p.136). Food is Western, with steaks and seafood plus a few Asian dishes and a small sushi selection. The set lunch and the weekend brunch are both good value at ¥198. Daily 11am–midnight; afternoon tea daily 3–5pm, Sat & Sun brunch 11am–3pm.

CAFÉS

Canil Café 狗窝, gǒu wō 3F, 1933 Millfun, 611 Liyang Lu, near Haining Lu ☎ 55233971; Ⓜ Hailun Lu; map pp.83. A good half a dozen showdogs pad around this café, fussed over by canine-crazy customers who buy them treats for ¥20. Arriving humans must wait in the holding pen until the dogs have vetted them. Once inside, there's a minimum spend of ¥50, which will just about get you a coffee. You can eat here but, having seen the dogs on the tables and in the kitchen, you probably won't want to. Daily 10am–6pm.

Ferrari Owners Club 1F, Unit 10, 1933 Millfun, 611 Liyang Lu, near Haining Lu ☎ 53154098; Ⓜ Hailun Lu; map p.83. Memorabilia such as race suits, steering wheels, models and helmets dot this fan café that isn't as elitist as it sounds – the real Ferrari-owners are probably on the Bund. The best features are the two driving rigs attached to a computer game that allow you to crank through a few simulated laps (¥50 a go). They serve coffee, cake, spirits and a basic food menu. Daily 10am–7pm.

★**Friends Café** Unit A105, 1913 Creative Park, 160 Harbin Lu, near Jiaxing Lu ☎ 186 01191315; Ⓜ Hailun Lu; map p.83. The One With the Chinese Knock Off! This little café, handy for Millfun, is a decent, clearly unauthorized, simulacrum of *Friends' Central Perk* – that sofa, that sign, and there's even a resident smelly cat. You can get your favourite character's name written across your cappuccino by staff who are fortunately much more efficient than Rachel ever was. They also serve every cake or dessert that has ever been mentioned on the show (¥25–58). Episodes are screened constantly, allowing you to play spot the replica with your surroundings. Daily 10am–9pm.

Old Film Café 老电影咖啡吧, lǎo diànyǐng kāfēi bā 123 Duolun Lu ☎ 56964763; Ⓜ Dongbaoxing Lu; map p.83. If you're in the area, this charming old house, full of period detail, is the place for refreshment, though a coffee will set you back ¥35. They screen black-and-white films upstairs at 7pm nightly. Daily 10am–1am.

BAR ROUGE

Drinking and nightlife

Shanghai's cosmopolitan population has long been famous for its unquenchable thirst for novelty, love of style and dedication to having a good time; this city has always been good at putting on a do. While times have changed, you'll find plenty of parallels with the glory days of "taxi girls", cabarets, flowerhouses and anything-but-innocent "tea dances" – so far as China goes, this is party central. There's nightlife here for all tastes, from spit-and-sawdust dives to exclusive cocktail bars, cheesy mega-discos to slick DJ clubs. That said, the scene is nothing if not capricious and places go in and out of fashion and open and close with the seasons; for bang up-to-date information, check out ⓦsmartshanghai.com or an expat listings magazine (see p.36).

ESSENTIALS

Names and addresses Note that lots of bars only have English names; if you're asking directions or getting a cab, the address is more useful than the name.

Opening hours Hours are flexible, with bars tending to close when the last barfly has lurched off – but everywhere will be open till at least midnight, and much later on the weekends. Clubs open at around 9pm, get going after midnight, and close at 4am or later. We've given the opening hours for all the places we review in this Guide.

Prices Though Chinese beer can be cheaper than bottled water in shops, bar prices can come as something of a shock; even in the shabbiest dive, a small bottle of Tsingtao will cost upwards of ¥25. In the swankiest venues it will be more than ¥50, and for a cocktail you won't get change from a ¥100 note. But just about everywhere has a happy hour (two drinks for the price of one), and these are generally long – sometimes 5pm to 8pm. Wednesday or Thursday is often ladies' night, with many places offering free drinks for women before midnight. Look out too for open bar nights – all you can drink for around ¥100 – advertised in expat magazines. Only the swankiest venues have cover charges, and those will usually include one free drink. However, one annoying practice common in upmarket clubs is having to pay to sit at a table – a waitress will soon shoo you off if you blanch at the (often ridiculous) price.

Fake alcohol Fake alcohol is really common in Shanghai, especially in the cheaper, divier venues. You probably won't know you've been drinking dodgy booze till the next day, when you feel like a run-over cat. If you're paranoid about it, stick to classy places and avoid the most commonly faked labels – famous brand spirits and wines.

Transport Note that a lot of places, generally those in the Old French Concession, are at least a 10min walk from the nearest metro station – and, as the metro stops running at around 11pm, you'll probably be getting a cab home at the end of the night.

BARS

Some of the venues listed as **cafés** in our Eating chapter (see pp.125–141) work very well after dark as bars, notably *Citizen Bar and Café* (see p.137), *Café des Stagiaires* (see p.137) and *Barbarossa* (see p.131). Most **fancy restaurants** have civilized bars attached, which can be great places for a quiet cocktail: particularly good are *Jade on 36* (see p.140), *Lost Heaven the Bund* (see p.129), *Mr and Mrs Bund* (see p.130) and *Char* (see p.131).

12

THE BUND AND NANJING DONG LU

Bar Rouge 7F, No. 18 The Bund, 18 Zhongshan Dong Yi Lu ☎63391199, ⓦbar-rouge-shanghai.com; Ⓜ Nanjing Dong Lu; map p.40. This cool place can feel a bit snooty at times – it's best to dress up – but it all looks fabulous and the terrace has great views over the Bund. Cover is ¥100 on weekends and you won't get change from a red bill for a drink, but go for one, check out the view, and then head on to somewhere less posey. Gets very dancey later. Happy hour daily 6–9pm; on ladies nights (Thurs 9.30–11.30pm) women get free cocktails and a complimentary manicure. Daily 6pm–3am.

Captain Bar 船长酒吧, chuánzhǎng jiǔbā 6F, Captain Hostel, 37 Fuzhou Lu ☎63235053, ⓦcaptainhostel.com.cn; Ⓜ Nanjing Dong Lu; map p.40. This relaxed, divey venue is one of the few in the area where you won't feel the need to dress up. Never mind the unremarkable interior, it's all about the terrace, with its fabulous view of Pudong. It sits atop a backpacker hostel (see p.122), though most hostel guests are put off by the prices: you're paying for the view, with draught beer at ¥50, cocktails around ¥70 and basic pizzas for ¥90 – pricey, but it's still the cheapest in the area. Happy hour daily till 8pm. Daily 5pm–late.

WHERE TO DRINK

There are a number of **bar districts** in Shanghai, and it's well worth taking in more than one over the course of the evening. The best nights in the city tend to involve a bit of bar-hopping – it's lucky that taxis are cheap. The biggest range of watering holes can be found in the **Old French Concession**. **Xintiandi** is upmarket, perhaps just a little too respectable, but a good place for a civilized drink if you can afford it. At the time of writing, **Yongkang Lu** is a great, laidback bar strip – but there is talk of the bars being closed down, so it may well be less fun by the time you read this. A promising new bar area is evolving at the junction of Yanping and Wuding Lu, in **Jing'an**. To the west, **Hengshan Lu** is a more diffuse zone, stretching for several kilometres, with bars catering to most tastes but veering towards expat-friendly, just-like-home pastiche. At the glam venues on the **Bund**, the air of exclusivity is reflected in the prices. Incidentally, if you're dumb enough to follow one of the ubiquitous touts promising to take you to a "lady bar", then you probably deserve the subsequent shakedown. Anyway, it's not as if there's a shortage of "independent female contractors" in the regular dive bars.

★ Long Bar Waldorf Astoria, Zhongshan Dong Yi Lu, near Guangdong Lu ☏ 63229988, ⊛ waldorfastoriashanghai .com/english/dine_in_style/Long_Bar; Ⓜ Nanjing Dong Lu; map p.40. Sophisticated, retro lounge with an Art Deco look and, as you might have guessed, a very, very long bar – more than 30m long, modelled on the original that once graced this address (see p.46). The drinks menu is lengthy too, with plenty of mellow whiskies, including Yamazaki. Live jazz from 10pm and no cover. Mon–Sat 4pm–1am, Sun 2pm–1am.

Peace Hotel Jazz Bar 和平饭店爵士酒吧, hépíngfàndiàn juéshìjiǔbā Fairmont Peace Hotel, 20 Nanjing Dong Lu, near the Bund ☏ 63216888, ⊛ fairmont.com/peace-hotel-shanghai/dining/the jazzbar; Ⓜ Nanjing Dong Lu; map p.40. Famous in the 1920s for its eight-piece dance band, this bar has been refitted in a retro, Art Deco style. The resident jazz band plays from 7pm; their average age is 80 years old, though when a female vocalist joins them at 10pm, that figure lowers considerably. There are rather too many columns in front of the stage, and the clientele is touristy; still, as a historical curiosity, it's worth dropping in for a couple of (pricey) drinks. Minimum spend is ¥200/person. Daily noon–2am.

★ Unico 2F, Three on the Bund, 3 Zhongshan Dong Yi Lu ☏ 53085399, ⊛ unico.cn.com; Ⓜ Nanjing Dong Lu; map p.40. This clubby Bund bar and restaurant gets the crowd hopping with its latin music – it all gets loud and funky, but there are quieter areas at the back. The barmen make some of Shanghai's best caiparinhas, and line the counter with free mojitos on Tues (salsa night) from 8.30pm to 9.30pm. Live Latin music on Sat. No flip-flops or shorts allowed. Mon–Thurs & Sun 6pm–2am, later on Fri & Sat.

PEOPLE'S SQUARE

Constellation 酒池星座, jiǔchí xīngzuò 251 Huangpi Bei Lu, near Jiangyin Lu ☏ 53752712; Ⓜ People's Square; map p.49. This branch of the elegant cocktail bar chain (see below) is by far the best place to drink in an area that has a dearth of decent bars. Daily 7pm–2am.

THE OLD FRENCH CONCESSION

★ The Apartment 47 Yongfu Lu, near Fuxing Xi Lu ☏ 64379478, ⊛ theapartment-shanghai.com; Ⓜ Shanghai Library; map pp.60–61. A New York-style loft bar that's become a city favourite. There's a big bare-brick bar area, a quieter dining room and an airy patio upstairs. It gets very clubby at weekends – expect to do some shouting and dancing. Happy hour 2–8pm daily, and nightly drinks deals – women get free wine from 9pm on Thurs. On Fri and Sat there's a ¥100 cover, which gets you two free drinks. Mon–Thurs & Sun 11am–2am, Fri & Sat 11am–4am.

The Bell Bar Lane 248, Taikang Lu ☏ 138 17778890, ⊛ bellbar.cn; Ⓜ Dapuqiao; map pp.60–61. This casual little backpacker bar is the best place to drink in the Tianzifang warren. Amiable bartenders create a homely atmosphere – try the strawberry martini, or a heated gluhwein in winter, browse the book exchange and swap travel stories with the staff. Draught beer is around ¥60, which seems pricey but is standard for the area; the top floor is a whisky bar. Happy hour daily 5–8pm. To get there head north up Lane 248, and take the third turning on the right. Daily 10am–2am.

Botanist No. 2, 17 Xiangyang Bei Lu, near Changle Lu ☏ 64330538; Ⓜ Shaanxi Nan Lu; map pp.60–61. This elegant bar specializes in rather girly cocktails, made using herbs and blooms picked fresh from the flower wall behind the bar: but there's a decent whisky selection if that doesn't appeal. No standing, and it's popular, so arrive early to guarantee a seat. Cocktails start at ¥80. Tues–Sun 7pm–2am.

Constellation 酒池星座, jiǔchí xīngzuò 96 Xinle Lu ☏ 54040970, Ⓜ Shaanxi Nan Lu; 33 Yongjia Lu, near Maoming Nan Lu ☏ 54655993, Ⓜ Shaanxi Nan Lu; both map pp.60–61. This chain of refined cocktail bars has a good reputation, thanks to the attentive, bow-tied staff who know what they're shaking up. Show up early if you want to be guaranteed a seat and be aware that it they can get very crowded. Whisky lovers will be impressed by the huge variety on offer. There's a handy branch in People's Square, too (see above). Both daily 7pm–2am.

Cotton Club 棉花俱乐部, miánhuā jùlèbù 1416 Huaihai Zhong Lu, near Fuxing Xi Lu ☏ 64377110, ⊛ thecottonclub.cn; map pp.60–61. A long-running, relaxed jazz club with none of that bristling Shanghai attitude. Music gets going at 9.30pm, a bit later at weekends. Jam sessions on Tues. Tues–Sun 7.30pm–1.30am.

★ Dada 115 Xingfu Lu, between Fahuazhen Lu and Pingwu Lu ☏ 150 00182212, ⊛ facebook.com/ DadaBarShanghai; Ⓜ Jiaotong University; map pp.60–61. It might be a bit off the beaten track, but this clubby dive-bar is worth searching out for its laidback atmosphere and hip young crowd. Music, mostly house and electro, comes courtesy of talented independent promoters Antidote. Drinks are cheap at around ¥35, and there are always promotions. Wed–Sat 8pm–late.

★ Kartel 5F, 1 Xiangyang Nan Lu, near Julu Lu ☏ 54042899, ⊛ kartel.com.cn; Ⓜ Shaanxi Nan Lu; map pp.60–61. Don't be put off by the dingy elevator: this casual French bar is a real find. The bar itself is nice enough, with its bare brick walls and wooden floors, but turn right out of the elevator and head upstairs for the real treat: a rooftop that boasts a full panorama of the neon jungle. There's plenty of seating up here, a good wine list and affordable drinks (¥40–80). Happy hour daily 6–8pm. Daily 6pm–2am.

Mardi Gras 372 Xingguo Lu, near Tai'an Lu ☎62807598, ⓦmardigrasshanghai.com; Ⓜ Jiaotong University; map pp.60–61. Ignore this Spanish-style colonial mansion's so-so French restaurant and head upstairs to the sunken bar, where you'll discover excellent cocktails and stoic attitude, courtesy of the resident Japanese bartender. Daily noon–2am.

★Parrot 7 Donghu Lu, near Huaihai Zhong Lu ☎54660026; Ⓜ Shaanxi Nan Lu; map pp.60–61. Head up the narrow alley on the south side of Donghu Lu, and you'll find this fun and friendly bar tucked away; an antidote to the dressier, stuffier places on the main street. Draught beer is ¥40 or so; despite being tiny, it gets clubby at weekends, when DJs play funk or house. Daily 6pm till late.

Paulaner Bräuhaus 宝莱纳, bǎoláinà House 19–20, North Block, Taicang Lu, Xintiandi ☎63203935, ⓦ paulaner-brauhaus.com/shanghai; Ⓜ Xintiandi; map p.63. This huge beer hall – with another branch in Pudong (see p.146) – is all *Lederhosen*, beer and German food. They run their own microbrewery, but the beer's not cheap, with the smallest lager costing ¥68 (a litre is ¥105). Happy hour daily 5–9pm. Daily 11am–2am.

People 7 人间银七, rénjiānyínqī 805 Julu Lu, near Fumin Lu ☎54040707; Ⓜ Shaanxi Nan Lu; map pp.60–61. This hip bar trades on its exclusivity. Not only is there no sign, there doesn't even appear to be a door – just nine illuminated holes. Put your hands in the holes in the right order (you'll have to ring for the code), and a door slides back revealing a two-storey lounge bar with walls of exposed concrete, spotlights, comfy white sofas and a long, eerily lit bar. Other quirky elements – glasses with curved bottoms so they keep rolling round, baffling toilet doors with fake handles – will either delight or annoy. Daily 6pm–midnight.

The Roof Surpass Court, 4F, Bldg 5, 570 Yongjia Lu, near Yueyang Lu ☎60737628, Ⓜ Hengshan Lu; map pp.60–61. Japanese *izakaya*-style lounge specializing in classic cocktails plus a good selection of single malt Scottish and Japanese whiskies, and premium teas. Daily 5pm–2am.

★Senator 98 Wuyuan Lu, near Wulumuqi Zhong Lu ☎54231330, ⓦsenatorsaloon.com; Ⓜ Shanghai Library; map pp.60–61. A stylish and sophisticated speakeasy from the people behind *Citizen* (see p.137). It's intimate and cosy and the staff really know their cocktails; tell them your mood and tastes and they'll suggest a drink to fit. They have a vast range of bourbons and most of the recipes date back to the Prohibition era. Daily 5pm–1am.

Shanghai Brewery 20 Donghu Lu, near Huaihai Lu ☎33563996; 15 Dongping Lu, near Hengshan Lu ☎34610717; both map pp.60–61; ⓦshanghaibrewery .com. Serving beer from their own microbrewery, these bars are popular with well-heeled locals looking for something a bit different. The strawberry cider is a little sweet but the White IPA hits the spot; drinks will set you back ¥60–90. The Donghu Lu branch, with an Art Deco theme, is less trendy than the other bars in the area, and quieter, which makes it a good place to start a night out; the Dongping Lu branch has more the feel of a sports bar. Discounts and specials Mon–Fri 2–8pm, Sat and Sun 4–8pm. The food is unremarkable. Both daily 5pm–midnight.

Taste Buds Cocktail Palace 2F, 368 Wukang Lu, Ferguson Lane, near Hunan Lu ☎18021597; Ⓜ Shanghai Library; map pp.60–61. This craft cocktail bar is certain to impress: the decor is inspired by the Qing dynasty, so expect a palatial vibe, and of course that great orientalist signifier, bamboo birdcages. They specialize in vintage cocktails, which will set you back three figures but are well regarded: try a rum- and herb-based Tale of Mulata. It's a place for a date rather than a party, and there are two chilled patios. Daily 6pm–2am.

12

BRIGHT LIGHTS, BIG CITY

Shanghai at night, between dusk and about 10pm, is lit up like a pinball machine. The city sucks up so much of China's energy that the national grid can't take it, and power cuts are endured in the sticks. The best places to appreciate the awesome spectacle are:

100 Century Avenue The cocktails are expensive at the world's highest bar, but the view makes it worth it. See p.146.

Captain Bar The only Bund bar that won't empty your wallet. See p.143.

Huangpu River night cruise Touristy, but fun. See p.45.

Kartel The rooftop bar here offers a 360-degree view of glittering corporate monoliths. See opposite.

JW Marriott lobby An awesome view of People's Square, but be discreet: if too many people begin turning up, they'll probably start charging. See p.117.

Nanjing Dong Lu You might not want to buy anything here, but the lights are spectacular. See p.46.

Vue Slick bar with great views of Pudong from its terrace. See p.147.

Yuyuan This olde-worlde Chinatown bazaar takes on a whole new aspect when the neon comes on. See p.55.

TOP 5 COCKTAIL BARS

Constellation Go for the Moscow Mule. See p.144.

Long Bar Try the signature Waldorf cocktail. See p.144.

Revolucion Cocktail 2 Shanghai's best mojitos. See below.

Senator An Old Fashioned fits the vibe nicely. See p.145.

Unico Great gin and tonics. See p.144.

Windows Scoreboard 11F, 527 Huaihai Zhong Lu, near Chengdu Lu ☎53827757, ⓦwindowsbars.com; Ⓜ Huangpi Nan Lu; map pp.60–61. With sports on the screens, foosball and pool tables on the floor, and rock and hip-hop on the sound system, this feels a bit like a frat boy clubhouse – though strangely, it is located near the top of an anonymous office building. Beers are much cheaper than elsewhere (bottles start at ¥15); that and the laidback atmosphere draw a young and unpretentious crowd. A good place to start or end a night out. Daily 5pm–4am.

Zapatas 萨帕塔, sà pà tǎ 5 Hengshan Lu, near Dongping Lu ☎64334104, ⓦzapatas-shanghai.com; Ⓜ Hengshan Lu; map pp.60–61. No Mexican anarchist would be seen dead in the company of the lascivious crowd here – it's a heaving party on Mon and Wed nights, when women are offered free margaritas before midnight and tequila gets poured into the mouths of anyone dancing on the bar. Enter through the garden of *Sasha's*, the nearby restaurant. Happy hour daily 5–9pm. Daily 5pm–late.

JING'AN

Big Bamboo 金桥店, jīn qiáo diàn 132 Nanyang Lu, near Tongren Lu ☎62562265, ⓦbigbamboo.asia; Ⓜ Jing'an Temple; map pp.70–71. This popular and long-running bar screens the important games in virtually all sports. They've also got pool tables, darts, foosball and a menu of pub food. Happy hour and special deals daily 2–8pm. Daily 9am–2am.

Kaiba 开巴, kāibā 479 Wuding Lu, near Shanxi Bei Lu ☎62889676, ⓦkaiba-beerbar.com; Ⓜ Changping Lu; map pp.70–71. A favourite with the after-work crowd, this big Belgian bar has a great beer selection, with more than fifty imported bottled European beers and plenty more on draught. It's not cheap – a Duvell will set you back ¥70 – but there is a happy hour (Mon–Fri 4–9pm, Sat and Sun 2–7pm). Daily 11am–2am.

Revolucion Cocktail 2 98 Yanping Lu, near Xinzha Lu ☎62667969, ⓦrevolucion-cocktail.com; Ⓜ Changping Lu; map pp.70–71. This casual and friendly Cuban cocktail bar keeps it colourful with parrot paintings on the walls. It gets very dancey at weekends, when they play latin sounds

in addition to the usual hip-hop. Their signature cocktails are rum based, but they have a good selection of bottled beers, too. If it's not to your liking, take a stroll – a lot of new bars are springing up around here. Daily 6pm–2am.

Windows Too 蕴德诗酒吧, yùndéshī jiǔbā I2F, City Plaza, 1618 Nanjing Xi Lu ☎62889007, ⓦwindowsbar .com; Ⓜ Jing'an Temple; map pp.70–71. Cheap beer at ¥15 a bottle, noisy hip-hop, no class and no pretensions. It's packed nightly with those at the bottom of the Shanghai foreigner food chain – students, teachers and backpackers – and those who'll deign to talk to them. ¥50 cover Fri and Sat, when it's clubby. Daily 10am–late.

PUDONG

100 Century Avenue 世纪,100 Shìjì yībǎi 91F, Park Hyatt, Shanghai World Financial Centre, 100 Shiji Dadao ☎38551428, ⓦ100centuryavenue.com; Ⓜ Lujiazui; map p.76. This is the world's highest bar. Fantastic views, obviously, and live music every night from a Filipino band. But it's pricey – a beer is ¥80, and there's a cover of ¥100. Daily 11.30am–2.30pm & 5.30–10.30pm.

The Brew Kerry Hotel, 1388 Huamu Lu, near Fangdian Lu ☎61698888, Ⓜ Huamu Lu; map p.80. This big pub is a long way out, beyond the southern tip of Century Park, but it attracts the city's boozehounds with great wheat and IPA beers brewed on the premises, a pint of which will set you back ¥80 or so. Decent bar food, too. Happy hour daily 3–8pm. Daily 11.30am–2am.

The Camel 116 Weifang Xi Lu, near Pudong Nan Lu ☎58795892, ⓦcamelsportsbar.com; Ⓜ Shangcheng Lu; map p.76. This huge Australian-run sports bar has a big draught-beer selection and a menu of pub staples, including decent fish and chips. It's popular with the after-work crowd. Happy hour daily 4–8pm. Daily 10am–2am.

Cloud Nine 九重天酒吧, jiǔchóngtiān jiǔbā 87F, Grand Hyatt, Jinmao Tower, 88 Shiji Dadao ☎50491234, ⓦshanghai.grand.hyatt.com/en/hotel/dining/Cloud9; Ⓜ Lujiazui; map p.76. Inside it's all rather dark and metallic, but the view is astonishing. Unfortunately staff steer anyone not staying at the *Hyatt* away from the coveted windowside tables facing the Bund. Minimum spend is ¥120/person, and cocktails start at ¥80. Mon–Fri 5pm–1am, Sat & Sun 2pm–1am.

Flair 58F, Ritz-Carlton Pudong, 8 Shiji Dadao ☎20201778, ⓦritzcarlton.com/en/hotels/china/ shanghai-pudong/dining/flair; Ⓜ Lujiazui; map p.76. The terrace at this suave lounge bar has a jaw-dropping view – right into the Pearl Tower. One drink will thin three digits, and beware, there's a ¥350 minimum spend/person. Tapas and seafood available. Spectacular, yes. Value for money, no. Daily 5pm–2am.

Paulaner Bräuhaus 宝莱纳 bǎoláinà Binjiang Dadao ☎68883935, ⓦpaulaner-brauhaus.com; Ⓜ Lujiazui; map p.76. A spacious branch of the

German-style pub chain (see p.145) with pricey Paulaner beer from its own microbrewery. Good views of the Bund make it worth considering, especially in nice weather, when you can relax on the patio. Daily 11am–2am.

HONGKOU

Vue 32 & 33F, Hyatt on the Bund, 199 Huangpu Lu, north of Suzhou Creek ☏ 63931234, ⓦ shanghaithebund.hyatt.com/en/hotel/dining/VueBar; ⓜ Tiantong Lu;

map p.83. This hotel bar looks sleek, but is pretty average in every respect – with its fantastic views of the Bund it knows it doesn't have to try too hard. There's a jacuzzi on the outdoor terrace upstairs, though it seems to be just for dipping your feet in. Non-guests pay ¥100 admission, which includes one free drink from a limited menu; cocktails start at ¥120 and you have to pay extra for a windowside seat. Drinks offers Mon–Fri 5.30–7pm. Mon–Thurs & Sun 6pm–1am, Fri & Sat 6pm–2am.

CLUBS

The **dance scene** in Shanghai will be familiar to anyone who's been clubbing in any Western capital – you won't hear any local sounds or much that's not mainstream – but at least the door prices are cheaper. Most places host international DJs, and plenty of famous faces have popped in for a spin of the decks. At clubs aimed at the **Chinese market**, you'll probably find a comparatively small dancefloor, with most space given over to tables and chairs, the best located of which will be pay-to-sit – a ridiculous amount, usually. That's where you'll see the *tuhao* (nouveaux riche) guys with their skinny *xiaomis* (literally, little honeys), probably drinking Chivas with green tea (red wine with Sprite is going out of fashion). It will be table service, and at the swankiest of such places you may witness the arrival of a "Shanghai champagne train" – a parade of waitresses delivering pricey bottles with much fanfare, including sparklers. Note that there are also dancefloors in many of the city's **bars**, among them *Zapatas* (see p.146), *Bar Rouge* (see p.143), *The Apartment* (see p.144), *Dada* (see p.144) *Unico* (see p.144) and *Windows Too* (see opposite).

★**Arkham** 1 Wulumuqi Lu, near Hengshan Lu ☏ 62580355, ⓦ arkhamshanghai.com; ⓜ Hengshan Lu; map pp.60–61. It's all about the dancing in these three dark caverns, beloved by impassioned promoters and punters, where sets are mostly techno with shows by international DJs and rappers. Drinks are pretty cheap at around ¥40. Occasional shows on weeknights; check the website. Fri & Sat 10pm till late.

M2 4F, Hong Kong Plaza, 283 Huaihai Zhong Lu, near Huangpi Nan Lu ☏ 62886222, ⓦ facebook.com/ M2Shanghai; ⓜ Huangpi Lu; map pp.60–61. This big

brassy club, a favourite with affluent millennials who just wanna have fun, is always crowded. Though it's got that "Chinese club" ambience – genre-hopping music, table service, pay-to-sit – it attracts a lot of foreigners, making for a mixed and up-for-it crowd. A drink will set you back ¥80 or so. Mon–Wed & Sun 8pm–2am, Thurs–Sat 8pm–4am.

Monkey Champagne 38 Donghu Lu, near Xinle Lu ☏ 62556000, ⓦ houseofmonkey.com; ⓜ Shaanxi Nan Lu; map pp.60–61. Head down the alley on the north side of Donghu Lu, then through *Bonobo* restaurant, and you will find this neon temple of bling at the back. It's popular

12

CHINESE INDIE MUSIC

The Chinese **indie rock scene** is well worth a look. Bands don't make any money from selling records, thanks to piracy, and they don't get any airplay from mainstream media, so the whole scene is based around live performance; most musicians have a daunting gig schedule. Meanwhile, the indie scene is regarded with suspicion by the authorities, and venues are at constant risk of being shut down. Lyrics have to be submitted to government censors, so any musicians with points to make rely on double meanings and ambiguity.

The roots of the scene were built around a collection of loud, post-punk guitar bands from Beijing; most notable among this older generation are Carsick Cars, Retros, PK14 and New Pants. But the scene has since diversified, and spread across the country. Today you'll hear all manner of sounds; look out for the gothy disco of Nova Heart, the folk rock of Second Hand Roses or the Bowie-like Queen Sea Big Shark. Good **Shanghai bands** to hunt down are indie popsters Cold Fairyland and folk-punk rockers Top Floor Circus. Some groups will seem pretty familiar, and it's common for bands to sing in English: they would argue that rock is an international language. Other groups, in contrast, attempt to create something local by including Chinese instruments or singing styles: for something with a distinctly Chinese flavour, look out for Mongolian folk punks **Hanggai**.

12

with moneyed young locals and foreign-born Chinese, and it's trendy but dressy. Fri is hip-hop night; the rest of the time the crowd politely nods to pounding techno. Drinks are pricey, but all are free for the lay-deez on Thurs. Tues–Thurs 8pm–3am, Fri & Sat 8pm–6am.

Myst 相关团购, xiāng guān tuán gòu 1123 Yan'an Zhong Lu, near Fumin Lu ☎ 64379999, ⓦ mystshanghai.com; Ⓜ Jing'an Temple; map pp.70–71. The ground floor of this multistorey cavern is loungey,

the floor above is dancey and the top floor is for the VIPs to look down on the bopping proles. There are too many tables for a properly unrestrained dancefloor, but the shows are fun – a stage rises out of the floor, and skimpily dressed dancers show everyone how it's done. Don't expect too much sophistication or elbow room and you'll have a good time. There's usually no cover, and drinks aren't expensive, so you can't really go wrong. Daily 9pm–late.

LIVE MUSIC

Shanghai's **music scene** doesn't yet rival Beijing's, but it's only a matter of time as more venues open, new talent is trained in the impressive music schools, more international artists make appearances and more disaffected kids buy electric guitars. The city has a long affinity with **jazz**, dating back to Concession times – devotees should head to the Peace Hotel Jazz Bar (see p.144) or the *Cotton Club* (see p.144). There's plenty of **hip-hop** around, but it's really all about fashion and posing and the scene has yet to produce any music of note. The **indie music** scene is not as good as Beijing's, but it's there, and it's worth dipping a toe into the venues listed here. There are also plenty of great places to catch **classical** music performances, by the best international and home grown artists – these are listed in our Entertainment and art chapter (see opposite).

ROCK AND POP VENUES

★**MAO Livehouse** 光芒, guāng máng 308 Chongqing Lu, near Jianguo Zhong Lu ☎ 64450086, ⓦ mao-music.com; Ⓜ Madang Lu; map pp.60–61. A decent, mid-sized, centrally located venue for local and international rock and indie bands. The sound system passes muster and drinks are cheap, at around ¥25 a beer. Variable cover charge, usually around ¥50. Open during events only.

Mercedes Benz Arena 梅赛德斯-奔驰文化中心, méisàidésī-bēnchí wénhuà zhōngxīn 1200 Expo Ave, near Gaoke Xi Lu, Pudong ☎ 4001816688, ⓦ mercedes-benzarena.com/index.php/enhome; Ⓜ China Art Museum; map p.76. A legacy of the 2010 Expo, this giant UFO-like building seats 18,000. It hosts big international names from Justin Bieber to Elton

John. It's a little far out, but is handy for Yaohua Lu metro station.

Shanghai Stadium 上海体育场, shànghǎi tǐyùchǎng 666 Tianyaoqiao Lu ☎ 64266666, ext 2567; Ⓜ Shanghai Stadium; map p.87. Venue for mega-gigs by visiting bands such as the Rolling Stones, as well as home-grown idols. Tickets are cheaper than they would be in the West, usually around ¥150.

★**Yuyintang** 育音堂, yùyīntáng 851 Kaixuan Lu ☎ 52378662, ⓦ yytlive.com; Ⓜ Yan'an Xi Lu; map p.87. This grungy venue is ground zero for the Converse shoes and black-nail-varnish set, hosting rock/punk and electro gigs every weekend with a varying cover of around ¥30. It's all pretty rough and ready, with concrete floors and graffitied walls, but the sound system is surprisingly good, and bottles of beer are just ¥15. Daily 9.30pm–late.

ACROBATS AT THE SHANGHAI CENTRE THEATRE

Entertainment and art

An early edition of this guide scoffed that in Shanghai, "culture was something that happened to pearls". That statement could not be less true now. The city today boasts a truly fantastic range of arts venues, many of them new – a good dozen massive art spaces have opened in as many years – with prestige government projects, such as the grand Power Station of Art and the Oriental Arts Centre, joined by private galleries opened by billionaires who want to show off their art collections. Add to this the fact that Shanghai's major music, literary and film festivals are building considerable reputations (see p.26) and you have a buzzing arts scene.

13

Most visitors take in an **acrobatics** show and perhaps an **opera**, but there is plenty to see in the world of music, dance and drama, and a flourishing **contemporary art** scene, too. Bear in mind, though, that when it comes to cutting-edge new work, Shanghai doesn't quite measure up on the international stage, as the government's heavy-handed censorship makes any contentious form of cultural production impossible.

ESSENTIALS

INFORMATION

To find out what's on, check an expat magazine such as *Time Out* (ⓦtimeoutshanghai.com) or *City Weekend* (ⓦcityweekend.com.cn/shanghai), or the website ⓦsmartshanghai.com.

BOOKING TICKETS

Credit card bookings haven't yet caught on in China, but you can still get tickets in advance without the hassle of going to the venue. A couple of services can deliver tickets to your home or hotel; you pay cash on arrival, plus a small delivery charge.

Shanghai Cultural Information and Booking Centre ☎62172426, ⓦculture.sh.cn/English. Tickets booked here are delivered at no extra charge provided you book more than three days before the performance.

SmartShanghai ⓦsmartshanghai.com/smartticket. Useful and easily navigated English-language website.

DRAMA AND DANCE

Most Shanghai **theatre** is light-hearted fare about the trials of urban dating life, in Chinese of course, though some troupes occasionally put on shows in English. **Dance** is popular, but it's almost always the conservative end of the spectrum – if you're into modern dance, look out for the work of choreographer **Jinxing**, China's highest-profile transsexual and one of the scene's few innovators. Imported **musicals** and **ballets** are worth investigating, as tickets will be cheaper in Shanghai than at home. One innovation that's proving hugely popular right now is the streaming, into theatres, of **livecasts** of plays from Western theatres, often in London or New York – these are in English, of course, with Chinese subtitles, and are often pretty affordable at ¥100 or so.

Majestic Theatre 美琪大剧院, měiqí dàjùyuàn 66 Jiangning Lu, near Nanjing Xi Lu ☎62174409; ⓜNanjing Xi Lu; map pp.60–61. One of Asia's best theatres when it was built in 1941. Today, musicals are the main fare, but the programme is interspersed with some English-language drama, dance competitions and Chinese opera.

Shanghai Art Theatre 艺海剧院, yìhǎi jùyuàn 466 Jiangning Lu, near Kangding Lu ☎64278199; ⓜChangping Lu; map pp.70–71. This airy modern complex tends to show classical Chinese opera and rather rusty old Chinese dramas.

Shanghai Culture Square 文化广场, wénhuà guǎngchǎng 225 Shanxi Nan Lu, near Fuxing Zhong Lu ☎54619961, ⓦshculturesquare.com; ⓜShaanxi Nan Lu; map pp.60–61. This prestigious venue seats more than two thousand, and is usually home to musicals, both imported and domestic.

Shanghai Dramatic Arts Centre 上海话剧艺术中心, shànghǎi huàjù yìshù zhōngxīn 288 Anfu Lu ☎51695229, ⓦchina-drama.com; ⓜChangshu Lu; map pp.60–61. Slick productions in a modern auditorium; performances are usually of classics or crowd-pleasers. Western plays performed in Chinese are accompanied by English supertitles on an electronic screen.

Shanghai Grand Theatre 上海大剧院, shànghǎi dàjùyuàn 300 Renmin Dadao ☎63273094, ⓦshgtheatre.com; ⓜPeople's Square; map p.49. Popular contemporary dramas, operas and classical ballet are staged at this lovely venue, designed by French architect Jean-Marie Charpentier; it also puts on visiting musicals and has frequent one-off livecasts. Regular performances by the in-house Shanghai Symphony Orchestra (see opposite).

ACROBATICS

Acrobatics have a long tradition in China and **acrobatic shows** are unmissable crowd-pleasers. The style may be vaudeville but the stunts are spectacular – a dozen people stacked on one bicycle and the like – and performances have a little bit of everything, from plate-spinning, hoop-diving and comedy to jugglng and extraordinary gymnastic feats. Many of the performers will have been trained for their roles since childhood in specialist schools devoted to the art.

Shanghai Centre Theatre 上海商城剧院, shànghǎi shāngchéng jùyuàn 1376 Nanjing Xi Lu, by Xikang Lu ☎62798948, ⓦshanghaicentre.com/theatre; ⓜJing'an Temple; map pp.70–71. Stacks of

stunning stunts. Daily performances, starting at 7.30pm and finishing by 9pm, with tickets costing ¥100–280.

★**Shanghai Circus World** 上海马戏城, shànghǎi mǎxìchéng 2266 Gonghe Xi Lu ☎66522395,

CHINESE OPERA

Chinese opera is a unique combination of song, dance, acrobatics and mime. It's highly stylized, with every aspect of the performance, from costumes and make-up to movements, imbued with a specific symbolic meaning. Colour is very significant, red, for example, signifying loyalty and blue cruelty. Plots feature straightforward goodies and baddies, often concerning young lovers who are forbidden to marry, supernatural interventions and so on. The main barrier to appreciation for the uninitiated is the percussive din of the accompanying orchestra and the high register of the performers. These days – with the fan base growing increasingly elderly and in the hopes of appealing to a younger audience – shows have been shortened from four hours to an hour or two, and include plenty of slapstick and martial arts. There are hundreds of **regional variations**, such as Yue opera from nearby Zhejiang province, Kun opera from Jiangsu and the local form, Hu.

VENUES

Wanping Theatre 宛平剧院, wǎnpíng jùyuàn 857 Zhongshan Er Lu ☎ 64392277; Ⓜ Longhua Zhong Lu; map p.87. Nightly, tourist-friendly show based on the adventures of the Monkey King, broadly adapted from the Chinese classic novel *Journey to the West*. Performances are at 7.30pm; tickets start at ¥80.

Yifu Theatre 天蟾逸夫舞台, tiānchán yìfū wǔtái 701 Fuzhou Lu ☎ 63225075; Ⓜ People's Square; map p.39. One of the few places in Shanghai where you can hear provincial opera forms. There's a different show every night of the week and a brisk English summary at the start explains the plot. Tickets – ¥30 to ¥300 – can be bought on the day and shows start at 7.15pm (there are also some afternoon performances).

Ⓦ era-shanghai.com; Ⓜ Shanghai Circus World. Never mind the daft name, *ERA, the Intersection of Time* – the shows held at this gold-coloured dome are good old-fashioned spectaculars, the city's best, with audiovisual trickery enhancing the awe-inspiring acrobatic cavortings. It's in the north of the city, and handily has its own metro station, Shanghai Circus World (on line #1). Performances daily at 7.30pm. Tickets range from ¥120 to ¥600, but the pricier seats don't seem to have that much of an advantage over the cheaper ones.

CLASSICAL MUSIC

In addition to the venues listed below, **classical concerts** are also held at the Shanghai Grand Theatre (see opposite) – check the website. Most performances are of European classical music, at the traditional end of the spectrum, though there is an increasing interest in local composers and more eclectic works. Visits from international orchestras are common.

Oriental Arts Centre 上海东方艺术中心, shànghǎi dōngfāng yìshù zhōngxīn 425 Dingxiang Lu, near Shiji Dadao ☎ 68541234, Ⓦ shoac.com.cn; Ⓜ Science and Technology Museum; map p.80. A fantastic 40,000-square-metre behemoth with superb acoustics. At night the ceiling sparkles and changes colour according to the tunes being played.

Shanghai Concert Hall 上海音乐厅, shànghǎi yīnyuètīng 523 Yan'an Zhong Lu near Xizang Zhong Lu ☎ 63862836, Ⓦ shanghaiconcerthall.org; Ⓜ Dashijie; map p.54. This lovely old building was moved at tremendous cost 60m east in 2003, in order to get it away from the din of Yan'an Lu. Today it's the city's premier venue for classical music. Tickets from ¥80.

Shanghai Symphony Orchestra Hall 上海交响乐团, shànghǎi jiāoxiǎng yuètuán 1380 Fuxing Zhong Lu, near Baoqing Lu ☎ 4008210522, Ⓦ shsymphony .com; Ⓜ Changshu Lu; map pp.60–61. This is home to both the Shanghai Symphony Orchestra and the Shanghai Orchestra. There are two performance spaces: the 1200-seater Concert Hall and the chamber music hall which seats four hundred.

FILM

When it comes to pulling in the box-office receipts, China is second only to the US. Most of the movies screened here are home-produced, as the country's notoriously prickly **censors** pass just 34 foreign films a year for domestic Chinese consumption (though that number is set to increase). Shanghai has many cinemas where you can see English-language films dubbed into Mandarin, with at least one screening a day of the original with Chinese subtitles. You'll find more varied offerings at the Shanghai Film Art Centre, and during the **Shanghai International Film Festival** (see p.26). Expat-oriented screenings of mainstream Western films are held at the *Vienna Café* (see p.138) every Thurs at 7.30pm.

13

SHANGHAI CINEMA

China's first-ever moving picture was shown in Shanghai in 1914, at a teahouse variety show, and the nation's **first cinema** was built here twelve years later. By the 1930s film had caught on both with the foreign population and with the locals and a number of **studios** had opened. Influenced by the May Fourth Movement, which challenged imperialism and social conservatism, filmmakers eschewed the formalism and abstractions of Chinese drama, and sought to make **naturalistic** films. One classic from the era, *Sister Flower* (1933), tells the story of twin sisters separated at birth, one of whom ends up in Shanghai while the other remains a poor villager. *Spring Silk Worm*, from the same year, portrays grim decline in Zhejiang province, and points the finger at Japanese colonialism. The most celebrated film of the time was *The Goddess* (1934), about the struggle of a prostitute to have her son educated; it features a standout performance from the tragic beauty **Ruan Lingyu**, China's Garbo, who killed herself a year later.

With the **Japanese invasion** of 1937 Shanghai's studios were closed, and filmmaking talent fled. Despite the turmoil, the Shanghai studios produced one last great work, the epic *The Spring River Flows East* (1947), telling the story of a family torn apart by the conflict. When the **Communists** took over things didn't get any easier. The studios, now officially derided as bourgeois, managed to release just one privately funded film, *The Life of Wu Xun* (1949), the story of a nineteenth-century philanthropist – Mao damned it as revisionist and closed the studios down. Though the studios have yet to return to Shanghai, the city does have a new film school and is often depicted in modern Chinese cinema, most memorably in Lou Ye's tragic love story *Suzhou Creek* (2002).

Shanghai's decadent prewar days have a perennial appeal for filmmakers, it would seem, providing the **setting** for the stilted Merchant Ivory boreathon *The White Countess* (2004), and the adaptation of Somerset Maugham's *The Painted Veil* (which includes a CGI Bund); but it is Zhang Yimou's *Shanghai Triad* (1995) that really set the standard for a whole "gangsters and *qipao*" Concession-era genre. The brutal end to Concession days is shown in Ang Lee's sultry *Lust, Caution* (2007) and Steven Spielberg's adaptation of J.G. Ballard's classic novel, *Empire of the Sun* (1987). Today, Shanghai has an intriguing new role as a city of the future – science-fiction films *Code 46* (2008), *Looper* (2012) and *Her* (2013) were all shot here.

You can buy Chinese classics on DVD from the Foreign Language Bookstore (see p.163) or the shop in the Shanghai Grand Theatre (see p.163).

Broadband International Cineplex 万裕国际影城, wànyù guójì yǐngchéng 6F, Times Square, 99 Huaihai Lu ☎63910701, ⍟swy99.com; Ⓜ Dashijie; map p.54. Multiplex showing Chinese releases – although unusually it has English-speaking staff. Tickets ¥80–100, half-price on Tues and Wed.

Cathay Theatre 国泰电影院, guótài diànyǐngyuàn 870 Huaihai Zhong Lu ☎54040415, ⍟guotaifilm.com; Ⓜ Shaanxi Nan Lu; map pp.60–61. Grand, rather creaky old venue with cheaper tickets than the multiplexes (from ¥30) for much smaller seats. Mainstream releases.

IMAX Science and Technology Museum ☎68622000, ⍟sstm.org.cn; Ⓜ Science and Technology Museum; map p.80. Daily science spectaculars – short films, in Chinese, about tigers, dinosaurs, and so on, on a huge curved screen or in a 3D theatre. Tickets ¥40 or so.

Palace IMAX 6F, IAPM Mall, 999 Huaihai Zhong Lu ☎51093988, ⍟www.b-cinema.cn/w14313.jsp; Ⓜ Shaanxi Nan Lu; map pp.60–61. The newest and probably best cinema in the city, with six screens, not all of them IMAX. It's also the most expensive, with tickets from ¥100 to ¥180; there are discounts before noon and after 10pm daily – excluding IMAX films – and half-price tickets, including IMAX films, all day Mon and Tues.

Peace Cinema 和平影都, hépíng yǐngdū 290 Xizang Zhong Lu ☎63612898, ⍟shdgm.com; Ⓜ People's Square; map p.49. Huge, centrally located cinema just off People's Square, with an IMAX screen. Tickets start at ¥50, but IMAX tickets can be as much as ¥180. Discounts on Tues and Wed.

Shanghai Film Art Centre 上海影院中心, shànghǎi yǐngyuàn zhōngxīn 160 Xinhua Lu, near Panyu Lu ☎62804088, ⍟filmcenter.com.cn; Ⓜ Jiaotong University; map p.60–61. The main venue for the Shanghai International Film Festival (see p.26) is the only vaguely art-house cinema in town, and offers some non-mainstream content on its nine screens. Look out for directors' Q and A sessions. Tickets from ¥65, half-price on Mon and Tues.

UME International Cineplex 新天地国际影城, xīntiāndì guójì yǐngchéng 5F, South Block, Xintiandi ☎ 63733333, ⓦ bs.ume.com.cn/tplt/20131225152739 .shtml; Ⓜ Xintiandi; map p.63. Foreign films, subtitled rather than dubbed. Tickets start at ¥100, and are half-price before 7pm on Tues.

ART

Of all the arts, the most thriving scene, and certainly the most accessible to the visitor, is **contemporary art**, with the **Shanghai Biennale** (see p.26) getting bigger each time. Chinese art is hot, and is being snapped up by international dealers, though it remains to be seen how worthwhile this hyped-up work will turn out to be; some is a sophisticated form of chinoiserie, selling an image of China for foreign consumption. Still, there's plenty of good stuff out there. There are more and more international shows here too, which is just as well as there is an awful lot of gallery space that needs filling. As well as **government-run art galleries** such as the staid Duolun (see p.83), the vast Power Station of Art (see p.57) and the bombastic China Art Palace (see p.81), are more exciting **private ventures**, among them MoCA (see p.52), Rockbund (see p.42) and the Long Museum (see p.81 and p.88). In recent years, an entire **"museum mile"** has sprung up on West Bund (see p.87) – this orderly riverside promenade holds two sumptuous private galleries, the Long Museum (see p.88) and the Yuz Museum (see p.88), as well the West Bund Art Centre and ShanghART, with plans for even more spaces. Another mandatory stop for the artily inclined has to be **50 Moganshan Lu**, a derelict suburban textile factory that was first taken over by artists in the 1990s when rents were cheap, and has since filled up with small private galleries (see p.73).

Around Space 703 Chuang Ye Bldg, 33 Sichuan Lu ☎ 33050100, ⓦ aroundspace.org; Ⓜ Nanjing Dong Lu; map p.40. This small space tucked behind the Bund shows contemporary painting by cool Chinese artists. Tues–Sun 10.30am–6.30pm.

Art Labor 画廊 huàláng Bldg 4, 570 Yongjia Lu, near Yueyang Lu ☎ 34605331, ⓦ artlaborgallery.com; Ⓜ Hengshan Lu; map pp.60–61. This is one of the best places to see emerging local artists, usually exhibited alongside artists from abroad. Tues–Sat 11am–7pm, Sun noon–6pm.

Galerie Beaugeste 比极画廊, bǐjí huàláng 519, Bldg 5, Lane 210, Taikang Lu ☎ 64669012, ⓦ beaugeste-gallery.com; Ⓜ Dapuqiao; map pp.60–61. Slick photography gallery among the boutiques in Tianzifang (see p.64). It's small, but the shows are always interesting. Mon–Fri call ahead, Sat & Sun 10am–6pm.

OCAT Shanghai 1016 Suzhou Bei Lu, near Wenan Lu ☎ 66085180, ⓦ ocatshanghai.com; Ⓜ Qufu Lu; map pp.70–71. This not-for-profit museum, down an alley by Suzhou Creek, close to Qufu Lu metro station, holds big, somewhat uneven themed shows that mix local and international artists. Mon–Fri & Sun 10am–5pm, Sat 10am–9pm.

Shanghai Centre of Photography 上海摄影艺术中心, shànghǎi shèyǐng yìshù zhōngxīn 2555

CHINESE CONTEMPORARY ART AND ARTISTS

As China opened up after the cultural puritanism of the Mao years, **artists** discovered and imitated Western forms, from Surrealism to Dada to Pop, but the best absorbed international trends to create something that is distinctly Chinese. Today, although it's hard to speak of any truly dominating "isms", **documentary realism** remains a strong strain in Chinese art, with artists given leeway to bring up, albeit obliquely, issues whose discussion is curtailed in other forums – pollution, corruption and the destruction of the urban environment are common themes. Shanghai-based artists who exemplify this subtly political approach include photographic duo Birdhead, the photographer Yuan Xiaopeng and video artist **Yang Fudong**, notable for his wistful images of city life and migrant workers. Just as strong is a theme of nostalgia, retreat or introspection – plenty of artists don't wish to be commentators. Artists like **Liu Wei**, with his decaying cities, or **Gu Dexin**, who makes fruit and flesh confections, embody this trend.

Other **artists** to look out for include Shanghai-based Liu Jianhua, who makes headless ceramic women; Zhang Huan, who uses his body as a canvas; and Cai Guo-Qiang, who makes art with gunpowder. The most recognizable figures are Yue Minjun, whose absurdist paintings of laughing figures have been much copied, and Xu Bing, who creates attention-grabbing installations, most notoriously an exhibition of painted and tattooed pigs. You won't see anything of China's most famous contemporary art impresario, **Ai Weiwei**, however, as his work is judged to be just too contentious.

13

Longteng Dadao, near Fenggu Lu ☎64289516, ⓦfacebook.com/Shanghai-Center-of-Photography; ⓜYunjin Lu; map p.80. This impressive public gallery is dedicated to photography, putting on temporary shows from local and international artists. There is no permanent display. Tues–Sun 10.30am–5.30pm.

Shanghai Gallery of Art 外滩三号沪申画廊, wàitānsānhào hùshēn huàláng 3F, Three on the Bund, Zhongshan Dong Yi Lu ☎63215757, ⓦshanghaigalleryofart.com; ⓜNanjing Dong Lu; map p.40. An impressive space in a beautiful and upscale building, which hosts safe shows of established big hitters. Daily 11am–9pm.

ShanghART Bldg 10, 2555 Longteng Dadao, West Bund ☎63593923, ⓦwww.shanghartgallery.com; ⓜYunjin Lu; map p.87. This pristine new gallery (basically a set of white boxes) is a showcase for contemporary art; its prestigious stable includes local artists Yan Fudong and Ding Yi. Tues–Sun 11am–6pm.

West Bund Art Centre 2599 Longteng Dadao, near Fenggu Lu ⓦwestbundshanghai.com; ⓜYunjin Lu; map p.87. A huge old aircraft hangar on the West Bund, used as a venue for major international art and design fairs. Daily 10am–5pm, when in use.

TIANZIFANG

Shopping

Shanghai is an excellent city for shopping. There's something here for all tastes, whether you like getting stuck into teeming street markets or swaggering about in swanky boutiques with the glitterati. And with the yuan artificially pegged at a lowish rate (at least for the moment), most foreign visitors find shopping to be pretty good value, too. Best buys include international designer labels from factory outlet stores; tailored clothes and made-to-order shoes; original pieces by local designers; fake name-brand labels; jewellery; and quirky homeware including handmade porcelain.

14

The Shanghainese themselves love **luxury goods** – a great way to advertise status in a society that only recently lost traditional forms of hierarchical display. It's not uncommon to encounter young women spending several months' salary on a handbag (guys, on the other hand, tend to save for the apartment and car that are a prerequisite for dating those girls). However, all those glitzy brand names that give the central shopping streets their sheen are not good value at all; high-end goods and international brands are generally 20 percent more expensive than they would be in the West. Ignore them, and instead plunge into the fascinating world of **boutiques and markets**, where you'll find goods that are quirky, original, bespoke – and a bargain.

ESSENTIALS

Payment Only in high-end shops will you be able to use a credit or debit card. You can generally exchange goods with a receipt except in small shops.

Regulations and customs Keep in mind that most Western countries take a dim view of designer knock-offs. If you're packing more than a couple of look-a-like Vuittons, they could be confiscated. Technically, you cannot take items out of China that are more than 200 years old, but you'd be hard-pressed to find anything that ancient in Shanghai anyway. If you do manage to find something that is more than 100 years old, it'll require authentication from the Antiques and Relics Bureau; the store should help you and the process shouldn't cost you anything.

MALLS

Malls have transformed the retail environment of modern China, and nowhere have they been embraced as enthusiastically as in Shanghai. Aspects of **mall culture** that Europeans regard with disdain – artificiality, the absence of the authentic bustle of the street, a veneer of exclusivity – are in China seen as advantages. Perceived as upscale, they display the most expensive brands on the ground floor, with the more affordable goods above; there's always a food court and a clutch of restaurants, and often a gym and cinema.

Grand Gateway 港汇广场, gǎnghuì guǎngchǎng 1 Hongqiao Lu ☎64070111, ⓦgrandgateway66.com/en/home; map p.87. A megalosaurus of a mall with direct access to Xujiazui metro. It's a little cheaper and busier than the others. Daily 10am–10pm.

★**IAPM Mall** 999 Huaihai Zhong Lu ☎33266700, ⓦiapm.com.cn; map pp.60–61. The city's newest mall has to be commended for being strikingly designed, glitzy but not over the top or too pricey. As well as international brands such as Apple, Miu Miu and Stella McCartney, it hosts plenty of good, affordable restaurants, City Shop – the city's best import supermarket (see opposite) – in the basement, an IMAX cinema on the top floor (see p.152) and even a yoga studio (see p.28). Daily 10am–11pm.

WHERE TO SHOP

For the best choice of souvenirs, head to **Yuyuan Bazaar** (see p.55), **Qibao** (see p.93) or **Tianzifang** (see p.64) where you can get all the perennial favourites: chopsticks, kites, fans, carved signature seals, tea and teapots, but there are plenty of other less obvious options (see p.162). Nanjing Dong Lu (see p.46), which used to be known as the golden mile, is these days pretty prosaic, with stores full of cheap clothes – although at least it's pedestrianized. Most foreign visitors will be more impressed with the retail opportunities offered around the corner on **the Bund**, where luxury brand names have opened showpiece stores – though all but the absurdly wealthy will have to make do with window-shopping. Pricey luxury goods are also available in the malls of **Nanjing Xi Lu** (see p.69) or yuppie playground **Xintiandi** (see p.59).

The most chic area to shop is the **Old French Concession**; central Huaihai Zhong Lu itself is full of familiar brands, but the streets off it, such as Nanchang Lu, Shanxi Nan Lu, Wukang Lu, Anfu Lu and Maoming Lu, are full of fascinating little boutiques, making this the place to forage for fashionable gear. For local crafts, and anything that's a bit more creative, head to the **Tianzifang** area (see p.64).

For stores geared to local tastes, check out **Xujiahui** (see p.86); as soon as you exit Xujiahui metro station you're bang in the middle of a dense concentration of retail outlets – the Grand Gateway (see above), Pacific Digital Plaza (see p.162) and the Oriental Department Store – aimed at the burgeoning middle classes. This is a good place to come for electronic equipment and affordable fashion.

Plaza 66 恒隆广场, hénglóng guǎngchǎng 1266 Nanjing Xi Lu ☎62790910, Ⓦplaza66.com; map pp.70–71. The high-end stores in this mall are characterized by sleek, glassy-eyed staff who outnumber the customers; you could spend hours here without seeing anyone buy anything. Daily 10am–10pm.

Raffles City Mall 莱福士广场, láifúshì guǎngchǎng 268 Xizang Zhong Lu, corner of Fuzhou Lu ☎63403333, Ⓦrafflescity-shanghai.com; map p.39. To draw just the right kind of aspirational clientele a good mall should be a cocktail of the fabulous and the affordable, and should keep shoppers lingering with a decent café and a food court – and for all this, Raffles scores the highest. Check out the *Fresh Everyday* juice bar in the basement, before heading up to local fashion stores aimed at those skinny millennials. Daily 10am–10pm.

Super Brand Mall 正大广场, zhèngdà guǎngchǎng 168 Lujiazui Xi Lu, Pudong ☎6887788, Ⓦsuperbrandmall.com; map p.76. This place is huge, with thirteen floors. Tourists checking out Pudong almost always end up here: they come down from a viewing platform, wander round for a bit, come to realize there's not much to see at ground level and then look for something to eat. At least there are plenty of places to do that – more than seventy, in fact. Daily 10am–10pm.

Xintiandi Style 新天地时尚, xīntiāndì shíshàng 245 Madang Lu ☎53820666, Ⓦxintiandistyle.com; map p.63. Focuses on lesser known luxury brands, and there are frequent events and promotions. Daily 10am–10pm.

14

SUPERMARKETS

City Shop Basement, Times Square, 93 Huaihai Zhong Lu, map p.54; 1F, Shanghai Centre, 1376 Nanjing Xi Lu, map pp.70–71; Basement 1, IAPM Mall, 999 Huaihai Zhong Lu, map pp.60–61; Ⓦcityshop .com.cn. City Shop sells quality Chinese groceries (including an organic range), imported Western goods (though these often have a high mark-up) and good meat and bread. The branch in the IAPM Mall is the biggest: it even has a seafood bar (see p.133) and cooking school. City Shop also offers online shopping with free same-day delivery; you pay cash upon delivery. All branches daily 8am–10pm.

Feidan 飞蛋, fēi dàn 158 Anfu Lu ☎54038501; 382 Dagu Lu ☎4008208786; both map pp.60–61; Ⓦfeidan .cn. These Old French Concession delis have an impressive range of imported food and deli items; the Anfu Lu branch is popular with expats, as you can buy beers inside then drink them on the patio. Both daily 9.30am–10pm.

Parkson Supermarket 百盛, bǎishèng Basement, 918 Huaihai Zhong Lu ☎64158818, Ⓦparkson.cn; map pp.60–61. A good selection of imported Western products at a hefty mark-up. Daily 10am–10pm.

Shanghai First Food Store 第一食品, dìyī shípǐn 720 Nanjing Dong Lu ☎63222777; map p.39. This Shanghai institution is where locals go for speciality festival foods such as moon cakes. There are also plenty of traditional snacks and dried, pickled and marinated food from all around China. A lot of it, to be blunt, is not to foreign tastes, but the displays make for good photos. There's a food hall on the third floor. You won't find any English spoken, or written on the packaging, for that matter. Daily 9am–10pm.

ANTIQUES

Touristy areas have **antique stalls** selling opium pipes, Cultural Revolution alarm clocks, carved screens, Mao's Little Red Book, silk paintings and the like – all fairly cheap but, whatever the vendor tells you, you should always assume you're buying a modern copy. Most of the stock at antique stores is reproduction too, but at least they'll tell you so. Anything more than 100 years old will need authentication (see p.31).

★**Antique Garden** 古董花园, gǔdǒng huāyuán 44 Sinan Lu, near Xiangshan Lu ☎53821055, Ⓦantique-cafe.com; map pp.60–61. This antique shop, full of furniture and bric-a-brac, doubles as a café; be careful where you put down your cup. Mon–Thurs & Sun 11am–11.30pm , Fri & Sat, 11am–midnight.

Gelin Casa 阁琳家居, gélín jiājū 577 Changde Lu, near Xinzha Lu ☎62535175, Ⓦgelincasa.com; map pp.70–71. Antique furniture and fittings, often rescued from houses slated for demolition, and modern reproductions of "old Shanghai style". Everything from ashtrays and wallpaper to Art Deco dining tables. Pricey, but not outrageously so. Mon–Fri 9am–8pm, Sat & Sun 10am–8pm.

Henry Antique Warehouse 亨利古典家具店, hēnglì gǔdiǎn jiājùdiàn 3F, Bldg 2, 359 Hongzhong Lu ☎64010831; map p.87. The English-speaking staff at this huge space show off antique Chinese furniture and furnishings; a carved Chinese bed costs around ¥13,000. Overseas shipping is available. It's in the southern outskirts of the city, so you'll have to take a taxi. Mon–Sat 9am–7pm.

Zhang's Textiles 绣花张, xiùhuā zhāng Shanghai Centre, 202A Nanjing Xi Lu ☎62798587, Ⓦzhangstextiles.com; map pp.70–71. Genuine framed Qing-dynasty embroidery, jade bracelets and silk pillows. It's not cheap, though – you'll spend thousands of yuan for anything of any size. Daily 10am–9.30pm.

14

FAKES

Quite a lot in China is not what it seems – 90 percent of the world's **counterfeit goods** originate here. It isn't just clothes, cigarettes and bags; you can buy counterfeit phones, medicine, computers, cars, fossils, eggs – there are even entire fake IKEA and Apple stores. In Shanghai there are several **fake markets**, though if you're buying a supposed antique, or just about anything from a backstreet market store, there's a good chance that it's a fake too. You'll have to bargain harder at the fake markets than anywhere else in the city (see box, below); the pushy vendors commonly start at ten or twenty times the price they'll accept and it pays to shop around as plenty of people are selling the same thing. The **Shanghai Fake Market app** (free, Android only) offers a regularly updated price guide for just about anything you could buy here; alternately check the **online price database** at Ⓦ shanghaishopping .org/fake-market-prices/ before you go. As a rough guide, a man's watch costs between ¥100 and ¥250, a woman's watch ¥50 to ¥150; "Converse" trainers can be had for ¥80, other brands for a little more. Handbags range from ¥80 to ¥200, a bit more for suitcases and backpacks. You can pick up fake computer games and software for ¥50 or so, DVDs for ¥10. All clothes should cost less than ¥250, and sunglasses, pens and belts are all around ¥30. There's also golf gear on sale, and some stalls just hawk souvenirs. Note that according to the **customs laws** of Western countries, you are only allowed to import one dubious item per brand; so one fake Armani watch is fine, but a dozen will be impounded.

Han City 假货市场, jiǎhuò shìchǎng 580 Nanjing Xi Lu; map pp.70–71. Not far from People's Square, with three storeys of dodgy shops – it's a little cheaper higher up. It's convenient, but the ambience is gloomy and the vendors tiresome; there are persistent rumours that it is about to close down. Daily 10am–8pm.

Qipu Lu Market 七浦路河南北路交汇口, qīpǔlù hénán běilù jiāohuìkǒu 183 Qipu Lu, just off Henan Bei Lu; map p.83. Giant stores here sell some cheap local fashion among all the counterfeits. Generally, the higher the floor, the better the quality, but you'll have to sift through so many dregs it's only worth it if you have a lot of time and patience. Daily 9am–5.30pm.

★**Yatai Xinyang Fashion & Gift Market** 亚太新阳服 饰礼品市场, yàtài xīnyáng fúshì lǐpǐn shìchǎng Underground, beside the Science and Technology Museum metro station (entrance close to the ticketing machines); map p.80. This is the city's biggest fake market, and conveniently located; the metro brings you into the underground warren of stalls. It's divided into zones, with maps on the walls. As well as the usual fake shoes, bags and clothes, you can get tasteless oddities such as Putin T-shirts and Osama Bin Laden papercuts. There are plenty of tailors (see p.160), and a whole zone for jewellery, notably pearls (though don't be convinced by the tests that the stallholders do to show you your wares are genuine). Daily 10am–9pm.

CLOTHES AND SHOES

Sartorial elegance is something of a local obsession, and there's an old Chinese joke that Shanghai men would rather have oil for their hair than their wok. So you're spoilt for choice if you're looking for some glad rags. Name brands and chain stores will cost the same as at home or more, but there's a surfeit of great **local shops** and designers, and getting something **tailor-made** is a bargain. Always try prospective purchases on, and bear in mind that a Chinese large size is equivalent to a Western medium. Shops don't usually stock anything much bigger than that, and no shoes bigger than a

---

BARGAINING

In malls and high-street stores, prices are fixed, but there is always leeway for **bargaining** in small shops and markets. Meanwhile, in touristy places such as the **fake markets** or Yuyuan, haggling is essential, as vendors can start at ten or even fifty times what they'll accept.

Always bargain good-naturedly, as confrontational behaviour will make the seller clam up. Feign a complete lack of interest in the object even if you've fallen in love with it. The seller (a girl, usually) will tap a price into a calculator. You then tap in your best price and she acts as if you just shot her puppy. After a little more discussion, walk away ruefully shaking your head, and she'll chase after you and give you a "last price". Then you start negotiating again.

The best way to get a reasonable price is to decide how much you want to pay for something and then keep obstinately repeating that figure, rather than getting drawn into incremental increases. Remember that in places like fake markets you are likely to see the same thing for sale in the next store along, so having got a price from one place, take it to another and ask if they will beat it. Another tactic is to take the stallholder's card and tell them you'll tell other people about their place. Remember, too, that you'll always get a better price if you buy several items.

(male) British size 10 (US size 10.5), so if you're looking for larger sizes you'll have to get something custom-made or head for one of the fake markets (see opposite). For **high-street fashions**, try Raffles City Mall, Nanjing Dong Lu or Huaihai Lu; if you just want something cheap and smart-looking head for a Giordano or a Uniqlo (there are branches of both at the eastern end of Nanjing Dong Lu). **Shanghai Fashion Week** (ⓦshanghaifashionweek.com), held annually in October, is no longer the joke it used to be, and draws some of the world's most famous names in fashion. Events are held in Xintiandi and the parks nearby.

DESIGNER CLOTHES

If you want to see international designer clothes in showpiece stores head to Plaza 66 (see p.69), Xintiandi Style (see p.157), IAPM Mall (see p.156) or the Bund. Shanghai has produced some great local designers, who deserve your support; for stylish one-off fashions, browse the boutiques in Tianzifang and on Maoming Nan Lu and Shanxi Nan Lu, or head up Fumin Lu.

★**10 Corso Como** North Annexe, 1717 Nanjing Xi Lu ⓣ62861018, ⓦ10corsocom.com; map pp.70–71. This Italian concept fashion store is billed as a lifestyle experience – there's a café, a restaurant, art gallery, bar and bookshop as well as plenty of pricey, quirky clothes from international designers. Daily 10am–10pm.

38 Capital Joy 158 Jinxian Lu, near Maoming Nan Lu ⓣ62560134; map pp.60–61. Smart, affordable menswear from a Hong Kong designer. Off-the-peg suits start at ¥900. Daily 10am–6pm.

Catie Lo 105 Wukang Lu, near Fuxing Lu ⓣ64734198; map pp.60–61. An eclectic, well-curated range of women's shoes, clothing, accessories and retro Art Deco furniture. Daily noon–7.30pm.

Cha Gang 茶缸, chágāng 70 Yongfu Lu, near Hunan Lu ⓣ64733104, ⓦchagang.cn; map pp.60–61. Wang Yigang's unique but restrained unisex fashions and accessories, sold in a space that resembles an art gallery, are deservedly popular, though they're not cheap at around ¥800 for a top. Tues–Sun 11am–7pm.

★**Culture Matters** CM飞跃回力国货鞋店, CM fēiyuè huílì guóhuò xiédiàn Shop 2, 15 Dongping Lu ⓣ13671882040, ⓦfromsh.com; map pp.60–61. This is the main outlet store for two Chinese shoe brands that have caught on with Western hipsters, Feiyue and Warrior sneakers: the cheap, comfortable and stylish shoes are available here in more than fifty designs, including high-top versions, and start at ¥65. Instant indie cred and practically *de rigueur* in Shanghai's cooler clubs. Daily 1–9pm.

Dong Liang Studio 栋梁的地图, dòngliáng de dìtú 184 Fumin Lu ⓣ34696926, ⓦen.dongliangchina.com/home; map pp.60–61. This elegant converted house has three floors that showcase the best Chinese designers, with the more expensive and exclusive on the highest floor. Look out for evening wear by Na(too), Miss Mean and Shang Xia, bags by Fan Fan, and coats from Uma Wang. Plenty of artisanal jewellery and cool retro sunglasses on display too. Daily noon–10pm.

La Vie Courtyard 7, Lane 210, Taikang Lu ⓣ64453585; 306 Changle Lu, near Ruijin Yi Lu ⓣ63847378; ⓦlavie .com.cn; both map pp.60–61. These two Old French Concession shops hold a diverse collection of women's clothes by famed local designer Jenny Li; it's well worth rooting around for the odd gem. Prices start at around ¥300 for a top. Both daily 10.30am–8.30pm.

★ **Nuomi** 糯米, nuòmǐ 196 Xinle Lu, near Donghu Lu ⓣ54034199; No. 12, Lane 274, Taikang Lu ⓣ64663952; ⓦbrownricedesigns.com; both map pp.60–61. Two Old French Concession stores selling eco-conscious high fashion for women, made from recycled materials by a design collective; look out for the purses made from old billboard paper and elegant cotton evening dresses. Both daily 10am–9.30pm.

Shanghai Tang 上海滩, shànghǎi tān 868 Huaihai Zhong Lu, Old French Concession, ⓣ54030580, map pp.60–61; Unit 15, North Block, Lane 181, Taicang Lu, Xintiandi ⓣ63841601, map p.63; Pudong Shangri-La, 33 Fucheng Lu, Pudong ⓣ58776632, map p.76; ⓦshanghaitang.com. This is the only international Chinese luxury fashion brand, offering colourful, stylish chinoiserie such as silk pyjamas with embroidered dragons and the like. Home accessories and gifts are also on sale. Never mind that all their designers are foreign, and it's overpriced – it's still a lovely place to gawp. Huaihai Zhong Lu daily 10.30am–9.30pm; Xintiandi Mon–Thurs 11am–midnight, Fri–Sun 11am–2am; Pudong Shangri-La daily 10am–10pm.

Shiatzy Chen 夏姿陈, xiàzī chén 9 Zhongshan Dong Yi Lu ⓣ63219155, ⓦshiatzychen.com; map pp.60–61. Pleated skirts, tailored shirts and lavish evening gowns by Taiwanese designer Shiatzy Chen combine East and West with a dash of Hollywood glamour. Daily 10am–8pm.

Shirt Flag 衫旗帜, shān qízhì 1F, Bldg 17, 50 Moganshan Lu ⓣ62986483, ⓦshirtflag.com; map pp.70–71. Retro, Cultural Revolution chic, casual wear and bags; so-called McStruggle images, such as lantern-jawed workers waving iPods rather than Little Red Books, predominate. This kind of stuff is regarded as pretty naff in China but it might look cool back home, and it's not too expensive, at ¥160 for a T-shirt. Tues–Sun 11am–6pm.

Triple-Major Lane 25, Shaoxing Lu ⓣ54247308, ⓦtriple-major.com; map pp.60–61. A diverse range of men's and women's clothes from local and international designers. Tues–Sun 1–8pm.

14

14

Xinlelu Boutique 新乐路, xīn lè lù 414 Shanxi Bei Lu ☎ 52133301, ⓦ xinlelu.com; map pp.60–61. Classic womenswear, some from local designers. The store also hosts regular launch parties and events; check the website. Daily noon–8pm.

Younik 2F, No. 18 The Bund ☎ 63238688, ⓦ bund18 .com; map p.40. A shiny boutique selling high-end clothes by Chinese designers. Look for Lu Lun's haute couture and Jenny Ji's embroidered textiles combined with modern shapes. Daily 10am–10pm.

TAILORS AND COBBLERS

Getting some clothes or shoes made up is a recommended Shanghai experience; it will cost much less than at home and the artisans are skilled (provided you're clear about exactly what you are after) and quick. Either head to the South Bund Fabric Market and haggle, or play it safe and spend more at one of the established places, which line Moaming Nan Lu, just south of Huaihai Lu.

Billy Shoes 比利王制作鞋工作室, bǐliwáng zhìzuòxié gōngzuòshì 1238 Changle Lu, near Huashan Lu ☎ 62484881, ⓦ billyshoes.com; map pp.60–61. This is *the* Shanghai cobbler. There are plenty of samples, or you can turn up with a picture from a magazine. You won't get much change from ¥1000, and you'll have to wait up to three weeks for your shoes to be finished. Daily 10.30am–8pm.

Dave's Custom Tailoring 上海不列颠西服, shànghǎi bùlièdiān xīfú Lane 6, 288 Wuyuan Lu ☎ 54040001, ⓦ tailordave.com; map pp.70–71. The men's dress shirts and wool suits made here are certainly not the cheapest in town (suits start at ¥4000) but English-speaking staff make it popular. Items require at least ten days and two fittings to complete. Daily 10am–7pm.

Hanyi Cheongsam 瀚艺旗袍店, hànyì qípáodiàn 221 Changle Lu ☎ 54042303; map pp.60–61. This *cheongsam* store isn't cheap, but it's regarded as the best; prices start at ¥1800. Daily 9.30am–9.30pm.

Silk King 真丝大王, zhēnsī dàwáng 66 Nanjing Dong Lu, near the Bund ☎ 63211869, map p.39; 1226 Huaihai Zhong Lu, Old French Concession, ☎ 62821533, map pp.60–61; 819 Nanjing Xi Lu,

Jing'an ☎ 62150706, map pp.70–71; ⓦ silkking.com. The top silk retailers in Shanghai can tailor a silk or wool suit or a *qipao* in as little as 24 hours. Silk starts around ¥120/m, while cashmere is almost ten times that. All branches daily 9.30am–10pm.

★**South Bund Fabric Market** 南外滩轻纺面料市场, nānwàitān qīngfǎng miànliào shìchǎng 399 Lujiabang Lu; map p.54. Never mind the run-down area, this market is decent, with a huge choice of textiles – from denim and corduroy to bouclé and gold lamé – that can be bargained down to ¥20–50/metre, a little more for cashmere or silk (be wary, though, as both are often fake). In addition, most shops also have an on-site tailor; shops that enjoy some kind of reputation include Rita at no. 129, Jennifer at no. 237, Mr Bing at no. 305 and the brothers at no. 309. Come with a good idea of what you want – a photo from a fashion magazine will do, but you'll get much better results if you ask them to directly copy something you give them. If you're interested in a man's suit they'll show you a catalogue of styles. Don't be talked into buying more material than you need; a man's suit requires about 5m of fabric, a shirt about 1.5m. Prices vary, but expect to pay roughly ¥100 for a linen shirt, ¥120 for wool trousers and ¥250 for a man's lined corduroy blazer. If you've haggled sharply, the total price for a man's wool suit with a spare pair of trousers will be around ¥600 – less than half what you'd pay in a local shop. It will take them around a week to make and they will deliver for a small fee. You may have to get them to make on-site alterations when you pick up. Daily 10am–7pm.

Suits de Heart 真挚祝, zhēnzhì fú Shop 1–3, 59 Maoming Nan Lu, near Huaihai Zhong Lu ☎ 34060822, ⓦ sh-zff.com; map pp.60–61. The experienced tailors here are known to have a fanatical eye for detail and good knowledge of Japanese styles. A suit will cost around ¥5000. Daily 10am–8pm.

Suzhou Cobblers 苏州鞋匠, sūzhōu xiéjiàng Room 101, 17 Fuzhou Lu ☎ 63217087, ⓦ suzhou-cobblers .com; map p.39. Hand-embroidered slippers, bags and hand-knitted children's clothing in charming traditional designs. A pair of embroidered slippers is around ¥500. Daily 10am–6.30pm.

KNICK-KNACKS, JEWELLERY AND ACCESSORIES

Shanghai does **curios**, accessories and knick-knacks much better than it does antiques, with something of a **crafts** renaissance going on. There is also some very well-designed mass-market homeware and porcelain that's worth investigating. The place to start is **Tianzifang** (see p.64), where you'll find a conveniently dense cluster of stores. The Yatai Market (see p.158) has a big jewellery and pearl section.

Annabel Lee 安梨家居, ānlí jiājū Unit 2, Bldg 3, North Block, 181 Taicang Lu, Xintiandi ☎ 63200045, ⓦ annabel-lee.com; map p.63. Chic boutique selling cashmere scarves and blankets, silk underwear and pricey

souvenirs such as tissue holders. Daily 10am–8pm.

Bai Sher 摆什, bǎishè 866 Yan'an Zhong Lu, near Shanxi Bei Lu ☎ 13817778455, ⓦ baisher.blogbus .com; map pp.60–61. All sorts of affordable vintage, from

MADE IN CHINA: CHINESE BRANDS

As fashion-conscious Shanghai locals like to be seen as outward looking and international, prestige is generally conferred by international labels, be they IKEA or Gucci. But there are also a number of local brands that are making "Made in China" cool again. Hipsters should check out **Feiyue** sneakers (Ⓦfeiyue-shoes.com). Bold, cheap and practical, these old-school sneakers have been made in Shanghai since the 1920s. Perennially popular with students and martial arts practitioners, they now have huge indie cred, too. The makers, Da Fu, finally cottoned on to their cool appeal and started producing pricier lines (and selling them abroad) – even so, most designs won't set you back more than ¥150.

Another Chinese brand that's taking advantage of its nostalgic appeal is **Forever** (Ⓦwww .forever-bicycle.com). They've been making bikes since the 1940s, and for decades saw no need either to change the design or offer any colour but black (they're nicknamed "old tanks"). Their new range cleverly combines the familiar classic fixed-gear look with great build quality, and has proved hugely popular with young locals. Pricier, but with the same kind of elegant retro simplicity, are the watches of the **Shanghai Watch Company**, which in the 1970s were sported by every Chinese cadre. They are much sought after, and you'll see them in antique shops – though there are plenty of fakes around. If you want a good modern Chinese watch, take a look at **Sea-Gulls** (Ⓦseagull.sg). They make a lot of the movements for more prestigious brands and their own watches are good value and high quality.

Finally, there has been an explosion of local fashion labels – wander around any mall and you'll discover dozens. Notable at the top end is China's first luxury brand **Shang Xia** (Ⓦshang-xia.com), which produces homeware, clothes and accessories for women. Perhaps more exciting, and certainly more affordable, is the bold work coming from young Shanghai designers such as Helen Lee, Gao Yuan, Chictopia, ChiarEYES or Xander Chou – all of whom can be found at Dong Liang Studio (see p.159). Any fashion devotees really keen to take in the local scene should check out Shanghai Fashion Week (see p.159).

14

Art Deco lamps to venerable doors and leather jackets. Look out for the jewellery made from old mah jong tiles, Mao badges and the like. Daily 10am–10pm.

Brocade Country 锦绣坊, jǐnxiùfǎng 616 Julu Lu ☎62792677; map pp.60–61. Hand-stitched tapestries (from ¥150) collected by owner Liu Xiao Lan in Miao villages, plus intricate Miao-made embroidery and handcrafted silver ornaments. Daily 10.30am–7pm.

Brut Cake 1F, 232 Anfu Lu, near Wulumuqi Lu ☎54488159, Ⓦbrutcake.com; map pp.60–61. Colourful, artsy homeware and knick-knacks, generally ceramic or textiles, from Taiwanese artist Nicole Teng. On the pricey side but you can get a handmade mug for ¥180. Daily 11am–8pm.

Feicui Yuan 翡翠园, fěicuì yuán 514 Huaihai Zhong Lu ☎53838099; map pp.60–61. A well-regarded jade jewellery store, more reliable and better value than the shops around the more touristy areas. Daily 10am–6pm.

★**Harvest Studio** 盈佳坊工作室, yíngjiàfǎng gōngzuòshì Room 118, No. 3, Lane 210, Taikang Lu, Tianzifang ☎64734566; map pp.60–61. Hand-embroidered clothing, soft furnishings, notebooks and wallets by eight resident Miao tribeswomen. Also offers embroidery classes. Daily 9.30am–8pm.

Lan Yin Hua Bu Guan 蓝印花布馆, lányìnhuā bùguǎn Lane 637, 24 Changle Lu ☎54037947; map pp.60–61. Boutique selling handmade bags, waistcoats, tablecloths and the like created from a traditionally produced blue-and-white batik-style nankeen fabric. Daily 10am–7pm.

Lolo Love Vintage 2 Yongfu Lu, near Wuyuan Lu ☎64331789; map pp.60–61. Vintage clothes, mostly from the West, plus jewellery, shoes and oddities, in a space decorated with antique dolls. Daily noon–10pm.

★**Madame Mao's Dowry** 毛太设计, máotài shèjì 207 Fumin Lu ☎54033551, Ⓦmadamemaosdowry .com; map pp.60–61. Cultural Revolution kitsch for the home, with Mao-related geegaws aplenty, sold alongside quirky, often retro, ceramics, clothes and accessories from a wide range of local designers. Propaganda posters from the Seventies will set you back at least ¥800, and come with a certificate of authenticity. Daily 10am–7pm.

Paddy Field 稻家居, dào jiā jū 30 Hunan Lu ☎64375567, Ⓦpaddy-field.com.cn; map pp.60–61. This design emporium sells Southeast Asian-inspired homeware made from stone, leather and mother of pearl. They can also create custom furniture in about three weeks and ship overseas. Daily 10.30am–6.30pm.

Piling Palang 噼呤啪啷, pīlíng pālāng 828 Julu Lu ☎63352978, Ⓦpilingpalang.com; map pp.60–61.

14

China's best homeware brand is worth seeking out for its bright and funky original porcelain, lacquerware and cloisonné. Old Chinese forms are given a contemporary twist with modern designs; a plate will cost around ¥100, a tray or snuffbox-shaped vase twice that. Daily 10am–9.30pm.

Simply Life 逸居生活, yìjū shēnghuó 9 Dongping Lu (Old French Concession) ☎ 34060509, map pp.60–61; 159 Madang Lu (Xintiandi) ☎ 63875100, map p.63; ☺ simplylife-sh.com. Good places for speedy souvenir shopping, with affordable Chinese-themed knick-knacks and homeware. Both Mon–Thurs & Sun 10.30am–10.30pm, Fri & Sat 10.30am–11.30pm.

★**Spin** 旋陶艺, xuàn táoyì 360 Kangding Lu, near Shanxi Bei Lu ☎ 62792545, ☺ spinceramics.com; map

pp.70–71. Modern ceramics from Jingdezhen – the capital of china in China, as it were. None of that chintzy "lovers on a willow bridge" stuff that your gran had, this is modern, chic and minimalist, sometimes playful. A dumpling-shaped paperweight will cost ¥60; tea sets go from around ¥800. Daily 11am–9.30pm.

Urban Tribe 城市山民, chéngshì shānmín 133 Fuxing Xi Lu ☎ 64335366, ☺ urbantribe.cn; map pp.60–61. Stylish clothing, pottery and jewellery, all sharing an ethnic minimalist design aesthetic. Good café, too (see p.138). Daily 9.30am–10pm.

Wholesale Pearl and Stone Market 城隍庙珍珠批发市场, chénghuángmiào zhēnzhū pīfā shìchǎng 3F, 288 Fuyou Lu, near Jiuxiachang Lu; map p.54. The stalls here sell lots of jewellery, mostly pearls. Remember to haggle. Daily 10am–6pm.

SOUVENIRS

For souvenirs, you can't go wrong with teapots, fans, papercuts, signature seals and chopsticks, and you can get them all at **Yuyuan Bazaar** (see p.55). But if you're in the market for something a bit different, how about silk slippers from Suzhou Cobblers (see p.160); Cultural Revolution picture postcards from the Propaganda Poster Centre (see p.66); a replica of a *ding* pot from the Shanghai Museum shop (see p.49); an Obama as Mao T-shirt from a fake market (see p.158); or a flashing Buddha from Yufo Temple (see p.73)?

Huangshan Tea Company 黄山茶业有限公司, huángshān cháyè yǒuxiàn gōngsī Basement, Hong Kong Plaza; map p.54. Teapots from the famous factories at Yixing, as well as loose Chinese teas sold by weight. Vendors will let you sample all the wares. Daily 10am–1pm.

Nantai Costume Company 南泰戏剧服装用品有

限公司, nántài xìjù fúzhuāng yòngpǐn yǒuxiàngōngsī 181 Henan Zhong Lu, near Fuzhou Lu ☎ 63238344; map p.39. With fake beards, tasselled hats and all manner of outlandish outfits, Nantai kits out local opera troupes and expats looking for Halloween costumes. The resident mynah bird can say *ni hao*. Daily 9am–5pm.

ELECTRONICS, COMPUTER AND PHOTOGRAPHY EQUIPMENT

There's not much point buying big-name-brand **electronics** here, or anything that's near the top of the range; prices are the same as in the West, and you'll get less after-sales support. But it is worth checking out the **local brands** that you've probably never heard of (Lenovo is the biggest) and mid-range brands from Japan, Korea and Taiwan such as Acer (though note that the smaller brands won't have international warranties). A basic **Chinese laptop** costs as little as ¥2000, though it may well have build-quality issues. For twice that you can pick up one from a Korean company that will usually have an international warranty and will still cost two-thirds what it would cost in the West. But the **best value** is in gadgets and add-ons such as memory sticks, USB fans, webcams and the like.

Apple Store 300 Nanjing Dong Lu ☎ 23131800, ☺ apple.com; map p.39. This is Asia's biggest Apple Store. Students feel social pressure to turn up to college with an "Apple three set" – Mac, iPad and iPhone – so you'll see plenty of parents blanching at the prices. Daily 10am–10pm.

Huanlong Department Store 黄龙百货, huánglóng bǎihuò 3F, 360 Meiyuan Lu, by the main train station; map pp.70–71. Prices for photography equipment are not as good as in Hong Kong but still cheaper than the West. Plenty of the stores here sell

second-hand and studio gear. Daily 9am–6pm.

Pacific Digital Plaza 太平洋数码广场, tàipíngyáng shùmǎ guǎngchǎng 117 Zhaojiabang Lu ☎ 54905900; map p.87. Plaza One is a huge, three-storey mall, with a new Plaza Two over the road – look for the English "Metro City" sign. In both, stalls sell international and local electronics, but Plaza Two is much nicer. There is plenty of leeway for bargaining – always compare prices. Plaza One daily 10am–8pm, Plaza Two daily 10am–7pm.

FURNITURE

Locals might be flocking to IKEA, but foreign expats, it would seem, just can't get enough **retro Chinese furniture**, with four-poster beds, carved screens, and lacquered chairs the most popular of many lines. All shops will arrange shipping home. The majority is, of course, reproduction. See also the Paddy Field homeware store (p.161).

Kava Kava Home 吉木坊, jímù fāng 810 Julu Lu, near Fumin Lu ☎62148313, ⓦkavakavahome.com; map pp.60–61. Traditional Ming dynasty furniture designs (including lovely medicine chests and bedframes) jazzed up with bright colours and simple lines. Daily 10am–5.30pm.

Pusu 朴素生活, pǔsù shēnghuó Number 15, Alley 188, Changshu Lu ☎34619855, ⓦinpusu.com; map pp.60–61. Elegant and well-crafted wooden furniture. The lines are distinctly Chinese but there's no twiddly ornamentation. A chair will cost ¥1800, a bed ten times that. Daily 10am–10pm.

14

BOOKS, CDS AND DVDS

It's not hard to find **English-language books** in Shanghai. You can pick up those printed by local presses – usually drily written guides, or classics – for around ¥20, though imported books are expensive at more than ¥100. Fuzhou Lu is known to locals as "Book Street", but there's not much English-language material in its huge bookshops. You can buy fake **CDs and DVDs** from roadside stalls. They cost ¥10 (Westerners might have to haggle the vendors down) and quality is unreliable; new releases almost never work, or are grainy prints filmed in a cinema. In addition, many Western films will be dubbed into Russian, with Chinese subtitles – because of anti-pirating measures in the West, the counterfeiters are now copying the Russian releases. The Shanghai Grand Theatre Shop and the Foreign Language Bookstore stock plenty of authentic DVDs.

Big Movie 158 Xinle Lu, near Donghu Lu ☎54038736; map pp.60–61. The fake DVDs here are ¥12 each and they have a huge selection. If your disc doesn't work you can bring it back and swap it. They also sell Western magazines. Daily 10am–11pm.

Foreign Language Bookstore 上海外文书店, shànghǎi wàiwén shūdiàn 390 Fuzhou Lu ☎23204994, ⓦsbt.com.cn; map p.39. Though it's no longer the main source of English-language material in the city, there's still a good range of books in English about China, plus plenty of fiction with an emphasis on the classics. On higher floors you'll find audiovisual material and textbooks for people learning Chinese, plus maps, kids books and (authentic) movie DVDs. There's a café on the ground floor. Daily 9.30am–7pm.

★**Garden Books** 韬奋西文书局, tāofèn xīwén shūjú 325 Changle Lu, near Shanxi Nan Lu (Old French Concession) ☎54048728, map pp.60–61; Shanghai Centre, 1376 Nanjing Xi Lu (Jing'an) ☎15800554636, map pp.70–71; ⓦgardenbooks .cn. The Changle Lu shop is one of the city's mellowest spaces, and not just a good place to browse – the attached coffee shop is a great spot to cast a discreet eye over both your new acquisitions and the other customers while sampling tasty ice cream. The second address in the Shanghai Centre is a book-crammed booth. Fiction, art and coffee-table books, in English. Both daily 10am–10pm.

Shanghai Grand Theatre Shop 上海大剧院, shànghǎi dàjùyuàn Shanghai Grand Theatre, 300 Renmin Dadao, People's Square ☎63728701, ⓦshgtheatre.com; map p.49. A good selection of genuine DVDs, mostly documentaries and old films, from ¥12 to ¥30. Daily 10am–5pm.

SHANGHAI URBAN PLANNING EXHIBITION HALL

Contexts

History

Shanghai's history as a metropolis is distinct from that of the nation as a whole, as the machinations of thousands of years of imperial dynasties have not much influenced its destiny. In fact, it's a young city (in Chinese terms) whose story is dominated by trade rather than politics, and which has been shaped by international forces as much as domestic ones.

The port on the Yangzi

Contrary to Western interpretations, Shanghai's history did not begin with the founding of the foreign concessions. Located at the head of the **Yangzi River**, Shanghai grew from a fishing village (Shanghai simply means "on the sea") into a major commercial port during the Song dynasty. By the time of the Qing dynasty, huge **mercantile guilds** dealing in lucrative local products – silk, cotton and tea – often organized by trade and bearing superficial resemblance to their Dutch counterparts, had established economic and, to some extent, political control of the city. The Yangzi basin reaches half of China, and this formidable route to the interior was bolstered by almost a million kilometres of **canals** – vital trade routes in a country with very few roads. It was this unprecedented accessibility, noted by its first Western visitor, Hugh Lindsay of the British East India Company, that was to prove so alluring to the foreign powers, and set the city off down its unique, tempestuous path. The story of **foreign intervention** in China began in morally murky waters (and, some would say, remained there): it started with a dispute over drugs and money.

Ocean barbarians

The **Qing dynasty**, established in 1644, followed the pattern of China's long and repetitive history; a rebellion, in this case by the Manchus from the north, overthrew the emperor and established a new dynasty which ran, as usual, on a feudal, Confucian social model – everyone from peasant to emperor knew their place in a rigid hierarchy. By the eighteenth century the Qing had lost their early vigour and grown conservative and decadent, the out-of-touch royal court embroiled in intrigue. As with all previous dynasties, they were little troubled by outsiders. For thousands of years, China had remained alone and aloof, isolated from the rest of the world; the only foreigners in the Chinese experience were nomadic tribesmen at the fringes of the empire – savages to be treated with disdain.

So when the **British East India Company** arrived in the early seventeenth century the Manchu officials were not much interested. The "ocean barbarians" began trading in Canton in the far south, China's only open port – they sold English textiles to India, took Indian cotton to China, and bought Chinese tea, porcelain and silk. The Chinese wanted no British manufacturing in return, only silver.

Even this much trade was begrudged by the Qing, whose policies ensured that the East India Company always bought more than it sold, with the result that the British

1644	1832	1839
Qing dynasty established	British East India Company arrives in Shanghai	First Opium War begins

exchequer reluctantly made up the balance with hard currency. The Company's infamous solution to this trade imbalance was to get the country hooked. **Opium** grown in India was exported to China, and proved a great success; in 1760 more than a thousand chests, each weighing more than a hundred pounds, were imported; fifty years later, this had grown to more than forty thousand. Stupefied addicts numbered more than two million and now the trade imbalance was firmly in the other direction.

In 1839, fearing a crippled economy, Emperor Daoguang abruptly declared the trade illegal and British merchants were forced to watch their opium cargo hurled overboard from their ships. It was a typically ill-judged response. The British countered by **seizing Hong Kong** (then a minor outpost) and sending an expeditionary force to attack Canton, triggering the **First Opium War**. Chinese tactics such as sending monkeys with fireworks to set enemy ships alight were inventive but hardly effective; the superior technology of the British meant that the result was never in doubt.

In 1842 the defeated Manchus were forced to sign the unequal **Treaty of Nanjing**, which ceded Hong Kong to the British and opened Shanghai, then a small fortified town, as well as four other ports (Fuzhou, Xiamen, Guangzhou and Ningbo), to

ARCHITECTURE IN SHANGHAI

Shanghai has a great mix of striking buildings, all rather jumbled together, with traditional Chinese temples abutting Art Deco classics in the shadow of looming, brutalist skyscrapers. It isn't always pretty or coherent – a "Shanghai skyline" is architects' slang for a poorly planned mess – but, at least in the centre, there is always some marvel, oddity or bizarre juxtaposition to appreciate. The city's **architectural wonders** date from two distinct periods: 1900 to the 1930s, when colonial powers were making their mark, and the late twentieth century to today, when formidable new commercial powers were making theirs.

THE COLONIAL PERIOD

Shanghai's first building boom began at the start of the twentieth century, when the foreigners set their stamp on their new concession. For their public buildings, they picked a style then much in vogue: Neoclassicism, which consciously echoes ancient Greek and Roman archetypes, implying that the new colonial powers were modern heirs to those ancient empires. The finest examples were built by the British firm Palmer and Turner, including the **HSBC building** (see p.44), the **Yokohama Bank building** (see p.42) and the **Customs House** (see p.44), all on the Bund. The French take on the rather po-faced style was lighter; known as Beaux Arts, the best example in Shanghai is the **Okura Garden hotel** (see p.65).

More intimate in scale were the villas that the new European merchant class built as luxurious reminders of home. These displayed all kinds of European styles, from Spanish hacienda to German castle, but the most popular was the Tudor half-timbered mansion. Though generally neglected in the twentieth century, many have been restored and reopened as offices, restaurants or hotels; striking examples include the **Hengshan Moller Villa** (see p.65) and **Ruijin Guesthouse** (see p.64).

It is fortuitous that the city's biggest colonial building boom, in the 1920s, coincided with the rise of one of the modern era's most elegant styles: Art Deco. Its design principles of streamlining, exuberance and assertive modernity created masterworks that still look contemporary, despite being dwarfed by newly built skyscrapers. Notable examples include

1842	1844	1854
Defeated Manchus sign the Treaty of Nanjing with the British	Sino-American Treaty of Wangxia allows for extra-territoriality	Taiping Rebellion begins

foreign trade. This, the first of many unequal treaties, marks the beginning of modern Chinese history, on a sour note of national humiliation.

The Concession era

Of the new open ports, Shanghai was the most ideally situated – at the midpoint of China's coast, close to established trading routes between the West and Japan, and offering a route straight into the heart of China. The town was soon booming, and other nations scrambled to get a foothold in the alluring new market that the British had prised open. France, Belgium, Norway and Russia all began to make their own demands on the Qing administration, but it was the **Americans** who proved most influential. An envoy sent by President Tyler "to save the Chinese from being an exclusive monopoly of England" managed, in the 1844 Treaty of Wangxia, to hack out the principle that was to prove vital to Shanghai's development, the idea of "**extra-territoriality**"; foreigners resident in the treaty ports would be subject to the laws of their own nation rather than those of China. This guaranteed the safety

the **Park hotel** (see p.169), **Broadway Mansions** (see p.40), **Grosvenor House** (see p.65) and the **Fairmont Peace Hotel** (see p.42).

MODERN ARCHITECTURE

Since the early 1990s Shanghai has been growing faster than anywhere else in the world, ever – at one point, a quarter of the world's cranes were in use here. In the rush to globalize, the city has become a construction free-for-all, a playground for the most celebrated names in architecture. The result has seen some of the world's most ambitious building projects – from spectacular high-rises to brand-new futuristic cities.

With Shanghai attempting to become a global power, thirty percent of new projects were awarded to foreign architects. They usually attempted at least a nod towards Chinese culture; one recurring theme has been the use of circles atop squares, as a reference to the Chinese idea that the earth is square and heaven round – this is notable in French architect Jean-Marie Charpentier's **Shanghai Grand Theatre** (see p.51). The most effectively Sinicized building has to be the **Jinmao Tower** (see p.78), whose proportions are built around the number eight – associated with prosperity in Chinese culture – and whose tiered form constantly references pagoda design.

Construction continues at a frantic pace. To get a taste of the newest grand projects, head to the Shanghai Urban Planning Exhibition Hall (see p.51).

SHANGHAI'S SATELLITES

Developments within the city are certainly eye-catching, but the most ambitious projects are happening outside the city centre. With its population expected to hit fifty million by 2050, and a population density four times greater than that of New York, Shanghai cannot simply build upwards – it needs to spread outwards, too. Accordingly, nine new **satellite cities** have been built from scratch, providing homes for half a million souls. Designed to appeal to the affluent and increasingly Westernized Chinese middle class, they are all pastiches of European cities and towns. **Pujiang** has an Italian flavour, **Fencheng** focuses on an adaptation of Barcelona's Ramblas and **Anting** is a German-themed town designed by Albert Speer, the son of Hitler's favourite architect. **Thames Town**, meanwhile, the faux-English centre to Song Jiang new town, features cobbled streets, half-timbered mock Tudor houses and a parish church (see p.94).

1863	1865	1870	1895
Americans join the British Concession, creating the International Settlement	Taiping Rebellion defeated	Shanghai's Chinese population tops seventy thousand	Japanese win the right to start manufacturing in Shanghai

and property of traders – and of course, set them completely apart from the local population.

Shanghai was divided up between trading powers, with each claiming a riverside frontage: the British along the Bund and the area to the north of the Chinese city, the **French** in an area to the southwest, centred on the site of a cathedral a French missionary had founded two centuries earlier. Later the Americans, in 1863, came to tack their own areas onto the British Concession, which expanded into the so-called **International Settlement**. Each section was a mini-state, with its own police force, and a municipal council voted in by prominent traders. The borders of these states had not been fixed, so the foreigners used every excuse to extend them. It was colonialism in all but name; but whereas in other colonial territories, such as British India, a degree of mixing occurred between people, in Shanghai the Chinese and the foreigners lived in isolation from each other, in a state of mutual contempt.

The Huangpu riverfront swelled as the **great trading houses** such as Jardine Matheson and Swire from Hong Kong rushed to open *godowns* (warehouses) and offices. Silk, tea and opium (still technically illegal) remained important but insurance and banking proved lucrative new moneymakers. Behind the river, homesick merchants built mansions in imitation of the ones they had left behind in Europe, with large gardens. By 1853 there were several hundred foreign ships making regular trips into the Chinese interior, and almost a thousand resident foreigners, most of them British. Still, even the largest firms had only a dozen or so foreign staff. It would take a catastrophic civil war to kick the city's development into a much higher gear.

The Taiping Rebellion and beyond

China's humiliation by foreigners, and the corruption and decadence of her ineffectual overlords, caused instability in Shanghai's giant, mysterious hinterland. Between 1740 and 1840 the Chinese population tripled, and vast numbers of peasantry became poverty-stricken and rootless. Arbitrary taxes and lawlessness compounded their plight. Resentment crystallized around the unlikely figure of charismatic cult leader **Hong Xiuquan**, a failed scholar who declared himself the younger brother of Jesus Christ. His egalitarian philosophy proved wildly popular, and he attracted millions of followers. Declaring their intention to build a Taiping Tianguo, or "Heavenly Kingdom of Great Peace", with Hong as its absolute ruler, these **Taipings** stormed across southern China, capturing Nanjing in 1854 and making it their capital. They abolished slavery, redistributed the land and replaced Confucianism with a heretical form of Christianity.

A sister organization, the **Small Sword Society**, took over the Chinese quarter at the centre of Shanghai. Alarmed by these fanatical revolutionaries, the city's foreign residents joined forces with the armies of the Qing against them. The fighting devastated the countryside around Shanghai, and more than twenty million are thought to have died (more than a hundred million if natural disasters and famine are added) – making this obscure rebellion, little known in the West, the world's bloodiest-ever civil war. Hong retreated into the sensual distractions of his harem, and the drive of the Taiping faltered; the final blows were administered with the help of foreign mercenaries in 1865.

For Shanghai, the crisis proved an opportunity. Chinese **refugees** from the conflict swarmed, for safety, into the city's foreign concessions. Previously, foreigners had

1908	1911	1920s	1921
Dowager Empress Cixi dies	Qing dynasty collapses	A construction boom in Shanghai brings a rash of elegant Art Deco buildings to the city	Chinese Communist Party founded in Shanghai

banned Chinese from living in their exclusive enclaves, but plenty of the new arrivals had gold enough to make them overcome any scruples. Now Shanghai's greatest asset became land, as the average price of an acre in the foreign concessions shot up from £70 to more than £10,000 in less than a decade. The merchants demolished their spacious villas, sold their grounds and annexed local farms in a feverish **real-estate boom**. The city's Chinese population exploded from fewer than a thousand souls in 1850 to more than seventy thousand by 1870.

A pattern was set: as Manchu misrule continued and warlords blighted millions of lives, Shanghai profited by offering haven under the racist but at least orderly rule of the foreigners. This is when the city began to take its modern shape, with Nanjing Lu emerging as the busiest shopping street and the French Concession providing the most desirable residences. The Chinese were not allowed any say in running the city, though their taxes paid for improvements such as gas lighting, electricity and tarmacked roads.

The seeds of revolution

It was the arrival of a new foreign power, who played by different rules to the old colonial nations, that caused Shanghai's next spurt of growth. For the **Japanese**, dealings with the West had proved much more positive than for the Chinese and by the mid-nineteenth century Japan had successfully transformed itself into a modern industrial nation. Following their defeat of the Qing in a conflict over the vassal state of Korea in 1895, the Japanese copied the Western tactic of extracting unequal treaties, and won for themselves the right to start **manufacturing** in Shanghai. It was a clever move; coal and electricity were cheap, and, with the city stuffed with desperate refugees, labour even cheaper. The Western powers followed, factories replaced the *godowns* along the Huangpu and the city grew from a trading port into an industrial powerhouse.

Squalid living conditions, outbreaks of unemployment and glaring abuses of Chinese labour by foreign investors made the city a natural breeding ground for **revolutionary**

LADISLAV HUDEC (1893–1958)

The most notable star of Shanghai's Art Deco architecture scene was Hungarian **Ladislav (László) Hudec** who, more than anyone else, created the city's distinctive Art Deco stamp. In 1918, he fought for the Hungarian army and was captured by the Russians; en route to a prison camp in Siberia, he jumped the train – and ended up in Shanghai. Having set up practice here, he built dozens of buildings, most famously the *Park* hotel, which was the city's tallest building well into the 1980s; the structure that now houses the Arts and Crafts Museum (see p.66); the lovely Grand Theatre at 216 Nanjing Xi Lu (now a cinema); and the striking, flatiron-style Normandie Apartments (see p.67). A block of flats that he designed and lived in for ten years has now been converted into a boutique hotel, the *Jinjiang MetroPolo Hotel Classiq Shanghai Jing'an Temple* (see p.119).

Hudec fans might want to track a couple more classics down in the backstreets behind the Bund: you'll find the Savings and Loan Building (though it's sadly rather dilapidated) at 259 Sichuan Zhong Lu, the Christian Literature Society building at 128 Huqiu Lu and, directly behind it at 209 Yuanmingyuan Lu, the China Baptist Publication Building.

1928	1931	1937
Chiang Kai-shek forms National Government in Nanjing	Civil war between Nationalists and Communists begins. Manchuria is lost to the Japanese	Japanese occupy the valley of the Yangzi River

ferment. But just as influential was first-hand experience of foreign technology, ideologies and administration. To Shanghai's urban intellectuals, especially those who had been educated abroad, it became clear that the old imperial order had to be overthrown. Just as clearly, the foreigner had to be expelled – from now on, far from being aloof from China's political life, the city was about to be thrown into the centre of it.

By the early twentieth century, mass **civil disorder** had broken out across the country. Attempts to reform the administration had been quashed by the conservative Dowager Empress Cixi, and her death in 1908 further destabilized the country. In 1911, the dynasty finally collapsed, in large part due to the influence of the Shanghai intellectual, **Sun Yatsen**, leader of the Nationalists and a champion of Chinese self-determination. Steeped in international culture, this ex-medical student was a fine product of the city's intellectual foment. Yet against men such as this, who understood the need to modernize, warlords maintained China's old ideological model and fought to establish a new dynasty. No one succeeded, and with the absence of central government, chaos reigned.

In 1921, the **Chinese Communist Party** (**CCP**) was founded in Shanghai. Four years later, in protest at the indiscriminate killing of protesting students by settlement police, the CCP organized China's first strike. Two hundred thousand workers downed tools; some even marched under the slogan "No taxation without representation!" Much to the chagrin of Shanghai's foreign overlords, the Chinese were beginning to develop political consciousness.

Nationalists versus Communists

The most powerful of the new groups, however, was the **Nationalist Party**, now led by the wily **Chiang Kai-shek**. In 1927 he attempted to unite the country in an alliance with the Communists. Curfews and labour unrest froze the city as the Nationalists and Communists fought Shanghai's own warlords. Having won that battle, Chiang promptly turned on his allies and launched a surprise attack against the Communists, with the help of the city's ruthless criminal mastermind, **Du Yuesheng**. In what came to be known as the White Terror, Du's hoods, dressed in Nationalist uniforms, rampaged across the city, killing anyone with any association with communism; at least twelve thousand died, most of them executed in cold blood.

But even during the chaos, the party continued, and the foreign concessions remained an enclave of privilege. Foreign Shanghai was at its decadent height in the 1920s and 1930s, and it was during this age of inequality and decadence that Shanghai got its reputation as the "**Paris of the East**" or, less politely, "whore of the Orient". A visiting missionary sniffed, "If God allows Shanghai to endure, he owes Sodom and Gomorrah an apology." For foreigners, no visa or passport was needed and every new arrival, it was said, had something to hide. White Russian *émigres* (see p.66) filled the chorus lines at the Paramount and the Majestic, and their unluckier sisters joined the Chinese girls at the only institutions more popular than the cabaret, the brothels. The traps that a destitute woman could fall into were many, yet only in Shanghai could a Chinese girl receive an education, reject an arranged marriage or carve out a career. Film stars such as Ruan Lingyu, China's Garbo, personified the new independent spirit, in her screen roles and her real life – though the latter ended in tragedy, with her suicide.

1941	1949	1966	1976
Japanese occupy Shanghai	Communists take over China	Mao Zedong launches the Cultural Revolution	Mao Zedong dies

Inevitably, the show could not last. By 1928 Chiang Kai-shek had defeated enough warlords to form a tentative **National Government**, with its capital in Nanjing. Now he courted the Western powers and, partly to prove that he was a modernizer, converted to Christianity and married Song Meiling, whose father had been a close ally of Sun Yatsen. Though he was explicit about his desire to rid China of the foreigners, the powers in Shanghai backed him as the man to control the country. They were forced to renege on some of the more outrageous racist policies, such as the ruling that kept the Chinese out of Shanghai's parks; more importantly, Chinese were allowed to vote in municipal elections.

But Chiang had not rooted out all of Shanghai's Communists; by 1931 they had regrouped, and a messy civil war began. To compound the nation's woes, the same year the **Japanese snatched Manchuria** (China's northeastern province, present-day Dongbei) and Chiang found himself fighting two conflicts. Believing the Communists to be the more serious threat, he fled west with his government to avoid a showdown that he feared losing. The Japanese now struck against the interior, and in 1937 succeeded in occupying the valley of the Yangzi River, thus cutting off river trade, and depriving Shanghai of its source of wealth. Hobbled by the depression at home, weary of fighting losing battles against China's resurgent nationalism, the Western powers lost their appetite for interference in the country's chaotic affairs, and Shanghai was left to decline. By the time the Japanese marched in 1941, the life had already drained from the metropolis.

Shanghai under the Communists

It took nearly a decade for China to become once more united, this time under the Communist Party, led by **Mao Zedong**. Communism might have come from abroad, but the manner of its triumph and rule – shrewd charismatic leader leads a peasants' revolt, then becomes an all-powerful despot – were a rerun of dynastic models. They might have been born there, but the Communists distrusted Shanghai; associating it with imperialism, squalor and bourgeois individualism, they deliberately ran the city down. The worst slums were replaced by apartments, the gangsters and prostitutes were taken away for "re-education", and foreign capital was ruthlessly taxed if not confiscated (although Chiang Kai-shek did manage to spirit away the gold reserves of the Bank of China to Taiwan, leaving the city broke). For 35 years Western influences were forcibly suppressed.

Perhaps eager to please its new bosses, the city became a centre of radicalism, and Mao, stifled by Beijing bureaucracy, launched his **Cultural Revolution** here in 1966 – officially a campaign to rid China of its counter-revolutionaries, but really a way to regain control of the party after a string of economic failures. Fervent Red Guards even proclaimed a Shanghai Workers' Commune, modelled on the Paris Commune, but the whole affair quickly descended into wanton destruction and petty vindictiveness. After Mao's death in 1976, Shanghai was the last stronghold of hardcore Maoists, the Gang of Four, in their struggle for the succession, though their planned coup never materialized.

The Shanghainese never lost their ability to make waves for themselves; their chance came when following the death of Mao – and the failure of his experiment – China's Communists became **one-party capitalists**. Its economic renaissance dates from 1990 when Shanghai became an autonomous municipality and the paddy fields of Pudong were designated a "Special Economic Zone". The pragmatic leader **Deng Xiaoping** declared an end to the destructiveness of ideological politicking by declaring "It doesn't

1990	**2003**	**2007**
Shanghai becomes an autonomous municipality and Pudong is designated a "Special Economic Zone"	China puts a man into space for the first time	Shanghai Party Secretary Chen Liangyu arrested on corruption charges

matter if the cat is black or white, as long as it catches mice" – though the dictum of his that Shanghai has really taken to heart is "To get rich is glorious".

Shanghai today

Since opening for business, **Shanghai's growth** has never dipped below ten percent a year. The city has been torn up and built anew (locals quip that its new mascot is the crane), and now has more skyscrapers than New York. The population has swelled to 24 million people and per capita incomes rose from US$1000 per year in 1977 to US$13,000 in 2013. Accounting for a third of China's foreign imports and attracting a quarter of all foreign investment into the country, Shanghai is the white-hot core of the nation's astonishing boom. In 2010 the city also garnered global attention with the glitzy **World Expo**, which brought in more than fifty million visitors; the beano was an excuse for yet more huge construction projects, including the regeneration of the Bund.

As well as batteries of skyscrapers, there has been massive investment in **infrastructure projects**, most notably the Maglev train, five new metro lines, the US$2 billion Pudong International Airport and Hongqiao Station and the high-speed lines that emanate from it. Prestige ventures such as the Oriental Arts Centre and Mercedes Benz Arena have joined high-profile projects such as the Shanghai Centre in epitomizing the city's breezy new swagger. With a huge stock exchange, its next target is to become Asia's biggest financial centre.

Of course there are problems. Shanghai's destiny is still controlled by outside forces, today in the form of the technocrats of Beijing. In recent history, many key modernizing officials in the central government were from the Shanghai area; Jiang Zemin and Zhu Rongji were both former mayors. But the arrest in 2007 of Shanghai Party Secretary Chen Liangyu on corruption charges spelled the end of the politically influential "Shanghai clique" and these days Beijing is firmly in charge. Despite huge gains economically, the city – and the nation as a whole – remains **politically stagnant**. Corruption is rife – more than US$15 billion is embezzled annually from state coffers. Most worrying for Shanghai's long-term prospects and reputation for business nous, China's uniquely opaque business environment means that government connections have replaced entrepreneurial spirit as the necessary prerequisite for high achievement.

Simply dealing with the products of success has become a considerable headache. The city is almost four times as dense as New York and the flow of new arrivals is constant, many of them poor migrant workers from the countryside in search of work. Not unionized, they are often exploited, and – though the majority are family men who send their wages home – widely resented.

Shanghai's attitude to the **environment**, along with the rest of China, is that the clean-up will start just as soon as the city gets rich; the result is that the air quality is poor and the rivers filthy. Finally, the city is becoming a victim of its own success – all those skyscrapers are causing it to **sink** at the rate of about 1.5cm a year.

All that said, however, Shanghai is a natural survivor, and will surely cope with whatever new vicissitudes history throws its way – it's not as if it hasn't had practice. As the business heart of the world's newest superpower, it's booming in all directions, and the sheer buzz of a city on the make is intoxicating. It might not have had much of a past, but it's guaranteed a future.

2008	2010	2015
Beijing hosts the Olympic Games	Shanghai hosts the World Expo, resulting in a huge range of construction projects	The Shanghai Tower, at the time the second-tallest building in the world, is erected in Pudong

Books

Don't expect too much variety in English-language reading material in Shanghai, and bear in mind that what is available will mostly be expensive imports. You will, though, find cheap editions of Chinese and Western classics published in English by Chinese publishers. In the reviews below, titles marked with a ★ are particularly recommended. Note that the Chinese put surnames before first names, and we've listed authors here in alphabetical order accordingly (though Westernized Chinese names follow the English format).

HISTORY

Robert Bickers *Empire Made Me: An Englishman Adrift in Shanghai*. This readable, carefully researched tale humanizes the Concession era by focusing on one English policeman who is both toughened and corrupted by his experiences.

★**Stella Dong** *Shanghai: The Rise and Fall of a Decadent City 1842–1949*. Excellent popular history, vivid and readable, with rather an anti-foreigner bias. Plenty of salacious stories of opium, flower girls, squalor and debauchery.

Reno Kresno *Strangers Always*. A first-hand account of the author's childhood as a exiled Russian Jew growing up in Hongkou amid the chaos of wartime Shanghai and the Japanese occupation.

Nien Cheng *Life and Death in Shanghai*. One of many "my years of hell in the Cultural Revolution" books, but better than most, with absorbing descriptions of life in Shanghai in the bad old days of dour ideological purity.

Lynn Pan *Old Shanghai: Gangsters in Paradise*. A riveting account of the dark side of a dirty time: Pan cleverly tells the story of prewar Shanghai by examining the lives of three larger than life figures: chief Inspector of the French Concession, Huang Jinrong; Dai Li, head of the secret police; and Big Eared Du, gangland overlord.

Harriet Sargeant *Shanghai*. Academic and broad-ranging exploration of the city during the Concession era, giving equal weight to Chinese and foreign inhabitants, and particularly good on their interrelations.

Various *Shanghai Walks*. This series of guides, written by local experts, enthusiasts and historians, describe intriguing city walks, with maps and photos throughout. Each book has four or five routes, mostly in Puxi, with plenty of information and anecdotes.

SOCIETY AND BUSINESS

★**Tim Clissold** *Mister China*. Engaging and eye-opening real-life horror story of how a Western venture capitalist lost US$400 million in China, thanks largely to fraud and malfeasance by his local partners. It's not Shanghai-specific but is a must for anyone thinking of tackling China's "eccentric" business environment.

James Farrer *Opening Up: Youth Sex Culture & Market Reform in Shanghai*. An original and engrossing piece of social anthropology, based on interviews, that uses an examination of Shanghai's sexual revolution to make some telling points.

Mark Kitto *China Cuckoo*. Another memoir from an old China hand who got his fingers burnt: Kitto was once riding high as the mogul behind China's first expat magazine, *That's Shanghai*, until the authorities forced him out of business and he retreated to run a guesthouse in Mogashan. Required

reading for any aspiring entrepreneurs.

Rob Shmitz *Street of Eternal Happiness*. Shmitz follows the lives of a few diverse characters who live on a single street in Shanghai; the engaging portraits offer valuable insights into modern China.

★**Sun Tzu** *The Art of War*. "Lure them with the prospect of gain, then take them by confusion"; this classic treatise on military strategy is as relevant now as it was when it was written, nearly three thousand years ago. Short and to the point, it's full of pithy maxims that can be applied to many aspects of life, particularly business.

Pamela Yatsko *New Shanghai*. This journalistic introduction to the vagaries of the twenty-first-century metropolis is an expat essential – breezy and well informed on business and culture.

FICTION

★**J.G. Ballard** *Empire of the Sun*. The best literary evocation of old Shanghai is a compelling tale of how the gilded life of expat Shanghai collapsed into chaos with the

onset of war, based on the author's own experience (see box, p.174). It was subsequently made into a film by Steven Spielberg.

COCKTAILS AND ATROCITIES: J.G. BALLARD IN SHANGHAI

The most interesting foreign novelist associated with Shanghai is **J.G. Ballard** (1930–2009), whose work was formed by his experience in the city. Ballard was born and raised in the French Concession, where he experienced a childhood of great privilege – living in a villa on what is now Panyu Lu – and then, following the Japanese invasion in 1941, a nightmare of total privation. He spent much of the war in a Japanese internment camp near the Longhua Temple, while the rest of his life was lived in comfortable suburban obscurity in England.

As a writer Ballard was known for visionary fiction concerning the psychological effects of technological developments and mass media; *Crash* (1973), for instance, is about a gang of car crash fetishists, while *Concrete Island* (1974) sets a Robinson Crusoe story on a traffic roundabout. His apocalyptic imagination was clearly formed by his experience of war as a teenager: as he wrote in his autobiography *Miracles of Life* (2008), "The memories of Shanghai that I had tried to repress had been knocking at the floorboards under my feet, and had slipped quietly into my fiction."

Late in his career, he finally dealt with the subject head on, in the semi-autobiographical **Empire of the Sun** (1984); it was described as "the best British novel about the Second World War" by the *Guardian* newspaper and made into a film by Steven Spielberg. Its description of wartime Shanghai's cocktail parties and atrocities feels very distant from the city today; on the other hand, his dystopian fiction about alienating urban environments – such as *High Rise* (1975; made into a movie in 2016), in which tower-block residents descend into tribal savagery – feels strangely prescient in the Shanghai of Pudong and Thames Town.

Tom Bradby *The Master of Rain*. A breathless, slightly overlong novel of murder and betrayal in 1920s Shanghai.

★ **Hergé** *The Blue Lotus*. One of the best Tintin yarns, a tale of drugs and derring-do set in Shanghai during the Sino-Japanese conflicts of the 1930s.

Kazuo Ishiguro *When We Were Orphans*. Ishiguro is a great writer but this postmodern detective story set in Shanghai between the wars is a little too clever and doesn't quite deliver.

Mian Mian *Candy*. Salacious, meandering *roman-à-clef*, with plenty of sex, drugs and rock 'n' roll, by one of China's modern *enfants terribles*. Set in the 1980s and 1990s, it already seems very dated.

★ **Qiu Xiaolong** *The Inspector Chen Series*. This series of nine procedural detective novels features the poetry-loving Inspector Chen of the Shanghai PSB. Though Qiu sometimes seems more interested in examining Shanghai society and morals than in weaving a mystery, his stories of corrupt officials, sharp operators and compromised cops are the best evocations of the city and its people written in English, and the plotlines are taken straight out of the headlines.

Neal Stephenson *The Diamond Age*. A brilliant and inventive science-fiction reinvention of Concession-era Shanghai, set in a future where the world has been transformed by nanotechnology.

Wei Hui *Shanghai Baby*. Infamous chick lit, banned in China for its louche moral tone, concerning a girl torn between her impotent Chinese boyfriend and married Western lover – though her true love is for designer labels. Self-absorbed, over-hyped and with rather more style than substance.

Zhang Henshui *Shanghai Express*. A pulp novel from the 1930s, very popular in its day. Lots of incidental detail enlivens a melodramatic tale of seduction and betrayal set on a train ride from Beijing to Shanghai.

Chinese

Though you'll certainly hear the local Shanghai dialect being spoken, Mandarin Chinese, derived from the language of officialdom in the Beijing area, is the city's primary tongue. It's been systematically promoted over the past hundred years as the official, unifying language of the Chinese people, much as modern French, for example, is based on the original Parisian dialect. It is known in mainland China as putonghua, "common language".

Chinese **grammar** is delightfully simple. There is no need to conjugate verbs, decline nouns or make adjectives agree – Chinese characters are immutable, so Chinese words simply cannot have different "endings". Instead, context and fairly rigid rules about word order are relied on to make those distinctions of time, number and gender that Indo-European languages are so concerned with. Instead of cumbersome tenses, the Chinese make use of words such as "yesterday" or "tomorrow" to indicate when things happen; instead of plural endings they simply state how many things there are. For English speakers, Chinese word order is very familiar, and you'll find that by simply stringing words together you'll be producing perfectly grammatical Chinese. Basic sentences follow the subject-verb-object format; adjectives, as well as all qualifying and describing phrases, precede nouns.

From the point of view of foreigners, the main thing that distinguishes Mandarin from familiar languages is that it's a **tonal language.** In order to pronounce a word correctly, it is necessary to know not only the sounds of its consonants and vowels but also its correct tone – though with the help of context, intelligent listeners should be able to work out what you are trying to say even if you don't get the tones quite right.

Pinyin

Back in the 1950s it was hoped eventually to replace Chinese characters with an alphabet of Roman letters, and to this end the **pinyin system**, a precise and exact means of representing all the sounds of Mandarin Chinese, was devised. It comprises all the Roman letters of the English alphabet (except "v"), with the four tones represented by diacritical marks, or accents, which appear above each syllable. The old aim of replacing Chinese characters with *pinyin* was abandoned long ago, but in the meantime *pinyin* has one very important function, that of helping foreigners pronounce Chinese words. However, there is the added complication that in *pinyin* the letters don't all have the sounds you would expect, and you'll need to spend an hour or two learning the correct sounds (see p.176).

You'll often see *pinyin* in Shanghai, on street signs and shop displays, but only well-educated locals know the system very well. The Chinese names in this book have been given both in characters and in *pinyin*; the pronunciation guide below is your first step to making yourself comprehensible. For more information, see the *Rough Guide Mandarin Chinese Phrasebook* or *Pocket Interpreter* (FLP, Beijing) – the latter is available at Shanghai's Foreign Language Bookstore (see p.163).

Pronunciation

There are four possible **tones** in Mandarin Chinese, and every syllable of every word is characterized by one of them, except for a few syllables, which are considered toneless. In English, to change the tone is to change the mood or the emphasis; in Chinese, to change the tone is to change the word itself. The tones are:

First or "high" *ā ē ī ō ū*. In English this level tone is used when mimicking robotic or very boring, flat voices.

Second or "rising" *á é í ó ú*. Used in English when asking a question showing surprise; for example "*eh?*"

Third or "falling-rising" *ǎ ě ǐ ǒ ǔ*. Used in English when echoing someone's words with a measure of incredulity; for example, "John's dead." "*De-ad?!*"

Fourth or "falling" *à è ì ò ù*. Often used in English when counting in a brusque manner – "*One! Two! Three! Four!*"

Toneless A few syllables do not have a tone accent. These are pronounced without emphasis, as in the English **u**pon.

Note that when two words with the third tone occur consecutively, the first word is pronounced as though it carries the second tone. Thus nǐ (meaning "you") and hǎo ("well, good"), when combined, are pronounced ní hǎo, meaning "how are you?"

CONSONANTS

Most consonants, as written in *pinyin*, are pronounced in a similar way to their English equivalents, with the following exceptions:

c as in ha**ts**

g is hard as in **g**od (except when preceded by "n", when it sounds like sa**ng**)

q as in **ch**eese

x has no direct equivalent in English, but you can make the sound by sliding from an "s" to an "sh" sound and stopping midway between the two

z as in su**ds**

zh as in fu**dge**

VOWELS AND DIPHTHONGS

As in most languages, the vowel sounds are rather harder to quantify than the consonants. The **examples** below give a rough description of the sound of each vowel as written in *pinyin*.

a usually somewhere between **fa**r and m**a**n

ai as in **eye**

ao as in c**ow**

e usually as in f**u**r

ei as in g**ay**

en as in hyph**en**

eng as in s**ung**

er as in b**ar** with a pronounced "r"

i usually as in b**ee**, except in *zi, ci, si, ri, zhi, chi* and *shi*, when *i* is a short, clipped sound, like the American military "sir".

ia as in **ya**k

ian as in **yen**

ie as in **yeah**

o as in s**aw**

ou as in sh**ow**

ü as in the German **ü** (make an "ee" sound and glide slowly into an "oo"; at the mid-point between the two sounds you should hit the *ü*-sound.

u usually as in f**oo**l, though whenever *u* follows *j, q, x* or *y*, it is always pronounced **ü**

ua as in s**ua**ve

uai as in **wh**y

ue as though contracting "you" and "air" together, **you'air**

ui as in **way**

uo as in w**ore**

Useful words and phrases

When writing or saying the name of a Chinese person, the surname is given first; thus Mao Zedong's family name is Mao.

BASICS

I	我	wǒ
You (singular)	你	nǐ
He	他	tā
She	她	tā

We	我们	wǒmen
You (plural)	你们	nǐmen
They	他们	tāmen
I want...	我要	wǒ yào...
No, I don't want...	我不要	wǒ bú yào...
Is it possible...?	可不可以...	kěbù kěyǐ...?
It is (not) possible	(不)可以...	(bù)kěyǐ
Is there any/Have you got any...?	你有没有...	nǐ yǒuméiyǒu...?
There is/I have	有...	yǒu...
There isn't/I haven't	没有...	méiyǒu
Please help me	请帮我忙...	qǐng bāng wǒ máng
Mr...	...先生	xiānshēng
Mrs...	...太太	tàitai
Miss...	...小姐	xiǎojiě

COMMUNICATING

I don't speak Chinese	我不会说中文	wǒ búhuì shuō zhōngwén
Can you speak English?	你会说英语吗?	nǐ huì shuō yīngyǔ ma?
Can you get someone who speaks English?	请给我找一个 会说英文的人?	qǐng gěi wǒ zhǎo yī gè huì shuō yīngyǔ de rén?
Please speak slowly	请说得慢一点	qǐng shuōde mànyīdiǎn
Please say that again	请再说一遍	qǐng zài shuō yībiàn
I understand	我听得懂	wǒ tīngdedǒng
I don't understand	我听不懂	wǒ tīngbùdǒng
I can't read Chinese characters	我看不懂汉字	wǒ kànbùdǒng hànzì
What does this mean?	这是什么意思?	zhè shì shénme yìsi?
How do you pronounce this character?	这个字怎么念?	zhègè zì zěnme niàn?

GREETINGS AND BASIC COURTESIES

Hello/How do you do/How are you?	你好	nǐhǎo
I'm fine	我很好	wǒhěnhǎo
Thank you	谢谢	xièxie
Don't mention it/You're welcome	不客气	búkèqi
Sorry to bother you...	麻烦你	máfan nǐ
Sorry/I apologize	对不起	duìbùqǐ
It's not important/No problem	没关系	méi guānxi
Goodbye	再见	zài jiàn
Excuse me	对不起	dùibùqǐ

CHITCHAT

What country are you from?	你是哪个国家的人?	nǐ shì nǎgè guójiā derén
Britain	英国	yīngguó
England	英国/英格兰	yīngguó/yīnggélán
Scotland	苏格兰	sūgélán
Wales	威尔士	wēi'ěrshì
Ireland	爱尔兰	ài'ěrlán
America	美国	měiguó
Canada	加拿大	jiā'nádà
Australia	澳大利亚	àodàlìyà
New Zealand	新西兰	xīnxīlán
South Africa	南非	nánfēi
China	中国	zhōngguó
Outside China	外国	wàiguó
What's your name?	你叫什么名字?	nǐ jiào shénme míngzi?

My name is...	我叫...	wǒ jiào...
Are you married?	你结婚了吗?	nǐ jiéhūn le ma?
I am (not) married	我(没有)结婚(了)	wǒ (méiyǒu) jiéhūn (le)
Have you got (children)?	你有没有孩子?	nǐ yǒu méiyǒu háizi?
Do you like...?	你喜不喜欢...?	nǐ xǐ bù xǐhuān...?
I (don't) like...	我不喜欢...	wǒ (bù) xǐhuān...
What's your job?	你干什么工作?	nǐ gàn shénme gōngzuò?
I'm a foreign student	我是留学生	wǒ shì liúxuéshēng
I'm a teacher	我是老师	wǒ shì lǎoshī
I work in a company	我在一个公司工作	wǒ zài yígè gōngsī gōngzuò
I'm retired	我退休了	wǒ tuìxiūle
Clean/dirty	干净/脏	gānjìng/zāng
Hot/cold	热/冷	rè/lěng
Fast/slow	快/慢	kuài/màn
Good/bad	好/坏	hǎo/huài
Big/small	大/小	dà/xiǎo
Pretty	漂亮	piàoliàng
Interesting	有意思	yǒuyìsi

NUMBERS

Zero	零	líng
One	一	yī
Two	二/两	èr/liǎng*
Three	三	sān
Four	四	sì
Five	五	wǔ
Six	六	liù
Seven	七	qī
Eight	八	bā
Nine	九	jiǔ
Ten	十	shí
Eleven	十一	shíyī
Twelve	十二	shíèr
Twenty	二十	èrshí
Twenty-one	二十一	èrshíyī
One hundred	一百	yībǎi
Two hundred	二百	èrbǎi
One thousand	一千	yīqiān
Ten thousand	一万	yīwàn
One hundred thousand	十万	shíwàn
One million	一百万	yībǎiwàn
One hundred million	一亿	yīyì
One billion	十亿	shíyì

* 两/liǎng is used when enumerating, for example "two people" (liǎnggè rén). 二 /èr is used when counting.

TIME

Now	现在	xiànzài
Today	今天	jīntiān
(In the) morning	早上	zǎoshàng
(In the) afternoon	下午	xiàwǔ
(In the) evening	晚上	wǎnshàng
Tomorrow	明天	míngtiān
The day after tomorrow	后天	hòutiān
Yesterday	昨天	zuótiān

Week/month/year	星期/月/年	xīngqī/yuè/nián
Next/last week/month/year	下/上 星期/月/年	xià/shàng xīngqī/yuè/nián
Monday	星期一	xīngqī yī
Tuesday	星期二	xīngqī èr
Wednesday	星期三	xīngqī sān
Thursday	星期四	xīngqī sì
Friday	星期五	xīngqī wǔ
Saturday	星期六	xīngqī liù
Sunday	星期天	xīngqī tiān
What's the time?	几点了?	jǐdiǎn le?
Morning	早上	zǎoshàng
Afternoon	中午	zhōngwǔ
10 o'clock	十点钟	shídiǎn zhōng
10.20	十点二十	shídiǎn èrshí
10.30	十点半	shídiǎn bàn

TRAVELLING AND GETTING AROUND TOWN

North	北	běi
South	南	nán
East	东	dōng
West	西	xī
Airport	机场	jīchǎng
Ferry dock	船码头	chuánmǎtóu
Left-luggage office	寄存处	jìcún chù
Ticket office	售票处	shòupiào chù
Ticket	票	piào
Can you sell me a ticket to...?	可不可以给我买到...的票?	kěbùkěyǐ gěi wǒ mǎi dào.... de piào?
I want to go to...	我要去...	wǒ yào qù...
I want to leave at (8 o'clock)	我想(八点钟)离开	wǒ xiǎng (bā diǎn zhōng) líkāi
When does it leave?	什么时候出发?	shénme shíhòu chūfā?
When does it arrive?	什么时候到?	shénme shíhòu dào?
How long does it take?	路上得多长时间?	lùshàng děi duōcháng shíjiān?
CITS	中国国际旅行社	zhōngguó guójì lǚxíngshè
Train	火车	huǒchē
(Main) train station	主要火车站	(zhǔyào) huǒchēzhàn
Bus	公共汽车	gōnggòng qìchēzhàn
Bus station	汽车站	qìchēzhàn
Long-distance bus station	长途汽车站	chángtú qìchēzhàn
Express train/bus	特快车	tèkuài chē
Fast train/bus	快车	kuài chē
Ordinary train/bus	普通车	pǔtōng chē
Timetable	时间表	shíjiān biǎo
Map	地图	dìtú
Where is...?	...在 哪里?	...zài nǎlǐ?
Go straight on	往前走	wǎng qián zǒu
Turn right	往右走	wǎng yòu zǒu
Turn left	往左拐	wǎng zuǒ guǎi
Taxi	出租车	chūzū chē
Please use the meter	请打开记价器	qǐng dǎkāi jìjiàqì
Underground/metro station	地铁站	dìtiě zhàn
Bicycle	自行车	zìxíngchē

Which bus goes to…?	几路车到...去?	jǐlù chēdào … qù?
Number (10) bus	(十)路车	(shí) lù chē
Does this bus go to…?	这车到...去吗?	zhè chē dào … qù ma?
When is the next bus?	下一班车几点开?	xiàyìbānchē jǐdiǎn kāi?
The first bus	头班车	tóubān chē
The last bus	末班车	mòbān chē
Please tell me where to get off	请告诉我在哪里下车	qǐng gàosù wǒ zài nǎlǐ xiàchē
Museum	博物馆	bówù guǎn
Temple	寺庙	sìmiào
Church	教堂	jiàotáng

ACCOMMODATION

Accommodation	住宿	zhùsù
Hotel (upmarket)	宾馆	bīnguǎn
Hotel (cheap)	招待所, 旅馆	zhāodàisuǒ, lǚguǎn
Hostel	旅社	lǚshè
Do you have a room available?	你们有房间吗?	nǐmén yǒu fángjiān ma?
Can I have a look at the room?	能不能看一下房间?	néngbùnéng kànyíxià fángjiān?
I want the cheapest bed you've got	我要你这里最便宜的床位	wǒ yào nǐzhèlǐ zuìpiányi de chuáng wèi
Single room	单人房	dānrén fáng
Twin room	双人房	shuāngrén fáng
Double room with a big bed	双人房间带大床	shuāngrén fángjiān dài dàchuáng
Three-bed room	三人房	sānrén fáng
Dormitory	多人房	duōrén fáng
Suite	套房	tàofáng
(Large) bed	(大)床	(dà) chuáng
Passport	护照	hùzhào
Deposit	押金	yājīn
Key	钥匙	yàoshi
I want to change my room	我想换一个房间	wǒ xiǎng huàn yígè fángjiān

SHOPPING AND MONEY

How much is it?	这是多少钱?	zhè shì duōshǎo qián?
That's too expensive	太贵了	tàiguìle
I haven't got any cash	我没有现金	wǒ méiyǒu xiànjīn
Have you got anything cheaper?	你没有便宜一点的?	yǒu méiyǒu piányi yìdiǎn de?
Do you accept credit cards?	可不可以用信用卡	kě bù kěyǐ yòng xìnyòngkǎ?
Department store	百货商店	bǎihuò shāngdiàn
Market	市场	shìchǎng
¥1 (RMB)	一块 (人民币)	yíkuài (rénmínbì)
US$1	一块美金	yíkuài měijīn
£1	一个英镑	yígè yīngbàng
Change money	换钱	huànqián
Bank	银行	yínháng
ATM	提款机	tíkuǎn jī
PSB	公安局	gōng'ān jú

COMMUNICATIONS

Post office	邮电局	yóudiàn jú
Envelope	信封	xìnfēng
Stamp	邮票	yóupiào
Airmail	航空信	hángkōng xìn
Surface mail	平信	píngxìn
Telephone	电话	diànhuà
Mobile phone	手机	shǒujī
SMS message	短信	duǎnxìn
International telephone call	国际电话	guójì diànhuà
Reverse charges/collect call	对方付钱电话	duìfāngfùqián diànhuà
Telephone card	电话卡	diànhuà kǎ
I want to make a telephone call to (Britain)	我想给（英国）打电话	wǒ xiǎng gěi (yīngguó) dǎ diànhuà
Internet	网吧	wǎngbā
Email	电邮	diànyóu

HEALTH

Hospital	医院	yīyuàn
Pharmacy	药店	yàodiàn
Medicine	药	yào
Chinese medicine	中药	zhōngyào
Diarrhoea	腹泻	fùxiè
Vomit	呕吐	ǒutù
Fever	发烧	fāshāo
I'm ill	我生病了	wǒ shēngbìng le
I've got flu	我感冒了	wǒ gǎnmào le
I'm (not) allergic to...	我对…(不)过敏	wǒ duì … (bù) guòmin
Antibiotics	抗生素	kàngshēngsù
Condom	避孕套	bìyùntào
Tampons	卫生棉条	wèishēng miántiáo

Menu reader

GENERAL

Restaurant	餐厅	cāntīng
House speciality	拿手好菜	náshǒu hǎocài
How much is that?	多少钱?	duōshǎo qián?
I don't eat (meat)	我不吃(肉)	wǒ bù chī (ròu)
I would like...	我想要…	wǒ xiǎng yào...
Local dishes	地方菜	dìfāngcài
Snacks	小吃	xiǎochī
Menu/set menu/English menu	菜单/套菜/英文菜单	càidān/tàocài/yīngwén càidān
Small portion	少量	shǎoliàng
Chopsticks	筷子	kuàizi
Knife and fork	刀叉	dāchā
Spoon	勺子	sháozi
Waiter/waitress	服务员	fúwùyuán
Bill/cheque	买单	mǎidān
Cook these ingredients together	一快儿做	yíkuài'r zuò
Not spicy/no chilli please	请不要辣椒	qǐngbúyào làjiāo
Only a little spice/chilli	一点辣椒	yìdiǎnlàjiāo
50 grams	两	liǎng

250 grams	半斤	bànjīn
500 grams	斤	jīn
1 kilo	公斤	gōngjīn

DRINKS

Beer	啤酒	píjiǔ
Coffee	咖啡	kāfēi
Milk	牛奶	niúnǎi
(Mineral) water	(矿泉)水	(kuàngquán) shuǐ
Wine	葡萄酒	pútáojiǔ
Tea	茶	chá
Black tea	红茶	hóngchá
Green tea	绿茶	lǜchá
Jasmine tea	茉莉花茶	mòlìhuā chá

STAPLE FOODS

Aubergine	茄子	qiézi
Bamboo shoots	笋尖	sǔnjiān
Bean sprouts	豆芽	dòuyá
Beans	豆	dòu
Beef	牛肉	niúròu
Black bean sauce	黑豆豉	hēidòuchǐ
Bread	面包	miànbāo
Buns (filled)	包子	bāozi
Buns (plain)	馒头	mántou
Carrot	胡萝卜	húluóbo
Cashew nuts	腰果	yāoguǒ
Chicken	鸡	jī
Chilli	辣椒	làjiāo
Crab	蟹	xiè
Cucumber	黄瓜	huángguā
Duck	鸭	yā
Eel	鳝鱼	shànyú
Eggs (fried)	煎鸡蛋	jiān jīdàn
Fish	鱼	yú
Fried dough stick	油条	yóutiáo
Garlic	大蒜	dàsuàn
Ginger	姜	jiāng
Green pepper (capsicum)	青椒	qīngjiāo
Green vegetables	绿叶蔬菜	lǜyè shūcài
Jiaozi (dumplings, steamed or boiled)	饺子	jiǎozi
Lamb	羊肉	yángròu
Lotus root	莲心	liánxīn
MSG	味精	wèijīng
Mushrooms	磨菇	mógū
Noodles	面条	miàntiáo
Omelette	摊鸡蛋	tānjīdàn
Onions	洋葱	yángcōng
Oyster sauce	蚝油	háoyóu
Pancake	摊饼	tānbǐng
Peanut	花生	huāshēng
Pork	猪肉	zhūròu
Potato (stir-fried)	(炒)土豆	(chǎo) tǔdòu
Prawns	虾	xiā

Preserved egg	皮蛋	pídàn
Rice, boiled	白饭	báifàn
Rice, fried	炒饭	chǎofàn
Rice noodles	河粉	héfěn
Rice porridge (aka congee)	粥	zhōu
Salt	盐	yán
Shuijiao (dumplings in soup)	水饺	shuǐjiǎo
Sichuan pepper	四川辣椒	sìchuān làjiāo
Soup	汤	tāng
Soy sauce	酱油	jiàngyóu
Squid	鱿鱼	yóuyú
Sugar	糖	táng
Tofu	豆腐	dòufu
Tomato	蕃茄	fānqié
Vinegar	醋	cù
Water chestnuts	马蹄	mǎtí
Yogurt	酸奶	suānnǎi

COOKING METHODS

Boiled	煮	zhǔ
Casseroled	焙	bèi
Deep-fried	油煎	yóujiān
Fried	炒	chǎo
Poached	白煮	báizhǔ
Red-cooked (stewed in soy sauce)	红烧	hóngshāo
Roast	烤	kǎo
Steamed	蒸	zhēng
Stir-fried	清炒	qīngchǎo

SHANGHAI SPECIALITIES

Beggars' chicken (baked)	叫花鸡	jiàohuā jī
Braised pig trotters	蹄膀	tí pang
Brine duck	盐水鸭	yánshuǐ yā
Crab soup	蟹肉汤	xièròu tāng
Crispy eel	香酥脆	xiāngsū cuì
Crystal prawns	水晶虾仁	shuǐjīng xiārén
Dongpo pork casserole (steamed in wine)	东坡焙肉	dōngpō bèiròu
Drunken chicken (chicken cooked in wine)	醉鸡	zuìjī
Drunken prawns	醉虾	zuìxiā
Fish-shred soup	鱼丝汤	yúsī táng
Five-flower pork (steamed in lotus leaves)	五花肉	wǔhuā ròu
Fried crab with eggs	蟹肉鸡蛋	xièròu jīdàn
Hairy crab	大闸蟹	dàzhá xiè
Pearl balls (rice-grain-coated, steamed rissoles)	珍珠球	zhēnzhū qiú
Shaoxing chicken	绍兴鸡	shàoxīng jī
Shengjian dumplings	生煎包	shēngjiān bāo
Smoked fish	熏鱼	xūnyú
Soup dumplings (steamed, containing jellied stock)	汤包	tāngbāo
Sour and hot soup with eel and chicken	龙凤酸辣汤	lóngfèng suānlà tāng
Steamed "lions' head" (mincemeat)	清蒸狮子头	qīngzhēng shīzitóu
Steamed sea bass	清蒸鲈鱼	qīngzhēng lúyú
Stuffed green peppers	馅青椒	xiàn qīngjiāo

Sweet and sour spareribs	糖醋小排	tángcù xiǎopái
West Lake fish (braised in a sour sauce)	西湖醋鱼	xīhú cùyú
White-cut beef (spiced and steamed)	白切牛肉	báiqiē niúròu
Xiaolong dumplings	小笼包	xiǎolóng bāo
Yangzhou fried rice	杨州炒饭	yángzhōu chǎofàn

EVERYDAY DISHES

Braised duck with vegetables	炖鸭素菜	dùnyā sùcài
Cabbage rolls (stuffed with meat or vegetables)	卷心菜	juǎnxīncài
Chicken and sweetcorn soup	玉米鸡丝汤	yùmǐ jīsī tāng
Chicken with cashew nuts	腰果鸡片	yāoguǒ jīpiàn
Claypot/sandpot (casserole)	沙锅	shāguō
Crispy aromatic duck	香酥鸭	xiāngsūyā
Egg flower soup with tomato	蕃茄蛋汤	fānqié dàn tāng
Egg fried rice	蛋炒饭	dànchǎofàn
Fish casserole	焙鱼	bèiyú
Fried shredded pork with garlic and chilli	大蒜辣椒炒肉片	dàsuàn làjiāo chǎoròupiàn
Kebab	串肉	chuànròu
Noodle soup	汤面	tāngmiàn
Pork and mustard greens	芥末肉片	jièmo ròupiàn
Pork and water chestnut	马蹄猪肉	mǎtí zhūròu
Prawn with garlic sauce	大蒜炒虾	dàsuàn chǎoxiā
Pulled noodles	拉面	lāmiàn
Roast duck	烤鸭	kǎoyā
Scrambled egg with pork on rice	滑蛋猪肉饭	huádàn zhūròufàn
Steamed rice packets wrapped in lotus leaves	荷叶蒸饭	héyè zhēngfàn
Stewed pork belly with vegetables	回锅肉	huíguōròu
Stir-fried chicken and bamboo shoots	笋尖炒鸡片	sǔnjiān chǎojīpiàn
Sweet bean paste pancakes	赤豆摊饼	chìdòu tānbǐng
Wonton soup	馄饨汤	húntun tāng

VEGETABLES AND EGGS

Aubergine with chilli and garlic sauce	大蒜辣椒炒茄子	dàsuàn làjiāo chǎoqiézi
Bean curd and spinach soup	菠菜豆腐汤	bōcài dòufutāng
Egg fried with tomatoes	蕃茄炒蛋	fānqié chǎodàn
Fried bean curd with vegetables	豆腐蔬菜	dòufu shūcài
Fried bean sprouts	炒豆芽	chǎo dòuyá
Spicy braised aubergine	香茄子条	xiāngqiézitiáo
Stir-fried bamboo shoots	炒冬笋	chǎo dōngsǔn
Stir-fried mushrooms	炒鲜菇	chǎo xiāngū
Vegetable soup	蔬菜汤	shūcài tāng

REGIONAL DISHES

NORTHERN

Aromatic fried lamb	炒羊肉	chǎo yángròu
Peking duck	北京烤鸭	běijīng kǎoyā
Fish with ham and vegetables	火腿蔬菜鱼片	huǒtuǐ shūcài yúpiàn
Fried prawn balls	炒虾球	chǎo xiāqiú
Hotpot	火锅	huǒguō
Lion's head (pork rissoles casseroled with greens)	狮子头	shīzitóu
Red-cooked lamb	红烧羊肉	hóngshāo yángròu

SICHUAN WESTERN CHINESE

Boiled beef slices (spicy)	水煮牛肉	shuǐzhǔ niúròu
Crackling-rice with pork	爆米肉片	bàomǐ ròupiàn
Crossing-the-bridge noodles	过桥面	guòqiáo miàn
Double-cooked pork	回锅肉	huíguōròu
Dry-fried pork shreds	油炸肉丝	yóuzhá ròusī
Gongbao chicken (with chillies and peanuts)	公保鸡丁	gōngbǎo jīdīng
Hot and sour soup (flavoured with vinegar and white pepper)	酸辣汤	suānlà tāng
Hot-spiced bean curd	麻婆豆腐	mápó dòufu
Smoked duck	熏鸭	xūnyā
Stuffed aubergine slices	馅茄子	xiàn qiézi

FRUIT

Honeydew melon	哈密瓜	hāmìguā
Lychee	荔枝	lìzhī
Mango	芒果	mángguǒ
Orange	橙子	chéngzi
Peach	桃子	táozi
Pear	梨	lí
Plum	李子	lǐzi
Pomegranate	石榴	shíliú
Watermelon	西瓜	xīguā

Glossary

Arhat Buddhist saint

Bei North

CCP Chinese Communist Party

Concession A section of Shanghai under the control of a foreign power during the nineteenth and twentieth centuries; a colonial territory in all but name

Cultural Revolution Ten-year period beginning in 1966 and characterized by destruction, persecution and fanatical devotion to Chairman Mao

Dagoba Another name for a stupa

Ding An ancient three-legged vessel, used for cooking and ceremonial purposes

Dingpeng Literally a nail shed – the cheapest kind of brothel in Concession-era Shanghai

Dong East

Dougong Ornate, load-bearing bracket used in temple roofs

Fen Smallest denomination of Chinese currency – there are one hundred fen to the yuan

Feng Peak

Feng shui A system of geomancy used to determine the positioning of buildings

Gong Palace

Gongyuan Park

Guan Temple

Guanyin The ubiquitous Buddhist Goddess of Mercy, who postponed her entry into paradise in order to help ease human misery. Derived from the Indian deity Avalokiteshvara, she is often depicted with up to a thousand arms

Guomindang (GMD) The Nationalist Peoples' Party. Under Chiang Kai-shek, the GMD fought Communist forces for 25 years before being defeated and moving to Taiwan in 1949, where it remains a major political party

Han Chinese The main body of the Chinese people, as distinct from other ethnic groups such as Uigur, Miao, Hui or Tibetan

Hu Lake

Jiao (or mao) Ten fen

Jie Street

Little Red Book A selection of "Quotations from Chairman Mao Zedong", produced in 1966 as a philosophical treatise for Red Guards during the Cultural Revolution

Longtang A narrow lane lined with *shikumen* houses

Lu Street

Maitreya Buddha The Buddha of the future, at present awaiting rebirth

Men Gate/door

Miao Temple

Ming Chinese dynasty that ruled from 1368 to 1644, before being overthrown by the Manchus from the north

Nan South

PLA The People's Liberation Army, the official name of the Communist military forces since 1949

PSB Public Security Bureau, the branch of China's police force which deals directly with foreigners

Pagoda Tower with distinctively tapering structure

Pipa A traditional string instrument

Pinyin The official system of transliterating Chinese script into Roman characters

Putonghua Mandarin Chinese; literally "Common Language"

Qiao Bridge

Qing The last of the great Chinese dynasties (1644–1911), administered from Beijing

Qipao The characteristic Chinese long fitted dress

Red Guards The unruly factional forces unleashed by Mao during the Cultural Revolution to find and destroy brutally any "reactionaries" among the populace

Renmimbi Literally "people's money"; the official Chinese term for the Chinese currency

Renmin The people

Shikumen Terraced housing created in the nineteenth century by the British

Shuyu A high-class courtesan, like a geisha, skilled in singing and dancing as well as the arts of love

Si Temple, usually Buddhist

Song A Chinese dynasty (960–1279 AD) administered first from Kaifeng and later from Hangzhou, regarded as mercantilist and progressive

Stele Freestanding stone tablet carved with text

Stupa Multitiered tower associated with Buddhist temples that usually contains sacred objects

Ta Tower or pagoda

Tai ji A discipline of physical exercise, characterized by slow, deliberate, balletic movements

Tang Arguably the greatest Chinese dynasty (618–907 AD), the Tang was outward looking and stable. The era also represented a high-water mark for the Chinese arts

Taxi girls Girls who danced for money in Concession-era Shanghai

Tea dances Organized dances in Concession Shanghai, rather less innocent than the name implies

Tian Heaven or the sky

Xi West

Yuan China's unit of currency. Also a courtyard or garden

Zhou Villa or manor

Small print and index

A ROUGH GUIDE TO ROUGH GUIDES

Published in 1982, the first Rough Guide – to Greece – was a student scheme that became a publishing phenomenon. Mark Ellingham, a recent graduate in English from Bristol University, had been travelling in Greece the previous summer and couldn't find the right guidebook. With a small group of friends he wrote his own guide, combining a contemporary, journalistic style with a thoroughly practical approach to travellers' needs.

The immediate success of the book spawned a series that rapidly covered dozens of destinations. And, in addition to impecunious backpackers, Rough Guides soon acquired a much broader readership that relished the guides' wit and inquisitiveness as much as their enthusiastic, critical approach and value-for-money ethos. These days, Rough Guides include recommendations from budget to luxury and cover more than 120 destinations around the globe, from Amsterdam to Zanzibar, all regularly updated by our team of roaming writers.

Browse all our latest guides, read inspirational features and book your trip at **roughguides.com**.

Rough Guide credits

Editor: Samantha Cook
Layout: Ankur Guha
Cartography: Ed Wright
Picture editor: Phoebe Lowndes
Proofreader: Jennifer Speake
Managing editor: Andy Turner
Assistant editor: Payal Sharotri

Production: Jimmy Lao
Cover photo research: Sarah Stewart-Richardson
Editorial assistant: Aimee White
Senior DTP coordinator: Dan May
Programme manager: Gareth Lowe
Publishing director: Georgina Dee

Publishing information

This fourth edition published July 2017 by
Rough Guides Ltd,
80 Strand, London WC2R 0RL
11, Community Centre, Panchsheel Park,
New Delhi 110017, India
Distributed by Penguin Random House
Penguin Books Ltd, 80 Strand, London WC2R 0RL
Penguin Group (USA), 345 Hudson Street, NY 10014, USA
Penguin Group (Australia), 250 Camberwell Road,
Camberwell, Victoria 3124, Australia
Penguin Group (NZ), 67 Apollo Drive, Mairangi Bay,
Auckland 1310, New Zealand
Penguin Group (South Africa), Block D, Rosebank Office
Park, 181 Jan Smuts Avenue, Parktown North, Gauteng,
South Africa 2193
Rough Guides is represented in Canada by DK Canada, 320
Front Street West, Suite 1400, Toronto, Ontario M5V 3B6
Printed in Singapore
© Rough Guides 2017
Maps © Rough Guides

208pp includes index
A catalogue record for this book is available from the
British Library
ISBN: 978-0-24127-902-1

Help us update

We've gone to a lot of effort to ensure that the fourth
edition of **The Rough Guide to Shanghai** is accurate
and up-to-date. However, things change – places get
"discovered", opening hours are notoriously fickle,
restaurants and rooms raise prices or lower standards. If
you feel we've got it wrong or left something out, we'd like
to know, and if you can remember the address, the price,
the hours, the phone number, so much the better.

Please send your comments with the subject
line "**Rough Guide Shanghai Update**" to mail@
uk.roughguides.com. We'll credit all contributions and
send a copy of the next edition (or any other Rough Guide
if you prefer) for the very best emails.

Find travel information, read inspiring features and book
your trip at roughguides.com.

ABOUT THE AUTHOR

Simon Lewis (Ⓦ simonlewiswriter.com) has worked as a travel writer specializing in Asia for nearly twenty years. In addition to this guide he has written the *Rough Guide to Beijing* and contributed to the *Rough Guide to China*. He is also a novelist and screenwriter; his crime novel *Bad Traffic* has been translated into seven languages and was shortlisted for the *LA Times* Book of the Year 2012. His produced feature film scripts include thrillers *Tiger House*, *Jet Trash* and *The Anomaly*.

Acknowledgements

Simon would like to thank Timesavers Cat, Jeremy, Mark, Du Yingnan, Cici, Polly, ace foodblogger Ivy, Sam, Sitang, top editor Samantha Cook and Noe and Hana.

Photo credits

All photos © Rough Guides, except the following:
(Key: t-top; c-centre; b-bottom; l-left; r-right)

1 SuperStock: Fabio Nodari
2 Robert Harding Picture Library: Tim Graham
4 Dreamstime.com: Aliaksandr Mazurkevich
7 Alamy Stock Photo: Alex Segre
9 Alamy Stock Photo: Hemis (t). **Getty Images:** Jon Arnold (c); Paul Souders (b)
11 123RF.com: Philip Lange (tl). **Robert Harding Picture Library:** Lucas Vallecillos (c)
12 Alamy Stock Photo: VIEW Pictures Ltd (b). **Getty Images:** Onest Mistic (t)
13 Alamy Stock Photo: Karl Johaentges (c). **AWL Images:** Alan Copson (b). **Chi-Q** (tl). **Dreamstime.com:** Hongtao926 (tr)
14 Alamy Stock Photo: Agencja Fotograficzna Caro (cr). **Getty Images:** Jon Arnold (b)
15 Alamy Stock Photo: Rolf Richardson (t). **Photoshot:** Tibor Bognar (b). **Pixattitude** (c)
16 Alamy Stock Photo: kpzfoto
38 Getty Images: China Span RM/Keren Su

53 Dreamstime.com: Mikhail Nekrasov
58 Getty Images: Rob Smith
68 Dreamstime.com: William Perry
82 Dreamstime.com: Ktree
86 Dreamstime.com: Bartlomiej Magierowski
91 Alamy Stock Photo: JTB MEDIA CREATION, Inc.
105 Alamy Stock Photo: dbimages (bl). **Dreamstime.com:** Badoff (t). **Robert Harding Picture Library:** Tao Images (br)
114 Fairmont Peace Hotel
125 Lost Heaven
135 Alamy Stock Photo: Kevin Foy (br). **Mr and Mrs Bund** (bl)
142 Alamy Stock Photo: LOOK Die Bildagentur der Fotografen GmbH
155 Alamy Stock Photo: Planetpix
164 Getty Images: Qilai Shen

Cover *Neon shop signs on Nanjing Street* **Alamy Stock Photo:** Asia Photopress

Index

Maps are marked in grey

Map index

Listings key

- Accommodation
- Eating
- Drinking and nightlife
- Shopping

City plan

The **city plan** on the pages that follow is divided as shown:

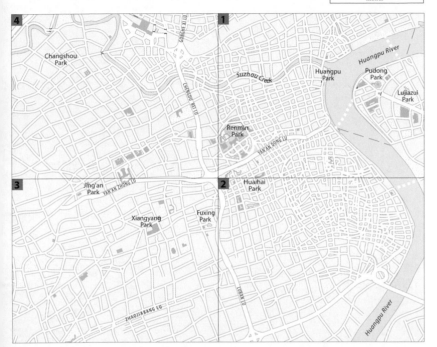

Map symbols

Pedestrianized road	⊠ Gate/park entrance	🌲 Pagoda
Railway	▲ Mountain peak	⚓ Ferry dock
Ferry route	✈ Airport	Building
Wall	⊖ Shanghai metro station	Church/cathedral/chapel
(i) Tourist information	(M) Other metro station	Market
⊠ Post office	(A) Bus station/depot	Park/cemetery
@ Internet access	★ Minibus stand/bus stop	Beach
✚ Hospital	✡ Synagogue	

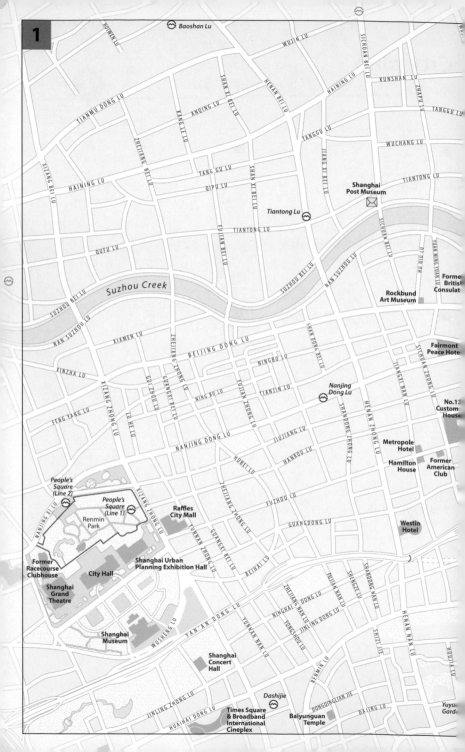

1

Baoshan Lu

HUMEN LU

TIANMU DONG LU

WUJIN LU

SICHUAN BEI LU

KUNSHAN LU

ZHAPU LU

TANGGU LU

SHAN XI BEI LU

ANQING LU

HENAN BEI LU

HAINING LU

KANG LU

ZHEJIANG BEI LU

TANG GU LU

JIANG XI BEI LU

TANGGU LU

WUCHANG LU

XIZANG BEI LU

HAINING LU

SHAN XI BEI LU

QIPU LU

TIANTONG LU

Shanghai Post Museum

SICHUAN BEI LU

QUFU LU

FUJIAN BEI LU

TIANTONG LU

Tiantong Lu

NAN SUZHOU LU

SUZHOU BEI LU

DI TIO TIH

YUAN MING YUAN LU

Former British Consulat

SUZHOU BEI LU

Suzhou Creek

SUZHOU BEI LU

Rockbund Art Museum

NAN SUZHOU LU

XIAMEN LU

ZHEJIANG ZHONG LU

BEIJING DONG LU

SHAN DONG BEI LU

Fairmont Peace Hote

XINZHA LU

NINGBO LU

GU ZHOU LU

GUANGXI BEI LU

NING BO LU

FUJIAN ZHONG LU

TIANJIN LU

SICHUAN ZHONG LU

JIANGXI NAN LU

Nanjing Dong Lu

HENAN ZHONG LU

No.13 Custom House

FENG YANG LU

XIZANG ZHONG LU

LU HE LU

NANJING DONG LU

JIUJIANG LU

SHANDONG ZHONG LU

Metropole Hotel

HUBEI LU

HANKOU LU

Hamilton House

Former American Club

People's Square (Line 2)

NANJING XI LU

People's Square (Line 1)

XIZANG ZHONG LU

Renmin Park

Raffles City Mall

HEJIANG ZHONG LU

FUZHOU LU

GUANGDONG LU

Westin Hotel

Former Racecourse Clubhouse

YUNNAN ZHONG LU

GUANGXI BEI LU

Shanghai Urban Planning Exhibition Hall

BEIHAI LU

SHANDONG NAN LU

City Hall

Shanghai Grand Theatre

WUSHENG LU

Shanghai Museum

YAN'AN DONG LU

YUNNAN NAN LU

ZHEJIANG DONG LU

NINGHAI NAN LU

JINLING DONG LU

YONGSHOU LU

FUJIAN NAN LU

SHENGEL LU

SHANDONG NAN LU

HENAN NAN LU

SHIZI JIE

HOUJIA LU

Shanghai Concert Hall

JINLING ZHONG LU

RENMIN LU

Dashijie

DONGQINGLIAN JIE

HUAIHAI DONG LU

Times Square & Broadband International Cineplex

Baiyunguan Temple

DAJING LU

Yuyu Gard

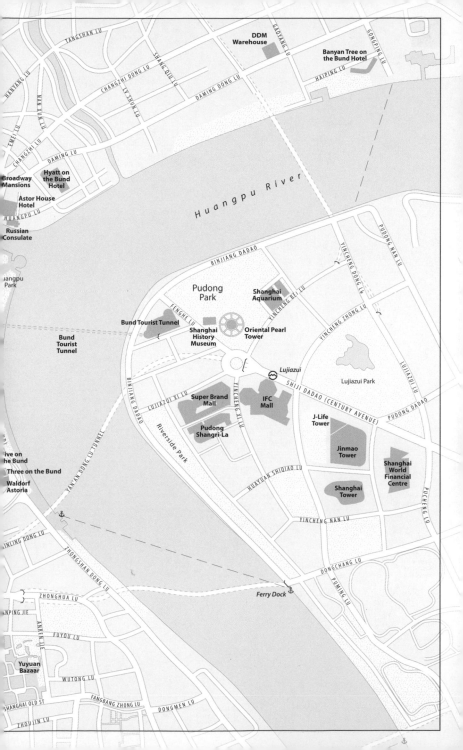

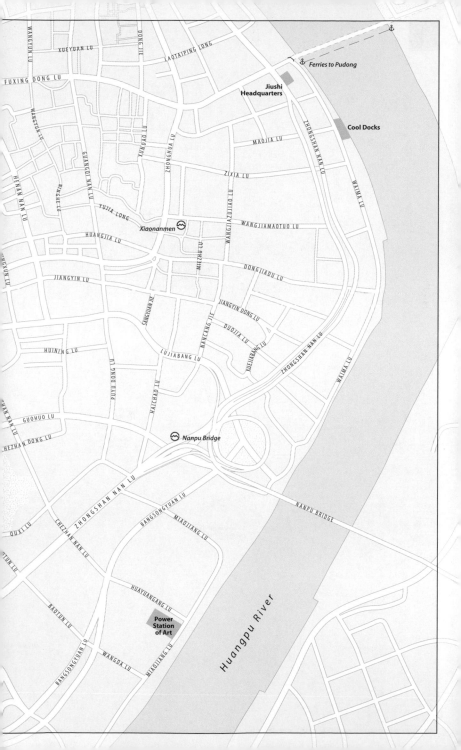

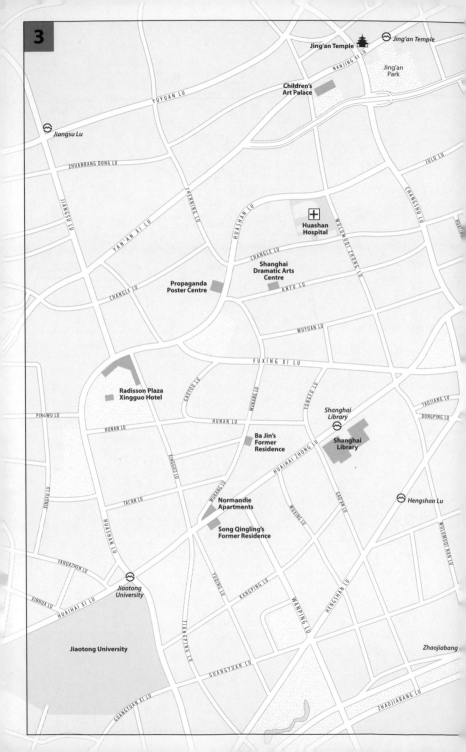

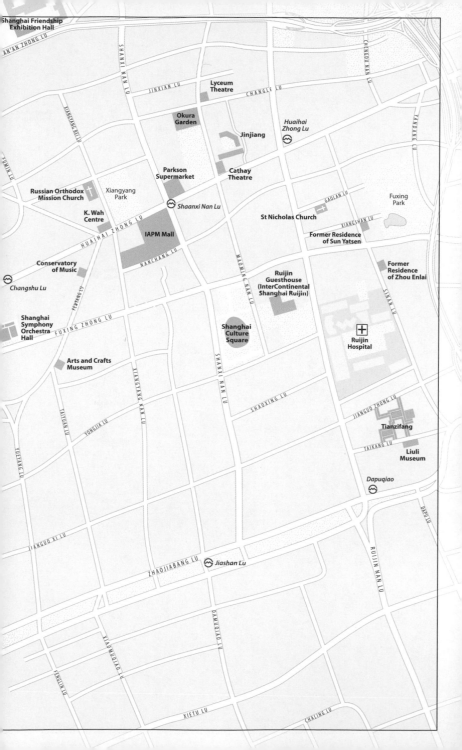

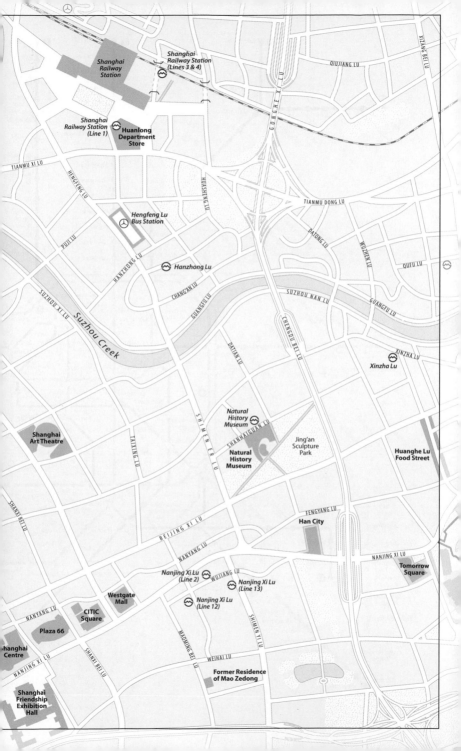

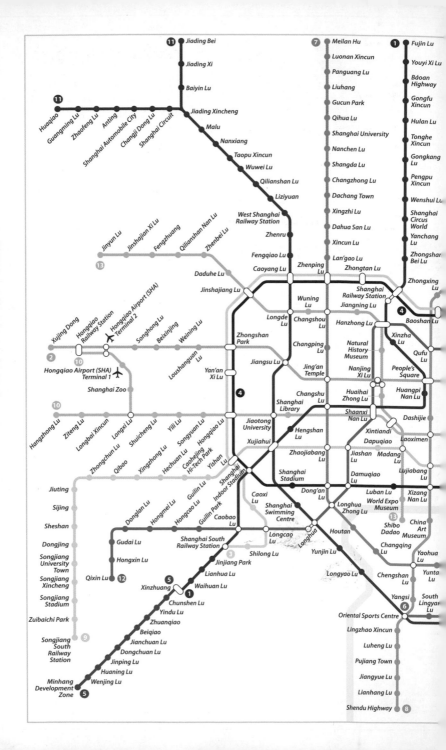

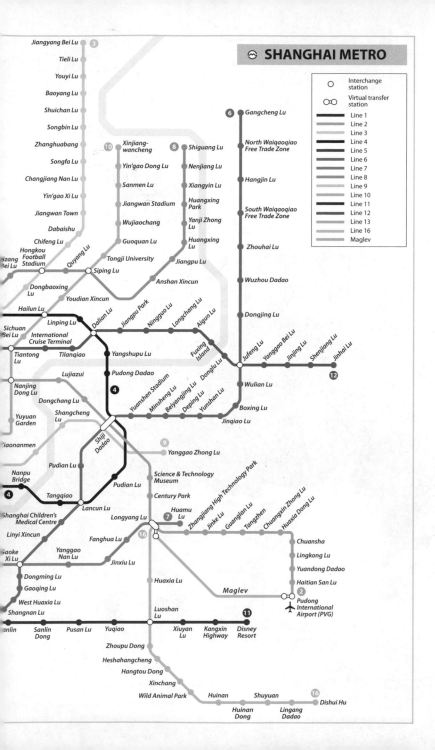

SHANGHAI METRO

Interchange station
Virtual transfer station
Line 1
Line 2
Line 3
Line 4
Line 5
Line 6
Line 7
Line 8
Line 9
Line 10
Line 11
Line 12
Line 13
Line 16
Maglev

Jiangyang Bei Lu
Tieli Lu
Youyi Lu
Baoyang Lu
Shuichan Lu
Songbin Lu
Zhanghuabang
Songfa Lu
Changjiang Nan Lu
Yin'gao Xi Lu
Jiangwan Town
Dabaishu
Chifeng Lu
Hongkou Football Stadium
izang Bei Lu
Dongbaoxing Lu
Hailun Lu
Linping Lu
Sichuan Bei Lu
International Cruise Terminal
Tiantong Lu
Tilanqiao
Nanjing Dong Lu
Dongchang Lu
Yuyuan Garden
Shangcheng Lu
Xiaonanmen
Shij Dadao
Nanpu Bridge
Pudian Lu
Tangqiao
Lancun Lu
Shanghai Children's Medical Centre
Linyi Xincun
Gaoke Xi Lu
Yanggao Nan Lu
Jinxiu Lu
Dongming Lu
Gaoqing Lu
West Huaxia Lu
Shangnan Lu
anlin
Sanlin Dong
Pusan Lu
Yuqiao

Xinjiang-wancheng
Yin'gao Dong Lu
Sanmen Lu
Jiangwan Stadium
Wujiaochang
Guoquan Lu
Tongji University
Siping Lu
Youdian Xincun
Quyang Lu
Dalian Lu
Jiangpu Park
Yangshupu Lu
Pudong Dadao
Lujiazui

Shiguang Lu
Nenjiang Lu
Xiangyin Lu
Huangxing Park
Yanji Zhong Lu
Huangxing Lu
Jiangpu Lu
Anshan Xincun
Ningguo Lu
Longchang Lu
Aiguo Lu
Fuxing Island
Donglu Lu
Yuanshen Stadium
Minsheng Lu
Beiyangjing Lu
Deping Lu
Yumshan Lu
Jinqiao Lu

Gangcheng Lu
North Waiqaoqiao Free Trade Zone
Hangjin Lu
South Waiqaoqiao Free Trade Zone
Zhouhai Lu
Wuzhou Dadao
Dongjing Lu
Jufeng Lu
Yanggao Bei Lu
Jinjing Lu
Shenjiang Lu
Jinhai Lu
Wulian Lu
Boxing Lu

Yanggao Zhong Lu
Science & Technology Museum
Century Park
Zhangjiang High Technology Park
Jinke Lu
Guanglan Lu
Tangzhen
Chuangxin Zhong Lu
Huaxia Dong Lu
Chuansha
Lingkong Lu
Yuandong Dadao
Haitian San Lu
Pudong International Airport (PVG)

Huamu Lu
Longyang Lu
Fanghua Lu
Huaxia Lu
Luoshan Lu
Xiuyan Lu
Kangxin Highway
Disney Resort
Maglev

Zhoupu Dong
Heshahangcheng
Hangtou Dong
Xinchang
Wild Animal Park
Huinan
Huinan Dong
Shuyuan
Lingang Dadao
Dishui Hu

ROUGH GUIDES

ESCAPE THE EVERYDAY

ADVENTURE BECKONS
YOU JUST NEED TO KNOW WHERE TO LOOK

roughguides.com